Kickstart Modern Data Structures and Algorithms

Foundational Principles of Data Structures and Algorithms in C++ and Python

Ms. Divyashree Mallarapu
Mr. Sandeep Telkar R
Dr. Yasmeen Shaikh
Dr. Guruprasad Konnurmath

www.orangeava.com

First Published: March 2026

Published By: Orange Education Pvt Ltd, AVA®

Address: 9, Daryaganj, Delhi, 110002, India

275 New North Road Islington Suite 1314 London,
N1 7AA, United Kingdom

ISBN (PBK): 978-93-49887-38-1

ISBN (E-BOOK): 978-93-49887-60-2

Scan the QR code to explore our entire catalogue

www.orangeava.com

Get a Free eBook

We hope you're enjoying your recent book purchase! Your feedback is incredibly valuable to us and helps other readers discover books that truly make a difference.

If you found this book useful or enjoyable, we'd greatly appreciate it if you could leave a short review with a 5-star rating on Amazon. Your review supports our work and allows us to reach more learners worldwide.

As a thank-you, we're happy to offer you a **free digital copy of this book** plus a **30% discount code** for your next purchase on our official websites:

www.orangeava.com

www.orangeava.in (For the Indian Subcontinent).

☑ **How it works:**

Leave your review on Amazon, take a screenshot of the confirmation or use the following link to submit the claim and email it to **info@orangeava.com.** Once received the required detail, we will send your rewards within 24 hours, **along with one month free subcription to the book on AVA SkillShelf!**

Claim Form
https://rebrand.ly/4d2477

Thank you for your support—it truly means a lot to us.

Enjoy 1 Month of Free Access to AVA SkillShelf!

The future belongs to lifelong learners. With AVA SkillShelf, you go beyond reading books and start building real, job-ready skills curated by industry experts.

Your membership unlocks **200+ learning products** covering AI, Cloud, Python, Cybersecurity, Data Science, DevOps, and more—all in one platform. Our bestselling technical books are transformed into structured courses designed for practical, real-world application.

Learn directly from experienced professionals and published authors, with no filler—just actionable insights. Earn **verified digital certifications** to strengthen your CV, LinkedIn profile, and professional credibility.

Learn anytime, anywhere, on any device, at your own pace. Ideal for students, professionals, career switchers, and tech leaders.

For full access to all current and future courses, choose our **Annual Membership**. Simply scan the QR to get started!

For 1 month Free access, simply refer to the steps on the previous page titled: Get a Free ebook!

https://www.avaskillshelf.com/

Downloading the code bundles and colored images

Please follow the links or scan the QR codes to download the
Code Bundles and Images of the book:

https://github.com/ava-orange-education/Kickstart-Modern-Data-Structures-and-Algorithms

The code bundles and images of the book are also hosted on
https://rebrand.ly/3ljipn2

In case there's an update to the code, it will be updated on the existing GitHub repository.

Errata

We take immense pride in our work at **Orange Education Pvt Ltd,** and follow best practices to ensure the accuracy of our content to provide an indulging reading experience to our subscribers. Our readers are our mirrors, and we use their inputs to reflect and improve upon human errors, if any, that may have occurred during the publishing processes involved. To let us maintain the quality and help us reach out to any readers who might be having difficulties due to any unforeseen errors, please write to us at :

errata@orangeava.com

Your support, suggestions, and feedback are highly appreciated.

Dedicated to

My Beloved Grandparents:
Late Sri. Mallarapu Ramaiah Naidu, Smt. Mallarapu Lakshmamma
And
Sri. Potthuri Siddaiah Naidu, Smt. Potthuri Prameela.

My Parents:
Sri. Mallarapu Anjaneyulu Naidu, Smt. Mallarapu Anjali.

And My Strength and Support:
Sri. Potthuri Venkateshwara Rao, Smt. Potthuri Sindhu
Sri. Cherapally Anjan Kumar, Smt. Cherapally Sasikala

—Ms. Divyashree Mallarapu

My Beloved Parents:
Late Smt. Nagarathna GR,
Sri. Ramachandra RT
And
My Wife, Mrs. Rashmi PK.
My Lovely Daughter, Ms. Sirisha ST and My Son, Ujjwal ST
And
Students of 2022 – 2026 Batch: Department of
Artificial Intelligence and Machine Learning,
PESITM Shivamogga.

– Mr. Sandeep Telkar R

My Loving Parents:
Mr. Ubedulla Khadar Shaikh,
Smt. Zainabbi U Shaikh.
And
My Beloved Husband, Mr. Mohammed Shafi Shaikh,
My Lovely Daughter, Tanazparveen Shaikh and
My Loving Son, Tawfeeqahmed Shaikh.

– Dr. Yasmeen Shaikh

My Beloved Parents:
Late Sri. S. R. Konnurmath and
Smt. Susheela S. Konnurmath.
And
My Wife, Mrs. Poornima Konnurmath and
My Lovely Daughter, Ms. Pranavi Konnurmath.

– Dr. Guruprasad Konnurmath

About the Authors

Ms. Divyashree Mallarapu is an AI/ML Engineer with hands-on experience in the design, development, and deployment of production-grade machine learning solutions. Her technical expertise spans Artificial Intelligence, Machine Learning, Deep Learning, Natural Language Processing, Computer Vision, Big Data Analytics, Data Analysis, Cloud Computing, and Networking Automation, with strong proficiency in Python. She is also proficient in C++ and has a solid foundation in Data Structures and Algorithms. She has contributed to several applied projects, including generative AI systems, document intelligence solutions, predictive maintenance platforms, industrial defect detection, and NeuroSense, an intelligent healthcare platform focused on the early detection and management of neurodegenerative diseases.

In addition to her technical work, she has mentored students in hackathons, and conducted multiple technical workshops, reflecting her commitment to applied learning and knowledge dissemination. She is the co-author of a technical book, *Kickstart to Compiler Design Fundamentals*, and is actively engaged in developing structured, accessible as well as technically rigorous learning resources.

Mr. Sandeep Telkar R is an accomplished academician, researcher, and textbook author, currently serving as an Assistant Professor in the Department of Artificial Intelligence and Machine Learning at the PES Institute of Technology & Management, Shivamogga. He holds an M. Tech in Digital Communication and Networking and a B.E. in Information Science and Engineering, with strong expertise in programming (C, Java, Python), machine learning, deep learning, system software, and emerging AI technologies.

He is the author of several internationally published textbooks, including *Kickstart to Compiler Design Fundamentals*, *Python for Machine Learning*, and *Conquering C Programming*, which are widely appreciated for their clear conceptual approach, practical orientation, and student-friendly presentation. His upcoming books on Data Structures and Internet of Things further reflect his commitment to building strong foundational knowledge among learners.

With multiple research publications in reputed IEEE, Springer, and Scopus-indexed journals, along with Best Paper and Best Research Awards, he actively integrates research insights into his authored textbooks.

Dr. Yasmeen Shaikh is an accomplished academician, researcher, and educator in the field of Computer Science, Artificial Intelligence and Data Science. She currently serves as Professor and Head of the Department of Artificial Intelligence and Data Science at S. G. Balekundri Institute of Technology, Belagavi. She holds Ph.D., M. Tech and B.E in Computer Science and Engineering, with strong expertise in programming languages (C, C++, Java, and Python), Machine Learning, emerging AI technologies, Cloud Computing and Big Data Analytics.

With extensive experience in teaching, research, and academic leadership, she has contributed significantly to curriculum design, student mentoring, and institutional development. Her core areas of expertise include Machine Learning, Deep Learning, IoT, Data Analytics, and Intelligent Systems, with a strong emphasis on applying AI-driven solutions to real-world societal and industrial challenges. She has authored numerous research publications in reputed IEEE, Springer, and Scopus-indexed journals and conferences, along with securing patents and funded research projects. She also serves as a reviewer for leading international journals and conferences, actively contributing to the global research community.

Dr. Guruprasad Konnurmath is an Assistant Professor in the Department of Computer Science and Engineering at KLE Technological University, Hubballi. He received his Ph.D. in Computer Science and Engineering from KLE Technological University, and holds M.Tech. and B.E. degrees in Computer Science and Engineering from Visvesvaraya Technological University. Dr. Guruprasad has more than 14 years of teaching experience, and has made sustained contributions to academic excellence through curriculum development and effective pedagogical practices.

His research record includes the publication of more than 30 peer-reviewed papers in reputed international conferences and journals. Dr. Guruprasad's academic and research interests encompass DBMS, Data Structures and Algorithms, Machine Learning, Deep Learning, and NLP with Generative AI. Beyond scholarly publications, his academic contributions include a patent, book chapter contributions in Generative AI and Machine Learning, professional memberships in recognized computer societies, and service as a reviewer for Springer and other reputed international journals.

About the Technical Reviewer

Dr. Sudin Baraokar is a globally recognized AI and Deep Tech innovator with decades of leadership across banking, technology, and digital transformation. He holds a Doctorate in Computer Science from Canterbury University, UK, and a Bachelor of Computer Engineering (Honours) from the University of Mumbai.

Dr. Baraokar has held senior leadership roles including Chief Innovation Officer (CIO/CTO), Global IT Advisor, and Technology Leader at renowned institutions such as the State Bank of India (SBI), Barclays, IBM, and GE. He currently serves as an AI and Digital Transformation Advisor to global enterprises and academia, and is the Founder of a deep-tech startup delivering AI Inferencing as a Service.

His work spans 70+ technologies and platforms, covering AI architecture and strategy, GenAI, MLOps, FinTech, RegTech, cybersecurity, IoT, HPC, quantum computing, smart manufacturing, data science, and autonomic systems. He was instrumental in transforming SBI's Core Banking Systems, enabling 24,000 TPS and 1.5 billion daily transactions for over 500 million customers, and led the development of SBI YONO, the world's first Autonomic AI Digital Banking and Lending Super App with over 50 million users.

Dr. Baraokar has also established global platforms such as Barclays' Global Innovation Application Platform, GE's Industrial Digital Cockpit, and contributed to IBM Watson AI for Global Banking. He founded the Bankchain Alliance, uniting more than 30 banks to co-innovate emerging technology solutions.

A passionate educator and mentor, he has trained over one million professionals, delivered 1,000+ workshops and keynotes, and mentored 1,000+ startups and MSMEs worldwide. Beyond technology, he is an avid golfer, singer, charity volunteer, and researcher in future technologies, economics, sports, and history.

Acknowledgments

First and foremost, I express my sincere gratitude to my parents for their unwavering support, encouragement, and belief in me. Their guidance and sacrifices have formed the foundation of my academic journey, and made this work possible.

I am grateful to my teachers and mentors for their valuable guidance, academic insight, and continued encouragement, which have significantly contributed to my learning and professional growth in the field of Data Structures and Algorithms.

I sincerely thank my co-authors for their dedication, collaboration, and meaningful contributions. This book reflects our collective effort and shared commitment to academic excellence.

I would like to acknowledge the invaluable support of Orange Education Pvt Ltd. and their editorial team for their professionalism, patience, and assistance in refining the manuscript. Their attention to detail and commitment to quality greatly enhanced the final work.

Finally, I extend my sincere thanks to everyone who supported me during this journey. This publication would not have been possible without your encouragement and trust.

-Ms. *Divyashree Mallarapu*

I express my profound gratitude to my parents for their unwavering support, encouragement, and guidance throughout the course of this academic endeavor. Their constant belief in me has served as a source of motivation and perseverance.

I extend my sincere appreciation to PES Institute of Technology and Management (PESITM), Shivamogga, for providing a structured academic environment and the essential infrastructural and learning resources that enabled the successful completion of this work.

I convey my respectful thanks to the faculty members of the Department of Artificial Intelligence and Machine Learning (AIML) for their invaluable instruction, academic mentorship, and continued support in strengthening my conceptual and practical understanding of Data Structures.

I also acknowledge the contributions of the non-teaching staff of the AIML department for their assistance and cooperation in maintaining an effective and supportive academic atmosphere.

Thus, this book stands as a culmination of the collective guidance, academic support, and institutional encouragement received during this journey, and I remain sincerely grateful to all who have contributed, directly or indirectly, to its successful completion.

-Mr. *Sandeep Telkar* R

I express my heartfelt gratitude to my parents and family for their unwavering support, encouragement, and guidance throughout my academic and professional journey. Their constant belief in me has been a source of motivation and strength at every stage.

I extend my sincere gratitude to my institution, S. G. Balekundri Institute of Technology, Belagavi, for providing a conducive academic environment and the necessary resources that have enabled my research, teaching, and scholarly contributions. I also express my sincere appreciation to my colleagues for their valuable discussions, cooperation, and encouragement. Their expertise, mentorship, and collaborative spirit have significantly contributed to my academic growth and professional development.

Finally, I extend my gratitude to my students and research scholars, whose curiosity, enthusiasm, and engagement continually inspire me to explore new ideas, and push the boundaries of knowledge.

This book is a reflection of the collective support, knowledge, and encouragement I have received, and I remain deeply grateful to everyone who has been part of this journey.

-Dr. Yasmeen Shaikh

I sincerely acknowledge the KLE Technological University and the School of Computer Science and Engineering, for providing a supportive academic environment, a strong collaborative research culture, and valuable academic exposure that enabled the successful completion of this work. The process of conceptualizing and authoring this Data Structures book significantly enhanced my understanding of the subject, and contributed to my academic and professional development.

I extend my sincere appreciation to my students, whose curiosity, dedication, and enthusiasm for learning continue to inspire and motivate my academic pursuits.

I sincerely thank my parents for their constant support and guiding values, my wife for her unwavering support, and my daughter for being a continual source of strength and inspiration.

-Dr. Guruprasad Konnurmath

Preface

Data Structures and Algorithms are the backbone of efficient computing. Every software system we build—from simple programs to large-scale applications—relies on structured data organization and well-designed algorithms to perform efficiently. This underlying logic, often invisible to the end user, is what enables modern software to be fast, scalable, and reliable. At the core of problem-solving in computer science lies the effective use of data structures and algorithms. This book serves as a comprehensive guide to Data Structures and Algorithms, taking readers from fundamental concepts to advanced problem-solving techniques. Hence, whether you are a student, an aspiring software engineer, or a professional seeking to strengthen your algorithmic foundation, this book provides clear explanations, practical insights, and implementation-oriented learning to build strong problem-solving skills.

Data Structures and Algorithms are often perceived as difficult and abstract, but in reality, they represent a logical and systematic approach to solving problems efficiently. This book aims to simplify these concepts while maintaining a structured and rigorous approach. Each topic is explained with clarity, focusing on intuition, performance analysis, and real-world relevance, enabling learners to understand not just how algorithms work, but why they are designed in a particular way. By the end of this book, readers will not only understand core data structures and algorithms but will also be able to analyze problems, choose appropriate approaches, and implement efficient solutions with confidence. The book is structured into 16 chapters, covering all essential aspects of Data Structures and Algorithms—from foundational concepts and linear data structures to advanced algorithms, applied patterns, and career-oriented preparation. Each chapter follows a progressive learning model, ensuring a smooth and logical build-up of knowledge.

Chapter 1. Introduction to Data Structures and Algorithms

This chapter provides a foundational introduction to Data Structures and Algorithms, explaining their importance in programming and real-world problem-solving. It covers algorithm basics, performance analysis, time and space complexity, and asymptotic notations. The chapter also guides readers in setting up C++ and Python environments for hands-on implementation.

Chapter 2. Arrays and Strings

This chapter explores arrays and strings as fundamental linear data structures. It discusses memory representation, basic operations, and common manipulation techniques. Problem-solving patterns such as prefix sums, two pointers, and sliding window methods are introduced with practical examples and interview-oriented problems.

Chapter 3. Linked Lists

This chapter focuses on linked lists, covering singly, doubly, and circular linked lists. It emphasizes dynamic memory usage, pointer manipulation, and common operations, along with classic problems such as reversal, loop detection, and merging techniques.

Chapter 4. Stacks, Queues and Deques

This chapter introduces stacks, queues, and deques, explaining their operational principles and applications. It covers implementation techniques and real-world use cases such as expression evaluation, recursion handling, and breadth-first search.

Chapter 5. Hash Tables and Unordered Maps

This chapter presents hash-based data structures, detailing hashing techniques, collision handling, and performance considerations. It highlights practical applications such as frequency counting, caching, and fast lookups.

Chapter 6. Trees and Binary Search Trees

This chapter introduces tree-based structures, including binary trees and binary search trees. It covers traversal methods, recursive processing, and key operations with real-world use cases.

Chapter 7. Heaps and Priority Queues

This chapter explains heaps and their role in implementing priority queues. Topics include heap operations, heapsort, and applications such as scheduling and Top-K problems.

Chapter 8. Graph Fundamentals

This chapter introduces graphs, their representations, and traversal techniques such as BFS and DFS, emphasizing real-world modeling and problem-solving.

Chapter 9. Graph Algorithms

This chapter focuses on essential graph algorithms, including shortest path and minimum spanning tree techniques, with performance analysis and applications.

Chapter 10. Sorting and Searching

This chapter covers fundamental and advanced sorting and searching algorithms, discussing efficiency, trade-offs, and practical applications.

Chapter 11. Greedy and Divide-and-Conquer Strategies

This chapter explores two major algorithmic paradigms, explaining when and how to apply them effectively to solve optimization problems.

Chapter 12. Dynamic Programming

This chapter introduces dynamic programming, covering problem identification, state formulation, and classic DP problems with optimization techniques.

Chapter 13. Backtracking and Recursion Patterns

This chapter focuses on recursion and backtracking techniques, highlighting constraint-based problem-solving and classic algorithmic challenges.

Chapter 14. Advanced Data Structures: Tries, Segment Trees and Fenwick Trees

This chapter presents advanced structures such as tries, segment trees, and Fenwick trees, emphasizing performance optimization and large-scale problem scenarios.

Chapter 15. Applied DSA Patterns and Standard Template Library

This chapter integrates common problem-solving patterns and practical usage of the C++ STL and Python utilities for efficient coding.

Chapter 16. Best Tips and Trends for Interviews

This final chapter prepares readers for technical interviews and real-world applications, covering smart coding practices, interview strategies, and emerging technology trends where DSA plays a critical role.

DID YOU KNOW

Did you know that Orange Education Pvt Ltd offers eBook versions of every book published, with PDF and ePub files available? You can upgrade to the eBook version at **www.orangeava.com** and as a print book customer, you are entitled to a discount on the eBook copy. Get in touch with us at: **info@orangeava.com** for more details.

At **www.orangeava.com**, you can also read a collection of free technical articles, sign up for a range of free newsletters, and receive exclusive discounts and offers on Print Books and eBooks.

PIRACY

If you come across any illegal copies of our works in any form on the internet, we would be grateful if you would provide us with the location address or website name. Please contact us at **info@orangeava.com** with a link to the material.

ARE YOU INTERESTED IN AUTHORING WITH US?

If there is a topic that you have expertise in, and you are interested in either writing or contributing to a book, please write to us at **business@orangeava.com**. We are on a journey to help developers and tech professionals to gain insights on the present technological advancements and innovations happening across the globe and build a community that believes Knowledge is best acquired by sharing and learning with others. Please reach out to us to learn what our audience demands and how you can be part of this educational reform. We also welcome ideas from tech experts and help them build learning and development content for their domains.

REVIEWS

Please leave a review. Once you have read and used this book, why not leave a review on the site that you purchased it from? Potential readers can then see and use your unbiased opinion to make purchase decisions. We at Orange Education would love to know what you think about our products, and our authors can learn from your feedback. Thank you!

For more information about Orange Education, please visit **www.orangeava.com**.

Table of Contents

Chapter 1

Introduction to Data Structures and Algorithms

Introduction

Welcome to the world of Data Structures and Algorithms (DSA)! This toolkit will transform how you think about and solve programming problems. Imagine opening your phone's contact list and finding a name in the blink of an eye. That seamless experience depends on the careful design of data structures and the clever logic of algorithms. In this chapter, we will gently guide you through these foundational concepts, while showing you how to organize data and the steps involved in processing it. After all, knowing these aspects makes the difference between code that crawls and the one that soars.

Thus, we will begin our journey by exploring the symbiotic relationship between data structures and algorithms: how choosing the right structure can simplify complex tasks, and how the right algorithm turns raw data into actionable results. You will learn to measure an algorithm's efficiency through `Big O`, `Big Ω`, and `Big Θ` notations, and recognizing common complexity classes such as constant, linear, and logarithmic time.

Thus, whether you are a fresh beginner coding your first programs; a job-seeker sharpening your interview skills; or an instructor seeking clear teaching examples, this chapter will provide a solid, self-contained foundation for more skills to follow. We will walk you through setting up C++ and Python on your machine and writing your very first DSA programs, so that you can immediately put theory into practice. By the end of this chapter, you will be ready to choose the right data structure for any problem, analyze and implement algorithms with confidence, and write code that is faster, leaner, and elegant.

Structure

In this chapter, we will cover the following topics:

- Foundations of Data Structures and Algorithms
- Significance of DSA in Software Development
- Classification of Data Structures
- Algorithm Categories and Components
- Introduction to Complexity Analysis
- Asymptotic Notation and Performance Measurement

- Common Algorithmic Complexity Classes
- Approach to Evaluating Algorithm Efficiency
- Preparing the Programming Environment
- Hands-on with Basic Programs

Foundations of Data Structures and Algorithms

Welcome to the first step of your journey into the world of **Data Structures and Algorithms (DSA)**! DSA is the core discipline that can transform ordinary code into efficient, scalable, and high-performing solutions. Whether you are a student taking your first course in computer science; a coding enthusiast preparing for technical interviews, or an educator looking for a clear and modern teaching reference, this chapter will address all your queries while guiding you through the intricacies of DSA.

DSA is not just about memorizing lists or syntax. It is about developing the ability to **think clearly**, **solve problems systematically**, and **build smarter software**. Just like how a carefully organized library makes it easier to find the right book, the right data structure and algorithm can make all the difference in how your code performs.

In this foundational section, we will set the stage with **what DSA means**, **why it matters**, and **how it shapes the way we approach programming challenges**. Hence, through real-world analogies and clean, practical explanations, you will gain the mental framework to understand how to write code well.

Let us begin building that foundation—step by step.

Data Structures and Algorithms

In programming, every solution starts with two core building blocks: **data** and **logic**. How we organize the data and process it directly impacts the efficacy and performance of the solution. This is where **data structures** and **algorithms** come into play.

A **data structure** is a way of organizing and storing data, so that it can be used efficiently. Just like a cabinet with different drawers for specific items, data structures help programmers categorize and manage information in a logical manner. Whether it is a simple list of numbers or a complex network of connected users, the choice of data structure determines how effectively that information can be accessed, updated, or searched.

An **algorithm** is a sequence of clear, well-defined steps designed to solve a specific problem or perform a task. Algorithms define the "how" of problem-solving. This includes queries such as how to search, how to sort, how to traverse, and how to optimize. Good algorithms are the difference between a sluggish program and a lightning-fast one.

Together, data structures and algorithms form the backbone of efficient programming. Therefore, we can say that data structures shape the data, while algorithms define how we interact with it.

Data and Logic in Problem Solving

Data and logic are inseparable companions in computer science. While **data structures** organize the information, **algorithms** provide the instructions to manipulate that information. Therefore, a good programmer does not just write code that works; they write code that works *well*, and that is where this combination becomes powerful.

Imagine building a food delivery app. You need to store user addresses (data), find the nearest delivery partner (algorithm), and update order status (data + logic). If your data is stored inefficiently—say, in a flat list—it may take too long to find relevant information. However, if it is organized in a location-aware structure like a tree or graph, an efficient searching algorithm can return the result in milliseconds.

This synergy becomes even more critical as data grows in size and complexity. A simple loop might work fine on ten items but fail miserably on ten million. Choosing the right structure (like a hash table instead of a list) and pairing it with an optimized algorithm (like binary search instead of linear search) ensures that your code remains reliable, fast, and scalable.

By learning how data and logic complement each other, you will be able to develop a deeper understanding of computational thinking and problem-solving. Therefore, these skills are essential for interviews, dealing with real-world software, and conducting advanced research.

Real-World Analogies

Now that you have seen how data and logic work together to solve problems, let us ground these abstract concepts in everyday examples. These analogies will help you form an intuitive understanding of how data structures and algorithms are used in real-life scenarios.

Think of a **data structure** as a **bookshelf**. You might have different shelves for fiction, nonfiction, and textbooks; this organizational structure helps you quickly find what you are looking for. Similarly, in programming, we use arrays, lists, stacks, or trees to organize information based on how we need to access or modify it.

An **algorithm** is like the **method** you use to find a specific book. Do you scan shelf by shelf (linear search)? Or do you go straight to the alphabetical section, and then to the author's name (binary search)? The way you search impacts how long it takes to get your book. That is the essence of algorithm efficiency.

Here is another one: imagine planning a trip. The **map** is your data structure—it holds all the places and routes. The **directions** you choose to get from point A to B are your algorithm. A smart GPS does not just show a path; it finds the **best** one. In software, the better your data structure and the smarter your algorithm, the faster and smoother your solution.

By viewing DSA through these familiar lenses, you will find it easier to grasp the purpose behind different techniques and develop the intuition to choose the right tools as you advance through the subject.

Significance of DSA in Software Development

After developing an initial intuition for data structures and algorithms, it is important to explore the role they play in the software systems that surround us. It is important to remember that DSA is not just theoretical; it is a practical cornerstone of real-world programming. Hence, whether you are developing a small utility tool or architecting an enterprise-grade application, the principles of DSA guide your decisions on efficiency, scalability, and maintainability. Therefore, this section highlights how DSA powers real applications, where it is used across industries, and why it is considered a critical skill in the tech world.

Role of DSA in Building Efficient Applications

In software development, performance is not just a luxury; it is a necessity. Users expect fast, responsive applications, and behind that smooth experience exists the invisible machinery of well-designed data structures and thoughtfully implemented algorithms. This is where DSA proves its unmatched value.

At its core, DSA is about solving problems in ways that are not only correct but efficient. Take, for example, searching for a product in an online store. A naive solution might scan the entire catalog every time a user types a keyword, but a system built with efficient search algorithms and well-organized data structures such as tries, hash tables, or binary search trees can deliver relevant results almost instantly, even when you are dealing with millions of entries.

Similarly, consider mobile apps that sync with cloud data. Without the use of queues and buffers (which manage data flow) and optimized algorithms for syncing, the app could easily crash or lag. It is DSA that ensures smooth data transfers, minimal memory use, and fast response times.

Efficient applications also mean scalable applications. As data grows, poorly chosen data structures or inefficient algorithms can turn a decent system into a bottleneck. Consider the example of a social media platform using an unoptimized way to suggest friends or fetch notifications; it might work for a few thousand users, but will crumble at scale. With proper use of graphs, heaps, or hash maps, such systems remain robust, even as user bases scale into the millions.

Ultimately, DSA empowers developers to think critically about *how* things are done. It is the difference between writing code that merely works, and writing code that *works well* under real-world constraints.

Real-World Use Cases of DSA

The real strength of DSA is seen not just in theory, but in the way they drive technology across countless real-world domains. Behind almost every software system you interact with—whether it is searching on Google, swiping through a music playlist, or booking a cab—DSA is at work. Its principles are applied to ensure speed, accuracy, scalability, and a seamless user experience.

In **search engines**, for instance, advanced data structures such as inverted indexes, tries, and graphs are used to index vast volumes of web pages. Algorithms such as PageRank, keyword matching, and relevance scoring ensure that users get the most accurate results within milliseconds.

E-commerce platforms like Amazon or Flipkart rely on hash maps to manage inventory, heaps to handle recommendation engines, and graphs for tracking user behavior. Priority queues can be used for processing high-value transactions quickly, and dynamic programming may optimize delivery routes.

In **navigation and maps applications**, graph algorithms such as Dijkstra's or A* (A-star) play a crucial role in finding the shortest path between two locations. These are implemented over graph-based data structures representing road networks, where each node is an intersection and edges represent roads.

Healthcare systems benefit from efficient storage and retrieval of patient records using trees or hash tables. Therefore, advanced applications like DNA sequencing or protein structure analysis use dynamic programming, pattern matching algorithms, and graph theory.

In **cybersecurity**, real-time threat detection often involves scanning logs and behaviors using algorithms that detect anomalies or apply pattern recognition. These functionalities and features are enabled by hashing techniques, stacks, and queue-based monitoring.

Even in **entertainment platforms** like Spotify or Netflix, DSA powers playlist generation, while caching popular content and analyzing user preferences through Machine Learning (ML) models trained on optimized data pipelines.

In modern data science and Artificial Intelligence (AI) systems, newer data representations such as **tuples and tensors** have also become increasingly important. Tuples are commonly used to group structured data like feature sets, coordinates, and database records, as they ensure immutability and data consistency in analytics pipelines. Tensors, which generalize arrays and matrices to higher dimensions, form the backbone of deep learning models. They enable efficient processing of images, text embeddings, audio signals, and video data. While classical data structures organize and manage data, tensors enable large-scale numerical computation on CPUs, GPUs, and specialized accelerators. Therefore, they effectively bridge traditional DSA concepts with modern AI-driven applications.

From these varied domains, it is clear that DSA is not a niche topic confined to coding interviews. In fact, it is the backbone of intelligent systems and smart applications, which quietly works behind the scenes to make digital life fast, reliable, and intelligent.

Industry Relevance and Expectations from DSA Knowledge

In the tech industry, DSA is more than just academic theory. Recruiters, engineers, and technical leaders alike understand that a solid grasp of DSA reflects a developer's ability to write clean, efficient, and scalable code. This line of thought is the force that builds great software.

Whether you are applying for a role as a software developer, data engineer, machine learning engineer, or even a system designer, one of the first filters you will encounter is a test of your DSA skills. Hence, this is not just about solving puzzles; it is about demonstrating the ability to break down problems, choosing the right approach, and implementing solutions that work well under constraints.

For example, in coding interviews, you are expected to identify when a hash table is more efficient than an array, or when recursion can simplify a tree traversal problem. These are not hypothetical exercises, but mirror real engineering challenges faced in production environments.

Beyond interviews, industry expectations extend into day-to-day work. Teams want developers who can optimize backend systems, reduce the time complexity of a feature rollout, or prevent bottlenecks in a database query. Therefore, these improvements often come from a deep, intuitive understanding of the underlying data structures and algorithms in play.

Startups look for engineers who can deliver fast, performant applications with limited resources. Big tech companies like Google, Microsoft, Amazon, and Meta evaluate problem-solving patterns rooted in DSA to gauge your adaptability and efficiency. Even non-tech industries such as finance, healthcare, and logistics value DSA knowledge because efficient data processing is essential for achieving success.

In short, mastering DSA not only makes you a better programmer; it signals to employers that you are equipped to tackle real-world challenges with thoughtfulness, precision, and creativity.

Classification of Data Structures

As we explore the core of DSA, it is important to understand how different data structures are organized based on how they manage, access, and store data. Much like arranging tools in a toolbox, every data structure serves a specific purpose—some are ideal for fast lookups, while others are good for dynamic insertion or hierarchical navigation.

At a high level, data structures are classified into **linear** and **non-linear** types based on the relationship between their elements. This classification, illustrated in *Figure 1.1*, will serve as a foundational guide throughout this book.

- **Linear Data Structures** such as Arrays, Linked Lists, Stacks, and Queues store elements sequentially and are easy to traverse.
- **Non-Linear Data Structures** like Trees, Heaps, and Graphs allow for more complex relationships, such as branching or interconnected nodes.

Each structure comes with its own set of strengths, limitations, and ideal use cases. In the following sections, we will explore both categories in depth, while examining their structure and behavior, as well as the occasions where they shine in real-world applications.

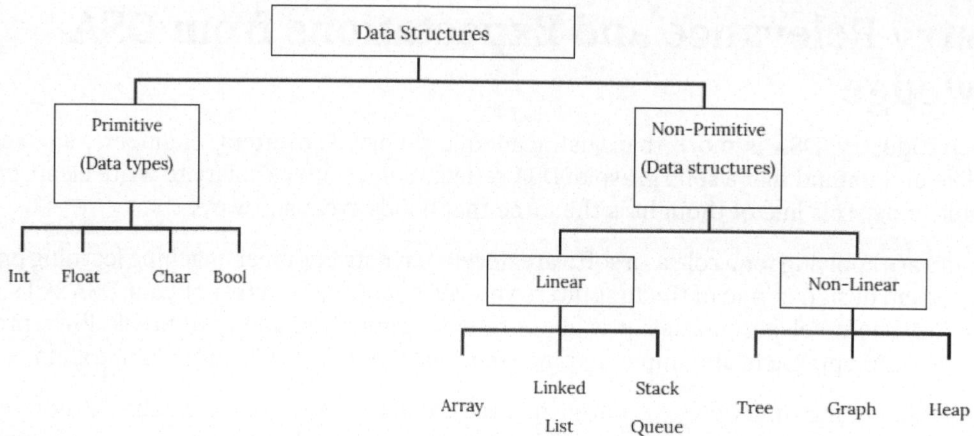

Figure 1.1: *Classification of Data Structures*

Linear Data Structures: Arrays, Linked Lists, Stacks, and Queues

Linear data structures organize data in a sequential, ordered manner. Each element follows the previous one and creates a logical chain of access and manipulation. Think of it like standing in a queue at a ticket counter: there is a beginning, an end, and everyone knows their place. This kind of structure is fundamental for solving a wide variety of programming problems with predictability and efficiency.

Let us begin by exploring the four core linear structures.

Arrays

An **array** is one of the simplest and most widely used data structures in computer science. It is a fixed-size, ordered collection of elements that are stored in contiguous memory locations. Arrays provide direct access to elements through indexing, which makes them especially efficient for read operations.

Key Characteristics

- **Fixed Size**: Once defined, its size cannot be altered (in most languages).
- **Random Access**: Any element can be accessed instantly using its index.
- **Homogeneous**: All elements must be of the same data type.

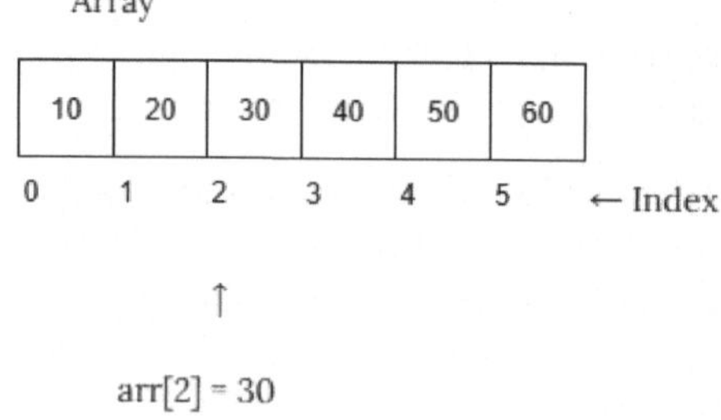

Figure 1.2: *Representation of an Array*

This diagram displays an array of integers with indices starting from 0. Each box in the diagram symbolizes a memory location and the labels beneath the boxes represent indices (for example, 0, 1, 2, and so on).

For instance, accessing arr[2] retrieves the third element in the array. This efficiency comes from the contiguous memory allocation as each index maps directly to a specific memory address.

Imagine a row of train coaches labeled A, B, C, D, and so on. Each coach has a fixed position, and to reach coach E, you simply count five steps from the beginning. That is precisely how arrays work; each element's location is mathematically calculated, which makes retrieval instantaneous.

Occasions to Use Arrays

- When the total number of elements is known in advance
- When frequent access or updates to specific elements are required using their index
- When memory needs to be tightly controlled and predictable

Consider storing marks of five students. An array of size 5 can hold all marks and allow constant-time retrieval.

In C++, it shows up as:

```
int marks[5] = {88, 76, 90, 85, 92};
cout << marks[2]; // Outputs 90
```

In Python, it looks like this:

```
marks = [88, 76, 90, 85, 92]
print(marks[2])  # Outputs 90
```

In both examples, the third element (index 2) is accessed in constant time—**O(1)**.

Linked Lists

A **linked list** is a linear data structure where each element (called a node) contains two parts: the actual data and a reference (or pointer) to the next node in the sequence. Unlike arrays, linked lists do not require contiguous memory locations. Instead, elements are linked using pointers, which offer flexibility in dynamic memory allocation.

This structure allows efficient insertions and deletions, especially when the exact position of elements is known. However, unlike arrays, accessing an element at a specific position requires traversing the list from the beginning.

Key Characteristics

- **Dynamic Size:** Grows or shrinks during runtime without memory reallocation
- **Sequential Access:** Accessing elements requires traversal from the head node.
- **Memory Efficiency:** Utilizes memory based on current need; no wastage due to fixed size
- **Flexible Insertion and Deletion:** Especially efficient at the beginning or middle.

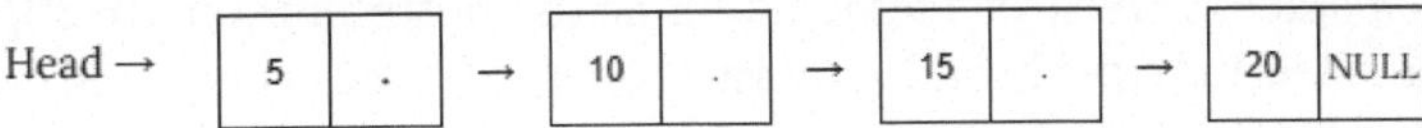

Figure 1.3: *Singly Linked List Representation*

This diagram represents a simple singly linked list of three nodes. Each node holds a data value (for example, 5, 10, 15, 20) and a pointer to the next node. The last node points to NULL, which indicates the end of the list. This structure visually illustrates how elements are connected in memory through references rather than being placed side-by-side.

Linked lists are best used when:

- The number of elements is unknown or changes frequently.

- Frequent insertions or deletions are expected at the beginning or middle of the sequence.
- Memory allocation needs to be dynamic and flexible.

Imagine a treasure hunt where each clue (node) contains a piece of information and a direction to the next clue. You cannot skip directly to the third clue; you must follow the sequence. That is how a linked list operates: you start at the head and move forward one node at a time.

Stacks

A **stack** is a linear data structure that follows the **Last-In, First-Out (LIFO)** principle. This means that the last element added is the first one to be removed. Think of it like a stack of plates: the last plate you place on top is the first one you take off. Stacks are widely used in function call management, undo mechanisms, parsing expressions, and more.

Unlike arrays and linked lists that allow access to any element, stacks restrict insertion and deletion to only one end, which is called the **top** of the stack.

Key Characteristics

- **LIFO Behaviour:** The last element added is removed first.
- **Single Access Point:** Only the top of the stack is accessible.
- **Operations:** `push` (add), **pop** (remove), and **peek** (view top without removing)
- Used in backtracking, recursion, and expression evaluation

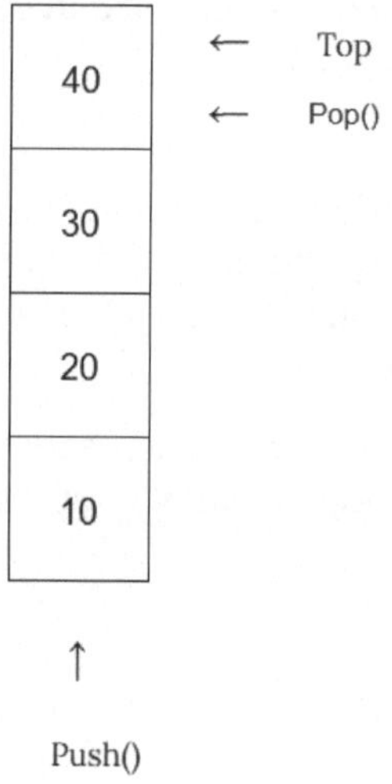

Figure 1.4: *Stack Representation*

This diagram shows a stack with three elements: 10 at the bottom, then 20, 30, and 40 at the top. The top is where both insertion (push) and removal (pop) take place. This visual emphasizes the LIFO order; only the most recent element (30) is accessible without removing others.

Stacks are best used when:

- You need to **reverse** a sequence of operations.
- Function **calls and recursion** must be tracked.
- The solution requires **backtracking** (for example, solving mazes, parsing).

Imagine a pile of books. You can only remove the book from the top without disturbing the rest. Similarly, in web browsers, the "**Back**" button works like a stack—you can return to the previous page by popping the most recently visited one from the history stack.

Queues

A **queue** is a linear data structure that operates on the **First-In, First-Out (FIFO)** principle. In a queue, the first element added is the first one to be removed, just like people waiting in a line at a ticket counter. The person who arrives first is served first, and new arrivals wait at the end of the line.

Unlike stacks where operations happen at one end, queues involve **two ends**:

- The **front**, where elements are removed (dequeued)
- The **rear**, where elements are added (enqueued)

Key Characteristics

- **FIFO Behavior:** First element in is also the first out.
- **Two Access Points:** Enqueue at the rear, dequeue from the front
- **Operations:** enqueue (insert), dequeue (remove), and sometimes peek (view front)
- Used in real-time systems, process scheduling, and simulations.

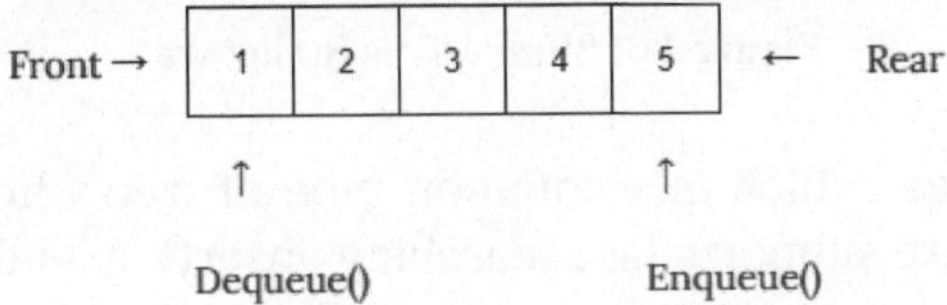

Figure 1.5: *Queue Representation*

This diagram represents a queue where 1 is added first and will also be the first to be removed. Elements enter from the rear (right side) and exit from the front (left side), while maintaining a strict order of processing. This makes queues ideal for systems that require orderly handling of tasks.

Queues are best used when:

- You want to maintain **order of processing** (for example, printing jobs).
- The task involves **buffering or queuing operations** (for example, network data packets).
- You need **level-order traversal** in trees or graph algorithms like **BFS** (Breadth-First Search).

Imagine a ticket booking counter at a railway station. People stand in a line and are served one by one in the order they arrived. You cannot cut the line or pick who goes next. Hence, it can be concluded that queues ensure fairness and sequence, and are crucial for processing tasks in many real-world systems like printers, CPU job scheduling, and customer service desks.

Non-Linear Data Structures: Trees, Heaps, and Graphs

Unlike linear data structures that organize data sequentially, **non-linear data structures** arrange elements in hierarchical or interconnected formats. These structures enable more complex relationships between data elements, which makes them essential for solving advanced computing problems. Instead of a straight line, imagine a branching tree or a web; similarly, non-linear structures allow for multiple paths and levels of connection.

Now, let us explore three major types of non-linear data structures: **trees**, **heaps**, and **graphs**—each uniquely powerful and suited for specialized tasks.

Trees

A **tree** is a hierarchical structure made up of nodes, where each node may point to multiple child nodes, but only one parent node (except the root). It begins at a single node called the **root** and branches out into **subtrees**.

Key Characteristics

- **Rooted Hierarchy:** Starts from a root node
- **Parent-child relationship** between elements
- **Acyclic:** No cycles, unlike graphs
- **Recursive Nature:** Trees can be broken into smaller trees.

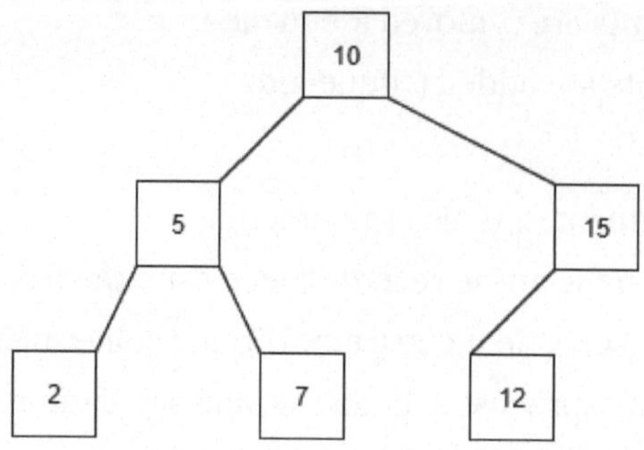

Figure 1.6: *Binary Tree Structure*

This figure shows a **binary tree**, which is a common type of tree where each node has up to two children. The hierarchical nature supports fast searching, insertion, and deletion when it is balanced properly.

Trees are best used when:

- Data needs **hierarchical representation** (for example, file systems, HTML/XML structure).
- Fast **search, insert, and delete** operations are required (for example, Binary Search Tree).
- Traversal in multiple orders (for example, in-order, pre-order, post-order) is needed.

Consider a **company's organizational chart** at the top is the CEO (root), Under them are department heads (children); under the heads are managers, and so on.

This hierarchy forms a tree, where each employee (node) reports to exactly one manager (parent), but can have several people reporting to them (children).

Other examples can be:

- **File Systems** on Your Computer (Folders within Folders)
- **Family Genealogy Charts**
- **Tournament Brackets**

Heaps

A **heap** is a specialized tree-based structure that satisfies the **heap property**:

- In a **max heap**, each parent is greater than or equal to its children.
- In a **min heap**, each parent is less than or equal to its children.

Heaps are **complete binary trees**, meaning all levels are fully filled, except the last, which is filled from left to right.

Key Characteristics

- **Priority-Based Structure**
- **Efficient Retrieval of min or max** Element
- Used in sorting and priority queues

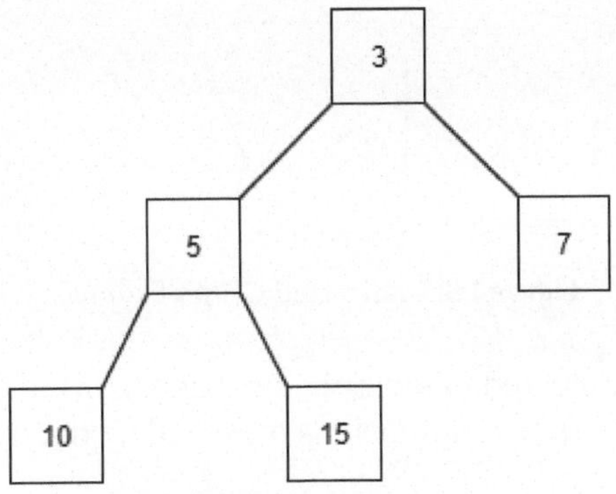

Figure 1.7: *Min Heap Example*

In this min heap, the root node has the smallest value. Every child node is greater than its parent, which makes it easy to access the minimum value at the top.

Heaps are best used when:

- You need **efficient priority handling** (for example, task schedulers, Dijkstra's algorithm).
- **Sorting operations** like heapsort are required.
- Implementing **priority queues**, where the highest (or lowest) priority element must be accessed quickly.

Think of a **priority boarding line at an airport.**

- Passengers are assigned boarding priorities (for example, Business Class > Frequent Flyers > Economy).
- The one with the highest priority always boards first.

This mirrors a **max heap** where the highest-priority element (root) is accessed and removed first.

Other examples can be:

- **Job Scheduling in Operating Systems**
- **Leaderboard Rankings** (Highest Score Always at the Top.)

Graphs

A **graph** is a powerful non-linear structure consisting of **nodes (vertices)** and **connections (edges)**. Unlike trees, graphs allow **cycles and multiple connections** between nodes, which makes them ideal for representing networks.

Graphs can be:

- **Directed** or **Undirected**
- **Weighted** or **Unweighted**
- **Cyclic** or **Acyclic**

Key Characteristics

- **Flexible representation** for complex relationships
- **Adjacency list or matrix** used for storage
- Nodes can connect to multiple others; even forming loops.

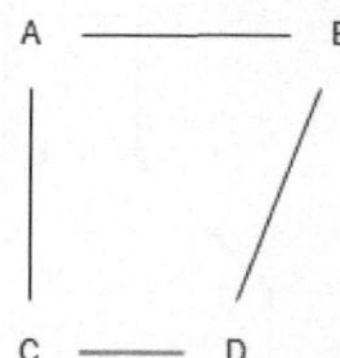

***Figure 1.8:** Undirected Graph Example*

This graph shows four nodes connected in multiple directions, forming a network. Graphs can model anything from roads between cities to relationships on social media platforms.

Graphs are best used when:

- Modeling **networks** (for example, roads, social networks, dependency graphs)
- Performing **pathfinding** (for example, GPS navigation, web crawling)
- Implementing **graph algorithms** like BFS, DFS, Dijkstra's, or Kruskal's

Consider **Google Maps** Locations as **nodes** (cities, intersections), The roads between them are **edges**, which are possibly weighted by distance or travel time.

Graphs can represent all possible routes. Algorithms like Dijkstra's help you find the **shortest path**.

Other examples can be:

- **Social Networks** (Consider People as Nodes, and Friendships as Edges)
- **Internet Link Structure** (Webpages Linked through Hyperlinks)
- **Electric Circuits or Supply Chain Systems**

Algorithm Categories and Components

Algorithms are the beating heart of computation. They are well-defined, step-by-step procedures that solve specific problems. Whether it is sorting numbers, searching for data, or navigating a route, algorithms are used everywhere in programming. In this section, we will break down what makes up an algorithm, the common categories you will frequently encounter, and how every algorithm follows a logical input-process-output structure.

Key Characteristics of Algorithms

Before diving into types, it is essential to understand what makes an algorithm "good" or even valid. Every algorithm shares the following fundamental traits:

- **Input:** It takes zero or more inputs.
- **Definiteness:** Every step is clearly defined.
- **Finiteness:** It terminates after a finite number of steps.
- **Output:** It produces at least one output.
- **Effectiveness:** Each operation must be basic enough to be carried out.

These properties ensure an algorithm not only works, but does so in a predictable and computable way.

Algorithm Types: Searching, Sorting, Traversal

Algorithms are usually categorized based on the problem they solve. Here are the three core ones that are foundational to many applications:

Searching Algorithms

Searching algorithms are used to **locate a specific item** in a data structure.

- **Linear Search:** Scans each element one by one
- **Binary Search:** Efficiently finds elements in a sorted list by repeatedly dividing the search space

Example: Looking for a contact on your phone by typing the first few letters of the name

Sorting Algorithms

Sorting algorithms arrange data in a particular order (ascending or descending).

- **Bubble Sort, Insertion Sort:** Simple, but less efficient for large data
- **Quick Sort, Merge Sort:** Divide-and-conquer techniques for optimal performance

Example: Sorting emails by date or name in your inbox

Traversal Algorithms

Traversal algorithms help **visit all elements** in a data structure, especially trees and graphs.

- **Tree Traversals:** Preorder, Inorder, Postorder
- **Graph Traversals:** Breadth-First Search (BFS), Depth-First Search (DFS)

Example: Viewing all folders and files on your computer systematically

Logical Structure: Input, Processing, Output

Every algorithm, regardless of its category, follows this simple but powerful flow:

- **Input:** The initial data needed to begin the task
- **Processing:** The actual steps or logic used to transform the input
- **Output:** The final result or solution after processing

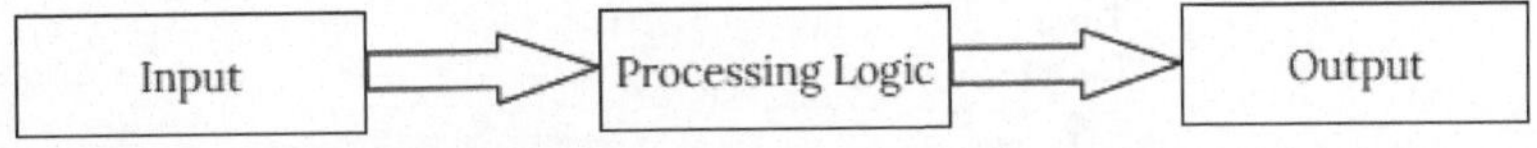

***Figure 1.9**: Logical Flow of an Algorithm*

Think of a coffee machine. The flow will look like this:

- **Input**: Coffee beans and water
- **Process**: Grinding, heating, brewing
- **Output**: A hot cup of coffee

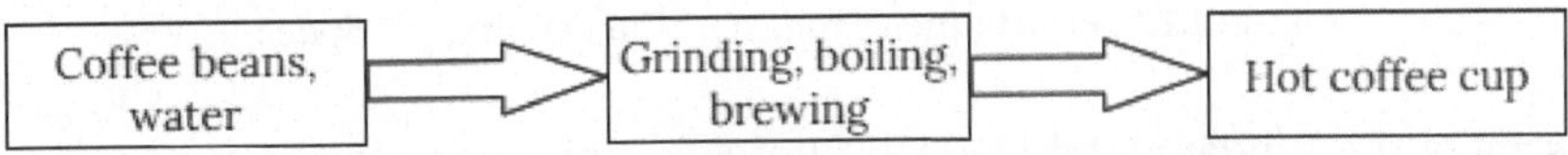

***Figure 1.10**: Coffee Machine Analogy for an Algorithm*

Therefore, this structured flow will help you visualize the algorithm's journey and plan your code efficiently.

Introduction to Complexity Analysis

As we dive deeper into algorithm design, it is not enough to ask, "*Does this solution work?*". We must also ask, "*How well does it work?*". This is where **complexity analysis** comes in. It allows us to evaluate the **efficiency** of an algorithm in terms of **time** and **space**, which are the two most critical resources in computing.

Whether you are coding a simple calculator or building a real-time recommendation engine, knowing how efficiently your code performs can make the difference between a responsive app and a sluggish one. Complexity analysis helps us choose or design the best algorithm for the job, especially when input sizes scale up.

Time and Space as Key Performance Metrics

Time complexity tells us how the running time of an algorithm increases with the size of the input. Think of it as how long it would take to solve a puzzle as it grows in size. For example, searching for a contact in your phone with 10 entries is easy, but what if there are 10,000 of them?

Space complexity refers to the amount of memory an algorithm needs during execution. It is like how much desk space you need while solving a jigsaw puzzle; the more pieces you lay out at once, the more room you will require.

Therefore, both metrics are often expressed using mathematical notation (which we will cover in the next section), but their purpose is intuitive: to compare different approaches and understand scalability.

Trade-Offs between Speed and Memory Usage

In real-world applications, there is often a trade-off between time and space. You can make an algorithm faster by using more memory or use less memory and accept a slower runtime.

Imagine that you are cooking. If you have multiple pans (more memory), you can cook dishes in parallel (faster). However, if you have just one pan, you will cook one dish at a time (slower), even though you are saving kitchen space.

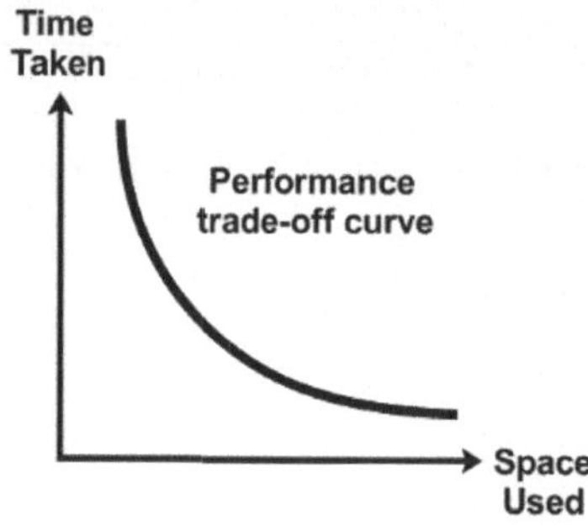

Figure 1.11: *Performance Trade-Off Curve: Time vs. Space*

This visual illustrates the fundamental trade-off between time complexity and space complexity in algorithm design. The X-axis represents the **space utilized (memory consumption)**, while the Y-axis indicates the **time taken (execution speed)** by an algorithm.

The curve shows an inverse relationship—**optimizing for faster execution time often requires more memory**, while **reducing space usage may lead to longer execution times**. For instance, caching intermediate results (as in Dynamic Programming) speeds up computations, but consumes additional memory.

This trade-off is crucial when designing algorithms for resource-constrained environments such as embedded systems or large-scale data processing tasks. Developers must balance between time and space based on the specific needs of their applications, while aiming for an optimal solution that neither wastes memory nor slows down excessively.

Here is a common example from computing:

- A **hash table** allows for constant-time data access, but consumes more space.
- A **linked list** saves space, but accessing an element may take longer.

Choosing the right algorithm involves balancing these factors based on the problem's constraints and available resources.

Understanding complexity helps in:

- Predicting performance before running code
- Optimizing for time-critical or memory-limited systems
- Succeeding in technical interviews and competitions
- Writing scalable, production-ready software

Asymptotic Notation and Performance Measurement

When analyzing how good or bad an algorithm is, we do not just rely on stopwatch timings. Instead, we use mathematical tools to express an algorithm's **performance relative to input size**. This abstraction helps us understand how algorithms can behave as the problem scales, without being tied to machine-specific execution times.

Asymptotic notation is the standard way to describe an algorithm's efficiency by focusing on its **growth rate**, rather than exact timing. It tells us how the resource usage (time or space) grows with increasing input size (*n*).

Let us explore the three most important notations that form the backbone of algorithm analysis:

Big O: Worst-Case Upper Bound

Big O represents the **upper bound** of an algorithm's running time or space requirement. It defines the **worst-case scenario**, ensuring that the algorithm will not perform worse than this rate as input grows. It guarantees performance limits and helps in choosing algorithms that will not become impractically slow, even with large datasets.

Imagine that you are searching for a file in a messy office. In the worst case, you might have to look through **every single drawer** before finding it. Big O describes this maximum possible effort.

Moreover, it describes the upper limit of an algorithm's runtime or space complexity. A function `f(n)` is `O(g(n))` if there exist positive constants c and n_0 such that:

$f(n) \leq c \times g(n)$ for all $n \geq n_0$

Therefore, beyond a certain input size n_0, $f(n)$ will not grow faster than $g(n)$ multiplied by a constant c.

Omega: Best-Case Lower Bound

Omega provides the **lower bound** of an algorithm's performance. It describes the **best-case scenario**, while indicating that the algorithm will take **at least** this much time or space. It can help understand how fast an algorithm could ideally perform under the most favorable conditions. However, the Omega curves will show the minimum growth rate beneath actual performance.

Let us go back to the office analogy—if the file you are searching for happens to be **right on the top of your desk**, it is the best case scenario. Omega captures this optimistic outcome.

It describes the lower limit of an algorithm's runtime or space complexity. A function *f(n)* is Ω(g(n)), if there are positive constants c and n_0 such that:

$f(n) \geq c \times g(n)$ for all $n \geq n_0$

Therefore, beyond a certain input size n_0, *f(n)* will grow at least as fast as *g(n)* multiplied by constant c.

Theta: Tight Bound for Average-Case

Theta defines the **tight bound**, which means that it describes both the **upper and lower bounds** simultaneously. It represents the scenario where the algorithm consistently performs at this rate for typical inputs. It gives a precise, reliable estimate of the algorithm's average behavior.

Think of regularly filing documents in alphabetical order. On average, you will go through a **reasonable portion of drawers** before finding any given file, which is not the worst, but also not the best. Theta captures this typical workload.

It represents the exact asymptotic behavior (both upper and lower bounds). A function *f(n)* is Θ(g(n)), if there are positive constants c_1, c_2, and n_0 such that:

$c_1 \times g(n) \leq f(n) \leq c_2 \times g(n)$ for all $n \geq n_0$

Therefore, beyond n_0, *f(n)* grows proportionally to *g(n)* within constant factors c_1 and c_2.

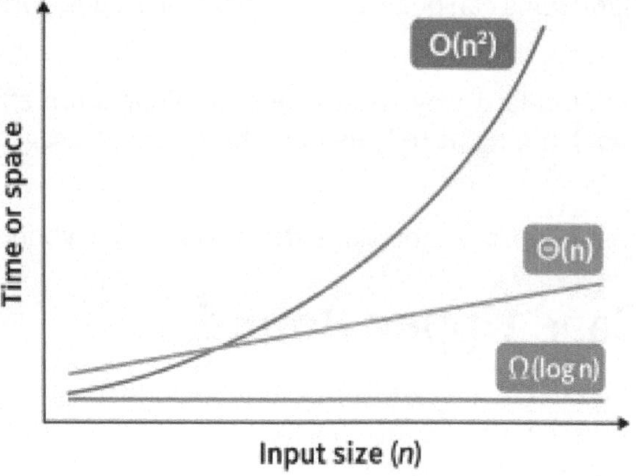

Figure 1.12: *Growth Comparison of Big O, Omega, and Theta*

This figure illustrates how different asymptotic notations describe algorithm efficiency as input size increases.

The curve `Big O (O(n²))` shows the upper bound, representing the worst-case scenario.

The line `Theta (Θ(n))` represents a tight bound that captures the average-case behavior.

The curve **Omega (Ω(log n))** depicts the lower bound, while denoting the best-case efficiency. Together, these curves help compare how algorithms grow under various conditions and highlight the importance of analyzing both upper and lower limits in performance.

Common Algorithmic Complexity Classes

When analyzing the performance of an algorithm, understanding its **time complexity** is essential. Time complexity helps estimate how the algorithm's runtime grows with the size of the input. Therefore, algorithms are classified into **complexity classes** with distinct performance characteristics and real-world implications, depending on how this growth behaves. Now, let us look at the most common classes that form the backbone of algorithm analysis:

Constant Time: `O(1)`

An algorithm has constant time complexity when its execution time does **not depend** on the input size. No matter whether you are dealing with 10 elements or 10 million, the time taken remains the same.

Think of it as switching on a light. Whether you are in a small room or a stadium, flipping the switch takes the same amount of time.

Therefore, accessing an element in an array using its index (for example, arr[5]) is a classic O(1) operation.

Linear Time: `O(n)`

An algorithm is said to operate in **linear time**, denoted as **O(n)**, when its running time increases directly in proportion to the size of the input. In such algorithms, each additional element in the input contributes a constant amount of extra work. Therefore, if the input size doubles, the execution time also grows approximately twofold.

A practical real-world analogy is searching for a particular book on a shelf by examining each book sequentially. As the number of books increases, the time required to locate the desired one increases at the same linear rate.

In programming, linear time commonly appears when every element of a data structure must be processed once. For example, calculating the total sum of numbers stored in an array requires visiting each element exactly one time, making the total work proportional to the number of elements.

Logarithmic Time: `O(log n)`

Logarithmic algorithms are extremely efficient. Instead of examining each item, they **cut the problem in half** with each step. This leads to incredibly fast execution even for large input sizes.

It is like searching for a name in a phonebook by flipping pages in the middle (binary search). You discard half the data at every step. Therefore, binary search on a sorted array is a prime example of `O(log n)` complexity.

Quadratic Time: $O(n^2)$

Algorithms with quadratic time complexity involve **nested iterations** over the input. As the input size grows, the time required grows exponentially faster and is specifically proportional to the square of the input size.

Suppose you are comparing every student in a class to every other student to find duplicates. As the number of students increases, the number of comparisons grows rapidly.

Therefore, bubble sort, selection sort, and other basic sorting algorithms often have `O(n²)` complexity.

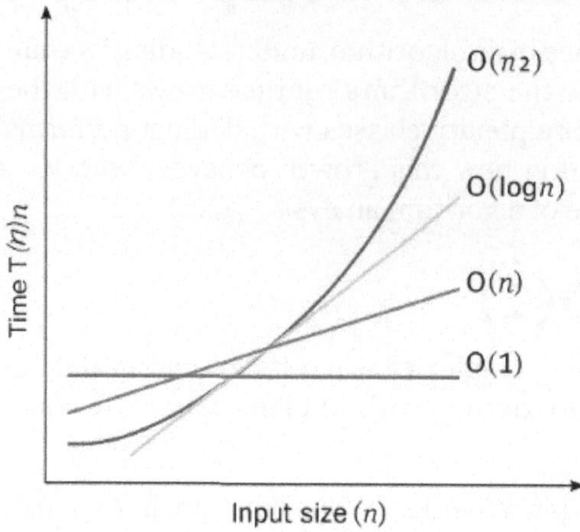

Figure 1.13: *Graphical Comparison of Common Complexity Classes*

The graph visually compares how different algorithmic complexities grow relative to the input size (**n**). The X-axis represents the input size, while the Y-axis shows the time (or space) taken by an algorithm as the input grows.

- **`O(1)` - Constant Time:** This is depicted as a flat, horizontal line. Regardless of the input size, the time taken remains constant. Typical examples include accessing an array element by index or performing a hash table lookup.
- **`O(log n)` - Logarithmic Time:** A slowly rising curve. This complexity grows much slower than linear time. It is common in algorithms like Binary Search, where the input size is repeatedly halved.
- **`O(n)` - Linear Time:** A straight diagonal line with a moderate slope. Time increases proportionally with the input size. Simple operations like traversing an array or linked list fall under this category.
- **`O(n²)` - Quadratic Time:** A steep curve rising sharply as input increases. Algorithms with nested loops over the data, like bubble sort or selection sort, exhibit quadratic complexity. For large datasets, `O(n²)` becomes impractically slow.

Approach to Evaluating Algorithm Efficiency

Algorithm efficiency is not just a theoretical exercise; it directly affects how fast and resource-friendly your programs are. Whether it is a search feature in a mobile app or a large-scale data processing task, knowing how to evaluate an algorithm's efficiency helps developers choose solutions that scale well and perform reliably.

To elaborate further, efficiency is typically analyzed through **three performance scenarios**: **best case**, **average case**, and **worst case**.

Best, Average, and Worst-Case Scenarios

- **Best-Case Scenario:** This refers to the most favorable situation for the algorithm, where it performs the minimum number of operations. For example, finding the target element at the first index in a linear search.
- **Average-Case Scenario:** This represents the expected performance over typical inputs. For a linear search, this would be finding the target somewhere in the middle of the list. Though a bit harder to compute than best and worst cases, it reflects real-world usage more accurately.

- **Worst-Case Scenario:** This is the scenario where the algorithm performs the maximum number of operations. For instance, when searching for a non-existent element in a list, the algorithm has to check every item.

Real-World Impact of Performance Analysis

Understanding these cases is crucial because:

A **worst-case efficient** algorithm ensures your application will not lag or crash when dealing with large or unexpected data inputs.

An **average-case optimized** algorithm ensures smooth everyday performance.

Even the **best-case scenario** matters when you are aiming for lightning-fast user experiences in specific use cases.

Consider the example of an online shopping platform. If the product search is not optimized for worst-case performance, it could frustrate users when the catalogue grows large. Similarly, real-time applications like stock trading platforms cannot afford algorithms that are only best-case efficient.

Introduction to Benchmarking and Profiling Basics

While theoretical analysis gives a general understanding of efficiency, real applications need **benchmarking** and **profiling** to measure actual performance.

Benchmarking involves running the algorithm with different input sizes and recording execution time and memory usage. This helps in comparing multiple algorithms in a controlled environment.

Profiling is a deeper analysis done on a running program to find bottlenecks, inefficient code segments, and resource-heavy operations. Tools like **gprof** (for C++) and **cProfile** (for Python) are commonly used for this.

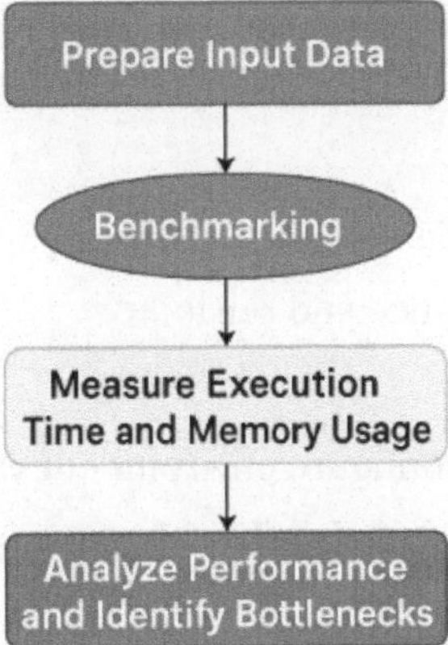

Figure 1.14: *Flowchart of Benchmarking and Profiling Process*

Figure 1.14 visually represents the step-by-step process of benchmarking and profiling an algorithm, which are critical practices in evaluating and improving code performance.

The process begins with **algorithm selection**, where a specific algorithm is chosen based on the problem requirements. Once selected, the next step is **input generation**, which involves preparing test data of varying sizes and complexities. This ensures that the performance is evaluated across different scenarios, from best-case to worst-case inputs.

Following this, the **benchmarking phase** measures the overall runtime of the algorithm. This involves executing the algorithm multiple times to gather consistent performance metrics such as execution time, CPU usage, and memory consumption. At the end, benchmarking provides a high-level overview of how efficiently the algorithm performs under given conditions.

However, benchmarking alone does not reveal internal performance bottlenecks. Hence, the next critical step is **profiling**, where tools are used to analyze finer details like function call frequency, time spent in each function, memory leaks, and I/O operations. Profiling helps identify specific sections of code that are performance hotspots.

The insights from profiling lead to the **optimization stage**, where developers refine the code to enhance efficiency—such as improving loops, while reducing redundant computations, or choosing better data structures.

After optimization, **re-benchmarking and validation** are essential to ensure that improvements have indeed resulted in better performance without breaking functionality. This is a cyclic process and may involve multiple iterations until satisfactory results are achieved.

Finally, the process concludes with **documentation and reporting**, where all findings, metrics, and improvements are recorded for reference, reproducibility, and future analysis.

Preparing the Programming Environment

Before you start exploring algorithms and data structures, you will need the right set of tools to write, compile, and run your programs. Whether you are using C++ for its fine-grained control and performance, or Python for its simplicity and readability, a well-configured programming environment will make your learning journey smoother and more productive.

Hence, this section will guide you through installing compilers, setting up IDEs, and optimizing your workspace to practice DSA effectively.

Installing and Configuring C++ Compilers

For C++ programming, you need a compiler that can translate your code into machine-executable form. Popular choices include:

GCC (GNU Compiler Collection):

- Available on Linux, Windows (via MinGW), and macOS
- Known for its standard compliance and reliability

Installation:

- **Windows:** Install MinGW and configure environment variables.
- **Linux/macOS:** Usually pre-installed; otherwise, use package managers like apt (Linux) or brew (macOS).

Use terminal commands like `g++ filename.cpp -o` output to compile programs.

Code::Blocks IDE:

- Beginner-friendly Integrated Development Environment (IDE)
- Bundled with GCC in the installation package
- Features project management, code completion, and debugging tools
- Installation is straightforward with official binaries for Windows.
- **C++** is a preferred language for DSA learning due to its performance, memory control, and standard libraries.

Option 1: GCC Compiler via MinGW (Windows)

a. Download the MinGW installer from: https://osdn.net/projects/mingw/.
b. During installation, check g++ for C++ support.
c. After installation, add the bin folder (for example, C:\MinGW\bin) to your system PATH.
d. Open **Command Prompt** and type g++ --version to verify installation.

Option 2: Code::Blocks IDE with Compiler (Recommended for Beginners)

a. Download Code::Blocks with included MinGW from: https://www.codeblocks.org/downloads.
b. Install and launch the IDE.
c. Go to **Create a New Project > Console Application > C++.**
d. Write a simple program and hit **Build and Run (F9).**

Option 3: GCC on Linux or macOS

Linux (Debian/Ubuntu):

```
sudo apt update
sudo apt install build-essential
```

macOS:

```
xcode-select --install
```

Python Setup using Anaconda, IDLE, or VS Code

Python offers flexibility and simplicity, which makes it a great companion for DSA learners. There are multiple ways to set up Python such as:

Anaconda Distribution:

- A one-stop solution for Python and its libraries
- Recommended for data science enthusiasts but also effective for DSA practice
- Comes with Jupyter Notebook and other useful tools
- Installation involves downloading the installer and following guided steps.

Python IDLE:

- A lightweight, built-in Python editor
- Simple interface, good for small scripts and beginners
- Accessible directly after installing Python from the official website

Visual Studio Code (VS Code):

- A powerful code editor with Python extension support
- Offers features like IntelliSense, debugging, version control integration, and terminal access
- Suitable for larger DSA projects

Python is ideal for those new to programming. It emphasizes clarity, which makes it perfect for learning algorithmic thinking.

Option 1: Installing Python via Official Site

a. Go to https://www.python.org/downloads.
b. Download and run the installer. On Windows, **check "`Add Python to PATH`".**

c. Verify the installation:

```
python --version
```

Option 2: Using Anaconda

a. Download Anaconda from https://www.anaconda.com.

b. Install it to access:

   i. Python

   ii. Jupyter Notebooks

   iii. Conda (Environment Manager)

c. Anaconda Navigator lets you open notebooks or scripts without using the terminal.

Option 3: Using VS Code

a. Download VS Code: https://code.visualstudio.com.

b. Install the **Python extension** from the Extensions panel.

c. Open a **`.py`** file and click **`Run Python File in Terminal`** to execute.

Option 4: Using IDLE

a. IDLE comes bundled with Python. It is simple and perfect for quick tests.

b. Open IDLE and type:

```
print("Hello, DSA!")
```

c. Hit **`F5`** to run.

IDE Tips and Environment Optimization for DSA Practice

A good development environment increases productivity. Here are some suggestions to get the best experience while learning:

Syntax Highlighting: Makes your code easier to read and debug

Auto-Completion: Use IDEs or extensions that suggest keywords, functions, and variable names.

Line Numbers and Bracket Matching: Helps in tracing logic and finding errors

Terminal Integration: Choose IDEs like VS Code or Code::Blocks that allow compiling and running from within the editor.

Debugging Tools: Learn to set breakpoints and inspect variables.

Project Structure: Organize problems into folders for each DSA topic or chapter.

Version Control (Optional): Tools like Git help you track your code over time and work collaboratively.

Hands-on with Basic Programs

Now that your programming environment is ready, it is time to write your first Data Structures and Algorithms (DSA) programs. This hands-on section is designed to give you immediate feedback and a sense of accomplishment. You will write a simple program in both C++ and Python, observe their syntax and behavior, and build confidence through comparison.

Whether you are a complete beginner or brushing up after a break, these small wins go a long way in reinforcing your learning mindset.

Writing and Running a Simple Program in C++

Let us begin with a basic C++ program that prints a message to the console:

```
#include <iostream>
using namespace std;

int main() {
    cout << "Welcome to Data Structures and Algorithms!" << endl;
    return 0;
}
```

`#include <iostream>`: Imports input/output functions

using **`namespace std;`**: Allows direct use of cout without prefixing with std::

`int main() { ... }`: The main function where execution starts

`cout << ...;`: Sends output to the console

To run:

a. Open C++ IDE (for example, **`Code::Blocks`** or VS Code with compiler).

b. Paste the code into a new file and save as welcome.cpp.

c. Compile and run (usually F9 in Code::Blocks or terminal: `g++ welcome.cpp -o welcome && ./welcome`).

Equivalent Program in Python

Let us achieve the same output using Python:

```
print("Welcome to Data Structures and Algorithms!")
```

`print()`: Built-in function to send output to the screen

Python requires no **`main()`** function or header files for such simple scripts.

To run:

a. Open your Python IDE (for example, IDLE, VS Code, Jupyter).

b. Paste and save the code as welcome.py.

c. Run it using the play/run button or terminal: python welcome.py.

Syntax and Output Behavior

One of the most empowering moments in learning programming is to understand how a single logic can be expressed in multiple languages. In this section, we focus on bridging the gap between **C++** and **Python**. These languages are often used in DSA education. While they serve the same purpose, their syntax and structure differ, while offering varied perspectives on problem-solving.

C++ is statically typed and closer to the hardware. It requires more explicit declarations, use of semicolons, curly braces for blocks, and a clearly defined main() function. Python, on the other hand, is dynamically typed, emphasizes indentation for blocks, and removes the need for syntactic clutter such as semicolons or type declarations.

Let us examine a simple "Hello, World!" program in both languages:

C++ Example:

```
#include <iostream>
using namespace std;

int main() {
    cout << "Hello, World!";
    return 0;
}
```

Python Example:

```
print("Hello, World!")
```

Notice the contrast in verbosity. C++ demands attention to structure, includes headers, and defines the entry point explicitly. Python achieves the same output in a single line. This simplicity is why many beginners prefer Python initially, but learning both of them will give you a stronger grasp of underlying concepts and language independence.

When dealing with **DSA**, the differences become more apparent in how arrays, loops, or memory management are handled. For example, arrays in C++ require predefined sizes and types, while Python lists can grow dynamically.

Therefore, understanding these patterns is important not only for syntax mastery, but also for interpreting performance implications, which is a core concern in algorithmic problem-solving.

Conclusion

In this opening chapter, we laid the essential groundwork for your journey into Data Structures and Algorithms (DSA). We began by understanding what data structures and algorithms truly are. They are not just definitions, but powerful tools behind real-world problem-solving. From the basic classifications of linear and non-linear structures to the types and components of algorithms, each concept has been designed to build your conceptual clarity and confidence. You also explored the critical role of performance analysis in writing efficient code. Through Big O, Omega, and Theta notations, we learned how to evaluate algorithmic efficiency in terms of both time and space, which gives you the vocabulary and mindset to reason about code beyond just "what works." Visual aids and real-world analogies helped demystify complex ideas, while hands-on sections introduced you to setting up your programming environment in C++ and Python. This will equip you with the tools needed to start coding right away. Now that you have a solid understanding of how DSA fits into the larger landscape of software development, we are ready to dig deeper. In the next chapter, we will explore **Arrays and Strings**—two of the most foundational and widely-used linear data structures. You will learn how they are stored in memory, how to manipulate them efficiently, and how to recognize common patterns like sliding windows and prefix sums that frequently appear in interviews and real-world applications. Let us move forward and start solving problems with confidence.

Points to Remember

- Arrays and strings are linear data structures that store data sequentially in memory.
- Arrays can be static or dynamic, and support operations like insertion, deletion, traversal, and updating.
- Multidimensional arrays extend the concept of arrays to 2D and beyond, and are useful in matrix operations and grid-based problems.

- Strings are arrays of characters and come with powerful built-in functions for manipulation in both C++ (**`std::string`**) and Python (**`str`**).
- Understanding memory layout and index access is the key to writing efficient code.
- Common problem-solving techniques include prefix sums, sliding window, and two-pointer approaches.
- Mastery of arrays and strings is crucial for coding interviews and foundational to understanding more advanced data structures.

Multiple Choice Questions

1. Which of the following is true about arrays in C++?
   a. Arrays can dynamically grow in size.
   b. Arrays are always stored in non-contiguous memory.
   c. Array elements are accessed using indices.
   d. Array elements cannot be updated once initialized.
2. What is the time complexity of accessing an element in an array using its index?
   a. `O(n)`
   b. `O(1)`
   c. `O(log n)`
   d. `O(n²)`
3. Which built-in function in Python is used to calculate the length of a string?
   a. `count()`
   b. `size()`
   c. `length()`
   d. `len()`
4. What is the output of the following Python code?

```
arr = [1, 2, 3]
print(arr[-1])
```

   a. 1
   b. 2
   c. 3
   d. IndexError
5. Which of the following best describes a character array in C++?
   a. An array that stores only integers
   b. An array that stores only strings
   c. An array of characters terminated by a null character
   d. A string data type in Python

6. What is the time complexity of inserting an element at the end of an array (if space is available)?
    a. `O(1)`
    b. `O(n)`
    c. `O(log n)`
    d. `O(n log n)`
7. Which method in Python can replace characters in a string?
    a. `change()`
    b. `update()`
    c. `replace()`
    d. `modify()`
8. Which of the following operations is not directly supported by arrays in most languages?
    a. Index-based access
    b. Random access
    c. Insertion at a specific index
    d. Dynamic resizing
9. What is the main use of prefix sum in array problems?
    a. Sorting elements
    b. Optimizing range queries
    c. Reducing array size
    d. Reversing elements
10. Which technique is best suited for solving problems like "maximum sum subarray of size k"?
    a. Recursion
    b. Sliding Window
    c. Hashing
    d. Brute Force

Answers

1. c
2. b
3. d
4. c
5. c
6. a
7. c
8. d
9. b
10. b

Questions

1. Explain the difference between static and dynamic arrays with examples in C++ or Python.
2. Describe how the sliding window technique works with a real-world analogy.
3. What are the advantages and disadvantages of using arrays over linked lists?
4. Write a Python program to reverse a string without using built-in functions.
5. Implement prefix sum logic for a given array and explain its use case.
6. Compare and contrast array and string data types in terms of memory and operations.
7. Solve this problem: given an array of integers, return the indices of the two numbers that add up to a specific target.

Key Terms

- **Array:** A linear data structure storing elements of the same type in contiguous memory locations
- **String:** A sequence of characters treated as a single data structure
- **Indexing:** Accessing elements of arrays/strings using their position in memory
- **Sliding Window:** An optimization technique to reduce the time complexity of certain problems by maintaining a subset window
- **Prefix Sum:** A technique used to preprocess array data for range sum queries
- **Two-Pointer Technique:** An approach used to solve problems involving pairs or subarrays
- **Dynamic Array:** An array that can grow or shrink in size at runtime
- **Multidimensional Array:** An array of arrays; useful for representing matrices or grids
- **Character Array:** A basic representation of strings in low-level languages like C and C++
- **Built-in Functions:** Language-provided utility functions for manipulating data structures efficiently

CHAPTER 2
Arrays and Strings

Introduction

In this chapter, we will learn about arrays and strings, which are two of the most fundamental data structures in programming. They are essential for storing, organizing, and manipulating data efficiently in almost every type of application. In programming, we often deal with large amounts of data, which can be numbers, text, or a mix of both. Without structured storage, managing this data can be an inefficient and error-prone process. Arrays and strings allow us to store multiple related values in an organized way, access them quickly, and perform operations such as searching, sorting, or modification without introducing unnecessary complexity.

Arrays provide a way to store multiple values of the same data type in a single, contiguous block of memory, while allowing for fast and direct access to each element through its index. This makes them ideal for handling large datasets such as student marks, sales figures, or sensor readings. Strings, on the other hand, are sequences of characters used to store and process text—from single words, to entire documents. In low-level languages such as C, strings are implemented as arrays of characters ending with a null terminator, while in high-level languages such as Python and Java, they are objects internally backed by arrays, with additional built-in features for manipulation. The relationship between arrays and strings is foundational; in many languages, strings are essentially specialized arrays of characters. This means that many of the concepts and operations used with arrays—such as indexing, iteration, and slicing—also apply to strings. Learning arrays therefore provides a natural pathway to mastering string manipulation. Almost every program—whether it is a simple calculator, a complex web browser, or an AI system—uses arrays and strings in some form for storing structured data, processing text, implementing algorithms, or managing multimedia content. Hence, understanding these structures is a crucial first step toward mastering more advanced data handling techniques in programming. In this chapter, readers will learn about the concepts, operations, advantages, and implementation of arrays and strings in both C++ and Python, along with their real-world applications and best practices.

Structure

In this chapter, we will cover the following topics:

- Arrays
- Characteristics of Arrays

- Declaration and Initialization of Arrays
- Accessing and Modifying Elements
- Multi-Dimensional Arrays
- Operations on Arrays
- Common Array Problem-Solving Patterns
- Strings
- Declaration and Initialization of Strings
- Basic String Operations
- Traversing Strings
- Strings in Various Languages
- Built-in String Functions
- Memory Representation
- Common String Problem-Solving Patterns

Arrays

An array is a collection of **homogeneous elements**, which means that all elements stored in it must be of the same data type to ensure consistent memory allocation and efficient access. It has a **fixed size**, which is determined at the time of declaration and generally cannot be changed during the program's execution in the case of static arrays. Elements in an array are accessed using **index-based addressing**, where the first element is typically stored at index 0, the second at index 1, and so on. This allows for direct and fast retrieval of any element.

Need for Arrays

In programming, we often need to store and process large amounts of related data. For example, consider storing the marks of 50 students in a class. Without arrays, you would have to declare 50 separate variables (mark1, mark2, mark3, ...mark50). This approach is inefficient and makes the code harder to maintain, besides being prone to errors. Arrays solve this problem by providing a single variable name that can store multiple values of the same type in contiguous memory locations. Each value can be accessed directly using an index. This results in simpler code, better organization, and improved performance.

Key Benefits of Arrays

- **Efficient Storage:** Arrays store elements in contiguous memory locations, which improves access speed, and reduces memory management overhead.
- **Fast Index-Based Access:** Accessing an element is done in `O(1)` time using its index, which makes retrieval and modification very fast.
- **Simpler Code Structure:** Instead of declaring multiple variables, a single array can store all the elements, which makes programs shorter and more readable.
- **Easy Iteration:** Loops can be used to easily process all elements, which is essential for tasks like sorting, searching, and performing calculations.
- **Foundation for Complex Structures:** Many advanced data structures (matrices, heaps, hash tables, graphs) are implemented using arrays.

Contiguous Memory Storage in Arrays

In arrays, the concept of **contiguous memory storage** implies that all elements are stored one after another in a single continuous block of memory. This arrangement ensures that if the base address of the array (the address of the first element) is known, the memory address of any other element can be quickly calculated using its index. For example, the address of element **`A[i]`** can be derived as:

`Address of arr[i]=Base Address+(i×Size of Element)`

This property allows for fast and direct access to any element using index-based addressing. It also makes arrays highly efficient for operations like searching, sorting, and traversal. However, as the memory is reserved in a contiguous block, resizing arrays can be difficult, and inserting or deleting elements in the middle may require shifting other elements.

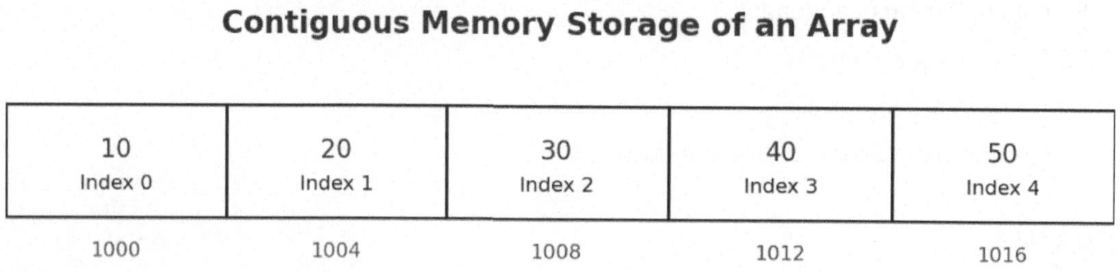

Contiguous Memory Storage of an Array

10 Index 0	20 Index 1	30 Index 2	40 Index 3	50 Index 4
1000	1004	1008	1012	1016

Figure 2.1: *Contiguous Memory Storage of an Array*

Figure 2.1 illustrates this by showing how array elements are stored side by side in consecutive memory addresses. The following C++ and Python code snippets demonstrate how memory addresses of array elements are managed in contiguous storage.

Example in C++:

```
#include <iostream>
using namespace std;
int main() {
    int arr[5] = {10, 20, 30, 40, 50};
    cout << "Array elements and their memory addresses:" << endl;
    for (int i = 0; i < 5; i++) {
        cout << "arr[" << i << "] = " << arr[i]
             << " at address " << &arr[i] << endl;
    }
    return 0;
}
```

Output

```
arr[0] = 10 at address 0x7ffee0c8
arr[1] = 20 at address 0x7ffee0cc
arr[2] = 30 at address 0x7ffee0d0
arr[3] = 40 at address 0x7ffee0d4
arr[4] = 50 at address 0x7ffee0d8
```

Notice how addresses increase by **4 bytes** each time (since int = 4 bytes).

In the preceding code:

We declared an integer array **`arr[5] = {10, 20, 30, 40, 50}`**.

Using a loop, we printed both the **value** of each element and its **memory address** using &arr[i].

The output shows that memory addresses increase in fixed steps (usually **4 bytes for int**). This step proved that the elements are stored **contiguously**.

Example in Python:

```
import ctypes
arr = (ctypes.c_int * 5)(10, 20, 30, 40, 50)

print("Array elements and their memory addresses:")
for i in range(5):
    print(f"arr[{i}] = {arr[i]} at address {ctypes.addressof(arr) + i * ctypes.
sizeof(ctypes.c_int)}")
```

Output

```
arr[0] = 10 at address 140728476393984
arr[1] = 20 at address 140728476393988
arr[2] = 30 at address 140728476393992
arr[3] = 40 at address 140728476393996
arr[4] = 50 at address 140728476394000
```

Here, addresses also increase by **4 bytes** because **`c_int`** = 4 bytes.

In the preceding code:

Python lists are dynamic and do not directly expose raw memory. Therefore, we used the **ctypes module** to create a C-style array.

`ctypes.c_int * 5` creates an array of 5 integers stored in contiguous memory.

`ctypes.addressof(arr) + i * ctypes.sizeof(ctypes.c_int)` calculates each element's address using the same formula as in C++.

Hence, the output confirms that memory addresses increase by the **size of each element**, and shows contiguous storage.

Fixed Size and Homogeneous Data Type

In arrays, all elements are of the same data type (homogeneous). This means an array can hold only integers, only floating-point numbers, or only characters, but not a mixture of different types. This property ensures that every element occupies the same amount of memory. It makes calculating the address of any element a straightforward process.

Another important property of arrays is their fixed size. Once the size of an array is declared, it generally cannot be changed during program execution (in static arrays). This allows the compiler to allocate a contiguous block of memory at compile-time or runtime, depending on the language.

For example,

- In C++, declaring **`int arr[5];`** reserves space for exactly 5 integers in memory.
- In Python, while lists are more flexible, arrays in the array module are closer to fixed-size structures, but still allow for resizing internally (which makes them dynamic in nature).

Therefore, this combination of fixed size and homogeneity makes arrays predictable and efficient, but also less flexible compared to dynamic data structures such as linked lists or Python lists.

Characteristics of Arrays

Arrays are one of the most widely used data structures because of their simplicity and efficiency. Here are some of their key characteristics:

Index-Based Access

Arrays store elements in contiguous memory locations, and each element can be accessed directly using an **index**. The first element is stored at index 0, the second at index 1, and so on. This makes locating elements straightforward and predictable. For instance, arr[3] refers to the fourth element in the array.

Random Access with Constant Time Complexity

Because arrays are stored in contiguous memory, the address of any element can be calculated directly from the base address using:

```
Address(A[i])=Base Address+( I × Size of Each Element)
```

This facilitates **direct or random access** in constant time **`O(1)O(1)O(1)`**. Therefore, unlike linked lists, there is no need to traverse elements sequentially to find a specific one.

Limitations

Despite their advantages, arrays also have certain limitations such as:

- **Fixed Size**: Once declared, the size of a static array cannot be easily changed. This makes arrays less flexible when the required size is not known in advance.
- **Costly Insertion/Deletion**: Inserting or deleting elements in the middle of an array requires shifting subsequent elements, which can be inefficient (O(n)O(n)O(n) time complexity).

Due to these properties, arrays are ideal for scenarios where the size of data is known in advance and frequent random access is required. However, when dynamic resizing or frequent insertions/deletions are needed, other data structures, such as linked lists or dynamic arrays (for example, Python lists, std::vector in C++), may be more suitable.

Declaration and Initialization of Arrays

Arrays must first be **declared** before they can be used in a program. Declaration specifies the data type of the elements and the size of the array. Initialization means assigning values to the elements at the time of declaration or later in the program. The syntax and behavior vary across programming languages such as **C++ and Python**. A simple visualization showing how a C++ array is declared, initialized, and stored in contiguous memory is shown in the given figure. Each element is placed side by side, with indices labeled as (arr[0], arr[1]) for clarity.

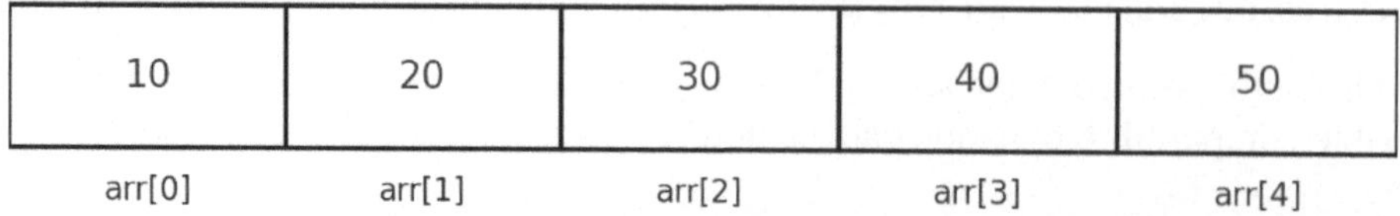

Figure 2.2: *Memory Representation of C++ Array*

The following C++ and Python code snippets demonstrate how the declaration and initialization using arrays:

Example Array Declaration:

```
// Declaration of an integer array of size 5
int arr[5];
```

This creates an array with 5 elements of type int. The values are **uninitialized** (contain garbage).

Example Array Initialization:

```
// Full initialization
int arr1[5] = {10, 20, 30, 40, 50};

// Partial initialization (remaining elements set to 0)
int arr2[5] = {1, 2};    // arr2 = {1, 2, 0, 0, 0}

// Size auto-detected
int arr3[] = {5, 6, 7, 8};    // size = 4
```

Example in C++:

```
#include <iostream>
using namespace std;
int main() {
    // Declaration without initialization
    int arr1[5];    // contains garbage values
    // Declaration with initialization
    int arr2[5] = {10, 20, 30, 40, 50};
    // Partial initialization (remaining elements = 0)
    int arr3[5] = {1, 2};    // {1, 2, 0, 0, 0}
    // Implicit size from initializer
    int arr4[] = {5, 10, 15};  // size = 3
    // Accessing elements
    cout << arr2[2] << endl; // Output: 30
    return 0;
}
```

Example in Python:

```
# In Python, arrays are usually implemented as lists
# Declaration without initialization (empty list)

arr1 = []
# Declaration with initialization
arr2 = [10, 20, 30, 40, 50]
# Partial initialization (simulate fixed size using * operator)
arr3 = [1, 2] + [0] * 3   # [1, 2, 0, 0, 0]
# Implicit size from initializer
arr4 = [5, 10, 15]
# Accessing elements
print(arr2[2])  # Output: 30
```

Static and Dynamic Allocation

When working with arrays, one of the first design decisions a programmer might have to take is **whether the size of the array should remain fixed, or should be adjusted as required**. This distinction gives rise to two approaches: **static allocation** and **dynamic allocation**. Static allocation fixes the array size at compile time, while ensuring simplicity and fast access; dynamic allocation allows for flexibility by determining the size at runtime. Understanding these two approaches is essential, as this choice directly affects memory usage, program efficiency, and the ability to handle varying amounts of data.

Static Allocation

In **static arrays**, the size of the array is fixed at compile time. Once declared, the number of elements cannot change.

Example in C++:

```
int marks[5];  // Creates an array of 5 integers
```

Here, marks can hold exactly 5 integers, no more and no less.

This is like reserving 5 lockers in advance; even if you only use 3, the remaining 2 stay reserved.

Advantages:

Fast Access (Contiguous Memory)

Simple to Implement

Limitations:

Wastes memory if the reserved space is not fully used

Cannot grow or shrink at runtime

Dynamic Allocation

In **dynamic arrays**, the size can be decided during program execution.

In C++, dynamic allocation is handled using **pointers** and the new keyword.

Example:

```
int* arr = new int[n];  // Creates an array of size 'n' at runtime
```

In Python, lists behave like dynamic arrays automatically:

```
arr = []          # Empty list
arr.append(10)    # Add elements dynamically
```

Advantages:

Can adapt to data needs as it is flexible

Efficient for problems where input size is unknown

Limitations:

Requires extra care in C++ to manage memory (use **`delete[]`**)

Slight overhead compared to static arrays

Analogy: It is like renting lockers on demand. You can decide how many lockers you need only when you arrive. If you need more later, you may also request additional ones.

Default Values and Partial Initialization

When working with variables or data structures, we may not always assign values to every element during initialization. In such situations, programming languages often provide **default values** to the uninitialized parts through a process known as **partial initialization**. This process ensures consistency, and prevents unexpected behavior in the program.

Default Values

In **C++**, arrays created inside functions may contain **garbage values** (random memory contents) until explicitly initialized.

Example:

```
int arr[5];  // May contain unpredictable values
```

In contrast, global arrays are automatically set to **zero**.

In **Python**, when you create a list with a fixed size, you typically set default values explicitly:

```
arr = [0] * 5   # Creates [0, 0, 0, 0, 0]
```

Partial Initialization

Arrays allow assigning only a few values, with the rest set to defaults.

Example in C++:

```
int arr[5] = {10, 20};  // arr = {10, 20, 0, 0, 0}
```

Example in Python:

```
arr = [10, 20] + [0] * 3   # arr = [10, 20, 0, 0, 0]
```

Analogy: Imagine filling only the first two shelves of a bookcase and leaving the rest empty for future use.

Static arrays are fixed in size and predictable in memory usage, while dynamic arrays offer flexibility at the cost of slightly more complexity. Therefore, partial initialization and default values help balance efficiency with convenience.

Accessing and Modifying Elements

Once an array is declared and initialized, the next important step is to learn how to work with its elements. Arrays provide a very structured way of storing data, but their true power lies in how efficiently we can retrieve and update individual values. Each element in an array is identified by an index, which acts like the address of a specific house in a street. This makes it possible to directly jump to the exact element we want without having to search through the entire structure.

Access operations let us read data from a given position, while modification operations allow us to overwrite existing values with new ones. These simple yet powerful capabilities form the basis for many higher-level algorithms such as searching, sorting, and pattern matching. Hence, whether it is looping through student marks, updating the stock price of a company in a dataset, or reading sensor values from a device, the ability to access and modify elements seamlessly is at the heart of problem-solving with arrays.

Indexing

One of the most important features of arrays is that their elements can be accessed and modified directly using **indexing**. An index is a numerical value that indicates the position of an element within the array, and in most programming languages such as C++ and Python, the index starts from zero. This means that the first element of an array is accessed using index 0, the second element using index 1, and so on until n-1 for an array of size n. For example, consider an array:

Index: 0 1 2 3 4

Value: 10 20 30 40 50

Here, the value 10 is stored at index 0, 30 is stored at index 2, and 50 is stored at index 4. Indexing provides **constant-time access (`O(1)`)**, which makes it highly efficient compared to sequential search methods. Moreover, the same indexing mechanism is used to modify elements; for instance, updating the value at index 2 will directly replace 30 with a new value. Thus, indexing not only enables quick retrieval of data, but also allows us to easily modify array elements without the need for traversal.

Example in C++:

```
#include <iostream>
using namespace std;

int main() {
    int arr[5] = {10, 20, 30, 40, 50};

    // Accessing elements
    cout << "Element at index 2: " << arr[2] << endl;

    // Modifying element
    arr[2] = 99;
    cout << "Modified element at index 2: " << arr[2] << endl;

    return 0;
}
```

Output

```
Element at Index 2: 30
Modified Element at index 2: 99
```

Example in Python:

```
arr = [10, 20, 30, 40, 50]

# Accessing elements
print("Element at index 2:", arr[2])

# Modifying element
arr[2] = 99
print("Modified element at index 2:", arr[2])
```

Output

```
Element at Index 2: 30
Modified Element at Index 2: 99
```

Loop-Based Traversal

Arrays are often traversed using **loops** because they allow us to systematically access each element in sequence. Since arrays store elements in contiguous memory locations and use index-based access, loops provide a convenient way to perform operations such as **searching, printing, updating, or applying computations** to every element. For instance, a 'for' loop can start from index 0 and continue up to n-1 (where n is the size of the array), while ensuring that every element is visited exactly once. This makes traversal both simple and efficient. Loop-based traversal is especially useful when we do not know beforehand which element needs to be modified, or when we want to apply the same operation—like doubling every number or checking for a condition—across the entire array. Additionally, languages such as Python and C++ also support enhanced loop constructs (for example, for-each loops), which make traversal more readable and less error-prone. Thus, loop-based traversal is a fundamental operation that enables programmers to process arrays effectively in a wide range of applications.

Updating Existing Elements in Arrays

Updating elements in an array refers to **changing the value** stored at a particular index. Since arrays use **contiguous memory storage,** and allow **direct index-based access**, updating any element takes **constant time O(1)**, regardless of the array size.

Each element in an array can be directly accessed using its **index.**

Once the index is located, you can assign a **new value** to replace the old one.

The original structure of the array remains intact; only the element's value changes.

Example in C++:

```
#include <iostream>
using namespace std;

int main() {
    int marks[5] = {70, 80, 65, 90, 85};

    // Updating the 3rd element (index 2)
    marks[2] = 75;

    cout << "Updated marks: ";
    for (int i = 0; i < 5; i++) {
        cout << marks[i] << " ";
    }
    return 0;
}
```

Output: `Updated Marks: 70 80 75 90 85`

Example in Python:

```
marks = [70, 80, 65, 90, 85]

# Updating the 3rd element (index 2)
marks[2] = 75

print("Updated marks:", marks)
```

Output: `Updated Marks: [70, 80, 75, 90, 85]`

Consider the example of a **class attendance register** where each student's attendance for a day is marked.

If the teacher made a mistake while entering a student's attendance, she simply **goes to the correct row (index)** and **updates the entry,** without disturbing the rest of the records.

This is exactly how **array updates** work—quickly, precisely, and efficiently.

Multi-Dimensional Arrays

A multi-dimensional array is a natural extension of the one-dimensional array, where elements are arranged in more than one dimension. Instead of storing data in a straight line, these arrays organize values into grid-like (2D) or cube-like (3D) structures. This allows for efficient representation of complex data such as tables, images, and models.

2D Arrays

A two-dimensional (2D) array can be thought of as a table with rows and columns, similar to a spreadsheet or a mathematical matrix. Each element is uniquely identified using two indices: one for the row and one for the column. Two-dimensional arrays are commonly used in applications where data needs to be represented in rows and columns, similar to a mathematical matrix or spreadsheet. For instance, they are used to **store student marks** in different subjects, where each row corresponds to a student, and each column to a subject. In **image processing**, 2D arrays are essential as images can be represented as a grid of pixels, with each element storing the color or intensity value of a pixel. They are also useful in **game development**, where 2D arrays represent game boards such as chess, tic-tac-toe, or Sudoku grids.

Example in C++:

```
#include <iostream>
using namespace std;

int main() {
    int marks[3][3] = { {85, 90, 78},
                        {88, 76, 92},
                        {90, 85, 88} };

    cout << "Marks of student 2 in subject 3: " << marks[1][2] << endl;
    return 0;
}
```

Output:

```
Marks of Student 2 in Subject 3: 92
```

In this example, **`marks[1][2]`** refers to the marks of the second student in the third subject.

3D Arrays

A **three-dimensional (3D) array** can be visualized as a stack of 2D arrays placed one behind another, forming a cube-like structure. Each element is accessed using three indices: depth (or layer), row, and column. For instance, **`arr[1][2][3]`** represents the element at depth 1, row 2, and column 3. Three-dimensional arrays extend the concept by stacking multiple 2D arrays to represent data in three dimensions. They are widely used in **computer games** for representing 3D graphics or objects, as they enable the creation of a realistic virtual environment. In **medical imaging**, such as MRI scans, 3D arrays store multiple layers of 2D images to form a complete three-dimensional representation of body organs. Similarly, in **weather forecasting models**, 3D arrays are applied to track parameters such as temperature, humidity, and pressure across three axes—time, latitude, and longitude—to provide accurate predictions and simulations.

Example in C++:

```
#include <iostream>
using namespace std;

int main() {
    int cube[2][2][2] = { { {1, 2}, {3, 4} },
                          { {5, 6}, {7, 8} } };

    cout << "Element at depth=1, row=0, col=1: " << cube[1][0][1] << endl;
    return 0;
}
```

Output:

```
Element at Depth=1, row=0, col=1: 6
```

Here, **`cube[1][0][1]`** refers to the element at **depth 1, row 0, and column 1.**

Operations on Arrays

Arrays support a variety of operations that allow programmers to access, manipulate, and organize data effectively. Some of the most important operations include traversal, insertion, deletion, searching, and sorting.

Traversal

Traversal refers to visiting each element of the array exactly once, usually for the purpose of displaying, modifying, or processing the data. This is commonly done using loops (such as for or while loops). For example, printing all elements of an array or updating each value by adding 10 requires traversal.

Example in C++:

```
#include <iostream>
using namespace std;

int main() {
    int arr[] = {10, 20, 30, 40, 50};
    int n = 5;

    cout << "Array elements: ";
    for (int i = 0; i < n; i++) {
        cout << arr[i] << " ";
    }
    return 0;
}
```

Example in Python:

```
arr = [10, 20, 30, 40, 50]

print("Array elements:", end=" ")
for i in arr:
    print(i, end=" ")
```

Insertion and Deletion

Insertion involves adding a new element into an array at a specific position. Since arrays are stored in contiguous memory, they may require shifting elements to make space for the new value.

Deletion involves removing an element from a given position, which also requires shifting the remaining elements to maintain the array's structure.

Due to this shifting process, insertion and deletion in arrays can be less efficient compared to dynamic structures like linked lists.

Example in C++ (Insertion):

```
#include <iostream>
using namespace std;

int main() {
    int arr[10] = {10, 20, 30, 40, 50};
    int n = 5, pos = 2, x = 25;  // Insert 25 at index 2

    for (int i = n; i > pos; i--) {
        arr[i] = arr[i - 1];  // Shift elements right
    }
    arr[pos] = x;
    n++;

    cout << "Array after insertion: ";
    for (int i = 0; i < n; i++) cout << arr[i] << " ";
    return 0;
}
```

Example in Python (Insertion):

```
arr = [10, 20, 30, 40, 50]
arr.insert(2, 25)  # Insert 25 at index 2

print("Array after insertion:", arr)
```

Example in C++ (Deletion):

```
#include <iostream>
using namespace std;

int main() {
    int arr[10] = {10, 20, 30, 40, 50};
    int n = 5, pos = 2;  // Delete element at index 2

    for (int i = pos; i < n - 1; i++) {
        arr[i] = arr[i + 1];  // Shift left
    }
    n--;

    cout << "Array after deletion: ";
    for (int i = 0; i < n; i++) cout << arr[i] << " ";
    return 0;
}
```

Example in Python (Deletion):

```
arr = [10, 20, 30, 40, 50]
arr.pop(2)  # Remove element at index 2

print("Array after deletion:", arr)
```

Searching

Searching is the process of finding whether a given element exists in the array and, if so, determining its position. Two common approaches within this category are:

- **Linear Search**: Each element is checked one by one until the desired value is found or the end of the array is reached. This method is simple, but is also less efficient for large arrays.
- **Binary Search**: A faster searching technique that works on sorted arrays. It repeatedly divides the array into halves, and checks in which half the element may lie. This reduces the search time significantly, with a time complexity of O(log n).

Example in C++ (Linear Search):

```
#include <iostream>
using namespace std;

int main() {
    int arr[] = {10, 20, 30, 40, 50};
    int n = 5, x = 30, pos = -1;

    for (int i = 0; i < n; i++) {
        if (arr[i] == x) {
            pos = i;
            break;
        }
    }

    if (pos != -1)
        cout << "Element found at index " << pos;
    else
        cout << "Element not found";
    return 0;
}
```

Example in Python (Linear Search):

```
arr = [10, 20, 30, 40, 50]
x = 30

if x in arr:
    print("Element found at index", arr.index(x))
else:
    print("Element not found")
```

Sorting

Sorting arranges the elements of an array in a specific order (ascending or descending). It is a fundamental operation used in data organization and searching. Some basic sorting methods include:

- **Bubble Sort**: Repeatedly compares adjacent elements and swaps them if they are in the wrong order
- **Selection Sort**: Finds the smallest (or largest) element and places it at the correct position in each iteration
- **Insertion Sort**: Builds the sorted portion of the array by inserting each element into its correct position

These simple sorting techniques are easy to implement but less efficient for large datasets compared to advanced algorithms such as Quick Sort or Merge Sort.

Example in C++ (Sorting):

```
#include <iostream>
using namespace std;

int main() {
    int arr[] = {50, 20, 40, 10, 30};
    int n = 5;

    for (int i = 0; i < n - 1; i++) {
        for (int j = 0; j < n - i - 1; j++) {
            if (arr[j] > arr[j + 1]) {
                swap(arr[j], arr[j + 1]);
            }
        }
    }

    cout << "Array after bubble sort: ";
    for (int i = 0; i < n; i++) cout << arr[i] << " ";
    return 0;
}
```

Example in Python (Sorting):

```
arr = [50, 20, 40, 10, 30]

for i in range(len(arr) - 1):
    for j in range(len(arr) - i - 1):
        if arr[j] > arr[j + 1]:
            arr[j], arr[j + 1] = arr[j + 1], arr[j]

print("Array after bubble sort:", arr)Element not found")
```

Built-in Array Functions

When working with arrays, we often perform common tasks such as **sorting, searching, reversing, summing up elements, or finding minimum and maximum values**. While these operations can be implemented manually, most modern programming languages provide **built-in functions** that make these tasks faster, simpler, and less error-prone.

Understanding these built-in utilities is essential because they not only save time during coding but also help you write **cleaner, optimized, and more efficient solutions**. In this section, we will explore the most commonly used functions in **C++** and **Python**, along with their practical examples.

Built-in Array Functions in C++

In C++, arrays are widely used for storing and processing large amounts of data. The Standard Template Library (STL) provides many powerful utilities in the **`<algorithm>`** and **`<numeric>`** headers, which make array operations much easier.

Sorting an Array: Sorting is one of the most frequently used operations. C++ provides the **`sort()`** function from the **`<algorithm>`** library, which sorts elements in ascending order by default.

```
#include <iostream>
#include <algorithm>
using namespace std;

int main() {
    int arr[5] = {40, 10, 30, 20, 50};
    sort(arr, arr + 5);

    cout << "Sorted Array: ";
    for (int i = 0; i < 5; i++) cout << arr[i] << " ";
    return 0;
}
```

Output: `Sorted Array: 10 20 30 40 50`

From this example, it is apparent that the time complexity of the **`sort()`** function is **`O(n log n)`**, which makes it highly efficient.

Reversing an Array: The **`reverse()`** function from **`<algorithm>`** reverses the order of elements.

```
reverse(arr, arr + 5);
```

Therefore, if the original array is {10, 20, 30, 40, 50}, after reversing, it becomes {50, 40, 30, 20, 10}.

Finding Minimum and Maximum

The functions **`min_element()`** and **`max_element()`** return pointers to the smallest and largest elements in the array.

```
int minVal = *min_element(arr, arr + 5);
int maxVal = *max_element(arr, arr + 5);
```

For {10, 20, 30, 40, 50},

`minVal = 10` and **`maxVal = 50`**

Calculating the Sum of Elements

The **`<numeric>`** header provides the **`accumulate()`** function, which adds up all elements in the way shown here:

```
#include <numeric>
int sum = accumulate(arr, arr + 5, 0);
```

For {10, 20, 30, 40, 50},

`Sum = 150.`

Searching in an Array: The **`binary_search()`** function can quickly check whether an element exists in a **sorted array.**

```
if (binary_search(arr, arr + 5, 30))
    cout << "Element found!";
else
    cout << "Element not found!";
```

In C++, the **`<algorithm>`** and **`<numeric>`** libraries provide powerful utilities for arrays.

Here are some commonly used functions:

Operation	Function	Example	Time Complexity
Sorting	sort(arr, arr+n)	sort(arr, arr+5);	O(n log n)
Reverse	reverse(arr, arr+n)	reverse(arr, arr+5);	O(n)
Minimum & Maximum	*min_element(arr, arr+n)	cout << *min_element(arr, arr+5);	O(n)
Sum of Elements	accumulate(arr, arr+n, 0)	int sum = accumulate(arr, arr+5, 0);	O(n)
Binary Search	binary_search(arr, arr+n, key)	if(binary_search(arr, arr+5, 90)) cout<<"Found";	O(log n)
Count Occurrences	count(arr, arr+n, key)	int c = count(arr, arr+5, 80);	O(n)

Table 2.1: *Built-in Array Functions in C++*

Built-in Array Functions in Python

Python provides an even simpler and more intuitive way to perform array operations using **lists** and the **NumPy library**.

Sorting an Array: Python's built-in **`sorted()`** function returns a new sorted list, while **`list.sort()`** modifies the original list in the following way:

```
arr = [40, 10, 30, 20, 50]
arr.sort()
print("Sorted Array:", arr)
```

Output: `Sorted Array: [10, 20, 30, 40, 50]`

Reversing an Array: Reversing can be done using the built-in **`reverse()`** method in the following manner:

```
arr.reverse()
print("Reversed Array:", arr)
```

Finding Minimum, Maximum, and Sum: Python provides built-in functions to find these easily, as demonstrated here:

```
arr = [10, 20, 30, 40, 50]
print("Minimum:", min(arr))
print("Maximum:", max(arr))
print("Sum:", sum(arr))
```

Output:

```
Minimum: 10
Maximum: 50
Sum: 150
```

Searching for an Element: Python uses the in keyword for membership checks, such as:

```
if 30 in arr:
    print("Element found!")
else:
    print("Element not found!")
```

Using NumPy for Faster Array Operations: For large datasets, Python developers prefer **NumPy**, a high-performance numerical computing library.

```
import numpy as np

arr = np.array([10, 40, 20, 30, 50])
sorted_arr = np.sort(arr)
total = np.sum(arr)

print("Sorted Array:", sorted_arr)
print("Sum of Elements:", total)
```

Furthermore, provides a **rich set of built-in methods** and the powerful **NumPy** library to handle arrays efficiently.

Operation	Method / Function	Example	Time Complexity
Sorting	`sorted(arr)`	`sorted([3,1,4,2]) → [1,2,3,4]`	`O(n log n)`
Reverse	`arr.reverse()`	`arr.reverse()`	`O(n)`
Sum of Elements	`sum(arr)`	`sum([1,2,3]) → 6`	`O(n)`
Minimum & Maximum	`min(arr) / max(arr)`	`min([4,2,7]) → 2`	`O(n)`
Searching	in operator	if 5 in arr:	`O(n)`
NumPy Array Tools	`numpy.sort()`, `numpy.mean()`	Faster operations on large arrays	`O(n log n)`

Table 2.2: *Built-in Array Functions in Python*

Common Array Problem-Solving Patterns

Arrays are one of the most versatile data structures, and many real-world problems are solved using **well-defined algorithmic patterns**. Among these, **prefix sum**, **two-pointer technique**, and **sliding window** are three of the most widely used strategies. Mastering these patterns allows you to write **efficient solutions** for competitive programming, interviews, and real-life data processing tasks.

Prefix Sum Problems

The **prefix sum technique** involves creating an auxiliary array where each element represents the **sum of all previous elements up to that index.**

This approach reduces repetitive summation operations and **optimizes time complexity**.

`prefix[i]=prefix[i-1]+arr[i]`

This allows us to calculate the sum of any subarray [L,R][L, R][L,R] in **O(1)** time. It is further represented as:

`sum(L,R)=prefix[R]-prefix[L-1]`

Example

Problem: Given an array `arr = [2, 4, 6, 8, 10]`, find the sum of elements from index 1 to 3.

Step 1: `Build prefix array → [2, 6, 12, 20, 30]`

Step 2: Use this formula:

`sum(1,3)=prefix[3]-prefix[0]=20-2=18`

C++ Code:

```
#include <iostream>
#include <vector>
using namespace std;

int main() {
    vector<int> arr = {2, 4, 6, 8, 10};
    int n = arr.size();
    vector<int> prefix(n);

    prefix[0] = arr[0];
    for (int i = 1; i < n; i++)
        prefix[i] = prefix[i - 1] + arr[i];

    int L = 1, R = 3;
    int sum = prefix[R] - (L > 0 ? prefix[L - 1] : 0);
    cout << "Sum from index " << L << " to " << R << " = " << sum;
    return 0;
}
```

Python Code:

```
arr = [2, 4, 6, 8, 10]
prefix = [0] * len(arr)
prefix[0] = arr[0]

for i in range(1, len(arr)):
    prefix[i] = prefix[i - 1] + arr[i]

L, R = 1, 3
sum_val = prefix[R] - (prefix[L - 1] if L > 0 else 0)
print(f"Sum from index {L} to {R} = {sum_val}")
```

Think of the **prefix sum technique** as keeping a running balance in your **bank account**. Each deposit adds to your **total balance**. To know how much money you had between January and March, you simply have to subtract your **January opening balance** from your **March balance**. This eliminates repetitive calculations.

Two-Pointer Technique

The **two-pointer technique** uses **two indices** that move towards each other, or in the same direction to solve problems efficiently. It is commonly applied to **sorted arrays,** and helps in reducing the time complexity from `O(n²)` to `O(n)` in many cases.

Example Problem

Find a pair of numbers in a sorted array that sums to a target.

Input: arr = [1, 3, 4, 5, 7, 10], target = 9

Approach:

Place one pointer left at the start and right at the end.

If arr[left] + arr[right] == target, we have found the pair.

If the sum is **less than target**, move left++.

If the sum is **greater than target**, move right--.

C++ Code:

```
#include <iostream>
#include <vector>
using namespace std;

int main() {
    vector<int> arr = {1, 3, 4, 5, 7, 10};
    int target = 9;
    int left = 0, right = arr.size() - 1;

    while (left < right) {
        int sum = arr[left] + arr[right];
        if (sum == target) {
            cout << "Pair found: " << arr[left] << ", " << arr[right];
            return 0;
        }
        if (sum < target) left++;
        else right--;
    }
    cout << "No pair found!";
    return 0;
}
```

Python Code:

```
arr = [1, 3, 4, 5, 7, 10]
target = 9
left, right = 0, len(arr) - 1

while left < right:
    s = arr[left] + arr[right]
    if s == target:
        print(f"Pair found: {arr[left]}, {arr[right]}")
        break
    if s < target:
        left += 1
    else:
        right -= 1
```

Imagine **two people searching for a lost ring**. One of them starts searching from the **left side** of the room, while the other begins from the **right side**. They move **towards each other** until they meet at the target. This is exactly how the **two-pointer method** works.

Sliding Window Problems

The **Sliding Window technique** is used when dealing with **contiguous subarrays or substrings**. Instead of recalculating sums, averages, or maximums repeatedly, we **reuse previous computations** by moving a **window** across the array.

Example Problem

Find the maximum sum of any subarray of size k.

Input: arr = [2, 1, 5, 1, 3, 2], k = 3

Approach:

Calculate the sum of the **first window**.

Slide the window by removing the **first element**, and then add the **next element**.

Keep track of the **maximum sum**.

C++ Code:

```
#include <iostream>
#include <vector>
using namespace std;

int main() {
    vector<int> arr = {2, 1, 5, 1, 3, 2};
    int k = 3, n = arr.size();
    int window_sum = 0;

    for (int i = 0; i < k; i++) window_sum += arr[i];
    int max_sum = window_sum;

    for (int i = k; i < n; i++) {
        window_sum += arr[i] - arr[i - k];
        max_sum = max(max_sum, window_sum);
    }

    cout << "Maximum sum of subarray of size " << k << " = " << max_sum;
    return 0;
}
```

Python Code:

```
arr = [2, 1, 5, 1, 3, 2]
k = 3
window_sum = sum(arr[:k])
max_sum = window_sum

for i in range(k, len(arr)):
    window_sum += arr[i] - arr[i - k]
    max_sum = max(max_sum, window_sum)

print(f"Maximum sum of subarray of size {k} = {max_sum}")
```

Imagine looking through a **train window**: you can only **see a limited number of trees** at a time. As the train moves, the **first tree disappears,** and a **new one enters** the view. Similarly, in arrays, the **sliding window method** continuously updates values, without recalculating everything from scratch.

Strings

Strings are an essential data type in programming, used to represent and manipulate text. A **string** is essentially a sequence of characters stored together, such as "`Hello`" or "`Computer`". Each character is stored in memory and can be accessed using an index, much similar to arrays.

In **C and C++**, strings are commonly implemented as **null-terminated character arrays**. This means that the sequence of characters ends with a special character '\0' (null character). For example, the string "Hello" is internally stored as:

```
['H', 'e', 'l', 'l', 'o', '\0']
```

This null terminator helps the program know where the string ends.

In contrast, **high-level languages like Python and Java** treat strings as **immutable objects**. This means that once a string is created, it cannot be changed directly. Any modification (such as concatenation or replacement) results in the creation of a new string. This immutability provides safety and efficiency in string operations, though it may lead to higher memory usage in some cases. Thus, strings serve as the foundation for text processing and manipulation in programming, with their implementation varying across different languages.

Example Strings in C++:

```
#include <iostream>
using namespace std;

int main() {
    char str1[] = "Hello";    // null-terminated string
    cout << "String: " << str1 << endl;

    // Accessing individual characters
    cout << "First character: " << str1[0] << endl;
    cout << "Last character before null: " << str1[4] << endl;

    return 0;
}
```

```
Internal memory representation of "Hello"
['H', 'e', 'l', 'l', 'o', '\0']
```

Example Strings in Python:

```
# Creating a string
str1 = "Hello"
print("String:", str1)

# Accessing individual characters
print("First character:", str1[0])
print("Last character:", str1[-1])

# Strings are immutable
new_str = str1 + " World"  # creates a new string
print("Modified string:", new_str)
```

Declaration and Initialization of Strings

Strings, like arrays, must first be declared before they can be used in a program. The way strings are declared and initialized depends on the programming language.

In **C and C++**, strings are typically declared as **character arrays**, or by using the **string class** (from the C++ Standard Library).

Memory Layout of C-style String: "Hello"

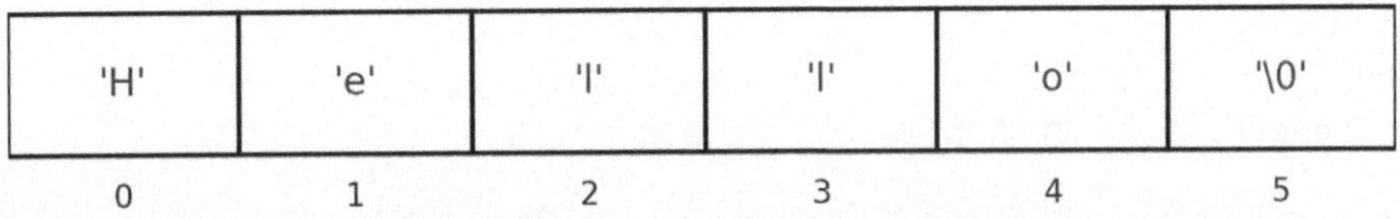

Figure 2.3: *Memory Layout of C-Style String*

Here is a clear diagram showing how the string **"Hello"** is stored in memory as a C-style string, including the **null terminator (\0)** at the end.

Using character arrays:

```
char str1[6] = "Hello";    // Automatically adds '\0' at the end
char str2[]  = "World";    // Size inferred, also null-terminated
```

Here, "Hello" takes 5 characters plus one extra space for the null character '\0'.

Using the string class in C++:

```
#include <iostream>
#include <string>
using namespace std;
string str3 = "Hello World";
```

The string class provides built-in functions for manipulation, such as concatenation, comparison, and substring extraction. Eventually, these functions make it easier to work with text.

In **Python**, strings are declared simply by enclosing characters within single (') or double (") quotes. Python also allows triple quotes (''' or """) for multi-line strings.

```
str1 = "Hello"
str2 = 'World'
str3 = """This is a multi-line string"""
```

Since Python strings are immutable, initialization defines their value at creation, and any modification results in the creation of a new string object.

Thus, declaration and initialization of strings provide the foundation for working with text data in different languages, with low-level languages like C requiring explicit handling of null characters, while high-level languages like Python offer simplicity and flexibility.

Basic String Operations

Strings are central to nearly every application in computer science—from storing usernames and passwords, to processing text in search engines. To work effectively with strings, we must first understand the most common operations: **finding their length, copying and concatenating them, and comparing or extracting substrings**.

Length Calculation

The **length of a string** refers to the number of characters it contains (excluding the terminating '`\0`' in C-style strings).

C-Style Strings: The strlen() function counts characters until it reaches '`\0`'.

```
#include <iostream>
#include <cstring>
using namespace std;

int main() {
    char word[] = "Hello";
    cout << "Length: " << strlen(word); // Output: 5
}
```

C++ String Class: The **`.length()`** or **`.size()`** method directly returns the number of characters.

```
string word = "Hello";
cout << word.length(); // Output: 5
```

Python: The built-in len() function makes it straightforward.

```
word = "Hello"
print(len(word))  # Output: 5
```

Imagine counting the number of books on a shelf. Each book is a character, and the total count gives the "length" of the shelf.

Copying and Concatenation

Copying allows us to duplicate a string, while concatenation combines two or more strings into one.

C-Style Strings: Functions such as **`strcpy()`** and **`strcat()`** (from **`<cstring>`**) handle these operations.

```
char str1[20] = "Hello";
char str2[20];
strcpy(str2, str1);    // Copy
strcat(str1, "World"); // Concatenate
```

C++ String Class: Much simpler using assignment (=) and addition (+)

```
strING S1 = "HELLO";
STRING S2 = S1;  // COPY
STRING S3 = S1 + " World"; // Concatenate
```

Python: Copying is done via assignment, and concatenation with +.

```
s1 = "Hello"
s2 = s1         # Copy
s3 = s1 + " World"  # Concatenate
```

Copying is like making a duplicate copy of a document, while concatenation is like binding two documents together into one.

Comparison and Substring Extraction

Comparisons are used to check equality or determine ordering (for example, for sorting). Substrings let us extract parts of strings, which is crucial in applications like parsing URLs or analyzing text.

C-Style Strings:

`strcmp(s1, s2)` compares two strings. It returns 0 if equal, negative if **`s1 < s2`**, and positive if **`s1 > s2`**.

It is also important to remember that substrings must be handled manually by copying parts into a new array.

C++ String Class:

Supports operators like ==, <, >.

Substrings can be obtained using **`.substr(start, length)`**.

```
string text = "DataStructures";
cout << text.substr(0, 4);  // Output: Data
```

Python:

Comparisons use relational operators (==, <, >).

Substrings are obtained using slicing.

```
text = "DataStructures"
print(text[0:4])   # Output: Data
```

Comparison is like checking two books to see if they are identical or if one comes before the other alphabetically.

Therefore, substring extraction is like tearing out a chapter from a larger book—you are focusing only on a section of the whole.

Traversing Strings

Traversing a string means visiting each character in the string one by one. This process is at the heart of many string operations such as searching for a character, counting vowels, or checking whether the string is a palindrome. By systematically moving through a string, programmers gain direct access to its contents. This makes manipulation and analysis possible.

Think of traversal as flipping through the pages of a book: you start at the first page and move forward, reading each page until you reach the end. Similarly, when traversing a string, you start at the first character, and keep moving until you reach the end marker.

Loop-Based Traversal

The most common way to traverse a string is by using loops. Thus, a '`for`' loop or '`while`' loop can be employed to process each character.

C-Style Strings:

```
#include <iostream>
using namespace std;

int main() {
    char word[] = "Hello";
    for (int i = 0; word[i] != '\0'; i++) {
        cout << word[i] << " ";
    }
    return 0;
}
```

Output: `H e l l o`

Here, the loop continues until the special null character '`\0`' is encountered, which signals the end of the string.

C++ String Class:

```
string word = "Hello";
for (int i = 0; i < word.length(); i++) {
    cout << word[i] << " ";
}
```

Python:

```
word = "Hello"
for ch in word:
    print(ch, end=" ")
```

As is apparent from the mentioned examples, loop traversal is like reading names from a class attendance list one by one, until the last student's name is read out.

End-of-String Detection

One crucial aspect of string traversal is to know when to stop. Unlike arrays with a fixed size, strings may vary in length. Therefore, a clear stopping condition is required.

C-Style Strings: Strings end with a special null character ('\0'). This invisible marker tells the program that there are no more characters to read.

C++ and Python Strings: These languages internally store the string length, so loops use this information rather than relying on a null terminator.

Example in **C** with explicit end detection:

```
char text[] = "DSA";
int i = 0;
while (text[i] != '\0') {
    cout << text[i];
    i++;
}
```

Output: DSA

Therefore, end-of-string detection is like reaching the last page of a book; the absence of another page signals that the reading is complete.

Strings in Various Languages

Strings are a universal concept across all programming languages, but the way they are represented and manipulated can differ significantly. Hence, understanding these differences is important for learners, as it builds flexibility, and prepares them to work across multiple platforms and coding environments.

C-Style Strings

In the C programming language (and in C++ when using legacy constructs), strings are represented as **arrays of characters** terminated by a special character '\0' (the null terminator). This null character acts as a sentinel that marks the end of the string. C-style strings, therefore, have these characteristics:

Stored in contiguous memory locations as character arrays

Ended explicitly with '**\0**'

Length is not stored separately, so the functions must traverse until they find the null terminator.

Mutable: Contents can be changed character by character.

Example in C++ (C-Style):

```
#include <iostream>
using namespace std;

int main() {
    char word[6] = "Hello";  // Automatically adds '\0'
    cout << word;            // Output: Hello
    return 0;
}
```

Here, "**Hello**" takes 6 memory slots: 5 for the characters **H e l l o**, and 1 for the null terminator \0.

Think of a C-style string as a **row of boxes in a shelf** where each box stores a letter, and the final box contains a red flag (\0) to signal "**stop reading further**".

Python Strings

In Python, strings are treated very differently. They are **immutable sequences of Unicode characters**, which means that once a string is created, it cannot be changed. Any modification results in the creation of a new string object.

Strings are objects of the built-in str class. They also have advantages like:

They support powerful operations such as slicing, concatenation, formatting.

They automatically manage memory; there is no need to worry about null terminators.

They are immutable, as they cannot modify characters directly.

Example in Python:

```
word = "Hello"
print(word)          # Output: Hello
print(word[0])       # Output: H
print(word[1:4])     # Output: ell
```

Here, slicing (**word[1:4]**) extracts a substring without altering the original string.

Moreover, a Python string is like a **printed word on paper**. You can read parts of it, copy it, or combine it with others, but you cannot erase or replace letters directly—you would have to rewrite the paper with a new word.

C++ String Class Methods

In C++, the **std::string** class from the **Standard Template Library (STL)** provides a rich set of **built-in methods** that make working with strings **simple, efficient, and powerful.** Unlike traditional **C-style character arrays**, std::string objects handle **dynamic memory management automatically**, which means that you do not need to worry about buffer sizes or manual allocation.

These methods allow programmers to **create, modify, search, compare, and analyze strings** easily, which is especially useful in solving **algorithmic and real-world problems** like text processing, data parsing, or pattern matching.

Key String Class Methods

Here is a comprehensive list of commonly used C++ string methods, grouped by their purpose:

Methods for Accessing String Data

length()/size()

Returns the **number of characters** in the string

```
#include <iostream>
#include <string>
using namespace std;

int main() {
    string str = "Data Structures";
    cout << "Length: " << str.length() << endl;
```

```
    cout << "Size: " << str.size() << endl;
    return 0;
}
```

Output:

```
Length: 15
Size: 15
```

It must be noted that **length()** and **size()** are interchangeable; therefore, both give the string length.

at(index)

Returns the **character at a specific index**

Unlike operator[], this method performs **bounds checking** to avoid runtime errors.

```
string str = "Algorithms";
cout << "Character at index 3: " << str.at(3);
```

Output: o

front() and **back()**

front() → Returns the **first character**

back() → Returns the **last character**

```
string str = "Coding";
cout << str.front() << endl;  // Output: C
cout << str.back() << endl;   // Output: g
```

Methods for Modifying Strings

append() / operator+=

Adds content to the end of a string

```
string s1 = "Hello";
s1.append(" World");
cout << s1 << endl;  // Output: Hello World

string s2 = "Hi";
s2 += " there!";
cout << s2 << endl;  // Output: Hi there!
```

insert(position, str)

Inserts a substring at a given position

```
string str = "Data Structures";
str.insert(5, "and ");
cout << str;
// Output: Data and Structures
```

replace(position, length, str)

Replaces part of the string with another string

```
string str = "I love Java";
str.replace(7, 4, "C++");
cout << str;
// Output: I love C++
```

`erase(position, length)`

Removes a specific portion of the string

```
string str = "Neural Networks";
str.erase(6, 9);
cout << str;
// Output: Neural
```

`clear()`

Deletes all characters, making the string **`empty`**

```
string str = "Hello";
str.clear();
cout << str;  // Output: (empty string)
```

`push_back()` and **`pop_back()`**

```
push_back(ch) → Adds a character at the end
pop_back() → Removes the last character
```

```
string str = "Data";
str.push_back('X');    // DataX
str.pop_back();        // Data
```

Methods for Extracting and Searching

substr(start, length)

Returns a **substring** starting from start with length characters

```
string str = "Artificial Intelligence";
cout << str.substr(0, 10);
// Output: Artificial
```

`find(str)`

Finds the **first occurrence** of a substring

```
string str = "Machine Learning";
cout << "Index: " << str.find("Learn");
// Output: 8
```

`rfind(str)`

Finds the **last occurrence** of a substring

```
string str = "abcabcabc";
cout << str.rfind("abc");
// Output: 6
```

`find_first_of()` and `find_last_of()`

`find_first_of()` → Finds the first occurrence of **any character** from a set

`find_last_of()` → Finds the last occurrence

```
string str = "hello world";
cout << str.find_first_of("aeiou");   // Output: 1 (first vowel: e)
cout << str.find_last_of("aeiou");    // Output: 7 (last vowel: o)
```

Methods for Comparing and Checking

`compare(str)`

Compares two strings **lexicographically** in the following manner:

```
Returns 0 → Strings are equal.
Returns >0 → The first string is greater.
Returns <0 → The second string is greater.
```

```
string s1 = "apple", s2 = "banana";
cout << s1.compare(s2);
// Output: Negative value (since "apple" < "banana")
```

`empty()`

Checks whether the string is empty

```
string str = "";
if (str.empty())
    cout << "String is empty!";
```

Methods for Conversion

`stoi()`, `stol()`, `stod()`

Converts a string to a numeric value

```
string num = "123";
int x = stoi(num);
cout << x + 10;
// Output: 133
```

Let us have a look at few important methods:

Category	Method	Purpose	Example
Access	`length()`	Returns size	`str.length()`
Modify	`append()`	Adds string	`s1.append("World")`
Insert/Replace	`insert()`	Inserts substring	`str.insert(5,"Hi")`
Erase	`erase()`	Removes part of string	`str.erase(2,3)`
Extract	`substr()`	Gets substring	`str.substr(0,5)`
Search	`find()`	Finds first match	`str.find("data")`
Compare	`compare()`	Lexicographic comparison	`s1.compare(s2)`
Check Empty	`empty()`	Tests if string is empty	`str.empty()`
Conversion	`stoi()`	String → int conversion	`stoi("123")`

Table 2.3: *Important String Class Methods*

Built-in String Functions

Strings are one of the most frequently used data types in programming and play a vital role in managing textual data effectively. They are used in almost every real-world application, from processing user inputs and handling files, to working with data storage and authentication systems.

Both **C++** and **Python** provide powerful **built-in string functions** that make string manipulation easier, faster, and more efficient. Hence, understanding these functions is crucial for **DSA**, **competitive programming**, and **interview preparation.**

Operation	Purpose	C++ Function and Example	Python Function and Example
Length of String	Returns the total number of characters in the string	`text.length() or text.size() cpp\nstring text="Hello";\ncout<<text.length();` **Output:** `5`	`len(text) python\ntext="Hello"\nprint(len(text))` **Output:** `5`
Concatenate Strings	Joins two or more strings into one	`str1 + str2 or str1.append(str2) cpp\nstring a="Data";\nstring b="Struct";\ncout<<a+" "+b;` **Output:** `Data Struct`	`a + b or " ".join([a,b]) python\na="Data"\nb="Struct"\nprint(a+" "+b)` **Output:** `Data Struct`
Extract Substring	Retrieves a portion of the string	`substr(start, len) cpp\nstring s="Algorithms";\ncout<<s.substr(0,5);` **Output:** `Algor`	`str[start:end] python\ns="Algorithms"\nprint(s[0:5])` **Output:** `Algor`
Search Substring	Finds the position of a substring	`find("word") cpp\nstring s="DSA with C++";\ncout<<s.find("C++");` **Output:** `8`	str.find("word") python\ns="DSA with Python"\nprint(s.find("Python")) **Output:** `9`
Change Case	Converts all letters to upper or lower case	`toupper(), tolower() cpp\nstring s=\"hello\";\nfor(char &c:s) c=toupper(c);\ncout<<s;` **Output:** `HELLO`	`upper(), lower() python\ns=\"hello\"\nprint(s.upper())` **Output:** `HELLO`
Replace Substring	Replaces a part of the string with another	`replace(pos,len,str) cpp\nstring s=\"I like C\";\ns.replace(7,1,\"C++\");\ncout<<s;` **Output:** `I like C++`	`replace(old,new) python\ns=\"I like C\"\nprint(s.replace(\"C\",\"C++\"))` **Output:** `I like C++`
Split & Join	Splits strings into parts or joins them back	Manual via loops or `stringstream cpp\n//` Not directly supported	`split(), join() python\ns=\"A B C\"\nprint(s.split())` **Output:** `['A','B','C']`
Compare Strings	Compares two strings	`str1.compare(str2) cpp\nstring a=\"abc\";\nstring b=\"xyz\";\ncout<<a.compare(b);` **Output:** -1	`==, <, > python\na=\"abc\";b=\"xyz\"\nprint(a==b)` **Output:** False

Table 2.4: *Built-in String Functions*

Memory Representation

How strings are stored in memory plays a crucial role in how they behave during execution. Therefore, different programming languages adopt different storage models depending on their design goals—some prefer efficiency and control, while others emphasize safety and simplicity.

Character Array Layout with Null Terminator

In low-level languages like **C**, strings are represented as **character arrays**. Each character occupies one memory cell, and the string ends with a special marker called the **null terminator (\0)**.

Every string is stored as consecutive bytes in memory.

The final byte is reserved for \0, which indicates the end of the string.

Hence, without the null terminator, functions like strlen() would keep scanning memory indefinitely, which can lead to errors.

Example:

```
char word[6] = "Hello";
```

Index	0	1	2	3	4	5
Value	H	e	l	l	o	\0

Figure 2.4: *Memory Layout*

Here, "`Hello`" occupies **6 memory cells**—five for the letters, and one for the terminator.

Imagine writing a word on a row of boxes. After finishing the last letter, you put a red "STOP" card (\0) in the next box to signal the end of the word.

Immutable and Mutable String Storage

When working with strings, an important concept to understand is whether the string is **immutable** (cannot be changed after it is created) or **mutable** (can be modified directly). This distinction affects both **memory usage** and **performance**, and is a key idea in programming.

Immutable Strings

In many programming languages such as **Python** and **Java**, strings are **immutable**. Therefore, once you create a string, its contents cannot be changed. If you attempt to modify it—say, by concatenating another string or replacing a character—a **new string object** is created in memory, while the old one remains unchanged. This behavior makes immutable strings **safe to use** in multi-threaded environments (since no other part of the program can alter the string unexpectedly).

Example in Python:

```
s = "Hello"
s = s + " World"   # Creates a new string "Hello World"
```

Here, "`Hello World`" is stored in a **new memory location**, while "Hello" remains untouched until garbage collection cleans it up.

Mutable Strings

Some languages, like **C++**, provide mutable string types (for example, std::string) where the characters can be modified in place. Similarly, Python offers a **bytearray** or lists of characters as mutable alternatives. Mutable strings are more **efficient for frequent modifications**, since they allow in-place editing without creating new objects.

Example in C++:

```
#include <iostream>
#include <string>
```

```
using namespace std;

int main() {
    string s = "Hello";
    s[0] = 'Y';    // Modify in place
    cout << s;     // Output: Yello
    return 0;
}
```

Here, the same memory block holding "`Hello`" is updated to "`Yello`" without allocating new space.

Immutable strings are ideal when you need reliability, security, and frequent string sharing (for example, dictionary keys, constants).

Mutable strings are better when building or editing strings dynamically, such as processing text documents or constructing large strings through repeated operations. Think of an **immutable string** as a sealed letter—you cannot change what is inside once it is written; if you want to send a new message, you write another letter. Therefore, a **mutable string** is like a whiteboard—you can erase, rewrite, and update content in the same place without needing a new board.

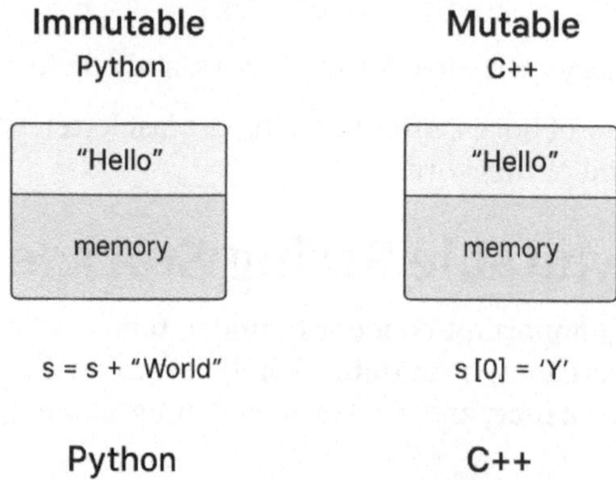

Figure 2.5: *Comparing Immutable and Mutable String Storage*

Figure 2.5 illustrates the difference between **immutable** and **mutable** string storage in programming:

- **Immutable String Storage:** The string "`Hello`" is stored in memory as [H][e][l][l][o]. When you modify it (for example, concatenating " `World`"), a **new memory block** is allocated: [H][e][l][l][o][ ][W][o][r][l][d]. The original string remains unchanged because immutable objects cannot be altered in place. This ensures **data integrity** and makes string handling safer, but it is less memory-efficient for repeated modifications.
- **Mutable String Storage**: The string "`Hello`" is stored in memory as [H][e][l][l][o]. When you modify a character (for example, `s[0] = 'Y'`), the **same memory block** is updated in place to [Y][e][l][l][o]. No new memory is allocated. This allows efficient modifications; however, programmers must be careful to avoid unintended overwrites or memory errors.

Common String Problem-Solving Patterns

Strings are one of the most frequently used data types in computer science. From handling user input and processing textual data, to implementing advanced algorithms in search engines and pattern matching, **string manipulation** forms the backbone of modern applications. To solve problems efficiently, certain **common problem-solving patterns** are widely used in competitive programming, interviews, and real-world systems.

In this section, we will discuss four essential string problem-solving techniques: **palindrome checks**, **anagram** detection, **substring search patterns**, and **sliding window techniques**.

Palindrome Checks

A **palindrome** is a string that reads the same forward and backward, such as "*madam*" or "*racecar*". Palindrome problems are popular in **coding interviews** and **real-world applications** such as validating DNA sequences, data mirroring in storage systems, or detecting symmetrical patterns in text. You may also use the **two-pointer technique here through the following checks**:

Place one pointer at the start (left) and another at the end (right).

Compare characters at both pointers.

Move inward until pointers meet.

If all corresponding characters match, the string is a palindrome. This is like holding a book open in the middle and comparing the left and right pages word by word. If everything matches, the text is symmetric, just like a palindrome.

Example

C++ Code:

```
#include <iostream>
using namespace std;

bool isPalindrome(string str) {
    int left = 0, right = str.length() - 1;
    while (left < right) {
        if (str[left] != str[right]) return false;
        left++;
        right--;
    }
    return true;
}
int main() {
    string s = "madam";
    cout << (isPalindrome(s) ? "Palindrome" : "Not Palindrome");
    return 0;
}
```

Python Code:

```
def is_palindrome(s: str) -> bool:
    return s == s[::-1]

print(is_palindrome("madam"))  # Output: True
```

Anagram Detection

An **anagram** is formed by rearranging the characters of one string to produce another. For example, "*listen*" → "*silent*".

Anagram detection is commonly used in **spell-checking**, **plagiarism detection**, and **data matching systems**.

- **Sorting Method**: Sort both strings. If the sorted versions are equal, they are anagrams.
- **Frequency Map Method** (*Optimized*): Count character occurrences using an array or hash map, and then compare them.

A fitting analogy is the case of two bags filled with letter tiles. If both the bags have **exactly the same letters in the same quantity**, they form an anagram.

Example Code

C++ Code:

```
#include <iostream>
#include <algorithm>
using namespace std;

bool isAnagram(string s1, string s2) {
    if (s1.length() != s2.length()) return false;
    sort(s1.begin(), s1.end());
    sort(s2.begin(), s2.end());
    return s1 == s2;
}

int main() {
    cout << (isAnagram("listen", "silent") ? "Anagram" : "Not Anagram");
    return 0;
}
```

Python Code:

```
def is_anagram(s1: str, s2: str) -> bool:
    return sorted(s1) == sorted(s2)

print(is_anagram("listen", "silent"))  # Output: True
```

Substring Search Patterns

Substring search involves finding whether a smaller string (**pattern**) exists inside a larger string (**text**).

This is essential in **search engines**, **plagiarism checkers**, **DNA matching**, and **auto-suggestion features**.

Naive Method: Slide the pattern over the text and compare character by character.

Efficient Method (*Recommended*): Use **KMP** or **Rabin-Karp** algorithms for faster searching.

Imagine flipping through a dictionary to find a word. You scan each page until you find the exact match.

Example Code

C++ Code:

```
#include <iostream>
using namespace std;

int substringSearch(string text, string pattern) {
    int n = text.length(), m = pattern.length();
    for (int i = 0; i <= n - m; i++) {
        int j;
        for (j = 0; j < m; j++)
            if (text[i + j] != pattern[j]) break;
        if (j == m) return i; // Match found
    }
    return -1;
}
```

```
int main() {
    cout << substringSearch("datastructures", "struct");
    return 0;
}
```

Python Code:

```
def substring_search(text: str, pattern: str) -> int:
    return text.find(pattern)

print(substring_search("datastructures", "struct"))  # Output: 4
```

Sliding Window Techniques in String Problems

The **sliding window** technique optimizes problems where you need to analyze **substrings** or **subarrays** continuously.

Instead of recalculating from scratch, the window "slides" to reuse previous computations. Common use cases include finding the **longest substring without repeating characters**, calculating **maximum or minimum substring length**, counting occurrences of specific patterns.

Imagine reading a book with a magnifying glass. The magnifier covers a fixed-width section of text—as you slide it, you can analyze the next portion without re-reading the old part.

Example Code

C++ Code:

```
#include <iostream>
#include <unordered_set>
using namespace std;

int longestUniqueSubstring(string s) {
    unordered_set<char> seen;
    int left = 0, maxLen = 0;
    for (int right = 0; right < s.length(); right++) {
        while (seen.count(s[right])) seen.erase(s[left++]);
        seen.insert(s[right]);
        maxLen = max(maxLen, right - left + 1);
    }
    return maxLen;
}

int main() {
    cout << longestUniqueSubstring("abcabcbb"); // Output: 3
    return 0;
}
```

Python Code:

```
def longest_unique_substring(s: str) -> int:
    seen, left, max_len = set(), 0, 0
    for right, char in enumerate(s):
        while char in seen:
            seen.remove(s[left])
            left += 1
        seen.add(char)
```

```
        max_len = max(max_len, right - left + 1)
    return max_len

print(longest_unique_substring("abcabcbb"))  # Output: 3
```

Common string problem-solving patterns are listed as follows:

Pattern	Use Case	Approach	Time Complexity
Palindrome Check	Verify symmetric strings.	Two-pointer comparison	`O(n)`
Anagram Detection	Compare rearranged words.	Sorting / frequency map	`O(n log n) / O(n)`
Substring Search	Find pattern in text.	Naive / KMP / Rabin-Karp	`O(n × m) / O(n+m)`
Sliding Window	Optimize substring problems.	Two-pointer dynamic window	`O(n)`

Table 2.5: *Common String Problem-Solving Patterns*

These string problem-solving patterns are widely used in real-world software systems beyond academic exercises. Palindrome checks are applied in DNA sequence analysis, text symmetry validation, and data integrity verification. Anagram detection is commonly used in spell-checking systems, plagiarism detection tools, and keyword matching engines. Substring search techniques form the backbone of search engines, text editors, log monitoring systems, and bioinformatics applications such as DNA pattern matching. The sliding window technique is extensively used in real-time text analytics, network traffic inspection, and stream-based data processing, where continuous evaluation of substrings is required without repeated computation.

Conclusion

In this chapter, we built a strong foundation by exploring **arrays and strings**, which are the most fundamental linear data structures. Arrays introduced us to the idea of contiguous memory storage, constant-time access, and structured organization of data, while also displaying their limitations in terms of size and flexibility. Strings, on the other hand, extended these ideas into handling textual data. We examined their operations, traversals, and differences across programming languages such as C, Python, and Java. Together, these concepts prepared us with the essential tools to store, manipulate, and process data efficiently at a fundamental level.

With this foundation in place, we will now move forward to ***Chapter 3: Linked Lists to*** explore a more dynamic and flexible approach to organizing data. Unlike arrays, linked lists do not rely on fixed, contiguous memory blocks; instead, they use nodes and pointers to achieve dynamic growth and flexibility. In the next chapter, we will study different types of linked lists, including singly, doubly, and circular linked lists, while learning their real-world applications, advantages over arrays, and common algorithmic patterns. By the end of Chapter 3, you will be equipped with the knowledge to handle dynamic data structures confidently. This will set the stage for solving more advanced problems in DSA.

Points to Remember

- Arrays store multiple values of the same data type in contiguous memory.
- Indexing starts at 0 in C, C++, and Python.
- Array access time is O(1), but insertion/deletion costs O(n).
- Static Arrays → Fixed size at compile time; Dynamic Arrays → Allocated at runtime.

- 2D/3D arrays in C/C++ are stored in row-major order.
- A C-style string is a char array terminated with '\0'.
- In C++, **`std::string`** is mutable, while in Python, strings are immutable.
- String operations: length, concatenation, copying, comparison, substring.
- Null terminator ('\0') signals the end of a C-style string.

Multiple Choice Questions

1. Which of the following is true about arrays?
   a. Arrays can store multiple data types.
   b. Arrays use contiguous memory locations.
   c. Array size can always be increased automatically.
   d. Array access time is `O(n)`.
2. If an integer array starts at address 2000, and each int is 4 bytes, what is the address of `arr[5]`?
   a. 2016
   b. 2020
   c. 2024
   d. 2025
3. Time complexity of binary search on a sorted array is:
   a. `O(1)`
   b. `O(log n)`
   c. `O(n)`
   d. `O(n log n)`
4. Which of these is a limitation of arrays?
   a. Random Access
   b. Contiguous Memory Requirement
   c. Homogeneous Data Type
   d. Index-Based Access
5. In Python, strings are:
   a. Mutable
   b. Immutable
   c. Stored in stack only
   d. Always character arrays
6. Which function is used to find length of C-style string?
   a. `len()`
   b. `sizeof()`
   c. `strlen()`
   d. `length()`

7. What is the main difference between `char str[] = "Hello";` and `string s = "Hello";` in C++?
    a. Both are the same.
    b. str is mutable, s is immutable.
    c. str is C-style (array), s is an object (`std::string`).
    d. None of these is applicable.
8. In C++, if `int arr[5] = {1,2};`, the values of remaining elements are:
    a. Garbage Values
    b. Zero
    c. Null
    d. Uninitialized
9. Which searching technique can only be applied to **sorted arrays**?
    a. Linear Search
    b. Binary Search
    c. Hashing
    d. Jump Search
10. If array size is n, what is the maximum index?
    a. n
    b. n-1
    c. n+1
    d. Undefined
11. Which of the following operations has `O(1)` complexity in arrays?
    a. Traversal
    b. Insertion
    c. Deletion
    d. Access by Index
12. In a **2D array** `a[m][n]`, how is element `a[i][j]` stored in row-major order?
    a. `Base + (i * n + j) * size`
    b. `Base + (j * m + i) * size`
    c. `Base + (i + j) * size`
    d. `Base + (i * j) * size`
13. Which data structure is better than arrays for frequent insertion/deletion?
    a. Stack
    b. Queue
    c. Linked List
    d. Hash Map

14. Which of the following is not a valid string operation in Python?
    a. Concatenation using +
    b. Checking substring with in
    c. String slicing `s[1:4]`
    d. Modifying a character `s[0] = 'A'`
15. What is stored in memory for `char str[10] = "Hi";`?
    a. `'H'` `'i'` `'\0'` and rest unused
    b. Only `'H'` `'i'`
    c. `'H'` `'i'` `'\0'` repeated till 10 cells
    d. Garbage values after `'i'`
16. Which of the following is true for Python strings?
    a. They are mutable and stored in stack.
    b. They are immutable and stored in heap.
    c. They are mutable and stored in heap.
    d. They are immutable and stored in stack.

Answers

1. b
2. c
3. b
4. b
5. c
6. b
7. c
8. c
9. b
10. b
11. b
12. d
13. a
14. c
15. d
16. a

Questions

1. Explain the need for arrays in programming. Why cannot we use simple variables for large data?
2. Describe the concept of contiguous memory allocation in arrays with an example.
3. What are the characteristics of arrays? Explain index-based access and random access complexity.

4. Differentiate between static allocation and dynamic allocation of arrays with syntax.
5. What are the advantages and disadvantages of arrays compared to linked lists?
6. Explain the time and space complexity of array operations (traversal, insertion, deletion, searching).
7. Differentiate between character arrays (C-style strings) and string objects in C++.
8. What is the role of the null terminator ('`\0`') in C-style strings? Explain with a memory diagram.
9. Compare mutable and immutable strings in C++, Java, and Python. Why are Python strings immutable?
10. Write a program to reverse a string without using built-in functions.
11. Write an algorithm to check if a given string is a palindrome.
12. How can you find the length of a string in C without using `strlen()`?
13. Explain the difference between string concatenation in C, C++, and Python.

Key Terms

- **Array:** Homogeneous collection in contiguous memory
- **Index:** Position of an element (0-based)
- **Static vs. Dynamic Allocation:** Compile-time vs runtime memory assignment
- **Row-major Order:** Storage order of multi-dimensional arrays
- **Traversal:** Sequential access of elements
- **C-style String:** Char array + '\0'.
- **Immutable:** Cannot change after creation (Python strings)
- **Mutable:** Can be changed (C++ std::string)
- **Null Terminator:** Special character ('\0') marking string end

Chapter 3
Linked Lists

Introduction

In modern software development, data is rarely static, and applications often need to manage collections of information that grow, shrink, and change dynamically. In the previous chapter, we explored arrays and strings, which work efficiently for fixed-size datasets stored in contiguous memory blocks. However, they have certain limitations, such as the need to define size at creation, and the overhead of shifting large portions of data during insertions or deletions. To overcome these challenges, we turn to **linked lists**, which refer to dynamic and flexible data structures that organize data into interconnected nodes, rather than relying on continuous memory allocation. Each node contains the data to be stored, and one or more pointers link it to other nodes. This enables efficient growth, shrinkage, and modification of data without costly memory reallocations. Therefore, a linked list can be imagined as a chain of train coaches, where each coach represents a node holding passengers (data), and a connector (pointer) to the next coach. It also allows coaches to be added, removed, or rearranged seamlessly. Therefore, in this chapter, we will explore linked lists in depth, starting from the basic structure of a node, and gradually moving on to various types such as **singly linked lists**, **doubly linked lists**, and **circular linked lists**. We will address their creation, traversal, insertion, deletion, merging, splitting, and reversal, along with essential pointer manipulation techniques, and comparisons with arrays to understand their advantages, limitations, and practical applications. By the end of this chapter, you will have a strong foundation in working with linked lists, a clear understanding of their memory representation, and the skills to implement and manipulate them efficiently using **C++** and **Python**. Hence, mastering these concepts will prepare you for solving real-world problems, and help you build your confidence to tackle more advanced data structures like **heaps, trees, and graphs**, that are explained in later chapters.

Structure

In this chapter, we will cover the following topics:

- Introduction to Linked Lists
- Structure of a Node
- Singly Linked Lists
- Doubly Linked Lists

- Circular Linked Lists
- Pointer Management in Linked Lists
- Loop Detection and Removal
- Reversal of Linked Lists
- Merging and Splitting Linked Lists

Introduction to Linked Lists

In the realm of data structures, linked lists play a crucial role in storing and managing data efficiently, especially when dealing with dynamic collections. Unlike arrays, which rely on contiguous memory allocation and have a fixed size, linked lists are built using independent nodes connected through pointers. Therefore, this structural difference gives linked lists the flexibility to grow or shrink during runtime, which makes them particularly useful when working with unpredictable data sizes.

The core strength of linked lists lies in their dynamic memory allocation. Since nodes are allocated independently in memory and linked using pointers, we can easily insert or delete elements without shifting existing data, as is required in arrays. Hence, this makes linked lists a preferred choice when the size of data cannot be predetermined, or when frequent insertions, deletions, and rearrangements are necessary.

For example, consider a music playlist application. When you add a new song or remove an existing one, the list updates seamlessly without the need to recreate or restructure the entire collection. This dynamic behavior is made possible by linked lists, which allow for smooth and efficient data manipulation.

Linked lists are widely used in modern **software systems, operating systems, and databases** due to their adaptability. Some practical applications include dynamic memory management, undo/redo functionality, implementing stacks, queues, and hash tables, web browsers, music or video streaming apps. In essence, arrays are ideal when fast random access is required, while linked lists are better suited for frequent modifications and dynamic storage requirements. Hence, understanding when to use each of them is important for writing efficient and optimized programs.

Structure of a Node

A linked list is fundamentally built using nodes, which act as the basic building blocks of the structure. Unlike arrays, where elements are stored in contiguous memory locations, a linked list organizes data in independent memory blocks called nodes, each connected to the next through pointers. These pointers create a logical sequence, even when the nodes are scattered across memory. To understand linked lists, we must first understand their smallest building block—the **node**. Every linked list, regardless of its type, is composed of a collection of these nodes that are logically connected to one another. Unlike arrays, where elements are stored in consecutive memory locations, the nodes of a linked list can be scattered anywhere in memory. What ties these nodes together is the **pointer mechanism**, which creates a **chain-like structure**. Moreover, each node acts as an independent unit, and typically consists of two core components:

Data Field

The data field is where the actual value or information is stored.

In a list of student records, the data field may store student IDs or names. In a music playlist, it may hold the song title or file path. The data stored can be of any type—integers, characters, strings, or even complex objects—depending on the application.

For example:

If we are storing numbers in a linked list, each node's data field could look like:

```
Data = 10, 20, 30, 40
```

These fields represent the values we want to manage in the list.

Pointer Field

The pointer field (also called the link field) stores the memory address of the next node in the sequence. This is what links one node to another and forms the chain-like structure of the linked list.

In a singly linked list, each node has one pointer, while connecting it to the next node. In a doubly linked list, each node has two pointers: one pointing to the next node, and another pointing to the previous node. In a circular linked list, the last node's pointer connects back to the first node, forming a loop.

Therefore, without this pointer, the linked list would lose its sequence, as the nodes are not stored in consecutive memory locations.

Memory Representation of Nodes

A node in a linked list may look simple conceptually—a data field and a pointer—but its representation in memory reveals why linked lists are so flexible, yet different from arrays.

When a node is created, the **data field** stores the actual information (for example, an integer value like 25). Right next to it in the node's structure is the **pointer field**, which stores the memory address of the next node in the sequence. Unlike arrays, where all elements occupy a single contiguous block of memory, nodes can be stored at **non-contiguous addresses**. The pointer ensures that the nodes remain logically connected, despite being scattered across memory.

For instance, consider the following nodes:

- The first node contains the value 25 and a pointer to the second node located at address 2004.
- The second node contains the value 40 and a pointer to the third node located at address 3012.
- The third node contains the value 55 and a pointer set to NULL, indicating the end of the list.

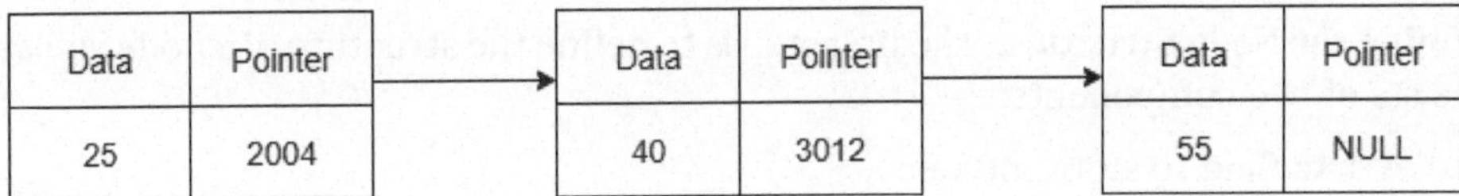

Figure 3.1: *Memory Representation of Nodes in a Linked List*

Visually, this can be thought of as a chain: each block has two parts—one is holding the data, and the other is pointing to the address of the next block. This structure allows insertion and deletion operations to be performed without shifting other elements, which is one of the **key advantages linked lists** offer over arrays.

Singly Linked Lists

A **singly linked list** is one of the simplest yet most powerful data structures in computer science. It is designed to store and manage data dynamically. Unlike arrays, where elements are stored in a **contiguous block of memory**, singly linked lists consist of individual **nodes** connected through **pointers**, while forming a flexible sequence of elements. Each node typically has two components: a **data field** that stores the actual value, and a **pointer field** that stores the memory address of the **next**

node in the sequence. The **first node** in the list is called the **head**, and the **last node** points to `NULL`, which indicates the **end of the list**. This design makes singly linked lists highly **dynamic**, **flexible**, and **efficient** for applications where the size of the dataset is unpredictable or subject to frequent changes. Unlike arrays, where memory must be pre-allocated, nodes in a singly linked list are created **on demand**, which optimizes memory utilization and avoids unnecessary allocation.

***Figure 3.2:** Structure of a Singly Linked List*

Singly linked lists are highly flexible data structures designed for **dynamic data storage and manipulation**. Unlike arrays, where elements are stored in continuous memory, linked lists consist of **nodes** connected through pointers, each containing **data** and a reference to the **next node**. The list begins at the **head** and ends when the last node points to **NULL**. One of their key strengths is **dynamic size management**; lists can easily **grow or shrink at runtime**, which makes them ideal when the number of elements is unpredictable. Traversal occurs **sequentially**, starting from the head and moving node by node, since **random access** like in arrays is not possible. Singly linked lists also provide **efficient insertion and deletion operations** because they avoid shifting elements as arrays do. Adding or removing nodes often involves just **updating pointers**, thereby making operations faster. However, due to their **unidirectional structure**, nodes only know about the **next node**. This makes **backward traversal** impossible without additional modifications. From a **memory perspective**, they are space-efficient since nodes are **allocated only when required**, while reducing wastage. Their flexibility makes them widely used in real-world systems, such as **memory management** in operating systems, **stacks** and **queues** implementation, **playlist handling** in media apps, **polynomial arithmetic**, **expression evaluation**, and **sparse matrix representation**, where they store only **non-zero values** efficiently.

Creation of Singly Linked Lists

Singly linked lists are created dynamically using memory allocation techniques, where nodes are generated during runtime instead of being allocated in contiguous memory blocks like arrays. This dynamic nature allows the linked list to grow or shrink as per the program's needs, and makes it highly flexible for handling unpredictable data sizes.

Here are the steps to create a singly linked list using dynamic memory allocation:

1. **Defining the Node Structure:** The first step is to define the structure of a node, which typically consists of two components:

    a. A **data field** to store the value

    b. A **pointer field** to store the address of the next node

    In C++, this is generally implemented using a struct or class.

2. **Allocating Memory Dynamically:** Using functions like new in C++ or constructors in Python, the memory for each node is allocated during runtime. This allows the list to grow as needed without wasting memory.

3. **Linking Nodes Together:** After creating nodes, each node's pointer field (next) is assigned the address of the subsequent node, forming a chain of connected nodes.

4. **Managing the Head and Tail:**

    a. **Head Pointer:** Stores the address of the first node in the list and acts as the entry point

    b. **Tail Pointer:** Keeps track of the last node, while ensuring that new nodes can be appended efficiently

Initialization of Head and Tail Pointers

Initially, both the **head** and **tail** pointers are set to NULL because the list is empty.

When the first node is created, both **head** and **tail** point to it.

For subsequent nodes, the **tail**'s next pointer is updated to the new node, and the **tail** pointer itself is shifted to the newly added node.

You may think of creating a singly linked list as forming a train:

- The **head** is the engine—the starting point of the journey.
- Each **node** is a coach connected to the previous one.
- The **tail** is the last coach, which makes it easy to attach a new one at the end when needed.

Traversal in Singly Linked Lists

Traversal in a singly linked list refers to the process of visiting each node in the list one by one, starting from the **head node** and following the links until the **end of the list**. Since linked lists are **sequential data structures**, accessing nodes happens by following the next pointer stored inside each node.

Unlike arrays, where elements can be accessed directly using their **index** (random access), linked lists **do not** provide direct indexing. Instead, we must **sequentially traverse** the list, and visit each node in order, until we reach the desired element or the end of the list.

a. **Start with the Head Node**: The **head** pointer points to the first node in the list.

b. **Process the Current Node**: At each step, we read or manipulate the data stored in the current node.

c. **Move to the Next Node**: Using the next pointer, we jump to the following node.

d. **Check for the End of the List**: Traversal stops when the next pointer is NULL, which indicates the **last node** has been reached.

Consider a **chain of connected railway coaches**. Each coach has a note showing where the **next coach** is. To reach the final coach, you start from the **first one** and follow the directions step by step until you find the last coach. Similarly, in linked lists, traversal happens **one node at a time**.

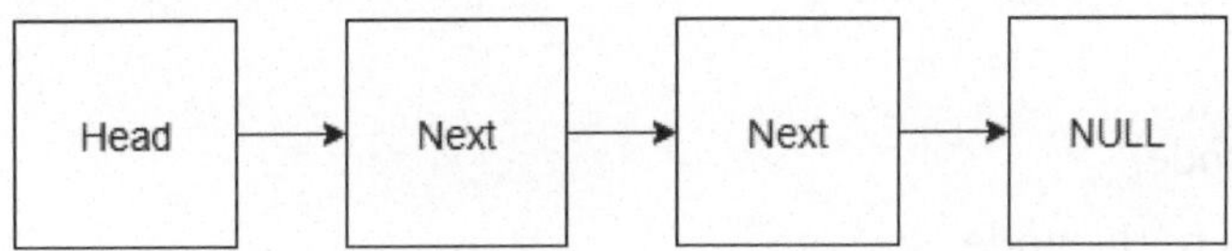

Figure 3.3: *Traversal in a Singly Linked List*

Insertion Operations

In a singly linked list, insertion refers to the process of **adding a new node** at a desired location within the sequence of existing nodes. Since nodes are connected through pointers rather than contiguous memory, inserting an element is generally more flexible than in arrays. Instead of shifting elements like in arrays, we can simply **manipulate the links** between nodes, which makes insertion operations more efficient in many scenarios.

However, the complexity and procedure for insertion depend on **where** the new node is placed. There are three primary cases to consider, which are elaborated as follows:

- Insertion at the **beginning** of the list
- Insertion at the **end** of the list

- Insertion at a **specific position** within the list

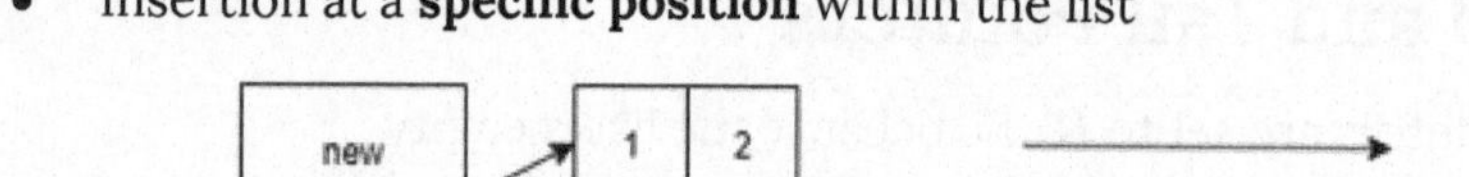

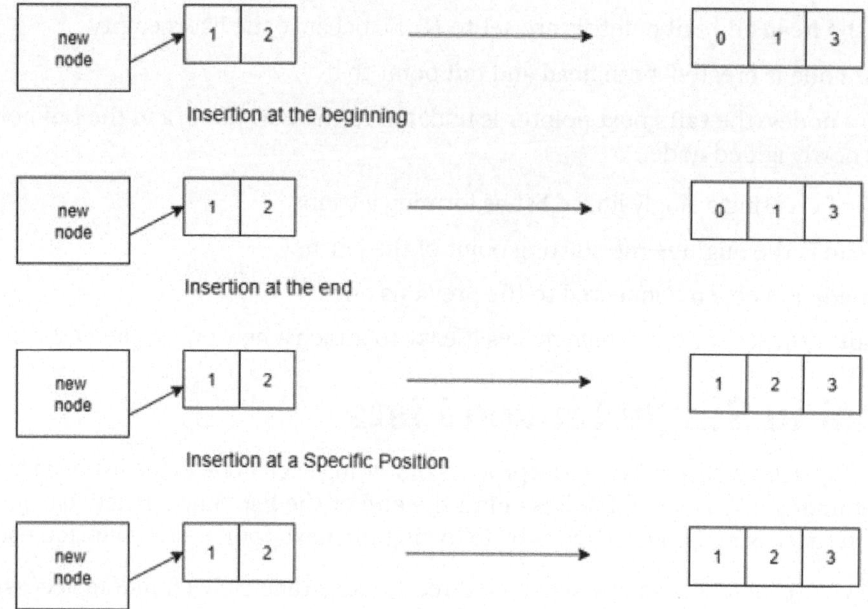

Figure 3.4: *Insertion in a Singly Linked List*

Insertion at the Beginning

Inserting a node at the beginning means placing the new node **before the current head** and updating the head pointer to this newly added node. This operation is **fast and efficient**, as it does not require traversing the list. When a new node is created, we assign it the desired value and set its next pointer to the current head node. Then, the head pointer is updated to point to this new node, which effectively makes it the **first element** in the list. Consider the instance of a line of people entering a cinema hall. If a VIP guest arrives, they are allowed to stand **right at the front of the queue** without disturbing others. Similarly, the new node takes the first position, while the rest of the list remains unchanged.

Time Complexity: `O(1)` → No traversal is needed.

Steps:

a. Create a new node.

b. Assign the data to the node.

c. Point the next of the new node to the current head.

d. Update the head pointer to the new node.

C++ Implementation:

```
void insertAtBeginning(Node* &head, int value) {
    Node* newNode = new Node();    // Step 1: Create a new node
    newNode->data = value;         // Step 2: Assign data
    newNode->next = head;          // Step 3: Link new node to current head
    head = newNode;                // Step 4: Update head to new node
}
```

Python Implementation:

```
def insert_at_beginning(head, value):
    new_node = Node(value)    # Step 1: Create a new node
```

```
    new_node.next = head          # Step 2: Link new node to current head
    head = new_node               # Step 3: Update head pointer
    return head
```

Insertion at the End

Inserting a node at the end involves adding a new node **after the current last node** in the list. Unlike insertion at the beginning, we must **traverse the entire list** to locate the final node before adding the new one. We first create a new node and set its next pointer to NULL (since it will become the last node). Then, starting from the head, we traverse until we reach the current last node, whose next pointer is updated to reference the new node. Imagine a **queue at a billing counter**. If a customer arrives last, they join **at the end of the line** without affecting the position of others. Similarly, the new node is added at the tail of the list.

Time Complexity: `O(n)` → Traversal through all n nodes is required in the worst case.

Steps:

a. Create a new node and assign data.
b. Set the new node's next to NULL.
c. Traverse the list until the last node.
d. Link the last node's next to the new node.

C++ Implementation:

```
void insertAtEnd(Node* &head, int value) {
    Node* newNode = new Node();
    newNode->data = value;
    newNode->next = NULL;

    if (head == NULL) {
        head = newNode;  // If list is empty, make newNode the head
        return;
    }

    Node* temp = head;
    while (temp->next != NULL) {
        temp = temp->next;  // Traverse to last node
    }
    temp->next = newNode;   // Link new node at the end
}
```

Python Implementation:

```
def insert_at_end(head, value):
    new_node = Node(value)
    if head is None:
        return new_node

    temp = head
    while temp.next:
        temp = temp.next
    temp.next = new_node
    return head
```

Insertion at a Specific Position

Inserting a node at a specific position requires careful **pointer manipulation** because the new node must be placed **between existing nodes,** while maintaining the integrity of the linked structure. We create a new node and traverse the list until we reach the node **just before the target position**. The new node's next pointer is linked to the node currently occupying that position, and the previous node's next pointer is updated to reference the new node. For example, to insert a node at position 3, we will traverse to the second node, make the new node point to the third, and update the second node to point to the new one. This is like **reserving a specific seat in a train**. If you book seat number 5, the railway system will not shuffle other passengers; instead, you will be **placed exactly at the desired position,** while the order of surrounding seats remains unchanged.

Time Complexity: `O(n)` → Traversal is required until the desired position.

Steps

a. Create a new node and assign data.

b. Traverse to the node **just before** the desired position.

c. Point the new node's next to the current node's **next**.

d. Update the previous node's **next** to the new node.

C++ Implementation:

```
void insertAtPosition(Node* &head, int value, int position) {
    Node* newNode = new Node();
    newNode->data = value;

    if (position == 1) {  // Insertion at beginning
        newNode->next = head;
        head = newNode;
        return;
    }

    Node* temp = head;
    for (int i = 1; i < position - 1 && temp != NULL; i++) {
        temp = temp->next;  // Move to (position-1)th node
    }

    if (temp == NULL) {
        cout << "Position out of range" << endl;
        return;
    }

    newNode->next = temp->next;
    temp->next = newNode;
}
```

Python Implementation:

```
def insert_at_position(head, value, position):
    new_node = Node(value)

    if position == 1:  # Insertion at beginning
        new_node.next = head
        return new_node

    temp = head
    for _ in range(position - 2):
```

```
        if temp is None:
            raise IndexError("Position out of range")
        temp = temp.next

    new_node.next = temp.next
    temp.next = new_node
    return head
```

Imagine **reserving a seat on a train**. You are placed **at a specific seat number**. Therefore, the railway system traverses through all seat numbers until it places you at the correct spot.

The following table summarizes the different insertion operations in a linked list, along with the steps involved and the necessary pointer updates for each case:

Insertion	Steps Involved	Pointer Updates
Insertion at the Beginning	Create a **new node.** Set `newNode->next = head` Update `head = newNode` If the list was empty, also set `tail = newNode`.	`newNode → next → headhead → newNode`
Insertion at the End	Create a **new node.** Set `newNode->next = NULL` Update `tail->next = newNode` Move `tail = newNode`	`tail → next → newNodetail → newNode`
Insertion at a Specific Position	Traverse the list to the node **before the desired position.** Set `newNode->next = prev->next` Update `prev->next = newNode`	`prev->next → newNodenewNode->next → nextNode`

Table 3.1: *Insertion Operations in a Singly Linked List*

Deletion Operations

Deletion is the process of **removing a node** from a linked list, while maintaining the structure and connectivity between the remaining nodes. Unlike arrays, where deleting an element shifts subsequent elements automatically, we must **manually adjust the node pointers** in a linked list to ensure that the list remains intact.

There are three primary deletion scenarios in singly linked lists:

- Deletion of the first node
- Deletion of the last node
- Deletion of a node at a specific position

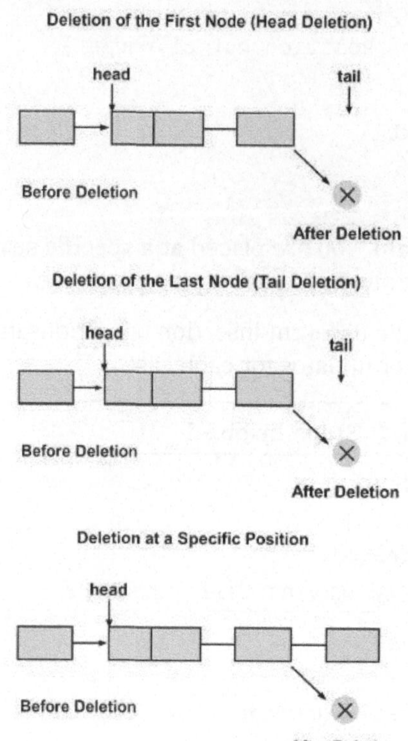

***Figure* 3.5:** *Deletion in a Singly Linked List*

Deletion of the First Node

The simplest deletion case occurs when we remove the **first node** (head) of the list. Since the head node is the entry point to the linked list, deleting it requires **reassigning the head pointer** to the next available node.

Steps Involved

a. **Store the reference** of the current head node in a temporary pointer.

b. **Update the head pointer** to point to the next node: **head = head->next**.

c. **Free the memory** allocated to the old head node.

Time Complexity: `O(1)` No traversal is needed since the head node is directly accessible. Imagine a queue at a ticket counter—when the first person gets the ticket and leaves, the **next person automatically becomes first** without affecting the rest of the line.

C++ Implementation:

```
#include <iostream>
using namespace std;

struct Node {
    int data;
    Node* next;
};

void deleteFirst(Node*& head) {
    if (head == nullptr) {
        cout << "List is empty. Nothing to delete." << endl;
        return;
```

```
    }

    Node* temp = head;        // Store the current head
    head = head->next;        // Move head to the next node
    delete temp;              // Free memory
    cout << "First node deleted successfully." << endl;
}
void display(Node* head) {
    Node* temp = head;
    while (temp) {
        cout << temp->data << " -> ";
        temp = temp->next;
    }
    cout << "NULL" << endl;
}
```

Python Implementation:

```
class Node:
    def __init__(self, data):
        self.data = data
        self.next = None

class LinkedList:
    def __init__(self):
        self.head = None

    def delete_first(self):
        if not self.head:
            print("List is empty. Nothing to delete.")
            return
        self.head = self.head.next
        print("First node deleted successfully.")

    def display(self):
        temp = self.head
        while temp:
            print(temp.data, end=" -> ")
            temp = temp.next
        print("None")
```

Deletion of the Last Node

Deleting the **last node** is slightly more complex because we must locate the **second-last node** to safely remove the tail.

Steps Involved

1. Start from the head and **traverse** the list until you reach the second-last node—the node whose next pointer points to the last node.
2. Set the next pointer of the second-last node to NULL.
3. Free the memory allocated to the last node.

Time Complexity: `O(n)` Traversal is required since we need to reach the node just before the last one.

Think of a **train with coaches;** if you want to remove the last coach, you first walk to the **second-last coach**, detach its connector, and remove the final one.

C++ Implementation:

```
void deleteLast(Node*& head) {
    if (head == nullptr) {
        cout << "List is empty. Nothing to delete." << endl;
        return;
    }

    if (head->next == nullptr) {
        delete head;
        head = nullptr;
        cout << "Last node deleted successfully." << endl;
        return;
    }

    Node* temp = head;
    while (temp->next->next != nullptr) {
        temp = temp->next;
    }

    delete temp->next;        // Delete the last node
    temp->next = nullptr;     // Set new tail's next to NULL
    cout << "Last node deleted successfully." << endl;
}
```

Python Implementation:

```
def delete_last(self):
    if not self.head:
        print("List is empty. Nothing to delete.")
        return

    if self.head.next is None:
        self.head = None
        print("Last node deleted successfully.")
        return

    temp = self.head
    while temp.next.next:
        temp = temp.next

    temp.next = None
    print("Last node deleted successfully.")
```

Deletion at a Specific Position

Sometimes, we need to delete a node from a **particular position** in the list—neither the first nor the last, but somewhere in the middle.

Steps Involved

1. Start from the head and **traverse** the list, until you reach the node **just before** the one to be deleted.
2. Store the reference of the **target node** in a temporary pointer.
3. Update the next pointer of the previous node to skip the target node, and connect directly to the following node.
4. Free the memory allocated to the deleted node.

Time Complexity: `O(n)` Traversal is needed to locate the node before the one being deleted.

Imagine a **chain of people holding hands**. If one person leaves the middle, the two people on either side simply **hold hands with each other**, which keeps the chain intact.

C++ Implementation:

```
void deleteAtPosition(Node*& head, int position) {
    if (head == nullptr) {
        cout << "List is empty. Nothing to delete." << endl;
        return;
    }
    if (position == 1) {
        deleteFirst(head);
        return;
    }
    Node* temp = head;
    for (int i = 1; temp != nullptr && i < position - 1; i++) {
        temp = temp->next;
    }
    if (temp == nullptr || temp->next == nullptr) {
        cout << "Position out of range." << endl;
        return;
    }
    Node* nodeToDelete = temp->next;
    temp->next = nodeToDelete->next;
    delete nodeToDelete;
    cout << "Node at position " << position << " deleted successfully." << endl;
}
```

Python Implementation:

```
def delete_at_position(self, position):
    if not self.head:
        print("List is empty. Nothing to delete.")
        return
    if position == 1:
        self.head = self.head.next
        print(f"Node at position {position} deleted successfully.")
        return
    temp = self.head
    for _ in range(position - 2):
        if not temp.next:
            print("Position out of range.")
            return
        temp = temp.next

    if not temp.next:
        print("Position out of range.")
        return

    temp.next = temp.next.next
    print(f"Node at position {position} deleted successfully.")
```

The following table summarizes the different deletion operations in a linked list along with the steps involved and the necessary pointer updates for each case:

Deletion	Steps Involved	Pointer Updates
Deletion at the Beginning	Check if the list is empty. If not, store the current head in a temporary pointer. Move head to head->next. Free/delete the temporary node.	`head = head->next`
Deletion at the End	Check if the list is empty. If only one node exists, delete it and `set head = NULL`. Otherwise, traverse until the **second last** node. Set the second last node's `next = NULL`. Free/delete the last node.	`second_last->next = NULL`
Deletion at a Specific Position	Check if the list is empty. If `position == 1`, delete the first node. Otherwise, traverse to the **(position - 1)th** node. Store the node to be deleted in a temporary pointer. Update the previous node's next to `temp->next`. Free/delete the temporary node.	`prev->next = temp->next`

Table 3.2: *Deletion Operations in a Singly Linked List*

Doubly Linked Lists

A Doubly Linked List (DLL) is a type of linear data structure used to store elements in a sequence while allowing navigation in both directions—forward and backward. Unlike a singly linked list, where each node only connects to the next node, a DLL introduces an additional connection: every node contains two pointers—one pointing to the next node, and another pointing to the previous node. This two-way linkage provides greater flexibility when managing data, and makes certain operations more efficient. In a doubly linked list, each node consists of three components:

- **Data Field**: Stores the actual information
- **Next Pointer**: Points to the next node in the sequence
- **Previous (`prev`) Pointer**: Points to the previous node in the sequence

The head pointer always refers to the first node, and the tail pointer refers to the last node. By design, the **`prev`** pointer of the first node is always **`NULL`** since there is no node before it, and the **next** pointer of the last node is also **`NULL`** because there is no node after it. This structure enables bi-directional traversal, and allows us to move freely between nodes without having to restart from the beginning.

To understand this better, imagine a train of coaches connected in both directions. You can move forward from one coach to the next, but if you forget something, you can also walk backward to the previous coach. Similarly, in a DLL, the **next** pointer moves you forward, while the **`prev`** pointer lets you retrace your steps backward. For example, in a music player playlist, you can move to the next song using the **next** pointer, or replay the previous song using the **`prev`** pointer—this is exactly how a doubly linked list works in practice.

One of the biggest strengths of DLLs is their efficiency. Unlike singly linked lists, you do not need to traverse the entire list to access the previous node. This makes operations like insertion, deletion, and traversal faster and more flexible. For instance, deleting a node becomes simpler because you can directly update the **`prev`** and **`next`** pointers without scanning the whole list.

However, this flexibility comes with a trade-off. Since each node stores two pointers instead of one, DLLs require slightly more memory than singly linked lists. Additionally, their implementation is a bit more complex because every insertion or deletion must carefully update both the **next** and **prev** pointers to maintain structural consistency.

Despite these challenges, doubly linked lists are widely used in real-world systems where dynamic data manipulation and two-way traversal are important. Examples include web browsers (for forward and backward navigation), undo-redo functionality in text editors, and media playlists that allow seamless switching between songs or videos.

Operations on Doubly Linked Lists

Doubly linked lists (DLLs) allow efficient manipulation of data thanks to their **two-way connections** using **prev** and **next** pointers. Unlike singly linked lists, DLLs make it easy to **traverse**, **insert**, and **delete** nodes from both ends and even from specific positions without needing to scan the entire list unnecessarily.

Let us see each of the major operations in detail:

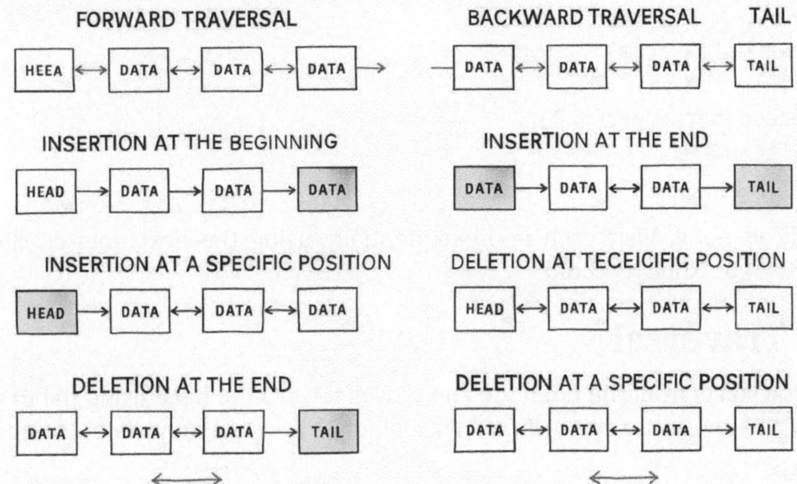

Figure 3.6: *Operations on Doubly Linked Lists*

Forward Traversal

Forward traversal means visiting each node in sequence from the **head** to the **tail** using the next pointer. Since DLLs maintain a direct reference to the first node, we start at the head and move ahead, until we reach the last node (where **next = NULL**).

This is like flipping through photos on your phone from **first to last**. Each swipe forward takes you to the next photo, which is similar to following the next pointer.

C++ Implementation:

```
#include <iostream>
using namespace std;

struct Node {
    int data;
    Node* prev;
    Node* next;
};

void forwardTraversal(Node* head) {
    Node* temp = head;
```

```
    cout << "Forward Traversal: ";
    while (temp != NULL) {
        cout << temp->data << " ";     // Print current node's data
        temp = temp->next;             // Move to next node
    }
    cout << endl;
}
```

Python Implementation:

```
class Node:
    def __init__(self, data):
        self.data = data
        self.prev = None
        self.next = None

def forward_traversal(head):
    temp = head
    print("Forward Traversal:", end=" ")
    while temp:
        print(temp.data, end=" ")
        temp = temp.next
    print()
```

Start from the head node. Visit each node sequentially using the next pointer. Stop when temp becomes NULL (C++) or None (Python).

Backward Traversal

Backward traversal starts from the **tail** node and moves toward the **head** using the **prev** pointer. This feature makes DLLs superior to singly linked lists, where backward movement is impossible without starting over.

Think of it like browsing a **web browser's history**—you can go forward to the next page or back to the previous one seamlessly.

C++ Implementation:

```
void backwardTraversal(Node* tail) {
    Node* temp = tail;
    cout << "Backward Traversal: ";
    while (temp != NULL) {
        cout << temp->data << " ";
        temp = temp->prev;      // Move backwards
    }
    cout << endl;
}
```

Python Implementation

```
def backward_traversal(tail):
    temp = tail
    print("Backward Traversal:", end=" ")
    while temp:
        print(temp.data, end=" ")
        temp = temp.prev
    print()
```

Insertion Operations in Doubly Linked Lists

Doubly linked lists are highly flexible when it comes to **inserting** and **removing** elements because each node maintains these two pointers:

prev → Points to the previous node

next → Points to the next node

This bidirectional structure allows us to perform insertion and deletion **efficiently** compared to singly linked lists, especially in the middle of the list.

Insertion in a doubly linked list can occur at three positions, which are explained here:

Insertion at the Beginning

When inserting at the start, we create a **new node**, and make it the **new head** of the list.

Process:

a. Create a new node and assign the data.

b. Set **newNode->next** to the current head.

c. Set **newNode->prev** to **NULL**.

d. If the list is not empty, update the old head's **prev** pointer.

e. Update the head pointer to the new node.

Consider the example of adding a **new coach** at the front of a train. The new coach connects to the existing first coach, and becomes the new starting point.

C++ Implementation:

```
void insertAtBeginning(Node*& head) {
    Node* newNode = new Node();
    cout << "Enter data: ";
    cin >> newNode->data;

    newNode->next = head;
    newNode->prev = NULL;

    if (head != NULL)
        head->prev = newNode;

    head = newNode;
}
```

Python Implementation:

```
def insert_at_beginning(head, data):
    new_node = Node(data)
    new_node.next = head
    if head:
        head.prev = new_node
    return new_node  # New node becomes the head
```

Create a new node. Set its next to the current head. If the list is not empty, update the old head's prev. Then, update the head pointer to the new node.

Insertion at the End

The new node becomes the **last node** of the list, when it is inserted at the end.

Steps:

a. Create a new node and assign the data.
b. Traverse the list until the last node.
c. Set the last node's next to the new node.
d. Set **`newNode->prev`** to the last node.
e. Set **`newNode->next`** to **`NULL`**.

Think of it like attaching a **new bogie at the back** of a train. It connects seamlessly and becomes the last compartment.

C++ Implementation:

```
void insertAtEnd(Node*& head) {
    Node* newNode = new Node();
    cout << "Enter data: ";
    cin >> newNode->data;

    newNode->next = NULL;

    if (head == NULL) {
        newNode->prev = NULL;
        head = newNode;
        return;
    }

    Node* temp = head;
    while (temp->next != NULL)
        temp = temp->next;

    temp->next = newNode;
    newNode->prev = temp;
}
```

Python Implementation:

```
def insert_at_end(head, data):
    new_node = Node(data)
    if head is None:
        return new_node

    temp = head
    while temp.next:
        temp = temp.next

    temp.next = new_node
    new_node.prev = temp
    return head
```

If the list is empty, make the new node the head. Otherwise, traverse to the last node and attach the new node.

Insertion at a Specific Position

Inserting at a given position involves adjusting the next and **`prev`** pointers carefully.

Steps:

a. Traverse the list until the node **before** the desired position.
b. Set the new node's next to that node's next.

c. Set the new node's **prev** to the current node.

d. Update the previous and next nodes' pointers accordingly.

This is like **inserting a new book** in the middle of a bookshelf. You shift the neighboring books slightly and place the new one at the desired spot.

C++ Implementation:

```
void insertAtPosition(Node*& head, int pos) {
    Node* newNode = new Node();
    cout << "Enter data: ";
    cin >> newNode->data;
    if (pos == 1) {
        insertAtBeginning(head);
        return;
    }
    Node* temp = head;
    for (int i = 1; i < pos - 1 && temp != NULL; i++)
        temp = temp->next;
    if (temp == NULL) {
        cout << "Invalid position!" << endl;
        return;
    }
    newNode->next = temp->next;
    newNode->prev = temp;
    if (temp->next != NULL)
        temp->next->prev = newNode;
    temp->next = newNode;
}
```

Python Implementation:

```
def insert_at_position(head, data, pos):
    new_node = Node(data)
    if pos == 1:
        return insert_at_beginning(head, data)
    temp = head
    for _ in range(pos - 2):
        if not temp:
            print("Invalid position!")
            return head
        temp = temp.next
    new_node.next = temp.next
    new_node.prev = temp
    if temp.next:
        temp.next.prev = new_node
    temp.next = new_node
    return head
```

You must traverse to the position where the node needs to be inserted. Update both **prev** and **next** pointers of surrounding nodes. Do not forget to handle edge cases, such as insertion, at the beginning or end.

Deletion Operations in Doubly Linked Lists

In a **Doubly Linked List (DLL)**, deletion operations are slightly more flexible and efficient compared to singly linked lists because each node maintains two pointers: **`prev`** (to the previous node) and **`next`** (to the next node). This bidirectional connectivity allows traversal in both directions and makes deletion operations faster and easier, especially when removing nodes from the **end,** or from a **specific position.**

Whether deleting the **first node**, **last node**, or a **node at any arbitrary position**, the key principle remains the same. This is articulated in the following steps:

Update the relevant **`prev`** and **`next`** pointers of the neighboring nodes.

Free or deallocate the node being removed.

Due to double links, there is **no need to traverse from the head** while deleting the last node—we can directly reach it using the **tail pointer** (if maintained). This makes DLLs more efficient than singly linked lists for certain deletion scenarios.

Next, we will break down each deletion case—**beginning**, **end**, and **specific position**—with explanations and visual representations for clear understanding.

Deletion at the Beginning

Removing the first node involves updating the head to the second node.

Steps:

a. Store a temporary pointer to the current head.
b. Move the head pointer to the next node.
c. Set the new head's **`prev`** to **`NULL`** (if it exists).
d. Delete the old head node.

This is like **removing the first coach** of a train. In that case, the second coach becomes the new first coach.

C++ Implementation:

```
void deleteAtBeginning(Node*& head) {
    if (head == NULL) return;

    Node* temp = head;
    head = head->next;

    if (head != NULL)
        head->prev = NULL;

    delete temp;
}
```

Python Implementation:

```
def delete_at_beginning(head):
    if head is None:
        return None
    temp = head
    head = head.next
    if head:
        head.prev = None
    return head
```

Deletion at the End

Removing the last node requires updating the previous node's next pointer.

Process:

a. Traverse the list until the last node.
b. Move to the second-last node.
c. Set the second-last node's next to NULL.
d. Delete the last node.

This is something like **detaching the last bogie** of a train; the one before it becomes the new end.

C++ Implementation:

```
void deleteAtEnd(Node*& head) {
    if (head == NULL) return;

    Node* temp = head;
    while (temp->next != NULL)
        temp = temp->next;

    if (temp->prev != NULL)
        temp->prev->next = NULL;
    else
        head = NULL;

    delete temp;
}
```

Python Implementation:

```
def delete_at_end(head):
    if head is None or head.next is None:
        return None
    temp = head
    while temp.next:
        temp = temp.next
    temp.prev.next = None
    return head
```

Deletion at a Specific Position

Deleting a node from a particular position involves carefully updating surrounding pointers.

Process:

a. Traverse the list until the target node.
b. Update the previous node's **`next`** to skip the target node.
c. Update the next node's **`prev`** to bypass the target node.
d. Delete the node.
e. Think of **removing a book** from the middle of a shelf. The neighboring books automatically close the gap.

C++ Implementation:

```
void deleteAtPosition(Node*& head, int pos) {
    if (head == NULL) return;
```

```
    Node* temp = head;
    for (int i = 1; i < pos && temp != NULL; i++)
        temp = temp->next;
    if (temp == NULL) {
        cout << "Invalid position!" << endl;
        return;
    }
    if (temp->prev != NULL)
        temp->prev->next = temp->next;
    else
        head = temp->next;
    if (temp->next != NULL)
        temp->next->prev = temp->prev;
    delete temp;
}
```

Python Implementation:

```
def delete_at_position(head, pos):
    if head is None:
        return None
    temp = head
    for _ in range(pos - 1):
        if temp is None:
            print("Invalid position!")
            return head
        temp = temp.next
    if temp.prev:
        temp.prev.next = temp.next
    else:
        head = temp.next
    if temp.next:
        temp.next.prev = temp.prev
    return head
```

Circular Linked Lists

A **circular linked list** is a special variation of a linked list where the **last node connects back to the first node**, thus forming a continuous loop. Unlike singly or doubly linked lists, circular lists do not have a NULL pointer at the end, which means that traversal can continue indefinitely unless a stopping condition is explicitly defined. This unique structure makes circular linked lists highly useful in real-time applications that require **continuous traversal**, such as **operating systems, memory management, and resource scheduling**. In a circular linked list, nodes are arranged in such a way that starting from any node allows you to **visit every other node** and eventually return to the starting point. This property makes it particularly efficient for scenarios where data must be **processed cyclically**. To better visualize this, imagine a **merry-go-round** in a park: after completing one full rotation, you return to the starting point without interruption. Similarly, traversal from the last node in a circular linked list naturally continues from the first node, which creates an **infinite loop,** unless the process is deliberately stopped.

Circular linked lists can be implemented in **two forms** based on how nodes are connected. In a **singly circular linked list**, each node contains a **data field** and a **next pointer**. The **next pointer** of the last node connects back to the **head**, thereby forming the circular structure. Traversal in this form is **unidirectional**, meaning that you can only move forward from one node to the next. This structure is simple, uses **less memory** compared to doubly circular lists, and is relatively easy to implement. This makes it suitable for **beginner-level problems**. A real-world example of its application can be seen in **multiplayer gaming servers**, where players are arranged in a circular manner. In this illustration the control automatically returns to the first player after the last player's turn. This pattern ensures smooth and continuous rotation.

In contrast, a **doubly circular linked list** enhances flexibility by including an additional **previous pointer** in each node, while facilitating **bidirectional traversal**. Each node, therefore, contains three components: the **data field**, a **next pointer** to the next node, and a **previous pointer** to the previous node. The **first node's previous pointer** links back to the **last node**, and the **last node's next pointer** links to the **first node**, which completes the circular connection. This structure simplifies **insertion** and **deletion** operations, as it allows direct access to both neighboring nodes. However, it requires **slightly more memory** than singly circular lists due to the additional pointer. A common example of its application is in **media players** that manage playlists; after the last song finishes, playback automatically loops back to the first, and users can seamlessly navigate **both forward and backward** through the playlist.

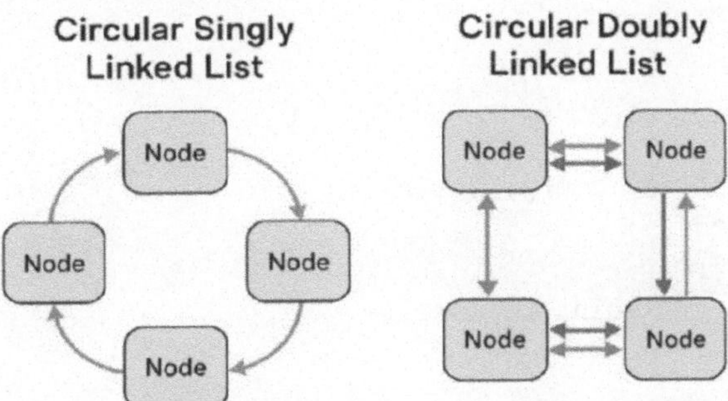

Figure 3.7: *Circular Linked Lists*

Circular linked lists are widely used in scenarios where **continuous traversal** and **dynamic data management** are essential. They form the backbone of several real-time systems and applications, including **CPU scheduling** using the **Round-Robin algorithm**, **buffered video streaming** where frames need to loop seamlessly, **multiplayer gaming systems** for managing players' turns, **resource allocation systems** for printers, memory blocks, or network packets, and **music or video playlists** that require infinite looping and smooth navigation.

Operations on Circular Linked Lists

Circular Linked Lists (CLLs) are an extension of regular linked lists where the **last node connects back to the first node**, while forming a closed loop. This unique structure allows continuous traversal and is especially useful in scenarios where data needs to be processed in a circular manner, such as **Round-Robin scheduling**, **multiplayer games**, or **media buffering**. In this section, we will explore the operations on circular linked lists, focusing on **creation**, **traversal techniques**, and **insertion and deletion operations**, along with examples for better clarity.

Creating Circular Linked Lists

Creating a circular linked list involves dynamically allocating nodes and linking them in such a way that the **next pointer of the last node** points back to the **head node**, thereby forming a circle.

Steps for Creation:

a. Create a new node dynamically.

   b. Assign data to the node.
   c. If the list is empty:
      i. Make the new node point to itself.
      ii. Set it as the **head**.
   d. If the list already has nodes:
      i. Traverse to the last node.
      ii. Link the new node to the **head**.
      iii. Update the last node's **next** pointer.

This is akin to a group of friends sitting around a **round table**. The first friend can pass an object to the next, and eventually, it comes back to the first. This is exactly how circular linked lists work.

C++ Implementation:

```
#include <iostream>
using namespace std;

struct Node {
    int data;
    Node* next;
};

Node* createCircularList(int arr[], int n) {
    Node* head = new Node();
    head->data = arr[0];
    head->next = head;  // Point to itself
    Node* last = head;

    for (int i = 1; i < n; i++) {
        Node* temp = new Node();
        temp->data = arr[i];
        temp->next = head;
        last->next = temp;
        last = temp;
    }
    return head;
}
```

Python Implementation:

```
class Node:
    def __init__(self, data):
        self.data = data
        self.next = None

def create_circular_list(arr):
    head = Node(arr[0])
    head.next = head
    last = head

    for i in range(1, len(arr)):
        temp = Node(arr[i])
        temp.next = head
        last.next = temp
        last = temp

    return head
```

Traversal Techniques

Traversal in CLLs is slightly different from singly or doubly linked lists because there is **no `NULL` pointer** to indicate the end. Instead, we **stop when we reach the starting node again**.

Algorithm

a. Start from the **`head`** node.

b. Visit and process the current node's data.

c. Move to the next node.

d. Stop when you return to the **`head`**.

Traversal is **endless** in CLLs unless you explicitly stop. Therefore, it is perfect for continuous data monitoring systems. In **Round-Robin CPU scheduling**, the traversal moves through all processes repeatedly until they are completed. Since there is **no `NULL` pointer**, we stop when we **reach the head node again**.

C++ Implementation:

```
void traverse(Node* head) {
    if (head == nullptr) return;
    Node* temp = head;
    do {
        cout << temp->data << " ";
        temp = temp->next;
    } while (temp != head);
    cout << endl;
}
```

Python Implementation:

```
def traverse(head):
    if not head:
        return
    temp = head
    while True:
        print(temp.data, end=" ")
        temp = temp.next
        if temp == head:
            break
    print()
```

Insertion Operations

We will now handle **three insertion scenarios**: **at the beginning**, **at the end**, and **at a specific position**.

Insertion at the Beginning

Create a new node. → Point it to the current head. → Update the last node's next. → Set the new node as the head.

C++ Implementation:

```
Node* insertAtBeginning(Node* head, int data) {
    Node* newNode = new Node();
    newNode->data = data;

    if (!head) {
```

```
        newNode->next = newNode;
        return newNode;
    }

    Node* temp = head;
    while (temp->next != head)
        temp = temp->next;

    temp->next = newNode;
    newNode->next = head;
    return newNode;  // New node becomes head
}
```

Python Implementation:

```
def insert_at_beginning(head, data):
    new_node = Node(data)

    if not head:
        new_node.next = new_node
        return new_node

    temp = head
    while temp.next != head:
        temp = temp.next

    temp.next = new_node
    new_node.next = head
    return new_node
```

Insertion at the End

Create a new node. → Point the last node's **next** to the new node. → Make the new node point to the **head**.

C++ Implementation:

```
Node* insertAtEnd(Node* head, int data) {
    Node* newNode = new Node();
    newNode->data = data;

    if (!head) {
        newNode->next = newNode;
        return newNode;
    }

    Node* temp = head;
    while (temp->next != head)
        temp = temp->next;

    temp->next = newNode;
    newNode->next = head;
    return head;
}
```

Python Implementation:

```
def insert_at_end(head, data):
    new_node = Node(data)

    if not head:
```

```
        new_node.next = new_node
        return new_node

    temp = head
    while temp.next != head:
        temp = temp.next

    temp.next = new_node
    new_node.next = head
    return head
```

Insertion at a Specific Position

Traverse to the desired position. → Insert the new node between two existing nodes. → Adjust the **next** pointers accordingly.

C++ Implementation:

```
Node* insertAtPosition(Node* head, int data, int pos) {
    Node* newNode = new Node();
    newNode->data = data;

    if (pos == 1)
        return insertAtBeginning(head, data);

    Node* temp = head;
    for (int i = 1; i < pos - 1 && temp->next != head; i++)
        temp = temp->next;

    newNode->next = temp->next;
    temp->next = newNode;
    return head;
}
```

Python Implementation:

```
def insert_at_position(head, data, pos):
    new_node = Node(data)

    if pos == 1:
        return insert_at_beginning(head, data)

    temp = head
    for _ in range(1, pos - 1):
        if temp.next == head:
            break
        temp = temp.next

    new_node.next = temp.next
    temp.next = new_node
    return head
```

Deletion Operations

We will now handle **three deletion scenarios, just like we did in the insertion section.**

Deletion at the Beginning

Move the head pointer to the second node. → Update the last node's **next** pointer. → Free the old head.

C++ Implementation:

```
Node* deleteAtBeginning(Node* head) {
    if (!head) return nullptr;

    Node* temp = head;
    while (temp->next != head)
        temp = temp->next;

    Node* toDelete = head;
    temp->next = head->next;
    head = head->next;
    delete toDelete;
    return head;
}
```

Python Implementation:

```
def delete_at_beginning(head):
    if not head:
        return None

    temp = head
    while temp.next != head:
        temp = temp.next

    temp.next = head.next
    head = head.next
    return head
```

Deletion at the End

Traverse to the **second-last node.** → Point its **next** to the head. → Free the last node.

C++ Implementation:

```
Node* deleteAtEnd(Node* head) {
    if (!head) return nullptr;

    Node* temp = head;
    Node* prev = nullptr;

    while (temp->next != head) {
        prev = temp;
        temp = temp->next;
    }

    prev->next = head;
    delete temp;
    return head;
}
```

Python Implementation:

```
def delete_at_end(head):
    if not head:
        return None

    temp = head
    prev = None

    while temp.next != head:
```

```
        prev = temp
        temp = temp.next

    prev.next = head
    return head
```

Deletion at a Specific Position

Traverse to the node before the target. → Link its next to the target's next. → Free the target node.

C++ Implementation:

```
Node* deleteAtPosition(Node* head, int pos) {
    if (!head) return nullptr;

    if (pos == 1)
        return deleteAtBeginning(head);

    Node* temp = head;
    Node* prev = nullptr;

    for (int i = 1; i < pos && temp->next != head; i++) {
        prev = temp;
        temp = temp->next;
    }

    prev->next = temp->next;
    delete temp;
    return head;
}
```

Python Implementation:

```
def delete_at_position(head, pos):
    if not head:
        return None

    if pos == 1:
        return delete_at_beginning(head)

    temp = head
    prev = None
    for _ in range(1, pos):
        prev = temp
        temp = temp.next
        if temp == head:
            break

    prev.next = temp.next
    return head
```

As we can see in the scenarios here, CLLs are powerful when continuous processing is required. Their creation and traversal differ slightly from linear lists, but insertion and deletion remain efficient because of their circular nature.

Pointer Management in Linked Lists

In linked lists, pointers are the foundation upon which the entire structure operates. Unlike arrays, where elements are stored in contiguous memory locations, linked lists rely on nodes that are scattered in memory and connected through pointers. Each node contains two parts: the data, and one or more pointers that link it to other nodes. Managing these pointers effectively is critical because any mistake, such as incorrect updates, improper initialization, or forgetting to deallocate memory, can result in serious issues like data loss, infinite loops, or memory leaks.

Pointers in linked lists act like bridges between nodes, while enabling traversal, insertion, deletion, and updates. If a pointer is mishandled, these operations can fail or produce unexpected results. Therefore, understanding how to manage the head, tail, next, and `prev` pointers is essential for writing reliable and efficient programs.

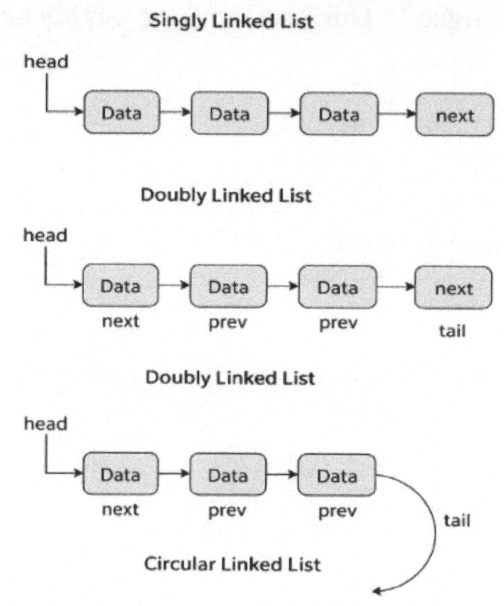

Figure 3.8: *Pointer Management in Linked Lists*

Handling Head, Tail, Prev, and Next Pointers

The **head** pointer plays a crucial role in linked lists. It always points to the **first node** in the list and serves as the entry point to access all other elements. Losing this pointer means losing the ability to access the list entirely. In some implementations, developers keep a **backup reference** to the head to prevent accidental data loss.

The **tail** pointer is equally important, especially when working with **circular** or optimized linked lists. It points to the **last node** in the list, which makes insertions at the end more efficient because there is no need to traverse the entire structure. In **circular linked lists**, the tail pointer's next always points back to the head, while forming a loop.

The **next** pointer, present in almost every type of linked list, connects a node to its immediate **successor**. It is the backbone of forward traversal and essential for operations like insertion and deletion. However, an incorrect update to the **next** pointer can lead to **broken links,** or even **infinite traversal loops**.

In **doubly linked lists**, the **prev** pointer comes into play, linking a node to its **previous** neighbor. It enables **reverse traversal** and simplifies operations like deletion and insertion, especially when modifying nodes in the middle of the list. However, maintaining consistency between **next** and **prev** is critical. If one pointer is updated incorrectly, the structure may become corrupted.

This is like a **train composed of various compartments, where**:

- The **head** pointer is the engine.
- The **tail** pointer is the last coach.
- The **next** pointer is the **coupling** that connects a coach to the next one.
- The **prev** pointer connects it to the **coach behind**.

- If one coupling (**`next`** or **`prev`**) is missing, the train **breaks**, which is similar to losing part of the linked list.

Avoiding Dangling and Null Pointers

One of the most common challenges when working with pointers is preventing **dangling references.** A dangling pointer occurs when a pointer still references memory that has already been **freed,** or is **invalid**. Accessing such memory can lead to program crashes or unpredictable behavior.

To avoid this problem, pointers should always be **initialized** to `NULL` (or **`nullptr`** in modern C++) before being used. After deleting a node, it is good practice to **reset its pointer to `NULL`** to indicate that it no longer refers to valid memory. Similarly, before traversing a list or updating a pointer, developers should always verify whether the pointer is `NULL` to prevent segmentation faults.

In languages like **Python**, memory management is handled automatically by the garbage collector, which reduces the likelihood of dangling pointers. However, explicitly assigning None to unused references is still considered a good programming habit.

Example in C++:

```
Node* temp = head;
delete temp;        // Memory freed
temp = nullptr;     // Prevents dangling pointer
```

In Python:

Python automatically manages memory via garbage collection. However, assigning 'None' to unused references is still a good habit.

```
temp = head
del temp
temp = None
```

Memory Deallocation and Cleanup

Proper **memory management** is vital when working with linked lists, especially in low-level languages like C and C++. If dynamically allocated memory is not released after use, it results in **memory leaks,** which can degrade system performance over time.

When deleting a node, developers must ensure two things:

The neighboring nodes should be reconnected correctly by updating their **`next`** and, if applicable, **`prev`** pointers.

The memory allocated for the node should be released using delete (in C++) or **`free()`** (in C).

For example, to **free an entire singly linked list**, the program traverses the list node by node, deletes each one, and moves to the next until the list becomes empty. In Python, the process is simpler. It is because removing references to nodes allows the garbage collector to reclaim memory automatically.

Example: Freeing the Entire Linked List in C++

```
void freeList(Node* &head) {
    Node* temp;
    while (head != nullptr) {
        temp = head;
        head = head->next;
        delete temp;  // Free node memory
    }
}
```

Example in Python:

```
def free_list(head):
    while head:
        temp = head
        head = head.next
        del temp
    return None
```

Efficient pointer management involves following a few key principles such as:

- Always **initialize pointers** before using them.
- After freeing memory, immediately **set the pointer to `NULL`** to prevent accidental access.
- During insertions and deletions, carefully update the next and `prev` pointers to maintain list integrity.
- Maintain a **backup of the head pointer** in case of accidental reassignment.
- In circular lists, ensure that the **`tail` pointer** correctly links back to the **head** to avoid traversal errors.

Pointer	Purpose	Common Issues	Best Practice
Head	Entry point to the list	Losing it makes the list inaccessible.	Always keep a backup reference if needed.
Tail	Points to the last node	Can lead to incorrect loops in circular lists	Update carefully during insertions and deletions.
Next	Connects to the next node	Incorrect assignment may cause broken links.	Always verify before updating.
Prev	Points to the previous node	Wrong updates cause traversal errors.	Maintain symmetry between next and prev.
Dangling pointers	Point to deleted memory	Causes crashes or undefined behavior	Set freed pointers to NULL / None.

Table 3.3: *Pointer Management Strategies*

Loop Detection and Removal

In linked lists, a **loop** (or cycle) occurs when a node's next pointer connects back to a previously visited node instead of NULL. This creates an **infinite traversal**, which means that if you keep following the pointers, you will never reach the end. Loops usually occur due to programming errors, improper pointer updates, or logical mistakes during **insertion, deletion, or merging** operations. Detecting and removing loops is essential to ensure that algorithms relying on traversals, such as searching or updating nodes, work correctly and do not cause infinite loops or excessive memory usage.

There are several ways to detect loops in linked lists, but one of the most efficient and widely used approaches is **Floyd's Cycle Detection algorithm**, which is also known as the **Tortoise and Hare algorithm**.

Floyd's Cycle Detection Algorithm

Floyd's algorithm uses **two pointers** moving at different speeds:

Slow Pointer (Tortoise) → Moves **one node** at a time

Fast Pointer (Hare) → Moves **two nodes** at a time

Steps Involved:

a. Initialize two pointers: **`slow = head`** and **`fast = head`**.

b. Move slow by one step and fast by two steps in each iteration.

c. If there is **no loop**, **`fast`** or **`fast->next`** will become **`NULL`**.

d. If there **is a loop**, slow and fast will eventually **meet at the same node** inside the loop.

Example in C++:

```
bool detectLoop(Node* head) {
    Node* slow = head;
    Node* fast = head;

    while (fast != nullptr && fast->next != nullptr) {
        slow = slow->next;          // Move slow by 1
        fast = fast->next->next;    // Move fast by 2

        if (slow == fast)           // Loop detected
            return true;
    }
    return false;  // No loop
}
```

Example in Python:

```
def detect_loop(head):
    slow = head
    fast = head

    while fast and fast.next:
        slow = slow.next        # Move slow by 1
        fast = fast.next.next   # Move fast by 2

        if slow == fast:        # Loop detected
            return True
    return False  # No loop
```

Techniques to Remove Loops Effectively

Once a loop is detected, it is important to **remove it** to restore proper traversal. The following steps are used:

Steps to Remove a Loop (Using Floyd's Algorithm):

a. **Detect Meeting Point:** Use Floyd's algorithm to find where slow and fast meet.

b. **Find Start of the Loop:**

   i. Keep one pointer at the **`head`** and another at the **meeting point**.

   ii. Move both pointers one step at a time; they will meet at the **start of the loop**.

c. **Break the Loop:**

   i. Traverse the loop until you find the **node pointing back to the start**.

   ii. Set this node's next pointer to **`NULL`**.

C++ Code for Loop Removal:

```
void removeLoop(Node* head) {
    Node *slow = head, *fast = head;

    // Detect loop
    while (fast && fast->next) {
        slow = slow->next;
```

```
        fast = fast->next->next;

        if (slow == fast)  // Loop detected
            break;
    }

    // If no loop
    if (fast == nullptr || fast->next == nullptr)
        return;

    // Find start of loop
    slow = head;
    while (slow->next != fast->next) {
        slow = slow->next;
        fast = fast->next;
    }

    // Break the loop
    fast->next = nullptr;
}
```

Python Code for Loop Removal:

```
def remove_loop(head):
    slow = head
    fast = head

    # Detect loop
    while fast and fast.next:
        slow = slow.next
        fast = fast.next.next
        if slow == fast:
            break
    else:
        return  # No loop found

    # Find start of loop
    slow = head
    while slow.next != fast.next:
        slow = slow.next
        fast = fast.next

    # Break the loop
    fast.next = None
```

This is like a **circular railway track** where a train keeps going around without ever reaching a terminal station. This is what happens in a linked list with a loop—you keep moving endlessly without an exit. Detecting and removing the loop is like **finding the exact point where the track reconnects,** and installing a **switch** to exit the circle.

Reversal of Linked Lists

Reversing a linked list is one of the most important and frequently used operations in data structures. It involves changing the direction of the links so that the head node becomes the tail, and the tail node becomes the head. Reversal is commonly used in applications like undo-redo functionalities, backtracking problems, and memory optimizations. There are two primary approaches: **iterative reversal** and **recursive reversal.**

Iterative Reversal Process

Reversing a linked list iteratively is one of the most commonly used techniques in data structure operations. The idea is to traverse the list **once** while continuously updating the next pointers of each node so that the links are reversed. In a singly linked list, each node has a data field and a next pointer pointing to the next node. To reverse the list, we need to **redirect these next pointers** so that they point to the previous node instead of the next one.

The process involves maintaining **three pointers** during traversal:

a. **`prev`** → Tracks the previously visited node. Initially set to **`NULL`**

b. **`current`** → Tracks the current node being processed; starts at the head

c. **`next`** → Temporarily stores the next node before updating links

Steps Involved:

1. Initialize **`prev = NULL`** and **`current = head`**.
2. Store **`next = current->next`** to avoid losing the remaining list.
3. Reverse the link: **`current->next = prev`**.
4. Move **`prev`** to current and current to next.
5. Repeat steps **2-4** until current becomes **`NULL`**.
6. Finally, **`set head = prev`**, as **`prev`** now points to the new first node.

C++ Implementation:

```
#include <iostream>
using namespace std;

struct Node {
    int data;
    Node* next;
};

Node* reverseIterative(Node* head) {
    Node *prev = NULL, *current = head, *next = NULL;

    while (current != NULL) {
        next = current->next;        // Save next node
        current->next = prev;        // Reverse the link
        prev = current;              // Move prev forward
        current = next;              // Move current forward
    }
    head = prev;                     // Update head
    return head;
}

// Utility function to print the list
void printList(Node* head) {
    while (head) {
        cout << head->data << " -> ";
        head = head->next;
    }
    cout << "NULL\n";
}
```

Python Implementation:

```
class Node:
    def __init__(self, data):
        self.data = data
        self.next = None
def reverse_iterative(head):
    prev = None
    current = head

    while current:
        next_node = current.next    # Save next node
        current.next = prev         # Reverse the link
        prev = current             # Move prev forward
        current = next_node        # Move current forward

    return prev  # New head

def print_list(head):
    while head:
        print(head.data, end=" -> ")
        head = head.next
    print("NULL")
```

Recursive Reversal Process

The **recursive reversal** of a linked list is an elegant technique that relies on the concept of **function call stacking**. Instead of iteratively changing pointers in a loop, we let the recursive function handle one node at a time, while breaking the problem into smaller subproblems. In simple terms, we:

- **Divide the problem** by separating the list into two parts: the first node, and the rest of the list.
- **Recursively reverse** the remaining list.
- **Reconnect the pointers** so that the reversed sublist connects back to the first node.
- **Update the head pointer** to point to the new first node of the reversed list.

Step 1: Base Case

If the list is **empty** (**`head == NULL`**) or has **only one node**, return the head, as it is already reversed.

Step 2: Recursive Step

Call the reversal function on the rest of the list:

```
newHead = reverse(head->next);
```

This continues until we reach the last node.

Step 3: Reconnect Pointers

Once the recursion unwinds, make the **next node** point back to the current node:

```
head->next->next = head;
```

Step 4: Mark the End

Break the original link to avoid cycles:

```
head->next = NULL;
```

Step 5: Return New Head

Finally, return the new head pointer (that is, the last node of the original list).

C++ Implementation:

```
#include <iostream>
using namespace std;

struct Node {
    int data;
    Node* next;
    Node(int value) : data(value), next(NULL) {}
};

Node* reverseRecursive(Node* head) {
    // Base case: empty list or single node
    if (head == NULL || head->next == NULL)
        return head;

    // Reverse the rest of the list
    Node* newHead = reverseRecursive(head->next);

    // Fix the current node's pointer
    head->next->next = head;
    head->next = NULL;

    return newHead;
}
```

Python Implementation:

```
class Node:
    def __init__(self, data):
        self.data = data
        self.next = None

def reverse_recursive(head):
    # Base case: empty list or single node
    if head is None or head.next is None:
        return head

    # Reverse the rest of the list
    new_head = reverse_recursive(head.next)

    # Fix the current node's pointer
    head.next.next = head
    head.next = None

    return new_head
```

Think of **recursive reversal** like **stacking plates**: you keep putting plates on top until you reach the last plate. When you start unstacking, you reverse the order. Similarly, recursion reaches the **end of the list,** and then **reconnects pointers** in reverse order.

Merging and Splitting Linked Lists

Linked lists are widely used in real-world applications where data needs to be **combined**, **reorganized**, or **partitioned** for efficient processing. Two fundamental operations that provide this flexibility are **merging** and **splitting** linked lists. These techniques are essential in various domains such as **search engines, database management systems**, **operating systems**, and **data analysis pipelines**.

Merging Two Sorted Linked Lists

Merging two sorted linked lists involves combining them into a **single sorted list** without unnecessarily creating additional data structures. This operation is commonly used in **merge sort algorithms**, **data aggregation systems**, and **real-time stream processing**. The merging process works as follows:

1. Start with two sorted linked lists, say **`list1`** and **`list2`**.
2. Compare the head nodes of both lists.
3. Select the node with the **smaller value** and attach it to the **merged list**.
4. Move the pointer forward in the list from which the node was chosen.
5. Repeat the process until all nodes from both lists are merged.
6. If any nodes remain in one list, link them directly to the merged list.

C++ Implementation:

```
Node* mergeSortedLists(Node* list1, Node* list2) {
    if (!list1) return list2;
    if (!list2) return list1;

    Node* result = nullptr;

    if (list1->data < list2->data) {
        result = list1;
        result->next = mergeSortedLists(list1->next, list2);
    } else {
        result = list2;
        result->next = mergeSortedLists(list1, list2->next);
    }

    return result;
}
```

Python Implementation:

```
def merge_sorted_lists(list1, list2):
    if not list1:
        return list2
    if not list2:
        return list1

    if list1.data < list2.data:
        result = list1
        result.next = merge_sorted_lists(list1.next, list2)
    else:
        result = list2
        result.next = merge_sorted_lists(list1, list2.next)

    return result
```

Splitting a Linked List

Splitting a linked list involves **dividing it into two or more parts** for better data management and parallel processing. This operation is useful in **load balancing**, **parallel computing**, **merge sort algorithms**, and **memory optimization**. There are two common approaches to splitting a linked list, which are:

Splitting into Two Equal Halves

a. This is achieved using the **`slow` and `fast` pointer technique**.
b. The **`fast` pointer** moves **two steps** at a time.
c. The **`slow` pointer** moves **one step** at a time.
d. When the fast pointer reaches the end, the slow pointer will be at the **midpoint**.
e. Break the list at the midpoint to create **two halves**.

C++ Implementation (Splitting into Two Halves):

```
void splitList(Node* head, Node** firstHalf, Node** secondHalf) {
    if (!head || !head->next) {
        *firstHalf = head;
        *secondHalf = nullptr;
        return;
    }
    Node* slow = head;
    Node* fast = head->next;
    while (fast && fast->next) {
        slow = slow->next;
        fast = fast->next->next;
    }
    *firstHalf = head;
    *secondHalf = slow->next;
    slow->next = nullptr;
}
```

Python Implementation (Splitting into Two Halves):

```
def split_list(head):
    if not head or not head.next:
        return head, None

    slow, fast = head, head.next

    while fast and fast.next:
        slow = slow.next
        fast = fast.next.next

    first_half = head
    second_half = slow.next
    slow.next = None
    return first_half, second_half
```

Splitting into k Segments

When the list must be divided into **k segments**:

a. Count the total number of nodes.
b. Divide the size by **k** to determine the segment size.
c. Break the list accordingly.

Merging and splitting linked lists play a crucial role in modern systems where dynamic data manipulation and efficient organization are required. Merging is widely used in applications such as **email and**

messaging systems, where multiple message threads are combined into a single chronological view; **search engines**, where datasets collected by different crawlers are merged into a comprehensive index; and **database management systems**, where sorted datasets are integrated seamlessly without the need for rearranging the entire collection. For example, when combining **customer transaction histories** from two different bank branches into a unified report, merging two sorted linked lists ensures smooth integration, while maintaining proper order, and minimizing time and memory overhead. On the other hand, splitting linked lists is equally important in scenarios where data needs to be distributed efficiently. It is used in **server load balancing**, where incoming requests are divided evenly across multiple servers; **social media feeds**, where large datasets are split into smaller chunks to enable infinite scrolling and faster content rendering; and **big data processing**, where breaking huge datasets into smaller linked lists allows parallel computation, and improves system performance. For instance, a **video streaming platform** that maintains a single linked list of all active users can split the list into **regional segments** during peak hours, which results in better server optimization and faster response times.

In large-scale systems, splitting linked lists plays a vital role in **load balancing and High-performance Computing** environments. For example, a web server handling millions of incoming requests may store them as a linked list in memory. To distribute the workload evenly, the list can be split into multiple smaller linked lists, each assigned to a different server or processing thread. This ensures that no single server becomes overloaded and improves response time. Similarly, in parallel computing applications such as scientific simulations or big data analytics, large datasets represented as linked lists are split into segments so that multiple processors can work on different portions simultaneously. This division enables efficient parallel execution, reduces processing time, and maximizes utilization of computational resources.

Hybrid Scenarios: Merging + Splitting

In modern applications, merging and splitting often **work together**.

- In **map-reduce frameworks**, data from multiple sources is **merged first**, and then **split into smaller tasks** for distributed computation.
- In **e-commerce platforms**, large product catalogs are **merged into a master list**, and later **split into personalized feeds** for individual users.

Conclusion

In this chapter, we explored **linked lists**, one of the most flexible and dynamic data structures in computer science. We learned about the **structure of a node** and examined different types of linked lists, including **singly, doubly, and circular variants**, understanding their unique properties and practical applications. Through detailed explanations, visuals, and code examples, we covered key operations such as **creation, traversal, insertion, deletion, merging, splitting, and reversal through** both **iterative** and **recursive approaches**. We also discussed **pointer management techniques**, **loop detection and removal using Floyd's algorithm**, and real-world use cases where linked lists provide efficient solutions. By the end of this chapter, you should now have a strong foundation in working with linked lists, understanding when to prefer them over arrays, and how to implement them effectively in **C++** and **Python**.

Building on this foundation, **Chapter 4: Stacks, Queues and Deques** takes us deeper into **linear Abstract Data Types (ADTs)** that play a critical role in **algorithmic problem-solving**. We will explore how **stacks** follow the **Last-In, First-Out (LIFO)** principle and are used in **recursion, expression evaluation, and undo-redo mechanisms**. Similarly, **queues**, based on the **First-In, First-Out (FIFO)** model, are essential for **task scheduling, buffering, and request handling**, while **deques** offer flexibility by supporting insertion and deletion at both ends, which makes them highly efficient in

sliding window problems and real-time applications. This upcoming chapter will combine theory, visual explanations, and practical code implementations, eventually preparing you to handle more complex **algorithmic challenges** effectively.

Points to Remember

- Linked lists are dynamic data structures that use nodes containing data and pointers, unlike arrays which use contiguous memory blocks.
- A node consists of a data field and one or more pointers; singly linked lists have one pointer (next), doubly linked lists have two pointers (**`prev`** and **`next`**).
- Singly linked lists support simple operations like insertion, deletion, and traversal, but have limitations in backward traversal.
- Doubly linked lists provide bidirectional traversal and easier node deletion, but require more memory due to an additional pointer.
- Circular linked lists connect the last node back to the first, and are useful in applications requiring cyclic iteration.
- Pointer management is critical to avoid memory leaks, dangling pointers, and to properly handle head and tail nodes.
- Loop detection in linked lists is important for avoiding infinite loops, and Floyd's Cycle Detection Algorithm (Tortoise and Hare) is an efficient method.
- Linked lists are preferred over arrays when frequent insertions/deletions are needed, and dynamic memory allocation is a requirement.

Multiple Choice Questions

1. What is the primary advantage of a linked list over an array?
   a. Fixed Size
   b. Dynamic Size
   c. Contiguous Memory Allocation
   d. Faster Access by Index
2. Which pointer is used in a singly linked list node?
   a. `prev`
   b. `next`
   c. `prev` and `next`
   d. `head`
3. In a doubly linked list, what is the purpose of the `prev` pointer?
   a. Point to the next node.
   b. Point to the previous node.
   c. Point to head node.
   d. Point to tail node.
4. Circular linked lists are particularly useful for:
   a. Static Memory Allocation
   b. Infinite Cyclic Traversal

   c. Random Access of Elements
   d. Sorting Algorithms

5. Which of the following is NOT a valid operation on a linked list?
   a. Insertion at the beginning
   b. Deletion at a specific position
   c. Direct access using index
   d. Traversal

6. Which algorithm is commonly used to detect a loop in a linked list?
   a. Binary Search
   b. Floyd's Cycle Detection Algorithm
   c. Merge Sort
   d. Quick Sort

7. What is the time complexity to insert a node at the end of a singly linked list without a tail pointer?
   a. `O(1)`
   b. `O(n)`
   c. `O(log n)`
   d. `O(n²)`

8. Which traversal is NOT possible in a singly linked list?
   a. Forward Traversal
   b. Backward Traversal
   c. Traversal from Head
   d. Traversal from the First Node

9. What is the space overhead per node in a doubly linked list compared to singly linked list?
   a. Same
   b. One extra pointer
   c. Two extra pointers
   d. Half the size

10. What happens if you forget to free the memory after deleting a node in a linked list?
    a. Memory Leak
    b. Program Crash
    c. Faster Execution
    d. None of the Above

11. Which operation is more efficient in linked lists compared to arrays?
    a. Access by Index
    b. Insertion and Deletion
    c. Sorting
    d. Searching

12. What type of linked list is best suited for a queue implementation?
    a. Singly Linked list
    b. Doubly Linked list
    c. Circular Linked list
    d. None of the Above
13. Which of the following is a key advantage of circular linked lists?
    a. They are easy to implement.
    b. They support infinite traversal without checking for null.
    c. They use less memory.
    d. They require no pointers.

Answers

1. b
2. b
3. b
4. b
5. c
6. b
7. b
8. b
9. b
10. a
11. b
12. c
13. b

Questions

1. Explain the difference between arrays and linked lists in terms of memory allocation and operations.
2. Describe the structure of a node in a singly linked list, and explain how dynamic memory allocation works during list creation.
3. Discuss the advantages and disadvantages of singly linked lists compared to the doubly linked lists.
4. How does a circular linked list differ from a singly linked list? Provide use cases where a circular linked list is preferable.
5. Describe the process of inserting a node at a specific position in a singly linked list.
6. Explain Floyd's Cycle Detection algorithm and its importance in linked list operations.
7. Describe the steps involved in reversing a singly linked list both iteratively and recursively.
8. Discuss the common pointer management issues in linked lists, and the ways to avoid memory leaks.

9. Explain how merging two sorted linked lists works and its applications.
10. What are the fast and slow pointer techniques? Give an example of their use in linked list problems.
11. How do you split a linked list into two halves? Explain the practical applications of this operation.
12. Compare the traversal and insertion time complexities of arrays versus linked lists.
13. What are the best practices for writing efficient and error-free linked list code in languages like C++ and Python?

Key Terms

- **Node**: A basic unit of a linked list containing data and one or more pointers.
- **Pointer**: A variable that stores the memory address of another variable or node.
- **Head Pointer**: A pointer that refers to the first node of a linked list.
- **Tail Pointer**: A pointer that refers to the last node of a linked list.
- **Dynamic Memory Allocation**: The process of allocating memory at runtime using pointers.
- **Traversal**: The process of visiting each node in a linked list sequentially.
- **Insertion**: Adding a new node at a specified position in a linked list.
- **Deletion**: Removing a node from a specified position in a linked list.
- **Floyd's Cycle Detection Algorithm**: An algorithm to detect loops in linked lists using two pointers moving at different speeds.
- **Loop Detection**: The process of identifying cycles in a linked list to prevent infinite traversal.
- **Reversal of Linked List**: Changing the direction of pointers so the list is traversed in reverse order.
- **Merging and Splitting**: Combining two linked lists into one or dividing a linked list into multiple parts.
- **Fast and Slow Pointer Technique**: Using two pointers moving at different speeds to solve linked list problems efficiently.
- **Memory Leak**: Unreleased memory due to failure in deallocating nodes, leading to wasted resources.
- **Dangling Pointer**: A pointer that refers to a memory location that has been freed or deallocated.

CHAPTER 4
Stacks, Queues, and Deques

Introduction

In the journey of mastering Data Structures and Algorithms (DSAs), understanding how information is stored, accessed, and processed is crucial for efficient problem-solving. Among the most important linear abstract data types are **stacks**, **queues**, and **deques**, which form the foundation for several real-world applications and advanced algorithms. A **stack** follows the **Last-In, First-Out (LIFO)** principle, which is why it is ideal for handling tasks such as function call management, undo operations, and expression evaluation. On the contrary, a **queue** operates on the **First-In, First-Out (FIFO)** principle, and is commonly used in task scheduling, process management, and Breadth First Search (BFS) traversal. To extend their respective capabilities, a **double-ended queue (abbreviated as deque)** offers enhanced flexibility by allowing insertions and deletions from both ends. This feature makes it highly efficient for solving problems such as sliding window computations and palindrome checking. Throughout this chapter, we will explore the **fundamental concepts, operations, step-by-step implementations, and the practical applications** of these data structures. Additionally, we will cover their **C++ STL and Python implementations,** and solve a collection of **common coding patterns as well as interview-focused problems** to strengthen your conceptual understanding and programming skills.

Structure

In this chapter, we will cover the following topics:

- Introduction to Linear Abstract Data Types
- Stack
- Queue
- Deque
- Common Coding Patterns and Interview Problems

Introduction to Linear Abstract Data Types

In computer science, a **data structure** defines an organized way of storing, managing, and accessing data to enable efficient processing. Among various data structures, **linear Abstract Data Types (ADTs)** are one of the most fundamental categories, as they arrange elements in a **sequential order**, where each element has a **unique predecessor** and a **unique successor** (except for the first and last elements). This sequential nature makes linear ADTs predictable and easier to implement in problem-solving scenarios.

Examples of linear ADTs include **stacks**, **queues**, and **deques**, which form the core of many algorithmic solutions. These structures are widely used in areas such as **recursion handling, task scheduling, memory management, expression evaluation, sliding window computations, and graph traversal**. Compared to **non-linear data structures** such as trees and graphs, where elements are arranged hierarchically or in networks, linear structures offer a **simpler flow of data,** and are often the first step toward mastering algorithm design. *Figure* 4.1 presents the classification of data structures and provides a clear overview of how they are organized into different categories.

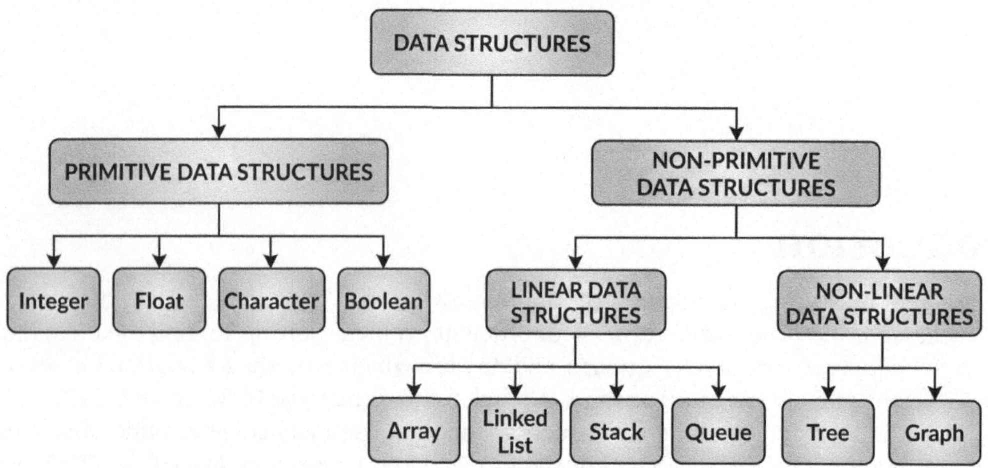

Figure 4.1: *Classification of Data Structures*

Stack

A **stack** is a fundamental data structure in computer science that stores data in an organized way but follows a special rule for accessing it—the **Last-In, First-Out (LIFO)** principle, where the most recently added item is always the first to be removed.

Stack Fundamentals

A **stack** is one of the most fundamental **linear Abstract Data Types (ADTs)** used in computer science and algorithm design. It sequentially organizes data but restricts how elements are inserted and removed, following the **Last-In, First-Out (LIFO)** principle. This means that the **last element added** to the stack is the **first one to be removed**, which is very similar to stacking plates in a kitchen.

Stacks play a crucial role in solving a variety of computational problems, including **function call management, expression evaluation, recursion handling, backtracking, syntax checking, and undo operations** in applications such as text editors and web browsers. Due to their structured nature, stacks are widely used in both **algorithm design** and **real-world problem-solving**. *Figure* 4.2 illustrates the Last-In-First-Out (LIFO) principle, while highlighting how the element inserted last is the first to be removed.

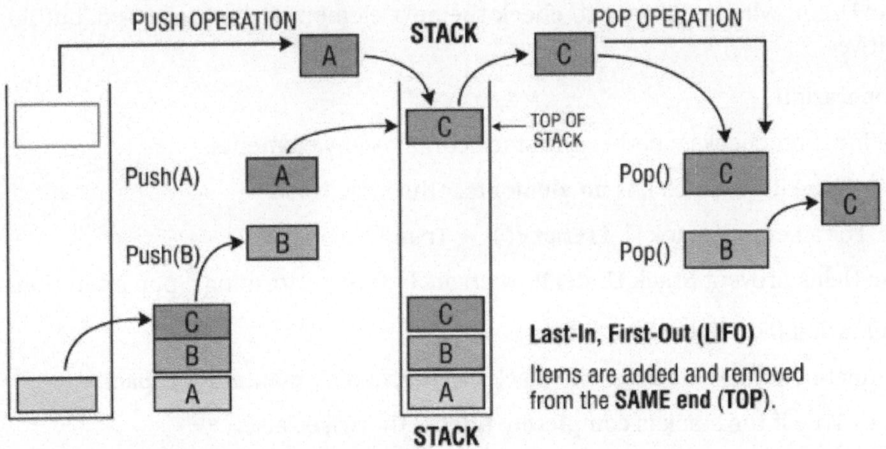

Figure 4.2: *LIFO Principle Representation*

Stack Operations

A **stack** follows the **Last-In, First-Out (LIFO)** principle. This means that the most recently added element is always removed first. To manage data effectively, stacks support a set of **core operations** that facilitate insertion, deletion, inspection, and validation of elements. Therefore, these operations form the foundation of stack-based problem-solving in programming.

Push Operation (Insertion)

The **push** operation adds a new element to the **top** of the stack.

Definition: Inserts an element at the **top** of the stack

Before Push: [10, 20, 30]

Push(40): Adds 40 at the top

After Push: [10, 20, 30, 40]

Edge Case: If the stack is already full (in a fixed-size implementation), **a stack overflow** occurs.

Analogy: Imagine adding a plate to the top of a plate stack in a cafeteria; the new plate always goes **on top**.

Pop Operation (Deletion)

The **pop** operation removes the **topmost** element from the stack.

Definition: Deletes and returns the element from the **top**

Before Pop: [10, 20, 30, 40]

`Pop()`: Removes 40

After Pop: [10, 20, 30]

Edge Case: If the stack is empty, a **stack underflow** occurs.

Analogy: Taking off the **topmost plate** from a stack—you cannot remove plates from the middle or bottom.

`Peek / Top` Operation (Inspection)

The **`peek`** (or **top**) operation returns the **value of the top element** without removing it.

Definition: Displays the topmost element without modifying the stack

Example: For [10, 20, 30], **`peek()`** → 30

Use Case: Useful when you want to **check** the next element to be processed, but do not want to remove it yet.

`isEmpty()` Operation

The **`isEmpty`** function checks whether the stack contains any elements.

Returns → True if the stack has **no elements**, otherwise False.

Example: For an empty stack [], **`isEmpty() → True`**

Use Case: Helps prevent **Stack Underflow** errors before performing a pop operation.

`isFull()` Operation (For Fixed-Size Stacks)

The **`isFull`** function checks whether the stack has reached its **maximum capacity**.

Returns → True if the stack is **completely filled**, otherwise False.

Example: For a stack of size 5 containing [10, 20, 30, 40, 50], **`isFull() → True`**

Use Case: Avoids **Stack Overflow** errors during insertion.

Figure 4.3 depicts the fundamental stack operations—**`Push`**, **`Pop`**, and **`Peek`**—while demonstrating how elements are added, removed, and accessed in a stack:

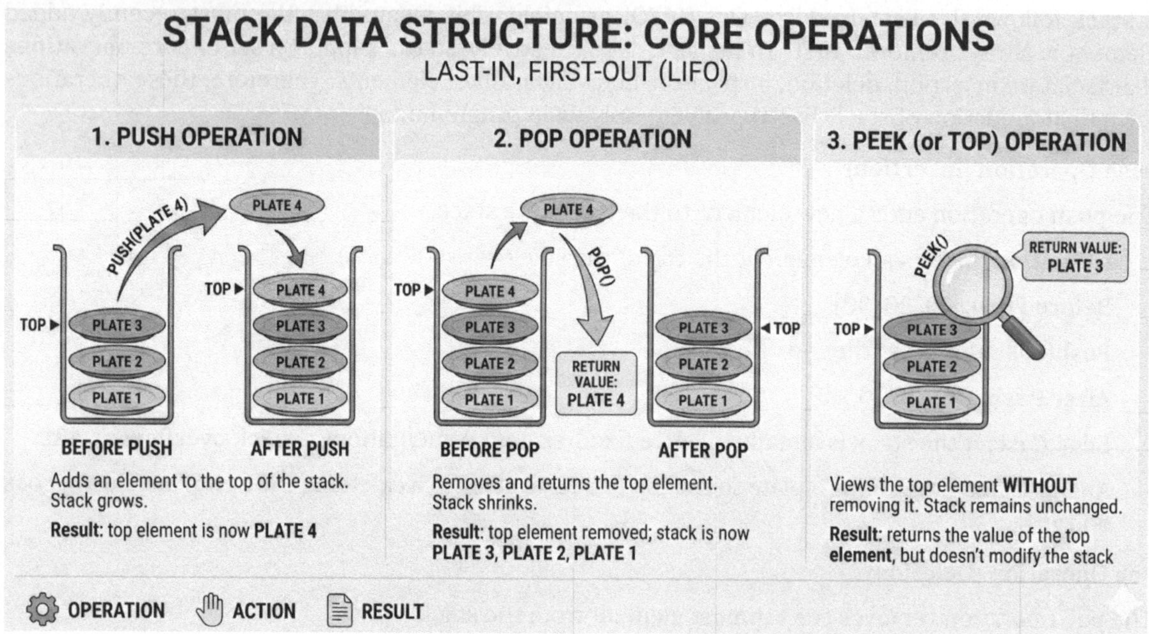

***Figure* 4.3:** *Push, Pop, and Peek Operations in a Stack*

Array-Based Stack Implementation

An **array-based stack** uses a **fixed-size array** to store elements. It is simple to implement and allows **constant-time (`O(1)`)** access to elements. However, the size of the stack must be predefined.

C++ Implementation:

```
#include <iostream>
using namespace std;

#define SIZE 5  // Maximum size of stack

class Stack {
    int arr[SIZE];
```

```
    int top;

public:
    Stack() { top = -1; }

    // Push operation
    void push(int x) {
        if (top == SIZE - 1) {
            cout << "Stack Overflow! Cannot push " << x << endl;
            return;
        }
        arr[++top] = x;
        cout << x << " pushed to stack\n";
    }

    // Pop operation
    void pop() {
        if (top == -1) {
            cout << "Stack Underflow! Cannot pop\n";
            return;
        }
        cout << arr[top--] << " popped from stack\n";
    }

    // Peek operation
    void peek() {
        if (top == -1) {
            cout << "Stack is empty\n";
            return;
        }
        cout << "Top element: " << arr[top] << endl;
    }

    // Display stack
    void display() {
        if (top == -1) {
            cout << "Stack is empty\n";
            return;
        }
        cout << "Stack elements: ";
        for (int i = 0; i <= top; i++) {
            cout << arr[i] << " ";
        }
        cout << endl;
    }
};

int main() {
    Stack st;
    st.push(10);
    st.push(20);
    st.push(30);
    st.display();
    st.pop();
    st.peek();
    return 0;
}
```

Python Implementation:

```
class Stack:
    def __init__(self, size=5):
        self.size = size
        self.stack = []

    def push(self, item):
        if len(self.stack) == self.size:
            print("Stack Overflow! Cannot push", item)
            return
        self.stack.append(item)
        print(f"{item} pushed to stack")

    def pop(self):
        if self.is_empty():
            print("Stack Underflow! Cannot pop")
            return
        print(f"{self.stack.pop()} popped from stack")

    def peek(self):
        return self.stack[-1] if not self.is_empty() else None

    def is_empty(self):
        return len(self.stack) == 0

    def display(self):
        print("Stack elements:", self.stack)

# Driver Code
st = Stack()
st.push(10)
st.push(20)
st.push(30)
st.display()
st.pop()
print("Top element:", st.peek())
```

Input Operations: `Push(10)`, `Push(20)`, `Push(30)`, `Pop()`, and `Peek()`

Table 4.1 demonstrates the sequence of stack operations, while showing how the stack state and top position change after each step.

Step	Operation	Stack State	Top
1	`Push(10)`	[10]	0
2	`Push(20)`	[10, 20]	1
3	`Push(30)`	[10, 20, 30]	2
4	`Pop()`	[10, 20]	1
5	`Peek()`	Top = 20	1

***Table 4.1**: Execution of Stack Operations (Push, Pop, and Peek)*

Linked List-Based Stack Implementation

An **array-based stack** has a **fixed size**, but a **linked list-based stack** uses **dynamic memory allocation**. This allows it to grow or shrink whenever needed. Each element is stored in a **node** containing the following:

- **Data Field**: Stores the value

- **Pointer Field**: Stores the address of the next node

This makes the linked list approach **more flexible** than arrays.

C++ Implementation:

```
#include <iostream>
using namespace std;

struct Node {
    int data;
    Node* next;
};

class Stack {
    Node* top;

public:
    Stack() { top = NULL; }

    // Push operation
    void push(int x) {
        Node* newNode = new Node();
        newNode->data = x;
        newNode->next = top;
        top = newNode;
        cout << x << " pushed to stack\n";
    }

    // Pop operation
    void pop() {
        if (top == NULL) {
            cout << "Stack Underflow! Cannot pop\n";
            return;
        }
        cout << top->data << " popped from stack\n";
        Node* temp = top;
        top = top->next;
        delete temp;
    }

    // Peek operation
    void peek() {
        if (top == NULL) {
            cout << "Stack is empty\n";
            return;
        }
        cout << "Top element: " << top->data << endl;
    }

    // Display stack
    void display() {
        if (top == NULL) {
            cout << "Stack is empty\n";
            return;
        }
        cout << "Stack elements: ";
        Node* temp = top;
        while (temp != NULL) {
            cout << temp->data << " ";
```

```
            temp = temp->next;
        }
        cout << endl;
    }
};
int main() {
    Stack st;
    st.push(10);
    st.push(20);
    st.push(30);
    st.display();
    st.pop();
    st.peek();
    return 0;
}
```

Python Implementation:

```
class Node:
    def __init__(self, data):
        self.data = data
        self.next = None
class Stack:
    def __init__(self):
        self.top = None
    def push(self, data):
        new_node = Node(data)
        new_node.next = self.top
        self.top = new_node
        print(f"{data} pushed to stack")
    def pop(self):
        if self.top is None:
            print("Stack Underflow! Cannot pop")
            return
        print(f"{self.top.data} popped from stack")
        self.top = self.top.next
    def peek(self):
        return self.top.data if self.top else None
    def display(self):
        temp = self.top
        elements = []
        while temp:
            elements.append(temp.data)
            temp = temp.next
        print("Stack elements:", elements)
# Driver Code
st = Stack()
st.push(10)
st.push(20)
st.push(30)
st.display()
```

```
st.pop()
print("Top element:", st.peek())
```

Applications of Stacks

Stacks are widely used in **computer science**, **software development**, and **real-life scenarios** due to their **LIFO nature**. Here are a few of these illustrations:

- **Expression Handling**
  - **Parenthesis Matching**: Checks if brackets `()[]{}` are balanced
  - **Expression Conversion:** Converts infix → postfix/prefix
  - **Expression Evaluation**: Evaluates postfix and prefix expressions
- **Function Call Management:** Uses a call stack to store function calls and handles recursion efficiently.
- **Backtracking Algorithms:** They are used in solving puzzles, mazes, and Sudoku.

  For example, if a wrong path is chosen, the algorithm **pops steps**, and then backtracks.
- **Undo/Redo Operations:** Text editors, IDEs, and graphics tools store recent actions in stacks.
- **Browser History Navigation:** Moving **backward pops** the current page, while going **forward** pushes it back.
- **Memory Management**: Operating systems and compilers manage function execution and variables using stacks.

Queue

A **queue** is a fundamental linear data structure that organizes elements sequentially and processes them according to the **First-In, First-Out (FIFO)** principle, meaning the element inserted first is always removed first. This behavior resembles real-world waiting lines, such as customers standing in a ticket queue, where service is provided in the order of arrival.

Queue Fundamentals

Understanding queue fundamentals is important because queues model situations where tasks must be handled in the exact order they arrive. Unlike stacks, where insertion and deletion occur at the same end, queues insert elements at the **rear,** and remove elements from the **front**, ensuring orderly processing.

The basic operations of a queue include:

Enqueue – adding an element to the rear of the queue

Dequeue – removing an element from the front

Peek/Front – viewing the first element without removing it

Queues are widely used in practical computing scenarios such as **task scheduling in operating systems, handling requests in web servers, buffering data streams, and managing printer jobs**, where maintaining arrival order is essential for fairness and efficiency.

Its key characteristics include:

- **FIFO Structure**: Insertions happen at the **rear** (enqueue), while deletions occur at the **front** (dequeue).
- **Sequential Storage**: It can be implemented using **arrays**, **linked lists**, or **pointers**.

- **Restricted Operations**: Insertion and deletion are performed only from **two ends.**
- **Real-Life Analogy**: It is like a ticket queue, cafeteria line, or printer job scheduling.

Queue Operations

A **queue** follows the **First-In, First-Out (FIFO)** principle, which means that the **first element** added to the queue is the **first one** to be removed. To manage data effectively, queues support a set of **core operations** that handle insertion, deletion, inspection, and validation of elements. Hence, these operations act as the foundation for solving more complex problems related to scheduling, buffering, and resource management.

Enqueue Operation (Insertion):

- The **enqueue** operation is used to **add** a new element to the **rear** (end) of the queue.
- **Definition** → Inserts an element at the **rear** of the queue
- **Before Enqueue:** [10, 20, 30]
- `Enqueue(40)`**:** Adds 40 at the **end**
- **After Enqueue:** [10, 20, 30, 40]
- **Overflow Condition:** If the queue is already full (in fixed-size implementations), a **Queue Overflow** occurs.
- **Analogy:** Think of joining a queue at a **ticket counter**—you **always** stand at the **end** of the line.

Dequeue Operation (Deletion)

- The **dequeue** operation **removes** an element from the **front** of the queue.
- **Definition** → Deletes and returns the element at the **front**
- **Before Dequeue:** [10, 20, 30, 40]
- `Dequeue()`**:** Removes 10
- **After Dequeue:** [20, 30, 40]
- **Underflow Condition:** If the queue is empty, **Queue Underflow** occurs.
- **Analogy:** Similar to people leaving a **movie ticket line**—the **first** person in the line is **served first**

Figure 4.4 illustrates the enqueue and dequeue operations in a queue, and shows how elements are inserted at the rear and removed from the front:

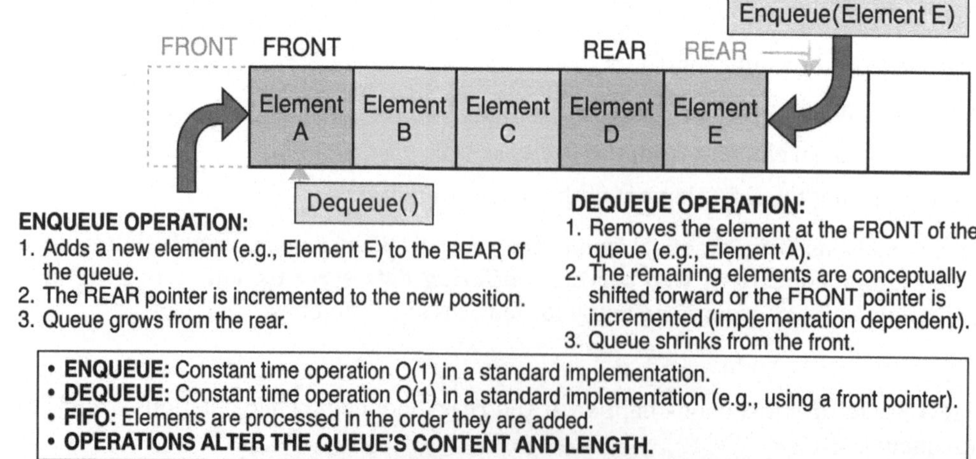

Figure 4.4: *Enqueue and Dequeue Operations*

`Peek/Front` Operation

- The **`peek`** (or **`front`**) operation returns the **value at the front** of the queue **without removing it.**
- **Definition** → Displays the element at the **front**
- **Example:** For [10, 20, 30], **`peek()`** → 10
- **Use Case:** It is useful when you want to **check** which element will be processed next without actually removing it.

`Rear/Back` Operation

- Some implementations provide a **rear** operation that returns the **last element** of the queue **without removing it.**
- **Example:** For [10, 20, 30], **`rear()`** → 30

Figure 4.5 depicts the Peek and Rear operations in a queue, while highlighting how the front and rear elements can be accessed without modifying the queue.

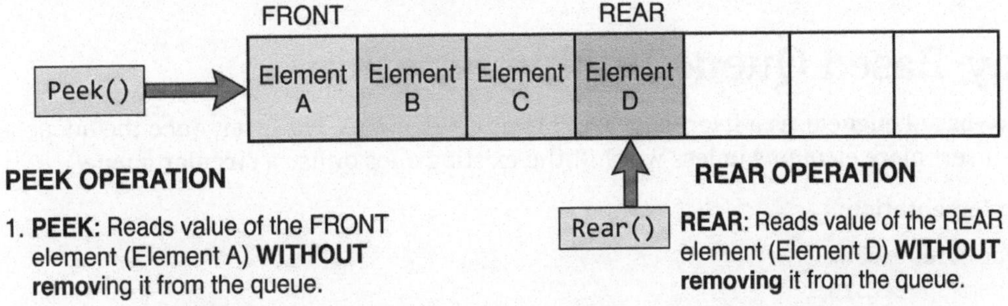

***Figure* 4.5:** *Peek and Rear Operations*

`isEmpty()` Operation

- The **`isEmpty`** function checks whether the queue has any elements.
- **Returns** → True if the queue is **empty**, else false
- **Example:** For **`[]`**, **`isEmpty() → True`**
- **Use Case:** Prevents **Queue Underflow** during a **dequeue** operation

`isFull()` Operation

- The **`isFull`** function checks whether the queue has reached its **maximum capacity**.
- **Returns** → True if the queue is **completely filled**, else false.
- **Example:** For a queue of size 5 containing [10, 20, 30, 40, 50], **`isFull()`** → True
- **Use Case:** Avoids **Queue Overflow** during an **enqueue** operation

Figure 4.6 illustrates the **`isFull`** and **`isEmpty`** operations, which are used to check whether a queue has reached its maximum capacity, or is completely empty.

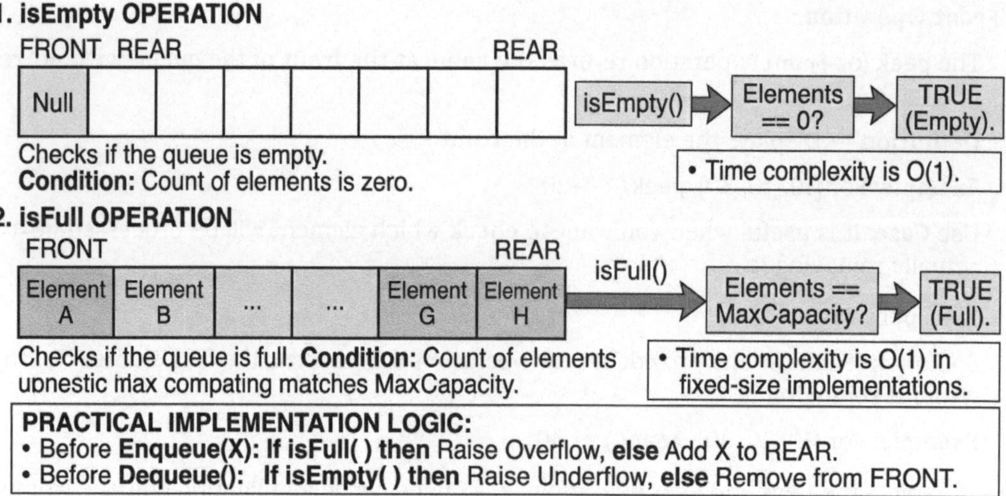

***Figure 4.6:** isFull and isEmpty Operations*

Array-Based Queue Implementation

An **array-based queue** uses a **fixed-size array** to store elements. However, once the queue is full, we cannot insert more elements unless we shift the existing ones or use a **circular queue**.

C++ Implementation:

```
#include <iostream>
using namespace std;

#define SIZE 5
class Queue {
    int arr[SIZE];
    int front, rear;

public:
    Queue() {
        front = rear = -1;
    }

    bool isFull() {
        return rear == SIZE - 1;
    }

    bool isEmpty() {
        return front == -1 || front > rear;
    }

    void enqueue(int x) {
        if (isFull()) {
            cout << "Queue Overflow! Cannot insert " << x << endl;
            return;
        }
        if (front == -1) front = 0;
        arr[++rear] = x;
        cout << x << " enqueued\n";
    }

    void dequeue() {
```

```
        if (isEmpty()) {
            cout << "Queue Underflow! Cannot delete\n";
            return;
        }
        cout << arr[front++] << " dequeued\n";
    }

    void display() {
        if (isEmpty()) {
            cout << "Queue is empty\n";
            return;
        }
        cout << "Queue elements: ";
        for (int i = front; i <= rear; i++)
            cout << arr[i] << " ";
        cout << endl;
    }
};

int main() {
    Queue q;
    q.enqueue(10);
    q.enqueue(20);
    q.enqueue(30);
    q.display();
    q.dequeue();
    q.display();
    return 0;
}
```

Python Implementation:

```
class Queue:
    def __init__(self, size=5):
        self.size = size
        self.queue = []

    def enqueue(self, item):
        if len(self.queue) == self.size:
            print("Queue Overflow! Cannot insert", item)
            return
        self.queue.append(item)
        print(f"{item} enqueued")

    def dequeue(self):
        if self.is_empty():
            print("Queue Underflow! Cannot delete")
            return
        print(f"{self.queue.pop(0)} dequeued")

    def peek(self):
        return self.queue[0] if not self.is_empty() else None

    def is_empty(self):
        return len(self.queue) == 0

    def display(self):
        print("Queue elements:", self.queue)
```

```
# Driver Code
q = Queue()
q.enqueue(10)
q.enqueue(20)
q.enqueue(30)
q.display()
q.dequeue()
q.display()
```

Circular Queue Implementation

A **circular queue** is an improved version of the **array-based queue** that solves the problem of **wasted space** in a normal queue. In a **linear queue**, once the **rear** reaches the end of the array, we cannot insert new elements even if there are empty spaces at the **front**. A **circular queue** overcomes this limitation by **connecting the rear back to the front**, forming a **circular structure**. Its key characteristics include:

- Uses the **modulus operator (%)** to wrap around
- **Front** → First element
- **Rear** → Last element
- Efficiently utilizes available space
- Commonly used in **CPU scheduling**, **buffer management**, and **network packet routing**
- Consider the example of a **Ferris wheel** where seats rotate in a **circle**; when the last seat passes, the first one comes back again. Similarly, the **rear pointer** loops back to the **front**.

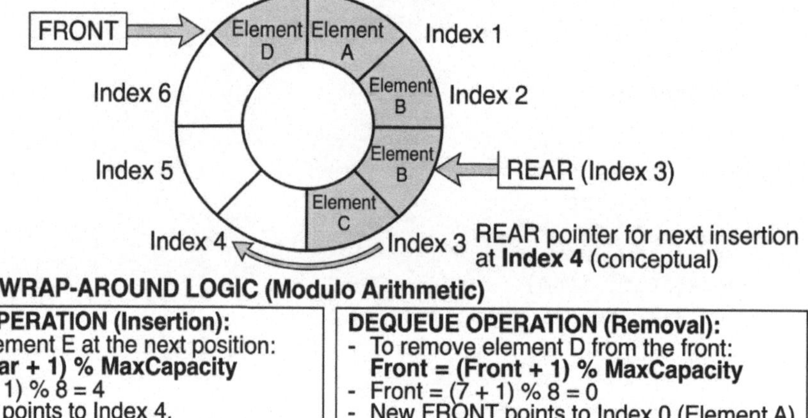

***Figure 4.7:** Circular Queue Implementation*

C++ Implementation:

```
#include <iostream>
using namespace std;

#define SIZE 5
class CircularQueue {
    int arr[SIZE];
    int front, rear;

public:
    CircularQueue() {
        front = rear = -1;
```

```
    }
    bool isFull() {
        return (front == 0 && rear == SIZE - 1) || (rear + 1) % SIZE == front;
    }
    bool isEmpty() {
        return front == -1;
    }
    void enqueue(int x) {
        if (isFull()) {
            cout << "Queue Overflow!\n";
            return;
        }
        if (front == -1) front = rear = 0;
        else rear = (rear + 1) % SIZE;
        arr[rear] = x;
        cout << x << " enqueued\n";
    }
    void dequeue() {
        if (isEmpty()) {
            cout << "Queue Underflow!\n";
            return;
        }
        cout << arr[front] << " dequeued\n";
        if (front == rear) front = rear = -1;
        else front = (front + 1) % SIZE;
    }
    void display() {
        if (isEmpty()) {
            cout << "Queue is empty\n";
            return;
        }
        cout << "Queue elements: ";
        int i = front;
        while (true) {
            cout << arr[i] << " ";
            if (i == rear) break;
            i = (i + 1) % SIZE;
        }
        cout << endl;
    }
};
int main() {
    CircularQueue cq;
    cq.enqueue(10);
    cq.enqueue(20);
    cq.enqueue(30);
    cq.enqueue(40);
    cq.display();
    cq.dequeue();
    cq.display();
    return 0;
}
```

Python Implementation:

```
class CircularQueue:
    def __init__(self, size=5):
        self.size = size
        self.queue = [None] * size
        self.front = self.rear = -1

    def is_full(self):
        return (self.rear + 1) % self.size == self.front

    def is_empty(self):
        return self.front == -1

    def enqueue(self, item):
        if self.is_full():
            print("Queue Overflow!")
            return
        if self.front == -1:
            self.front = self.rear = 0
        else:
            self.rear = (self.rear + 1) % self.size
        self.queue[self.rear] = item
        print(f"{item} enqueued")

    def dequeue(self):
        if self.is_empty():
            print("Queue Underflow!")
            return
        removed = self.queue[self.front]
        if self.front == self.rear:
            self.front = self.rear = -1
        else:
            self.front = (self.front + 1) % self.size
        print(f"{removed} dequeued")

    def display(self):
        if self.is_empty():
            print("Queue is empty")
            return
        i = self.front
        elements = []
        while True:
            elements.append(self.queue[i])
            if i == self.rear:
                break
            i = (i + 1) % self.size
        print("Queue elements:", elements)

cq = CircularQueue(5)
cq.enqueue(10)
cq.enqueue(20)
cq.enqueue(30)
cq.enqueue(40)
cq.display()
cq.dequeue()
```

```
cq.enqueue(50)
cq.display()
```

Linked List-Based Queue Implementation

A **linked list-based queue** overcomes the limitations of array-based queues, such as fixed size and wasted space. It uses a **dynamically allocated singly linked list** where:

The **front pointer** points to the **first node** (element to be dequeued next).

The **rear pointer** points to the **last node** (element to be enqueued next).

Therefore, memory is allocated only when needed, which makes the queue **flexible** and **efficient**.

Key advantages include:

- A linked list has no fixed size. Therefore, it can grow or shrink dynamically.
- No shifting of elements is required.
- Efficient memory utilization is observed.

Figure 4.8 illustrates a queue implemented using a linked list, while showing how nodes are dynamically connected to maintain the queue structure.

VISUALIZATION: Linked List Nodes as Queue Elements

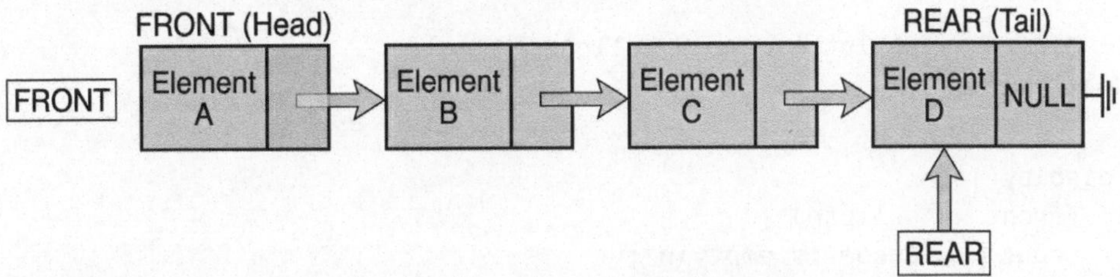

PRACTICAL QUEUE OPERATIONS (Pointer Manipulation)

ENQUEUE OPERATION (Insertion):	DEQUEUE OPERATION (Removal):
- To insert element E at the next position: **Current Rear -> Next = New Node(E)** - Rear is updated to point to the new node E. - New Rear points to Node E. - Queue content after enqueue: A→B→NULL	- To remove element A from the front: **Front = Front -> Next** - Front is updated to point to the next node B. - Element A is returned/deleted. - Queue content after dequeue: B→C–NULL

Figure 4.8: *Linked List-Based Queue*

C++ Implementation:

```
#include <iostream>
using namespace std;

struct Node {
    int data;
    Node* next;
};

class Queue {
    Node* front;
    Node* rear;

public:
    Queue() {
        front = rear = nullptr;
    }
```

```
    void enqueue(int value) {
        Node* newNode = new Node();
        newNode->data = value;
        newNode->next = nullptr;
        if (rear == nullptr) {
            front = rear = newNode;
            cout << value << " enqueued\n";
            return;
        }
        rear->next = newNode;
        rear = newNode;
        cout << value << " enqueued\n";
    }
    void dequeue() {
        if (front == nullptr) {
            cout << "Queue Underflow!\n";
            return;
        }
        Node* temp = front;
        cout << front->data << " dequeued\n";
        front = front->next;
        if (front == nullptr) rear = nullptr;
        delete temp;
    }
    void display() {
        if (front == nullptr) {
            cout << "Queue is empty\n";
            return;
        }
        Node* temp = front;
        cout << "Queue elements: ";
        while (temp != nullptr) {
            cout << temp->data << " ";
            temp = temp->next;
        }
        cout << endl;
    }
};
int main() {
    Queue q;
    q.enqueue(10);
    q.enqueue(20);
    q.enqueue(30);
    q.display();
    q.dequeue();
    q.display();
    return 0;
}
```

Python Implementation:

```
class Node:
    def __init__(self, data):
```

```
        self.data = data
        self.next = None
class Queue:
    def __init__(self):
        self.front = None
        self.rear = None

    def enqueue(self, item):
        new_node = Node(item)
        if self.rear is None:
            self.front = self.rear = new_node
            print(f"{item} enqueued")
            return
        self.rear.next = new_node
        self.rear = new_node
        print(f"{item} enqueued")
    def dequeue(self):
        if self.front is None:
            print("Queue Underflow!")
            return
        print(f"{self.front.data} dequeued")
        self.front = self.front.next
        if self.front is None:
            self.rear = None
    def display(self):
        if self.front is None:
            print("Queue is empty")
            return
        temp = self.front
        print("Queue elements:", end=" ")
        while temp:
            print(temp.data, end=" ")
            temp = temp.next
        print()
# Driver Code
q = Queue()
q.enqueue(10)
q.enqueue(20)
q.enqueue(30)
q.display()
q.dequeue()
q.display()
```

Priority Queues

A **priority queue** is a special type of queue in which **each element is associated with a priority**, and elements are **served based on their priority,** rather than just their insertion order. Unlike a normal queue that follows the **First-In, First-Out (FIFO)** principle, a priority queue ensures that the **highest-priority element is always processed first**. Its key characteristics include:

- Every element has two attributes: **data** and **priority**.
- The element with the **highest priority** is dequeued first.

- If two elements have the **same priority**, they are processed in **FIFO order**.
- Priority queues can be implemented using arrays, linked lists, heaps *(most efficient implementation), and* STL (C++ Standard Template Library).

Types of Priority Queues

Priority queues are mainly divided into two categories:

Max-Priority Queue: The element with the **highest priority** is dequeued first. This is commonly used in scheduling tasks where the **most critical job** must be completed first.

Example: Consider hospital emergency room systems—patients with severe conditions are treated first.

Min-Priority Queue: The element with the **lowest priority** is dequeued first. Often used in algorithms where **minimum-cost solutions** are required.

Example: Dijkstra's algorithm for finding the **shortest path** in a graph

C++ STL Implementation:

Using **`std::priority_queue`** from the **C++ Standard Template Library**:

```
#include <iostream>
#include <queue>
using namespace std;

int main() {
    priority_queue<int> pq;  // Max-priority queue

    // Inserting elements
    pq.push(40);
    pq.push(20);
    pq.push(60);
    pq.push(10);

    cout << "Elements in priority order: ";
    while (!pq.empty()) {
        cout << pq.top() << " ";  // Highest priority element
        pq.pop();
    }
    return 0;
}
```

Output:

```
Elements in Priority Order: 60 40 20 10
```

Python Implementation:

Using **heapq** (default min-priority queue):

```
import heapq

# Creating a min-priority queue
pq = []
heapq.heappush(pq, 40)
heapq.heappush(pq, 20)
heapq.heappush(pq, 60)
heapq.heappush(pq, 10)

print("Elements in priority order:", end=" ")
```

```
while pq:
    print(heapq.heappop(pq), end=" ")
```

Output:

```
Elements in Priority Order: 10 20 40 60
```

Applications of Queues

Queues play an essential role in solving real-world problems and are widely used in operating systems, networking, data processing, and algorithm design. Due to their **First-In, First-Out (FIFO)** nature, queues are ideal for situations where tasks or data need to be processed in the exact order they arrive. The following are some of the most significant applications of queues:

- **Task Scheduling and Process Management:** Operating systems use queues to manage processes, and also allocate CPU time effectively.

  For example, the **ready queue** in an OS stores processes waiting for execution, while the **job queue** manages background tasks.

  Example: In a multi-tasking system, processes enter the queue, and are then executed based on arrival order or priority.

- **Printer Job Scheduling**: In a multi-user environment, multiple print requests are handled using a queue.

  The first request in the queue is processed first, which ensures fairness among users.

- **Call Center and Ticketing Systems:** Customer service centers manage incoming calls using queues so that customers are served in the order they are called.

  Similarly, online ticket booking systems process requests sequentially to avoid conflicts.

- **CPU and Disk Scheduling**: In CPU scheduling, tasks waiting for execution are stored in a **queue**.

  Disk scheduling algorithms also use queues to manage read/write requests efficiently.

- **Network Data Management:** Queues are used in routers and switches to manage data packets before forwarding them.

  This ensures smooth data transmission, and prevents congestion in high-traffic networks.

- **Breadth-First Search (BFS) in Graphs:** In graph traversal algorithms, queues are used to explore nodes level by level.

  Example: BFS uses a queue to store nodes and ensures that each node is visited in the correct order.

- **Simulation and Real-Time Systems:** Queues are used in simulations, such as traffic management systems, airport check-ins, and customer flow monitoring where events must be processed chronologically.

Deque

A **deque** (pronounced "*deck*") is a linear data structure whose name comes from **double-ended queue**. It allows insertion and deletion of elements at both the **front** and the **rear**. Unlike a standard queue, which typically enforces strict First-In, First-Out (FIFO) processing, a deque offers greater operational flexibility because elements can be accessed and modified from either side.

Because of this dual-ended capability, a deque can be viewed as a generalized structure that combines the behavioral properties of both **queues** and **stacks**. This makes it particularly valuable in algorithmic problems such as sliding-window computations, palindrome verification, task buffering, and cache management.

Deque Fundamentals

Understanding deque fundamentals is important because this structure provides controlled access from both ends while still maintaining an ordered sequence of elements. This dual accessibility enables developers to design efficient solutions for problems that require dynamic insertion or removal at either boundary of the data structure.

The key characteristics of a deque include:

Bidirectional access – elements can be inserted or removed from both the front and the rear. **Adaptive behavior** – inserting at the rear and deleting from the front simulates queue behavior,

inserting and deleting from the same end simulates stack behavior.

Constant-time end operations – insertions and deletions at either end generally take **O(1)** time.

Flexible implementation – deques may be implemented using arrays, linked lists, or built-in containers such as std::deque in C++ and collections.deque in Python.

A useful real-world analogy is a special queue at a cinema entrance where people may join from either the front or the back, and attendants may process entries from either side. This operational flexibility mirrors how a deque manages elements in computing systems.

When to Use Deques:

- When you need **flexibility** for insertion and deletion from **both ends**
- When implementing **sliding window problems**, **palindrome checking**, or **caching mechanisms**
- When designing **algorithms requiring double-ended access**, like **BFS optimizations**

Types of Deques

A double-ended queue (**deque**) provides the flexibility to insert and delete elements from **both ends**. However, depending on certain restrictions imposed on operations, deques are classified into two main types:

- **Input-Restricted Deque**

  An **Input-Restricted Deque** allows for:

  Insertion → Only at one end (either front or rear)

  Deletion → From both ends

  This type is useful when data comes from a **single source**, but we want the freedom to remove elements **from either side**. Consider a **printer queue** where all print jobs are added **only at the rear**, but an **administrator** can remove urgent jobs from **either the front or rear**.

- **Output-Restricted Deque**

  An **Output-Restricted Deque** allows for:

  Deletion → Only at one end (either front or rear)

  Insertion → From both ends

  This type is useful when you want **flexibility in adding data**, but control over **how data is removed**. In a **ticket booking system**, new booking requests can be added **from both ends** (multiple counters), but cancellations or completions are processed **only from the front**.

Operations on Deques

A **deque** (double-ended queue) allows inserting and deleting elements **from both front and rear ends.** Due to its flexibility, it can be used as **queues**, **stacks**, or even a combination of both. The basic operations on deques are categorized into **insertion**, **deletion**, **access**, and **utility** operations.

Insertion Operations

Insertion operations in a deque allow us to add elements either at the front or the rear, which makes a deque more flexible than a normal queue.

- **`insertFront()` / `push_front()`**
  - **Inserts an element at the** front **of the deque.**
  - **Useful when** high-priority tasks **must be added at the beginning.**
  - **Imagine a** VIP queue **at an airport—VIP passengers are added at the** front **without disturbing others.**
- **`insertRear()` / `push_back()`**
  - **Inserts an element at the** rear **of the deque.**
  - **Is similar to a** normal queue, **where new tasks are added at the end.**

C++ STL Example (Insertion):

```
#include <iostream>
#include <deque>
using namespace std;

int main() {
    deque<int> dq;

    dq.push_back(10);    // Insert at rear
    dq.push_front(20);  // Insert at front
    dq.push_back(30);

    cout << "Deque elements after insertion: ";
    for (int x : dq)
        cout << x << " ";

    return 0;
}
```

Output: `Deque Elements after Insertion: 20 10 30`

Python Example (Insertion):

```
from collections import deque

dq = deque()

dq.append(10)        # Insert at rear
dq.appendleft(20)    # Insert at front
dq.append(30)

print("Deque elements after insertion:", list(dq))
```

Output: `Deque Elements after Insertion: [20, 10, 30]`

Deletion Operations

Deletion operations in a deque allow us to **remove elements** from **both ends**—either from the **front** or the **rear**, depending on the requirement.

`deleteFront()` / `pop_front()`

- Removes an element from the **`front`** of the **deque**
- Commonly used in **task scheduling,** where the earliest job is processed first

`deleteRear()` / `pop_back()`

- Removes an element from the **`rear`** of the **deque**
- Useful when removing the **most recently added** element

C++ STL Example (Deletion):

```
#include <iostream>
#include <deque>
using namespace std;

int main() {
    deque<int> dq = {20, 10, 30};

    dq.pop_front(); // Remove from front
    dq.pop_back();  // Remove from rear

    cout << "Deque elements after deletion: ";
    for (int x : dq)
        cout << x << " ";

    return 0;
}
```

Output: `Deque Elements after Deletion: 10`

Python Example (Deletion):

```
from collections import deque

dq = deque([20, 10, 30])

dq.popleft()  # Remove from front
dq.pop()      # Remove from rear

print("Deque elements after deletion:", list(dq))
```

Output: `Deque Elements after Deletion: [10]`

Access Operations

Access operations in a deque allow us to **view elements** stored at the **front** or **rear** without removing them, which makes it easy to check data without modifying the structure.

`getFront()`: Returns the element at the **`front`** without removing it

`getRear()`: Returns the element at the **`rear`** without removing it

C++ STL Example:

```
#include <iostream>
#include <deque>
```

```
using namespace std;
int main() {
    deque<int> dq = {10, 20, 30};
    cout << "Front element: " << dq.front() << endl;
    cout << "Rear element: " << dq.back() << endl;

    return 0;
}
```

Output:

```
Front Element: 10
Rear Element: 30
```

Python Example:

```
from collections import deque
dq = deque([10, 20, 30])
print("Front element:", dq[0])
print("Rear element:", dq[-1])
```

Output:

```
Front Element: 10
Rear Element: 30
```

Utility Operations

The following utility operations provide quick ways to manage and monitor a deque, such as checking its size, verifying whether it is empty, and accessing its elements efficiently:

Operation	C++ STL Method	Python Method	Description
Check if empty	`dq.empty()`	`len(dq) == 0`	Returns **true** if the deque is empty
Get size	`dq.size()`	`len(dq)`	Returns the **number of elements**
Clear deque	`dq.clear()`	`dq.clear()`	Removes **all elements**

Table 4.2: *Utility Operations*

Applications of Deques

Double-ended queues (or Deques) are highly versatile data structures because they allow insertion and deletion from **both ends** efficiently. Their flexibility makes them suitable for a wide range of real-world applications and algorithmic solutions. Some of the most common applications of deques include:

- **Sliding Window Problems:** Deques are widely used in solving sliding window problems where elements need to be added and removed dynamically, while maintaining the maximum or minimum value within a fixed window.

  Example: Finding the maximum of all subarrays of size *k*.

- **Implementing Both Stacks and Queues:** Since deques support operations at both ends, they can function as a **stack** (LIFO) or a **queue** (FIFO) depending on how you manage insertions and deletions.

- **Palindrome Checking:** Deques are ideal for checking whether a string is a palindrome by comparing characters from both ends simultaneously, which ensures efficient performance.

- **Task Scheduling:** In CPU and process scheduling, deques are used to manage tasks dynamically, where tasks can be added or removed from either end, based on priority or availability.
- **Undo and Redo Operations:** Text editors, drawing applications, and browsers often rely on deques to implement **undo/redo** functionality by efficiently tracking user actions from both ends.
- **Caching and Memory Management:** Deques are also used in implementing caching algorithms like **Least Recently Used (LRU)**, where elements are frequently added or removed from both ends to maintain efficient memory usage.

Common Coding Patterns and Interview Problems

Stacks, queues, and deques form the foundation of many algorithmic techniques and problem-solving approaches. They are frequently assessed in **technical interviews**, **competitive programming**, and **real-world applications**. Therefore, this section will explore some of the most common and important coding problems that leverage these data structures. The explanations will help you understand their practical use cases and develop your intuition to solve problems.

Balanced Parentheses Problem

This problem checks whether every opening bracket has a corresponding closing bracket in the correct order using a **stack**.

Example Input:

"{[()]}" → **Balanced**

"{[(])}" → **Not Balanced**

Approach:

- Use a **stack** to push opening brackets.
- For every closing bracket, check the top of the stack.
- If they match, pop; otherwise, return false.
- At the end, if the stack is empty → It is balanced.

C++ Implementation:

```
#include <iostream>
#include <stack>
using namespace std;

bool isBalanced(string s) {
    stack<char> st;
    for (char ch : s) {
        if (ch == '(' || ch == '{' || ch == '[')
            st.push(ch);
        else {
            if (st.empty()) return false;
            char top = st.top();
            if ((ch == ')' && top != '(') ||
                (ch == '}' && top != '{') ||
                (ch == ']' && top != '['))
                return false;
            st.pop();
```

```
        }
    }
    return st.empty();
}
int main() {
    string expr = "{[()]}";
    cout << (isBalanced(expr) ? "Balanced" : "Not Balanced");
    return 0;
}
```

Python Implementation:

```
def is_balanced(s: str) -> bool:
    stack = []
    mapping = {')': '(', '}': '{', ']': '['}
    for ch in s:
        if ch in mapping.values():
            stack.append(ch)
        elif ch in mapping:
            if not stack or stack[-1] != mapping[ch]:
                return False
            stack.pop()
    return not stack
expr = "{[()]}"
print("Balanced" if is_balanced(expr) else "Not Balanced")
```

Time Complexity: `O(n)`

Space Complexity: `O(n)`

Applications:

- Syntax Validation in Compilers
- Expression Parsing in Interpreters

Next Greater Element

Given an array, find the **Next Greater Element** (NGE) for each element. The NGE is the first element to the right that is greater than the current element.

Approach:

- Use a **stack** to store elements.
- Traverse the array **from right to left.**
- Pop smaller elements from the stack.
- If the stack is empty → NGE = -1; otherwise, the stack's top is the NGE.

C++ Implementation:

```
#include <iostream>
#include <stack>
#include <vector>
using namespace std;
vector<int> nextGreater(vector<int>& nums) {
    int n = nums.size();
    vector<int> result(n, -1);
    stack<int> st;
```

```
    for (int i = n - 1; i >= 0; i--) {
        while (!st.empty() && st.top() <= nums[i])
            st.pop();
        if (!st.empty())
            result[i] = st.top();
        st.push(nums[i]);
    }
    return result;
}

int main() {
    vector<int> arr = {4, 5, 2, 25};
    vector<int> ans = nextGreater(arr);
    for (int x : ans) cout << x << " ";
    return 0;
}
```

Python Implementation:

```
def next_greater(nums):
    n = len(nums)
    result = [-1] * n
    stack = []

    for i in range(n - 1, -1, -1):
        while stack and stack[-1] <= nums[i]:
            stack.pop()
        result[i] = stack[-1] if stack else -1
        stack.append(nums[i])
    return result

arr = [4, 5, 2, 25]
print(next_greater(arr))
```

Time Complexity: O(n)

Space Complexity: O(n)

Applications:

- Stock Price Analysis
- Temperature Tracking Systems

Stock Span Problem

Given daily stock prices, the goal is to determine the **span** of the stock's price for each day—that is, the number of consecutive previous days the price was less than or equal to today's price.

Approach:

- Use a **stack** to store indices of previous prices.
- For each price, pop elements from the stack while the current price is greater than the price at the stack's top index.

C++ Implementation:

```
#include <iostream>
#include <stack>
```

```
#include <vector>
using namespace std;

vector<int> stockSpan(vector<int>& prices) {
    int n = prices.size();
    vector<int> span(n);
    stack<int> st;

    for (int i = 0; i < n; i++) {
        while (!st.empty() && prices[st.top()] <= prices[i])
            st.pop();
        span[i] = st.empty() ? (i + 1) : (i - st.top());
        st.push(i);
    }
    return span;
}

int main() {
    vector<int> prices = {100, 80, 60, 70, 60, 75, 85};
    vector<int> result = stockSpan(prices);
    for (int x : result) cout << x << " ";
    return 0;
}
```

Python Implementation:

```
def stock_span(prices):
    n = len(prices)
    span = [0] * n
    stack = []

    for i in range(n):
        while stack and prices[stack[-1]] <= prices[i]:
            stack.pop()
        span[i] = i + 1 if not stack else i - stack[-1]
        stack.append(i)
    return span

prices = [100, 80, 60, 70, 60, 75, 85]
print(stock_span(prices))
```

Time Complexity: O(n)

Space Complexity: O(n)

Applications:

- Financial Analysis Tools
- Trend Monitoring in Stock Markets

Evaluate Reverse Polish Notation

The Reverse Polish Notation (Postfix Expression) evaluation uses a **stack** to compute mathematical expressions efficiently.

Example:

Expression: ["2", "1", "+", "3", "*"]

Evaluation: (2 + 1) * 3 = 9

Approach:

- Use a **stack** to store operands.
- Traverse tokens one by one:
  - If the token is a number → **Push** it.
  - If it is an operator → **Pop two operands**, perform the operation, and **push** the result.
- The top of the stack will hold the final result.

C++ Implementation:

```
#include <iostream>
#include <iostream>
#include <stack>
#include <vector>
#include <string>
using namespace std;

int evalRPN(vector<string>& tokens) {
    stack<int> st;
    for (string token : tokens) {
        if (token == "+" || token == "-" || token == "*" || token == "/") {
            int b = st.top(); st.pop();
            int a = st.top(); st.pop();
            if (token == "+") st.push(a + b);
            else if (token == "-") st.push(a - b);
            else if (token == "*") st.push(a * b);
            else st.push(a / b);
        } else {
            st.push(stoi(token));
        }
    }
    return st.top();
}

int main() {
    vector<string> expr = {"2", "1", "+", "3", "*"};
    cout << "Result: " << evalRPN(expr);
    return 0;
}
```

Python Implementation:

```
def eval_rpn(tokens):
    stack = []
    for token in tokens:
        if token in "+-*/":
            b = stack.pop()
            a = stack.pop()
            if token == '+':
                stack.append(a + b)
            elif token == '-':
                stack.append(a - b)
            elif token == '*':
                stack.append(a * b)
            else:
                stack.append(int(a / b))  # Ensure integer division
```

```
        else:
            stack.append(int(token))
    return stack[-1]

expr = ["2", "1", "+", "3", "*"]
print("Result:", eval_rpn(expr))
```

Time Complexity: `O(n)`

Space Complexity: `O(n)`

Applications:

- Expression Evaluation in Compilers
- Implementation of Calculators

Min Stack Implementation

A **min stack** is a special stack that supports standard operations such as **push** and **pop,** but also allows you to retrieve the **minimum element** in **`O(1)`** time.

Approach:

- Use these **two stacks**:
  - **Main stack** → Stores all elements.
  - **Min stack** → Stores the minimum element at each level.
- While pushing, you must remember that:
  - If the min stack is empty or new element ≤ min, push onto the min stack.
- While popping, you must remember that:
  - Pop **from** the min stack, if the popped element equals the current min.

C++ Implementation:

```
#include <iostream>
#include <stack>
using namespace std;

class MinStack {
    stack<int> st, minSt;
public:
    void push(int x) {
        st.push(x);
        if (minSt.empty() || x <= minSt.top()) minSt.push(x);
    }
    void pop() {
        if (st.top() == minSt.top()) minSt.pop();
        st.pop();
    }
    int top() {
        return st.top();
    }
    int getMin() {
        return minSt.top();
    }
};
```

```
int main() {
    MinStack s;
    s.push(5);
    s.push(3);
    s.push(7);
    cout << "Min: " << s.getMin() << endl;
    s.pop();
    cout << "Min: " << s.getMin();
    return 0;
}
```

Python Implementation:

```
class MinStack:
    def __init__(self):
        self.stack = []
        self.min_stack = []

    def push(self, x: int):
        self.stack.append(x)
        if not self.min_stack or x <= self.min_stack[-1]:
            self.min_stack.append(x)

    def pop(self):
        if self.stack[-1] == self.min_stack[-1]:
            self.min_stack.pop()
        self.stack.pop()

    def top(self):
        return self.stack[-1]

    def get_min(self):
        return self.min_stack[-1]

# Example usage
s = MinStack()
s.push(5)
s.push(3)
s.push(7)
print("Min:", s.get_min())
s.pop()
print("Min:", s.get_min())
```

Time Complexity: O(1) per operation

Space Complexity: O(n)

Applications:

- Real-Time Minimum Tracking in Data Streams
- Efficient Decision-Making Algorithms

Sliding Window Maximum Using Deque

Find the maximum element in every contiguous subarray (window) of size **k**.

Approach:

- Use a **deque** to store indices of useful elements.
- Maintain decreasing order in the deque.
- Remove indices that are out of the window.

- Remember that the front of the deque always holds the maximum.

Example:

Input: `nums = [1,3,-1,-3,5,3,6,7], k = 3`

Output: `[3,3,5,5,6,7]`

C++ Implementation:

```
#include <iostream>
#include <deque>
#include <vector>
using namespace std;
vector<int> maxSlidingWindow(vector<int>& nums, int k) {
    deque<int> dq;
    vector<int> result;
    for (int i = 0; i < nums.size(); i++) {
        if (!dq.empty() && dq.front() <= i - k)
            dq.pop_front();
        while (!dq.empty() && nums[dq.back()] < nums[i])
            dq.pop_back();
        dq.push_back(i);
        if (i >= k - 1)
            result.push_back(nums[dq.front()]);
    }
    return result;
}
int main() {
    vector<int> nums = {1,3,-1,-3,5,3,6,7};
    int k = 3;
    vector<int> ans = maxSlidingWindow(nums, k);
    for (int x : ans) cout << x << " ";
    return 0;
}
```

Python Implementation:

```
from collections import deque
def max_sliding_window(nums, k):
    dq = deque()
    result = []
    for i in range(len(nums)):
        while dq and dq[0] <= i - k:
            dq.popleft()
        while dq and nums[dq[-1]] < nums[i]:
            dq.pop()
        dq.append(i)
        if i >= k - 1:
            result.append(nums[dq[0]])
    return result
nums = [1,3,-1,-3,5,3,6,7]
print(max_sliding_window(nums, 3))
```

Time Complexity: `O(n)`

Space Complexity: `O(k)`

Applications:

- Signal Processing
- Performance Monitoring Systems
- Financial Data Analysis

BFS Traversal Using Queue

Breadth-First Search (BFS) is a graph traversal technique that explores all nodes level by level using a **queue**.

Approach:

- Use a **queue** to store nodes level by level.
- Start from the source node, mark it visited.
- Dequeue, process the node, and enqueue all unvisited neighbors.

C++ Implementation :

```
#include <iostream>
#include <vector>
#include <queue>
using namespace std;

void bfs(vector<vector<int>>& graph, int start) {
    vector<bool> visited(graph.size(), false);
    queue<int> q;

    visited[start] = true;
    q.push(start);

    while (!q.empty()) {
        int node = q.front();
        q.pop();
        cout << node << " ";

        for (int neighbor : graph[node]) {
            if (!visited[neighbor]) {
                visited[neighbor] = true;
                q.push(neighbor);
            }
        }
    }
}

int main() {
    vector<vector<int>> graph = {
        {1, 2},
        {0, 3, 4},
        {0, 5},
        {1},
        {1},
        {2}
    };

    cout << "BFS Traversal: ";
```

```
    bfs(graph, 0);
    return 0;
}
```

Python Implementation:

```
from collections import deque

def bfs(graph, start):
    visited = [False] * len(graph)
    q = deque([start])
    visited[start] = True

    while q:
        node = q.popleft()
        print(node, end=" ")
        for neighbor in graph[node]:
            if not visited[neighbor]:
                visited[neighbor] = True
                q.append(neighbor)

graph = [
    [1, 2],
    [0, 3, 4],
    [0, 5],
    [1],
    [1],
    [2]
]
print("BFS Traversal:", end=" ")
bfs(graph, 0)
```

Time Complexity: `O(V + E)`

Space Complexity: `O(V)`

Applications:

- Shortest Path Algorithms
- Network Routing Systems
- Social Network Friend Suggestions

Conclusion

In this chapter, we explored three essential linear abstract data types—stacks, queues, and deques, —and understood how they play a critical role in algorithm design and real-world problem-solving. We began this chapter by learning the core principles behind these structures, such as the LIFO behavior of stacks, the FIFO nature of queues, and the bidirectional flexibility of deques. We implemented them using arrays, linked lists, and built-in libraries in both C++ STL and Python, while making their practical usage more intuitive. Through various examples and applications, we discovered how these structures support tasks such as recursion handling, expression evaluation, parenthesis matching, sliding window problems, BFS traversal, and undo/redo functionalities. Additionally, we solved several common coding patterns and interview problems, including balanced parentheses, next greater element, stock span, reverse Polish notation evaluation, min stack design, sliding window maximum, and BFS traversal using queues. These hands-on examples demonstrated how mastering these structures equips you with strong problem-solving skills, and prepares you for both competitive programming and technical interviews.

In the next chapter, we will move beyond sequential data organization and explore hash-based data structures in *Chapter 5, Hash Tables and Unordered Maps*. We will understand the concept of hashing and hash functions, learn different collision handling techniques such as chaining and open addressing, and study load factors and rehashing for optimized performance. We will also implement unordered maps in C++ STL and dictionaries in Python while exploring real-world applications such as frequency counting, duplicate detection, and caching. To strengthen our understanding, we will tackle interview-focused problems such as two-sum, grouping anagrams, and finding the longest substring without repetition. Hence, mastering the next chapter will enable us to design high-performance applications where efficient data retrieval and optimized key-value mapping are essential.

Points to Remember

- **Stacks** follow the **Last-In, First-Out (LIFO)** principle. Insertion and deletion happen from the **top**.
- **Queues** follow the **First-In, First-Out (FIFO)** principle. Insertion happens at the **rear**, and deletion happens at the **front**.
- **Double-Ended Queues (Deques)** allow **insertion and deletion** from **both ends**, which makes them more flexible.
- **Array-based implementations** are simple but require a fixed size and may waste memory.
- **Linked list-based implementations** provide dynamic memory usage but require additional pointer handling.
- **Stacks** are widely used in **recursion**, **expression evaluation**, **undo/redo features**, and **backtracking**.
- **Queues** are essential for **task scheduling**, **BFS traversal**, **resource management**, and **real-time systems**.
- **Deques** are highly efficient for **sliding window problems**, **palindrome checking**, and **cache implementation**.
- **C++ STL** provides ready-to-use classes such as `std::stack`, `std::queue`, `std::deque`, and `std::priority_queue`.
- **Python** offers built-in implementations using `lists`, `collections.deque`, and `queue.Queue`.

Multiple Choice Questions

1. Which of the following best describes the behavior of a stack?
   a. FIFO
   b. LIFO
   c. Random Access
   d. Priority-Based
2. Which of these applications commonly uses stacks?
   a. Task Scheduling
   b. Undo Operations in Text Editors
   c. BFS Traversal
   d. Message Queues
3. Which data structure is most suitable for **breadth-first search**?
   a. Stack
   b. Queue

c. Deque

d. Priority Queue

4. What will be the time complexity of inserting an element into a stack implemented using an array?

   a. `O(1)`

   b. `O(n)`

   c. `O(log n)`

   d. `O(n²)`

5. Which of the following operations is **not** possible in a simple queue?

   a. Insert at the rear.

   b. Delete from the front.

   c. Insert at the front.

   d. Check if empty.

6. A deque allows insertion and deletion from:

   a. Front only

   b. Rear only

   c. Both ends

   d. Neither end

7. Which STL class is best for implementing a **priority queue** in C++?

   a. `std::queue`

   b. `std::deque`

   c. `std::priority_queue`

   d. `std::stack`

8. In Python, which module provides an efficient deque implementation?

   a. Array

   b. List

   c. Collections

   d. Queue

9. Which of the following is a typical use of a **priority queue**?

   a. Undo Operations

   b. Cache Memory

   c. CPU Job Scheduling

   d. Expression Evaluation

10. The sliding window maximum problem can be solved efficiently using:

    a. Stack

    b. Simple Queue

    c. Deque

    d. Linked List

Answers

1. b
2. b
3. b
4. a
5. c
6. c
7. c
8. c
9. c
10. c

Questions

1. Define a stack and explain its LIFO principle with an example.
2. What are the basic operations performed on a stack?
3. Differentiate between a simple queue and a circular queue.
4. What is the difference between input-restricted and output-restricted deques?
5. List two real-life applications of queues.
6. Explain the array-based and linked list-based implementations of stacks with diagrams and code.
7. Describe the working of circular queues with an example and implementation.
8. Explain priority queues, their importance, and real-world use cases.
9. Discuss the role of deques in solving the sliding window maximum problem.
10. Compare stacks, queues, and deques based on operations, performance, and applications.

Key Terms

- **Last-In, First-Out (LIFO):** The last inserted element is removed first (stack behavior).
- **First-In, First-Out (FIFO):** The first inserted element is removed first (queue behavior).
- **Deque:** A double-ended queue allowing insertion and deletion from both ends.
- **Push:** Operation to insert an element into a stack.
- **Pop:** Operation to remove an element from a stack.
- **Enqueue:** Inserting an element into a queue.
- **Dequeue:** Removing an element from a queue.
- **Priority Queue:** A queue where elements are served based on priority.
- **Circular Queue:** A queue that connects the rear to the front for efficient space utilization.
- **Sliding Window Problem:** A coding pattern where deques are used for optimized computations over subarrays.

CHAPTER 5
Hash Tables and Unordered Maps

Introduction

In the world of data structures, speed and efficiency are often the most decisive factors, as they influence which approach to use. While arrays, stacks, and queues allow us to organize data in structured ways, they can become slow when we need to frequently search for or retrieve information. Imagine looking up a person's phone number in a contact list: if the list is long, scanning each entry one by one takes time. Would it not be better if we could instantly jump to the correct entry, almost as if we had its exact location memorized? This is where the power of **hashing asserts its importance**. By using a mathematical function, called a **hash function**, we can transform a piece of information (like a name or an ID) into an index that directly points to where its associated data is stored. The result is **constant-time access on average**, which makes hash tables one of the most efficient tools for data retrieval. Therefore, hash-based structures form the backbone of many real-world systems; from storing passwords securely, to building caches for faster web browsing, and detecting duplicate records in large datasets. Programming languages and libraries provide ready-made implementations such as **unordered maps in C++ STL** and **dictionaries in Python**. These implementations enable developers to harness hashing without building everything from scratch. Therefore, in this chapter, we will explore the **foundations of hashing**, understand how **hash tables** are built and maintained, address challenges such as **collisions**, and examine practical implementations in both C++ and Python. We will also highlight their applications, limitations, and common interview problems where a thorough mastery of hash tables is essential. By the end, you will be able to see why hashing is regarded as a cornerstone of modern algorithm design and software development.

Structure

In this chapter, we will cover the following topics:

- Introduction to Hashing
- Hash Functions and Hash Tables
- Collision Handling
- Load Factor and Rehashing
- Implementations in C++ STL and Python
- Applications of Hash Tables

- Limitations and Pitfalls
- Interview Problems

Introduction to Hashing

Hashing is a powerful technique designed to make data access extremely fast and efficient. It forms the backbone of hash tables, which organize information in a way that supports quick insertion, deletion, and retrieval.

Importance of Efficient Data Retrieval

One of the most common tasks in computer science is searching for information. Whether it is finding a record in a database, checking if a username already exists, or counting the frequency of words in a text, fast data retrieval can make a huge difference in performance. Traditional data structures like arrays or linked lists often require linear-time searches, which means that the time grows proportionally with the number of elements. For large datasets, this becomes costly. Hashing addresses this challenge by offering a direct way to access data using a key, and reduces the average search time to near constant, regardless of dataset size.

Key–Value Pair Organization

At the heart of hashing lies the idea of **associating data (value) with a unique identifier (key)**. For example, consider a dictionary where words are keys and their meanings are values. Instead of scanning the dictionary page by page, hashing allows us to jump directly to the page containing the word we want. In programming, this structure is implemented as a **hash table**, where each key is passed through a **hash function** that computes an index. The value is then stored at this index, while allowing quick insertion, lookup, and deletion operations.

Hash Functions and Hash Tables

Hash tables derive their power from two central ideas: **hash functions** and the **arrangement of key-value pairs**. Together, these enable constant-time performance for most operations. Hence, this makes hash tables one of the most efficient data structures in practice.

Hash Functions

A **hash function** is the core of hashing. It transforms a given key (like a number, string, or object) into an index within a fixed-size table. The index points to the location where the associated value is stored. Thus, the efficiency of a hash table heavily depends on how well its hash function distributes keys across the table.

Role of Hash Functions in Indexing

Hash functions act as a "bridge" between keys and their storage location. When a key is passed to the hash function, it generates an integer value (the hash code). This hash code is then mapped to an index within the hash table's range. For example, In an employee database, the employee ID can be used as a key. A hash function will map this ID to a specific index, while allowing near-instant retrieval of employee details.

Properties of Effective Hash Functions

An effective hash function should satisfy the following properties:

- **Uniform Distribution**: Keys should be spread evenly across the table to avoid clustering.

- **Determinism**: The same key must always produce the same hash value.
- **Efficiency**: The hash computation should be quick, even for large datasets.
- **Low Collision Probability**: While collisions cannot be fully avoided, a good function minimizes their frequency.

C++ Example (Modular Hash Function):

```
#include <iostream>
using namespace std;

int hashFunction(int key, int tableSize) {
    return key % tableSize;
}

int main() {
    int key = 12345;
    int tableSize = 100;
    cout << "Hash index: " << hashFunction(key, tableSize) << endl;
    return 0;
}
```

Python Example (Hash Function for Strings):

```
def hash_function(key, table_size):
    return sum(ord(c) for c in key) % table_size

key = "Alice"
table_size = 10
print("Hash index:", hash_function(key, table_size))
```

Here, both examples show how a key (number or string) is mapped to an index. This simple method is often combined with collision handling strategies to maintain performance.

Structure of Hash Tables

A **hash table** is a data structure designed to store data in the form of **key-value pairs**. Unlike arrays or linked lists where searching for an element may require scanning through multiple entries, hash tables allow **direct access** by computing the index of a key using a hash function. This structural organization is what makes them so efficient.

Arrangement of Key-Value Pairs

In a hash table, each location (often called a *bucket* or *slot*) can hold a pair of data:

Key: A unique identifier such as an ID number, username, or word.

Value: The actual information associated with the key, such as a student's grade, account balance, or dictionary meaning:

Key (Student ID)	Value (Grade)
101	A
102	B+
103	A-

Here, the student IDs are the keys, and the grades are the values.

Indexing Process in Hash Tables

The **hash function** determines where in the table a key-value pair is stored. The steps for index processing are as follows:

- A key is passed to the hash function.
- The hash function generates a hash code (an integer).
- This hash code is mapped to a valid index within the table's size.
- The key-value pair is stored at that index.

Example: Suppose the key is "`Alice`", the table size is 10, and the hash function computes the value 4.

The pair ("`Alice`", "`Grade A`") is stored at index 4 in the table. Later, when "`Alice`" is searched, the same hash function recomputes the index 4. The value can then be retrieved directly.

Hence, the process eliminates the need for sequential searching.

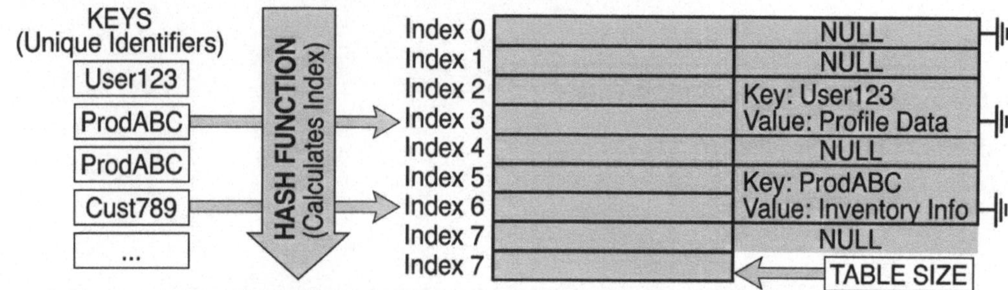

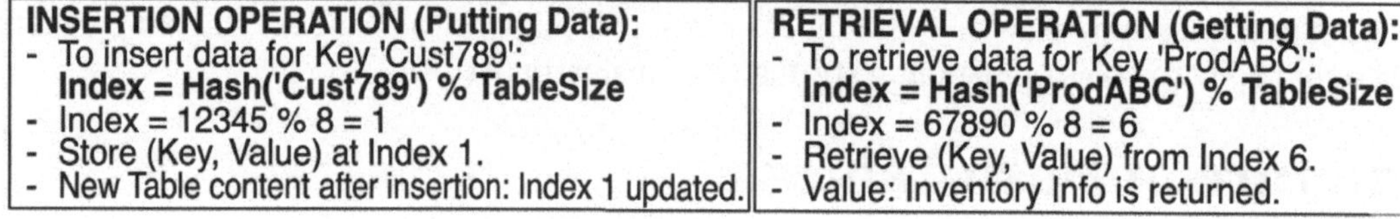

***Figure 5.1:** Indexing in a Hash Table*

Average-Case Constant-Time Performance

The true strength of hash tables lies in their **O(1) average time complexity** for insertion, deletion, and lookup.

Insertion: Directly map the key to an index and place the value.

Lookup: Pass the key to the hash function and jump to the correct index.

Deletion: Locate the key using the hash function and remove it.

This constant-time efficiency makes hash tables ideal for real-world applications such as **database indexing, symbol tables in compilers, and caching mechanisms.**

Note: *Although average performance is* `O(1)`, *collisions (when two keys map to the same index) may impact performance. Handling collisions effectively is covered in the next section.*

Collision Handling

Even with a well-designed hash function, it is inevitable that two different keys may map to the same index in a hash table. This situation is called a **collision**. Since collisions cannot be avoided completely, hash tables rely on systematic strategies to manage them. Effective collision handling ensures that the performance advantage of constant-time operations is preserved even when the table becomes crowded. Two widely used approaches to handle collisions are **chaining** and **open addressing, which are explained in this section**.

Chaining

Chaining is one of the simplest and most intuitive methods of handling collisions. Instead of forcing each table slot to store a single key-value pair, every slot maintains a small linked structure, which can be a **linked list** or **dynamic container**. When multiple keys hash to the same index, they are appended to the list at that slot.

Working Principle

Chaining resolves collisions by allowing each slot in the hash table to store a collection of entries rather than just one. Typically, this collection is implemented as a **linked list** or a **dynamic container** like a vector or list in modern languages. When two or more keys map to the same index:

The hash function is applied to each key.

If multiple keys result in the same index, all of them are inserted into the linked list (or container) at that index.

During search, the hash function determines the index, and then the corresponding list is scanned to find the required key-value pair.

Example: Suppose we are storing student IDs with grades in a hash table of size 5. The key indices will look like:

Key 101 → A → Index 1

Key 111 → B → Index 1

Both 101 and 111 map to index 1. Instead of overwriting, index 1 holds a chain: [(101, A) → (111, B)].

Strengths and Limitations

Like any technique, chaining has its own set of benefits and drawbacks. Understanding these helps in deciding when chaining is the right strategy for handling collisions and when other methods may be more suitable.

Strengths:

- Very simple and intuitive to implement.
- Can handle multiple collisions gracefully.
- The load factor (ratio of stored elements to table size) can exceed 1, as each slot can hold multiple items.
- Performance remains good if the hash function distributes keys evenly.

Limitations:

- Requires extra memory for pointers in linked lists.
- In the worst case (when all keys map to the same index), search time degrades to `O(n)`.
- Cache performance may be lower compared to open addressing, as linked lists scatter memory access.

C++ Example (Chaining Using `std::list`):

```
#include <iostream>
#include <list>
#include <vector>
using namespace std;

class HashTable {
    int size;
    vector<list<pair<int, string>>> table; // index -> list of key-value pairs
public:
    HashTable(int s) : size(s), table(s) {}

    int hashFunction(int key) {
        return key % size;
    }
    void insert(int key, string value) {
        int index = hashFunction(key);
        table[index].push_back({key, value});
    }
    string search(int key) {
        int index = hashFunction(key);
        for (auto &p : table[index]) {
            if (p.first == key) return p.second;
        }
        return "Not Found";
    }
};

int main() {
    HashTable ht(5);
    ht.insert(101, "A");
    ht.insert(111, "B");
    cout << ht.search(101) << endl;  // Output: A
    cout << ht.search(111) << endl;  // Output: B
}
```

Python Example (Chaining Using Lists):

```
class HashTable:
    def __init__(self, size):
        self.size = size
        self.table = [[] for _ in range(size)]

    def hash_function(self, key):
        return key % self.size

    def insert(self, key, value):
        index = self.hash_function(key)
        self.table[index].append((key, value))

    def search(self, key):
        index = self.hash_function(key)
        for k, v in self.table[index]:
            if k == key:
                return v
```

```
        return "Not Found"

ht = HashTable(5)
ht.insert(101, "A")
ht.insert(111, "B")
print(ht.search(101))  # Output: A
print(ht.search(111))  # Output: B
```

Chaining allows multiple keys to map to the same index without overwriting, by storing them in a linked list (C++) or list of tuples (Python). Both versions clearly show how hash tables can store and retrieve key-value pairs efficiently, even when collisions occur.

Open Addressing

In open addressing, each slot in the hash table can hold **only one key-value pair**. When a collision occurs, the algorithm searches for the next available slot using a probing strategy. Unlike chaining, no separate linked structure is used; everything is stored within the table itself. The general process is laid out in the following steps:

Compute the index using the hash function.

- If the slot is free → Insert the key-value pair.
- If the slot is occupied → Use a probing method to find the next available slot.
- The main strategies for open addressing are **linear probing, quadratic probing, and double hashing**. We have also explained them in detail.

Linear Probing

Linear probing resolves collisions by checking the next slots **sequentially** until an empty one is found. If a key collides at index i, the algorithm checks i+1, i+2, and so on (wrapping around the table), until a free slot is located.

Example:

Table Size = 5

Insert keys 10, 15, 20.

Hash Function: key % 5

10 % 5 = 0 → Index 0 → Empty → Insert 10

15 % 5 = 0 → Index 0 → Occupied → Check 1 → Insert 15

20 % 5 = 0 → Index 0 → Occupied → Check 1 → Occupied → Check 2 → Insert 20

C++ Code Example:

```
#include <iostream>
using namespace std;

class HashTable {
    int size;
    int* table;

public:
    HashTable(int n) {
        size = n;
        table = new int[size];
        for (int i = 0; i < size; i++) table[i] = -1; // -1 means empty
```

```
    }
    int hashFunction(int key) { return key % size; }
    void insert(int key) {
        int index = hashFunction(key);
        int start = index;
        while (table[index] != -1) {
            index = (index + 1) % size; // linear probing
            if (index == start) return; // table full
        }
        table[index] = key;
    }
    void display() {
        for (int i = 0; i < size; i++)
            cout << i << " --> " << table[i] << endl;
    }
};
int main() {
    HashTable ht(5);
    ht.insert(10);
    ht.insert(15);
    ht.insert(20);
    ht.insert(7);
    ht.display();
}
```

Collisions are resolved by checking **next sequential slots**. If the table is full, the insertion stops. This might look simple and cache-friendly, but can result in **primary clustering** (groups of filled slots).

Python Code:

```
class HashTable:
    def __init__(self, size):
        self.size = size
        self.table = [-1] * size  # -1 indicates empty slot
    def hash_function(self, key):
        return key % self.size
    def insert(self, key):
        index = self.hash_function(key)
        start = index
        while self.table[index] != -1:
            index = (index + 1) % self.size  # move sequentially
            if index == start:  # table full
                return
        self.table[index] = key
    def display(self):
        for i, val in enumerate(self.table):
            print(i, "-->", val)
# Example
ht = HashTable(5)
ht.insert(10)
ht.insert(15)
```

```
ht.insert(20)
ht.insert(7)
ht.display()
```

The preceding illustration checks the next sequential slot if a collision occurs. This looks rather simple, but can form clusters if many keys collide.

Quadratic Probing

Quadratic probing reduces clustering by using **quadratic jumps,** instead of sequential slots.

```
index = (hash(key) + i^2) % table_size
```

If a collision occurs, the next probe moves 1^2, 2^2, 3^2, ... steps ahead rather than 1 by 1.

Example:

Table Size = 7

Keys 10, 17, 24

Hash Function: **`key % 7 → All map to 3`**.

Probing Sequence: 3, 4, 7 (wraps to 0), 12 (wraps to 5), and so on

C++ Code Example:

```
#include <iostream>
using namespace std;

class HashTable {
    int size;
    int* table;

public:
    HashTable(int n) {
        size = n;
        table = new int[size];
        for (int i = 0; i < size; i++) table[i] = -1;
    }

    int hashFunction(int key) { return key % size; }

    void insert(int key) {
        int index = hashFunction(key);
        int i = 0;
        while (table[(index + i*i) % size] != -1) i++;
        table[(index + i*i) % size] = key;
    }

    void display() {
        for (int i = 0; i < size; i++)
            cout << i << " --> " << table[i] << endl;
    }
};

int main() {
    HashTable ht(7);
    ht.insert(10);
    ht.insert(17);
    ht.insert(24);
    ht.display();
}
```

Uses quadratic steps to reduce clusters still keeps all elements inside the table, no external storage. It also avoids consecutive filled slots forming large clusters like in linear probing.

Python Code:

```
class HashTable:
    def __init__(self, size):
        self.size = size
        self.table = [-1] * size

    def hash_function(self, key):
        return key % self.size

    def insert(self, key):
        index = self.hash_function(key)
        i = 0
        while self.table[(index + i*i) % self.size] != -1:
            i += 1
        self.table[(index + i*i) % self.size] = key

    def display(self):
        for i, val in enumerate(self.table):
            print(i, "-->", val)

# Example
ht = HashTable(7)
ht.insert(10)
ht.insert(17)
ht.insert(24)
ht.display()
```

This example uses quadratic jumps (i^2) to reduce clustering. It is better than linear probing for crowded tables.

Double Hashing

Double hashing uses a **second hash function** to calculate step size for probing.

The probing formula is:

`index = (hash1(key) + i * hash2(key)) % table_size`

This ensures better distribution, and reduces clustering more effectively than linear or quadratic probing.

Example:

Table Size = 7

Keys 10, 17, 24

`hash1(key) = key % 7, hash2(key) = 5 - (key % 5)`

If a collision occurs, move i * hash2(key) steps ahead.

C++ Code Example:

```
#include <iostream>
using namespace std;

class HashTable {
    int size;
```

```
    int* table;

public:
    HashTable(int n) {
        size = n;
        table = new int[size];
        for(int i=0;i<size;i++) table[i]=-1;
    }

    int hash1(int key) { return key % size; }
    int hash2(int key) { return 5 - (key % 5); } // step size

    void insert(int key){
        int i=0;
        int index;
        while(true){
            index = (hash1(key) + i*hash2(key)) % size;
            if(table[index]==-1){
                table[index] = key;
                break;
            }
            i++;
        }
    }
    void display(){
        for(int i=0;i<size;i++)
            cout << i << " --> " << table[i] << endl;
    }
};

int main(){
    HashTable ht(7);
    ht.insert(10);
    ht.insert(17);
    ht.insert(24);
    ht.display();
}
```

This illustration uses **two hash functions**: one for index, and the other for step size. Therefore, the function reduces both primary and secondary clustering, and requires two good hash functions for even distribution.

Python Code:

```
class HashTable:
    def __init__(self, size):
        self.size = size
        self.table = [-1] * size

    def hash1(self, key):
        return key % self.size

    def hash2(self, key):
        return 5 - (key % 5)  # step size

    def insert(self, key):
        i = 0
```

```
        while True:
            index = (self.hash1(key) + i * self.hash2(key)) % self.size
            if self.table[index] == -1:
                self.table[index] = key
                break
            i += 1

    def display(self):
        for i, val in enumerate(self.table):
            print(i, "-->", val)

# Example
ht = HashTable(7)
ht.insert(10)
ht.insert(17)
ht.insert(24)
ht.display()
```

This example uses a second hash function to calculate the probing step size. It reduces both primary and secondary clustering, and also requires two hash functions for good distribution.

Comparative Analysis of Probing Strategies

When using **open addressing** in hash tables, collisions are resolved by probing for the next available slot. The main strategies are **linear probing**, **quadratic probing**, and **double hashing**. Each has distinct advantages and limitations.

Strategy	Simplicity	Clustering Risk	Performance under high load	Notes
Linear Probing	Very easy	High (primary)	Degrades quickly	Best for small load factors
Quadratic Probing	Moderate	Medium (secondary)	Better than linear	Requires careful table sizing
Double Hashing	Moderate	Low	Remains efficient	Needs two hash functions

Table 5.1: *Comparative Analysis of Probing Strategies*

- **Linear probing** is simple but suffers from long clusters.
- **Quadratic probing** reduces clustering, but may leave some slots unreachable if table size is poorly chosen.
- **Double hashing** distributes keys more uniformly, and also offers the best performance for high load factors.

Therefore, choosing the right strategy depends on **load factor, table size, and the expected number of insertions**.

Load Factor and Rehashing

Hash tables work best when they are not too crowded. The **load factor** measures how full a table is, and as it increases, collisions become more frequent. To maintain fast and efficient operations, tables are sometimes **resized and rehashed**, while redistributing the keys to a larger table. Therefore, this section explores how load factor affects performance, and how rehashing keeps hash tables efficient.

Load Factor and Its Effect on Performance

The **load factor** measures how full a hash table is, and is calculated as:

Load Factor = Number of Elements

Table Size

A low load factor means that there are plenty of empty slots. This leads to faster insertions, searches, and deletions, as collisions are less frequent. As the load factor increases, more collisions occur, which can slow down operations.

In chaining, a high load factor results in longer linked lists at each index, which increases search time.

In open addressing, a high load factor means more probing steps are required to find an empty slot, which also increases insertion and lookup time.

Thus, maintaining a **load factor below 0.7 to 0.75** generally ensures efficient performance, while balancing memory usage and speed.

Example:

`Table Size = 10, Elements Inserted = 5 → Load Factor = 0.5 → Few Collisions → Fast Operations.`

`Table Size = 10, Elements Inserted = 9 → Load Factor = 0.9 → More Collisions → Slower Operations.`

Hence, this shows why monitoring the load factor is crucial for maintaining efficient hash table performance.

Rehashing and Resizing Strategy

When a hash table becomes too full, collisions increase, which slows down insertions and lookups. To maintain efficiency, the table is **resized and rehashed**. This process is known as **rehashing**.

How Rehashing Works:

- **Detect Threshold Breach**: When the load factor exceeds a pre-defined limit (commonly 0.7)
- **Create a New Table**: Usually double the original size (ideally a prime number for better distribution)
- **Recompute Hash Indices**: Each key is hashed according to the new table size.
- **Insert the Existing Elements**: All elements from the old table are reinserted into the new table.

Why Rehashing Matters:

- Keeps the **load factor under control,** and prevents excessive collisions.
- Ensures **average-case constant-time performance** for insertions and searches.
- Helps maintain **balanced distribution** of keys, thereby reducing clustering in open addressing and long chains in chaining.

Example in Python:

```
class HashTable:
    def __init__(self, size):
        self.size = size
        self.table = [[] for _ in range(size)]
        self.num_elements = 0
```

```
    def hash_function(self, key):
        return key % self.size

    def insert(self, key, value):
        if (self.num_elements + 1) / self.size > 0.7:
            self.rehash()
        index = self.hash_function(key)
        self.table[index].append((key, value))
        self.num_elements += 1

    def rehash(self):
        old_table = self.table
        self.size = self.size * 2 + 1
        self.table = [[] for _ in range(self.size)]
        self.num_elements = 0
        for chain in old_table:
            for key, value in chain:
                self.insert(key, value)
        print(f"Rehashing done. New table size: {self.size}")

    def display(self):
        for i, chain in enumerate(self.table):
            print(i, "-->", chain)

# Usage
ht = HashTable(3)
ht.insert(10, "A")
ht.insert(11, "B")
ht.insert(12, "C")  # triggers rehash
ht.insert(13, "D")
ht.display()
```

Initially, the table has three slots.

- Inserting three elements exceeds the load factor threshold (>0.7) and triggers rehashing.
- Table size increases, and all elements are reinserted based on the updated hash function.

Therefore, this keeps operations efficient even as more elements are added.

Example in C++:

```
#include <iostream>
#include <list>
#include <vector>
using namespace std;

class HashTable {
    int size;
    int numElements;
    vector<list<pair<int, string>>> table;

public:
    HashTable(int s) : size(s), numElements(0), table(s) {}

    int hashFunction(int key) { return key % size; }

    void insert(int key, string value) {
        double loadFactor = (double)(numElements + 1) / size;
        if (loadFactor > 0.7) rehash();
```

```
        int index = hashFunction(key);
        table[index].push_back({key, value});
        numElements++;
    }

    void rehash() {
        vector<list<pair<int, string>>> oldTable = table;
        size = size * 2 + 1; // new size
        table.clear();
        table.resize(size);
        numElements = 0;

        for (auto &chain : oldTable)
            for (auto &p : chain)
                insert(p.first, p.second);

        cout << "Rehashing done. New table size: " << size << endl;
    }

    void display() {
        for (int i = 0; i < size; i++) {
            cout << i << " --> ";
            for (auto &p : table[i])
                cout << "(" << p.first << "," << p.second << ") ";
            cout << endl;
        }
    }
};

int main() {
    HashTable ht(3);
    ht.insert(10, "A");
    ht.insert(11, "B");
    ht.insert(12, "C");  // triggers rehash
    ht.insert(13, "D");
    ht.display();
}
```

This works the same as the Python version.

It resizes the table and reinserts elements when the load factor exceeds the threshold.

Therefore, it maintains **efficient insert and search operations**.

Implementation Considerations

Threshold Selection: Choose a load factor limit (commonly 0.7).

Table Size: Prefer prime numbers for table sizes to reduce clustering.

Automatic Resizing: Most high-level languages handle this automatically (**`std::unordered_map`** in C++ and **`dict`** in Python).

Chaining vs. Open Addressing: Both benefit from rehashing but in different ways, which are:

Chaining: Shortens chains at each index

Open Addressing: Reduces probe sequences, minimizing clustering

C++ Example: Rehashing with Chaining

```
#include <iostream>
```

```
#include <list>
#include <vector>
using namespace std;

class HashTable {
    int size;
    int numElements;
    vector<list<pair<int, string>>> table;

public:
    HashTable(int s) : size(s), numElements(0), table(s) {}

    int hashFunction(int key) { return key % size; }

    void insert(int key, string value) {
        double loadFactor = (double)(numElements + 1) / size;
        if (loadFactor > 0.7) {
            rehash();
        }
        int index = hashFunction(key);
        table[index].push_back({key, value});
        numElements++;
    }

    void rehash() {
        vector<list<pair<int, string>>> oldTable = table;
        size = size * 2 + 1;  // new size (prefer prime)
        table.clear();
        table.resize(size);
        numElements = 0;

        for (auto &chain : oldTable) {
            for (auto &p : chain) {
                insert(p.first, p.second);  // reinsert existing elements
            }
        }
        cout << "Rehashing done. New table size: " << size << endl;
    }

    void display() {
        for (int i = 0; i < size; i++) {
            cout << i << " --> ";
            for (auto &p : table[i]) {
                cout << "(" << p.first << "," << p.second << ") ";
            }
            cout << endl;
        }
    }
};

int main() {
    HashTable ht(3);
    ht.insert(10, "A");
    ht.insert(11, "B");
    ht.insert(12, "C");  // triggers rehash
    ht.insert(13, "D");
    ht.display();
}
```

This illustration starts with a table of size 3.

Inserting three elements triggers load factor > 0.7; thereafter, rehashing occurs.
New Table Size = 2*3 + 1 = 7.

All elements are reinserted into the new table according to the updated hash function.

Python Example: Rehashing with Chaining

```
class HashTable:
    def __init__(self, size):
        self.size = size
        self.table = [[] for _ in range(size)]
        self.num_elements = 0

    def hash_function(self, key):
        return key % self.size

    def insert(self, key, value):
        # Check load factor
        if (self.num_elements + 1) / self.size > 0.7:
            self.rehash()

        index = self.hash_function(key)
        self.table[index].append((key, value))
        self.num_elements += 1

    def rehash(self):
        old_table = self.table
        self.size = self.size * 2 + 1  # new size (prime recommended)
        self.table = [[] for _ in range(self.size)]
        self.num_elements = 0

        for chain in old_table:
            for key, value in chain:
                self.insert(key, value)
        print(f"Rehashing done. New table size: {self.size}")

    def display(self):
        for i, chain in enumerate(self.table):
            print(i, "-->", chain)
V# Example Usage
ht = HashTable(3)
ht.insert(10, "A")
ht.insert(11, "B")
ht.insert(12, "C")  # triggers rehash
ht.insert(13, "D")
ht.display()
```

This example operates on the same logic as C++; the table resizes when load factor exceeds 0.

Existing keys are **reinserted** to the new table.

Thus, it ensures **average constant-time performance** even as the table grows.

Implementations in C++ STL and Python

Hash tables are widely used in modern programming; both C++ and Python provide built-in implementations that simplify coding. Moreover, these structures allow **efficient key-value storage and retrieval** without having to manually handle collisions or rehashing.

Unordered Maps in C++ ST

C++ provides the **unordered_map** container as a built-in implementation of a hash table. It allows you to **store and retrieve key-value pairs efficiently** without manually handling collisions or resizing. Unlike map, which stores elements in a sorted order using a balanced tree, **unordered_map offers average constant-time access**, which makes it ideal for situations where speed matters more than ordering.

Features and Advantages

The key advantages and features of unordered maps include:

- **Fast Access:** Average-case O(1) time for insertions, searches, and deletions
- **Automatic Handling of Collisions and Resizing:** The container grows dynamically and rehashes internally.
- **Flexible Key Types:** Keys can be integers, strings, or other hashable types.
- **Convenient Functions:** Includes **insert()**, **erase()**, **find()**, and iterators for easy manipulation
- **Dynamic Size:** There is no need to specify the final size in advance, as it grows automatically.

Syntax and Usage Examples

Using **unordered_map** is rather straightforward as you can insert, access, and iterate elements with simple syntax. The following examples reiterate this fact:

C++ Example:

```
#include <iostream>
#include <unordered_map>
using namespace std;

int main() {
    unordered_map<int, string> umap;

    // Insert elements
    umap[101] = "Alice";
    umap[102] = "Bob";
    umap.insert({103, "Charlie"});

    // Access element
    cout << "Key 102 maps to " << umap[102] << endl;

    // Iterate through elements
    for (auto &pair : umap) {
        cout << pair.first << " -> " << pair.second << endl;
    }

    // Check existence
    if (umap.find(101) != umap.end())
        cout << "Key 101 exists" << endl;
}
```

As is seen in this example:

- The **[]** operator inserts or updates elements.
- **insert()** adds a new key-value pair if it does not exist.
- **find()** checks if a key exists.

Here, the iteration order is not sorted, and instead focuses on speed.

Python Example:

```
# Create a dictionary
d = {101: "Alice", 102: "Bob"}

# Insert elements
d[103] = "Charlie"

# Access element
print("Key 102 maps to", d[102])

# Iterate through elements
for key, value in d.items():
    print(key, "->", value)

# Check existence
if 101 in d:
    print("Key 101 exists")
```

Here, we can see that:

- The dictionary keys must be hashable.
- Average insertion, lookup, and deletion are very fast.

Therefore, the iteration order is arbitrary, which is similar to **`unordered_map`**.

Complexity Analysis

Understanding time complexity helps in selecting hash-based containers for different scenarios.

Operation	C++ `unordered_map`	Python dict
Insert	`O(1)` average, `O(n)` worst	`O(1)` average, `O(n)` worst
Search	`O(1)` average, `O(n)` worst	`O(1)` average, `O(n)` worst
Delete	`O(1)` average, `O(n)` worst	`O(1)` average, `O(n)` worst

Table 5.2: *Complexity Analysis*

Dictionaries in Python

Python dictionaries provide a high-level, built-in hash table implementation. They allow **fast key-value mapping** without worrying about collisions or resizing. Dictionaries are versatile, widely used for counting, caching, and fast lookups in real-world applications.

Features and Advantages

The key features and advantages of Python dictionaries include:

- **Fast Access**: Average-case O(1) time for insert, search, and delete operations.
- **Automatic Handling**: Hashing, collision resolution, and resizing are handled internally.
- **Dynamic Sizing**: There is no need to predefine size, as the dictionary grows automatically.
- **Flexible Keys**: Keys must be hashable (immutable types like int, string, tuple).
- **Convenient Operations**: Supports in operator, **`items()`**, **`keys()`**, **`values()`**, and comprehensions.

Syntax and Usage Examples

Dictionaries provide an intuitive way to store and access key-value pairs. This is apparent in the following examples:

Python Example:

```
# Create a dictionary
d = {101: "Alice", 102: "Bob"}

# Insert elements
d[103] = "Charlie"

# Access element
print("Key 102 maps to", d[102])

# Update element
d[101] = "Alicia"

# Iterate through dictionary
for key, value in d.items():
    print(key, "->", value)

# Check if a key exists
if 101 in d:
    print("Key 101 exists")
```

- Keys are unique because values can be of any type.
- Average insert, search, and delete are extremely fast here.
- Dictionaries can handle rehashing internally when the load factor increases.
- The iteration order in Python 3.7+ is the insertion order, but not sorted by key.

C++ Comparison Example:

```
#include <unordered_map>
#include <iostream>
using namespace std;

int main() {
    unordered_map<int, string> umap;
    umap[101] = "Alice";
    umap[102] = "Bob";

    cout << "Key 101 maps to " << umap[101] << endl;

    for (auto &p : umap)
        cout << p.first << " -> " << p.second << endl;
}
```

We can observe that Python dictionaries behave similarly to **`unordered_map`** in C++ when it comes to efficiency, but Python syntax is simpler and far more dynamic.

Comparison Analysis

Knowing that the time complexity helps in selecting dictionaries for large-scale applications, this is articulated in the table here:

Operation	Python dict	C++ unordered_map
Insert	O(1) average, O(n) worst	O(1) average, O(n) worst
Search	O(1) average, O(n) worst	O(1) average, O(n) worst
Delete	O(1) average, O(n) worst	O(1) average, O(n) worst

Table 5.3: *Comparison Analysis*

Applications of Hash Tables

Hash tables are highly versatile due to their **fast key-value lookup** capabilities. They are widely used in real-world systems, algorithms, and programming challenges. Here are some of the most common applications of hash tables:

Frequency Counting

Hash tables make it easy to **count occurrences of elements** such as words, characters, or numbers. You can see this factor in the examples here:

C++ Example:

```
#include <iostream>
#include <unordered_map>
using namespace std;

int main() {
    string text = "hello world hello";
    unordered_map<string, int> freq;

    for (int i = 0; i < text.size(); i++) {
        if (text[i] != ' ') {
            string ch(1, text[i]);
            freq[ch]++;
        }
    }

    for (auto &p : freq) {
        cout << p.first << " : " << p.second << endl;
    }
}
```

Python Example:

```
text = "hello world hello"
freq = {}

for ch in text:
    if ch != ' ':
        freq[ch] = freq.get(ch, 0) + 1

for key, value in freq.items():
    print(key, ":", value)
```

Each unique element is stored as a key, and its count is the value. Therefore, the average insertion and lookup remain O(1), which makes this approach highly efficient.

Duplicate Detection

Hash tables can quickly check for **duplicate elements** in datasets. This can be observed in the following illustrations:

C++ Example:

```
#include <iostream>
#include <unordered_map>
#include <vector>
using namespace std;

int main() {
    vector<int> nums = {1, 2, 3, 2, 4, 1};
    unordered_map<int, bool> seen;

    for (int num : nums) {
        if (seen[num])
            cout << "Duplicate: " << num << endl;
        else
            seen[num] = true;
    }
}
```

Python Example:

```
nums = [1, 2, 3, 2, 4, 1]
seen = {}

for num in nums:
    if num in seen:
        print("Duplicate:", num)
    else:
        seen[num] = True
```

Thus, by storing each element as a key, duplicates can be detected in **linear time**.

Caching Techniques

Hash tables are widely used in **caching systems**, where frequently accessed data is stored for faster retrieval. They are a key component in **memoization for algorithms** and **LRU caches** in operating systems or web applications.

C++ Example:

```
#include <iostream>
#include <unordered_map>
using namespace std;

unordered_map<int, int> cache;

int fibonacci(int n) {
    if (cache.find(n) != cache.end())
        return cache[n];
    if (n <= 1)
        return n;
    cache[n] = fibonacci(n-1) + fibonacci(n-2);
    return cache[n];
```

```
}

int main() {
    cout << fibonacci(10) << endl;  // Output: 55
}
```

Python Example:

```
cache = {}

def fibonacci(n):
    if n in cache:
        return cache[n]
    if n <= 1:
        return n
    cache[n] = fibonacci(n-1) + fibonacci(n-2)
    return cache[n]

print(fibonacci(10))  # Output: 55
```

Therefore, hash tables store intermediate results for fast retrieval, which avoids repeated computation.

User Data Management

Hash tables are commonly used in **databases and applications** to manage user profiles efficiently.

Key: User ID or unique identifier

Value: User data (name, email, preferences)

C++ Example:

```
#include <iostream>
#include <unordered_map>
#include <string>
using namespace std;

struct User {
    string name;
    string email;
};

int main() {
    unordered_map<int, User> users;
    users[101] = {"Alice", "alice@example.com"};
    users[102] = {"Bob", "bob@example.com"};

    cout << users[101].email << endl;  // Output: alice@example.com
}
```

Python Example:

```
users = {
    101: {"name": "Alice", "email": "alice@example.com"},
    102: {"name": "Bob", "email": "bob@example.com"}
}

# Access a user profile
user_id = 101
print(users[user_id]["email"])  # Output: alice@example.com
```

We can see that hash tables allow **instant access** to user information. Therefore, they are the most efficient choice for login systems, profile lookups, and personalization features.

Real-World Systems

Hash tables support many critical applications in industry, such as:

- **Databases:** You can quickly access rows using primary keys.
- **Compilers:** Symbol tables map variable names to memory addresses or types.
- **Web Caching:** Hash tables can be used to store frequently requested URLs or API responses for fast retrieval.
- **Spell Checkers / Dictionaries:** Fast word lookup for validation or auto-completion.

Hash tables provide **fast and reliable access** in caching, user management, and system-level applications. Both C++ **`unordered_map`** and Python **`dict`** simplify implementation, while maintaining high performance. Therefore, proper hash function design and collision management ensure consistent efficiency in production systems.

Limitations and Pitfalls

While hash tables are highly efficient, they are **not a one-size-fits-all solution**. Thus, understanding their limitations is essential for designing robust and scalable applications.

Situations Where Hash Tables are Less Effective

Hash tables are not ideal when data needs to be ordered or datasets are very small. Here are some more situations where they are less effective:

- **Ordered Data Requirements:** Hash tables do not maintain sorted order. For instance, if you need elements in ascending order, a tree-based map will be better.
- **Small Datasets:** For very small datasets, linear search or arrays can sometimes be faster due to lower overhead.
- **Memory-Sensitive Systems:** Hash tables require extra memory for hashing structures, which may be inefficient in constrained environments.

Memory Overhead Issues

Extra memory usage can become significant due to table size and collision management.

Hash tables allocate extra space to reduce collisions, which increases **memory usage** compared to arrays or linked lists. Moreover, excessive resizing or a large initial table size can lead to **wasted memory**.

To better understand the impact of hash table allocation on memory consumption, consider the following example, where a dictionary is created with a large number of sparsely used keys.

```
# Large dictionary with mostly empty keys
sparse_dict = {i: None for i in range(1000000)}  # consumes significant memory
```

Problems with Weak Hash Functions

- Poorly designed hash functions can cause clustering, which eventually slows down operations.
- Poorly designed hash functions can cause **clustering**, where many keys map to the same index.

Therefore, weak hash functions can lead to degraded performance (`O(n)` operations, instead of `O(1)` average).

C++ Example: Poor Hash Function

```
#include <unordered_map>
#include <iostream>
using namespace std;

struct PoorHash {
    size_t operator()(int key) const {
        return 0; // All keys map to same bucket → worst-case
    }
};

int main() {
    unordered_map<int, string, PoorHash> umap;
    umap[1] = "A";
    umap[2] = "B";

    // Lookup becomes O(n) instead of O(1)
    cout << umap[1] << endl;
}
```

In this example, all keys end up in a single bucket, which will result in slow lookups and insertions.

Clustering in Open Addressing

Consecutive filled slots in open addressing can increase probe times, and also reduce efficiency.

In open addressing schemes, all keys are stored directly within the hash table array. Thus, whenever a collision occurs, the algorithm searches for the next available slot using a probing strategy such as linear probing, quadratic probing, or double hashing.

A common issue in this method is **clustering**, where consecutive slots become filled with keys. This creates groups of occupied slots that increase the number of probes required for insertion, search, or deletion. As a result, the performance **may degrade from average `O(1)`** to **`O(n)`** in extreme cases.

Example Concept: In linear probing, if three consecutive slots are filled, any new key colliding with this cluster must probe through all three slots before finding an empty one. This effect is called **primary clustering**, and it can be mitigated using **quadratic probing** or **double hashing**. Clustering increases probe sequences, therefore, choosing an appropriate probing strategy, and maintaining a low load factor are crucial considerations to ensure consistent performance.

Debugging Challenges

Errors in hashing or collisions can be subtle and hard to detect in large datasets. Hash tables are extremely efficient, but debugging them can be tricky due to their internal operations. Common challenges include:

- **Collision Handling Errors:** Mistakes in chaining or probing logic can cause lost or overwritten data.
- **Weak Hash Functions:** Poorly designed functions may cause many keys to collide, leading to unexpected behavior.
- **Key Handling Issues:** Using mutable objects as keys in Python, or inconsistent hashing in C++, can introduce subtle bugs.

- **Resizing and Rehashing Errors:** Improper rehashing during table growth can result in lost keys or lookup failures.

Example Concept:

- In Python, using a list as a dictionary key will raise a **TypeError** because lists are mutable and not hashable.
- In C++, overriding the hash function incorrectly in a custom key type can make **unordered_map** behave unpredictably.

Therefore, meticulously designing hash functions, key types, and collision resolution strategies is necessary to ensure reliability, and also make debugging easier.

Interview Problems

Hash tables are commonly used to solve popular interview problems efficiently. The following are some standard problems, along with example implementations in C++ and Python:

Two-Sum Problem

Problem: Given an array of integers, find two numbers that add up to a target sum.

C++ Code:

```
#include <iostream>
#include <unordered_map>
#include <vector>
using namespace std;

vector<int> twoSum(vector<int>& nums, int target) {
    unordered_map<int, int> hash;
    for (int i = 0; i < nums.size(); i++) {
        int complement = target - nums[i];
        if (hash.find(complement) != hash.end())
            return {hash[complement], i};
        hash[nums[i]] = i;
    }
    return {};
}

int main() {
    vector<int> nums = {2, 7, 11, 15};
    int target = 9;
    vector<int> result = twoSum(nums, target);
    cout << result[0] << ", " << result[1] << endl;  // Output: 0, 1
}
```

Python Code:

```
def two_sum(nums, target):
    hash_map = {}
    for i, num in enumerate(nums):
        complement = target - num
        if complement in hash_map:
            return [hash_map[complement], i]
        hash_map[num] = i
    return []
```

```
nums = [2, 7, 11, 15]
target = 9
print(two_sum(nums, target))  # Output: [0, 1]
```

The hash table stores numbers as keys and their indices as values. Therefore, the lookup for the complement is **O(1)** on average, and results in linear-time complexity.

Grouping Anagrams

Problem: Group words that are anagrams of each other.

C++ Code:

```
#include <iostream>
#include <vector>
#include <unordered_map>
#include <algorithm>
using namespace std;

vector<vector<string>> groupAnagrams(vector<string>& strs) {
    unordered_map<string, vector<string>> hash;
    for (auto &s : strs) {
        string key = s;
        sort(key.begin(), key.end());
        hash[key].push_back(s);
    }

    vector<vector<string>> result;
    for (auto &p : hash)
        result.push_back(p.second);
    return result;
}

int main() {
    vector<string> strs = {"eat", "tea", "tan", "ate", "nat", "bat"};
    auto groups = groupAnagrams(strs);
    for (auto &group : groups) {
        for (auto &word : group)
            cout << word << " ";
        cout << endl;
    }
}
```

Python Code:

```
from collections import defaultdict

def group_anagrams(strs):
    hash_map = defaultdict(list)
    for s in strs:
        key = "".join(sorted(s))
        hash_map[key].append(s)
    return list(hash_map.values())

strs = ["eat", "tea", "tan", "ate", "nat", "bat"]
groups = group_anagrams(strs)
for group in groups:
    print(group)
```

Sorting each word provides a unique key for anagrams. Therefore, words with the same key are grouped together efficiently using a hash table.

Longest Substring without Repeating Characters

Problem: Find the length of the longest substring without repeating characters.

C++ Code:

```
#include <iostream>
#include <unordered_map>
#include <string>
using namespace std;

int lengthOfLongestSubstring(string s) {
    unordered_map<char, int> hash;
    int left = 0, max_len = 0;
    for (int right = 0; right < s.size(); right++) {
        if (hash.find(s[right]) != hash.end())
            left = max(hash[s[right]] + 1, left);
        hash[s[right]] = right;
        max_len = max(max_len, right - left + 1);
    }
    return max_len;
}

int main() {
    string s = "abcabcbb";
    cout << lengthOfLongestSubstring(s) << endl;  // Output: 3
}
```

Python Code:

```
def length_of_longest_substring(s):
    hash_map = {}
    left = max_len = 0
    for right, char in enumerate(s):
        if char in hash_map:
            left = max(hash_map[char] + 1, left)
        hash_map[char] = right
        max_len = max(max_len, right - left + 1)
    return max_len

s = "abcabcbb"
print(length_of_longest_substring(s))  # Output: 3
```

The hash table tracks the most recent index of each character.

Therefore, the sliding window adjusts its left boundary whenever a duplicate character is encountered, while maintaining `O(n)` time complexity.

Additional Practice Problems

Now that we have seen key hash table problems with examples, it is your turn to **apply these concepts**! Try solving the following challenges on your own to strengthen your understanding and prepare for interviews:

- **Element Frequency Counter:** Given an array, count the frequency of each element using a hash table.
- **First Non-Repeating Character:** Find the first character in a string that appears only once.
- **Permutation Check:** Determine if two strings are permutations of each other.
- **LRU Cache Implementation:** Build a Least Recently Used (LRU) cache using a hash table and linked list.
- **Subarray with Zero Sum:** Detect whether a subarray with sum zero exists in an integer array.
- **Top K Frequent Elements:** Find the K most frequent elements in an array.
- **Two-Sum Variations:** Solve variations where multiple pairs can sum up to the target.

Tip:

- *Try solving each problem* ***first on paper*** *to plan the hash table structure.*
- *Then implement it in* ***C++ or Python****, while testing with different inputs.*
- *Think about* ***time and space complexity*** *for each solution.*

These exercises will reinforce your **concepts of key-value mapping, collision handling, and efficient lookups**. Hence, practicing them will give you the required confidence to tackle real-world coding challenges.

Conclusion

In this chapter, we explored the fundamentals of hash tables and unordered maps, and gained clarity on how key-value pairs can be stored and retrieved efficiently through hashing techniques. We also understood the role of hash functions, load factor, rehashing, and collision resolution methods such as chaining and open addressing, along with the practical advantages of using built-in implementations like C++ STL's `unordered_map` and Python's `dict`. The concepts were further reinforced through real-world applications such as frequency counting, duplicate detection, and caching, as well as interview-oriented problems like two-sum, grouping anagrams, and longest substring without repeating characters. These problems demonstrated the power of hashing in solving diverse computational challenges. With this strong foundation in hash-based structures, we are now ready to progress to *Chapter 6, Trees and Binary Search Trees*, where the focus will shift from flat key-value systems to hierarchical structures. The upcoming chapter will cover tree terminology, recursive definitions, traversal techniques, and operations on Binary Search Trees (BST), while also addressing practical applications like expression trees, directory management, and sorted data processing. Therefore, it will prepare us to handle more advanced data organization, besides implementing apt problem-solving strategies.

Points to Remember

- Hash tables store data in **key-value pairs**, which allows **average `O(1)` access**.
- A **good hash function** distributes keys uniformly and reduces collisions.
- **Chaining and open addressing** are the main techniques to handle collisions.
- **Load factor** affects performance. Therefore, rehashing is necessary when the table becomes too full.
- **C++ `unordered_map`** and **Python `dict`** provide ready-made implementations with built-in optimizations.
- Hash tables are widely used in **frequency counting, caching, user data management, and real-world systems**.

- Be aware of **limitations such as** memory overhead, clustering, weak hash functions, and debugging challenges.

Multiple Choice Questions

1. Which of the following is a primary collision handling method in hash tables?
   a. Linear Search
   b. Chaining
   c. Binary Search
   d. Stack
2. What is the average-case time complexity for searching an element in a hash table?
   a. `O(n)`
   b. `O(log n)`
   c. `O(1)`
   d. `O(n²)`
3. Which probing method is used to reduce primary clustering in open addressing?
   a. Linear Probing
   b. Quadratic Probing
   c. Chaining
   d. Random Probing
4. What happens when a hash table exceeds its load factor threshold?
   a. Data is deleted.
   b. Rehashing occurs.
   c. Hash table stops working.
   d. Duplicate keys are allowed.
5. In C++, which STL container provides a hash table implementation?
   a. `Map`
   b. `unordered_map`
   c. `Vector`
   d. `Set`
6. In Python, which data structure implements a hash table?
   a. `List`
   b. `Tuple`
   c. `Dict`
   d. `Array`
7. What is the key requirement for a hash function?
   a. It must always return 0.
   b. It should distribute keys uniformly.
   c. It must store keys in sorted order.
   d. It should only handle integers.

8. Which of the following operations may degrade to O(n) in a hash table?
   a. Insert in Empty Table
   b. Lookup with Clustering
   c. Delete in a Perfect Hash
   d. Traversal in a Linked List
9. In chaining, what is stored at each hash table index?
   a. A single key only
   b. A linked list of key-value pairs
   c. An array of integers
   d. A stack of keys
10. Why is load factor important in hash tables?
    a. It determines the size of key values.
    b. It affects performance and triggers rehashing.
    c. It sorts the table.
    d. It allows duplicate keys.
11. Which problem can be solved efficiently using hash tables?
    a. Binary Tree Traversal
    b. Two-Sum Problem
    c. Bubble Sort
    d. Depth-First Search
12. Which of the following is a limitation of hash tables?
    a. They are always sorted.
    b. They require large memory overhead.
    c. They cannot store key-value pairs.
    d. They cannot handle collisions.
13. In Python, which of these operations is **`O(1)`** on average for a **`dict`**?
    a. Iteration
    b. Key Lookup
    c. Sorting
    d. Slicing
14. What is the worst-case time complexity of searching in a hash table with chaining?
    a. `O(1)`
    b. `O(n)`
    c. `O(log n)`
    d. `O(n log n)`
15. Which real-world application often uses hash tables?
    a. Cache Systems
    b. Inorder Traversal

   c. Stack Undo Operations
   d. Breadth-First Search

16. What is **primary clustering**?
    a. It refers to the process where collisions are resolved by a stack.
    b. It refers to consecutive filled slots in open addressing.
    c. It refers to duplicate key insertion.
    d. It refers to hash function failure.

17. What is **rehashing** in hash tables?
    a. It refers to deleting all elements.
    b. It refers to the process of increasing table size and recalculating indices.
    c. It refers to sorting the keys.
    d. It refers to using a stack to store collisions.

Answers

1. b
2. c
3. b
4. b
5. b
6. c
7. b
8. b
9. b
10. b
11. b
12. b
13. b
14. b
15. a
16. b
17. b

Questions

1. Explain the structure of a hash table, and how key-value pairs are stored.
2. Describe the difference between **chaining** and **open addressing** for collision handling.
3. How does the **load factor** affect the performance of a hash table? Provide an example.
4. Implement a hash table in C++ or Python to **count the frequency of words** in a text.
5. Explain **primary clustering**, and describe how **quadratic probing** or **double hashing** can help reduce it.

6. Discuss the advantages of using **`unordered_map`** in C++ and **`dict`** in Python over arrays or linked lists.
7. Solve the **two-sum problem** using a hash table, and explain why it is efficient.
8. What are the limitations of hash tables, and in which scenarios should they be avoided?
9. How can hash tables be used in **caching** and **duplicate detection** applications?
10. Explain the concept of **rehashing**, and describe its necessity in dynamic hash tables.

Key Terms

- **Hash Table:** A data structure that stores key-value pairs for fast access and retrieval
- **Hash Function:** A function that converts a key into an index for storing in a hash table
- **Collision:** Occurs when two keys map to the same index in a hash table
- **Chaining:** A collision resolution method using linked lists to store multiple items at the same index
- **Open Addressing:** A collision resolution method that finds the next available slot using probing
- **Linear Probing:** A probing technique where the next consecutive slot is checked sequentially
- **Quadratic Probing:** A probing technique where the next slot is determined by a quadratic function of the step number
- **Double Hashing:** A probing technique that uses a second hash function to calculate step size
- **Load Factor:** The ratio of the number of elements to the size of the hash table that affects performance
- **Rehashing:** Increasing the table size and recalculating indices when the load factor exceeds a threshold
- **`unordered_map` (C++ STL):** A hash table implementation in C++ supporting O(1) average lookups
- **`dict` (Python):** Built-in Python hash table supporting fast insertion, lookup, and deletion
- **Primary Clustering:** Formation of consecutive filled slots in open addressing, which results in longer probe sequences

CHAPTER 6

Trees and Binary Search Trees

Introduction

Trees are one of the most fundamental data structures in computer science, as they are used to represent hierarchical relationships, and organize data efficiently. Unlike linear structures such as arrays, stacks, or queues, trees allow each element, called a node, to have multiple connections. This makes them ideal for modeling real-world systems such as family trees, organizational charts, and file directories. Hence, in this chapter, we will begin with the basics of tree structures, and will cover key terminologies such as root, leaf, height, and depth. We will also explore different ways to represent trees in memory using arrays and linked structures. We will then focus on binary trees, where each node has at most two children. Additionally, we will discuss their types, construction, and traversal techniques. Building on this foundation, we will touch upon the concept of Binary Search Trees (BSTs), which maintain ordered data to enable efficient searching, insertion, and deletion. From there on, we will examine balanced versus unbalanced BSTs, as well as their impact on performance. Finally, we will explore practical applications such as expression trees, BST validation, and finding the Lowest Common Ancestor (LCA) to equip you with a solid understanding of hierarchical data structures, recursive processing, and tree-based algorithms, as it is essential for both theoretical knowledge and practical problem-solving.

Structure

In this chapter, we will cover the following topics:

- Introduction to Trees
- Binary Trees
- Binary Search Trees

Introduction to Trees

In computer science, a **tree** is a widely used **non-linear data structure** that simulates a hierarchical tree-like structure with a set of connected nodes. It is widely used in computer science for efficiently storing, managing, and retrieving hierarchical data. A tree is a (possibly non-linear) data structure made up of nodes, vertices, and edges without having any cycles. A tree with no nodes is called the

null or **empty** tree. A tree that is not empty consists of a root node and many levels of additional nodes that form a hierarchy. *Figure* 6.1 presents examples of graphs that are not trees, and illustrates various structural violations such as disconnected components, multiple paths between vertices, and cycles.

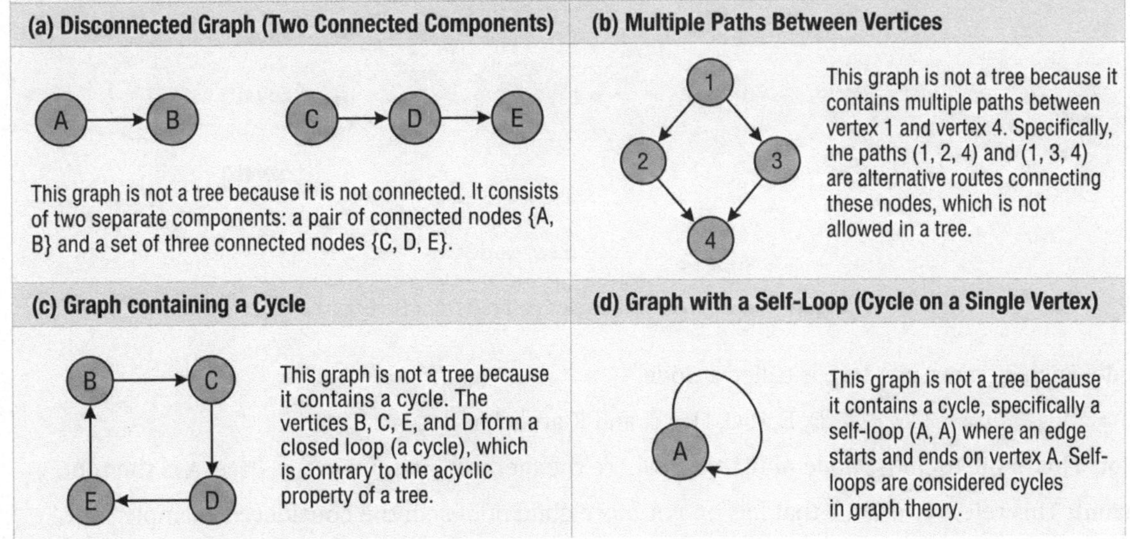

***Figure* 6.1:** *(a) Not a Tree: Two Non-Connected Parts, A->B, C->D->E; (b) Not a Tree: Two Paths (1,2,4) and (1,3,4) Connecting at Vertex B; (c) Not a Tree: Cycle (B, C, E, D, B); (d) Not a Tree: Cycle (A, A)*

Unlike linear data structures such as arrays, linked lists, or stacks, trees allow for more complex relationships between data elements. Therefore, they are ideal for representing data with a hierarchical nature, such as file systems, organization charts, XML/HTML documents, and Abstract Syntax Trees (ASTs) in compilers.

Definition:

A tree is defined as a finite set of one or more nodes such that:

- There is a specially designated node called the root.
- The remaining nodes are partitioned into $n \geq 0$ disjoint sets T1, T2, ..., Tn, where each of these sets is a tree. Therefore, T1, T2, ...Tn are called the subsets of the root.

Moreover, each node in a tree may have **zero or more child nodes** and exactly **one parent** except for the root node, which has no parent.

Basic Terminology

Understanding the basic terminology associated with trees is essential before we consider their implementation and operations. Trees are hierarchical data structures, and each component within them plays a specific role in storing and organizing data efficiently. *Figure* 6.2 illustrates the key concepts, such as nodes, root, edges, paths, height, and depth, which form the foundation for working with trees. It also illustrates the key terminologies in tree data structures, and highlights the nodes that form the basic elements of a tree.

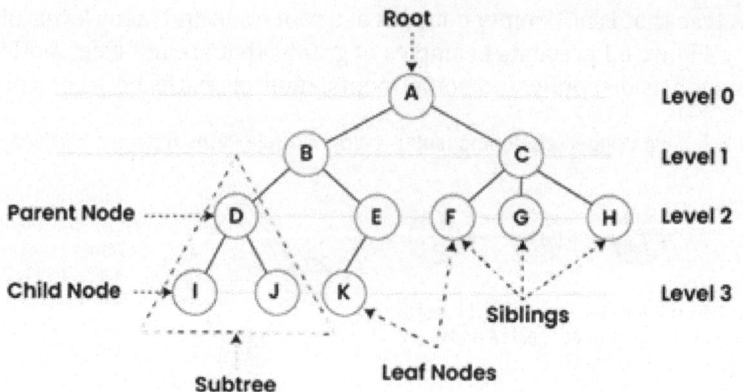

Figure 6.2: *Key Terminologies in Tree Data Structures*

Node: Each element in a tree is called a node.

- In *Figure* 6.2, A, B, C, D, E, F, G, H, I, J, and K are all nodes.

Root: This is the topmost node of the tree, where the hierarchy starts. In this case, A is the root.

Parent: This refers to a node that has one or more child nodes. In the considered example:

- A is the parent of B and C.
- B is the parent of D and E.
- C is the parent of F, G, and H.
- D is the parent of I and J.
- E is the parent of K.

Child: It refers to a node that descends from another node (its parent). Hence, according to the diagram:

- B and C are the children of A.
- D and E are the children of B.
- F, G, and H are the children of C.
- I and J are the children of D.
- K is the child of E.

Siblings: These are nodes that share the same parent. As per the diagram:

- B and C are siblings (Children of A).
- D and E are siblings (Children of B).
- F, G, and H are siblings (Children of C).
- I and J are siblings (Children of D).

Leaf Node (or External Node): This is a node with no children.

- In *Figure* 6.2, F, G, H, I, J, and K are leaf nodes.

Internal Node: This refers to a node that has at least one child (that is, not a leaf).

- A, B, C, and D are internal nodes.

Edge: This is the connection between a parent and a child node.

- For example, there are edges from A to B, A to C, B to D, and so on.

Path: This refers to a sequence of nodes and edges that connect a node with a descendant.

- For example, path from A to F is A → C → F

Depth of a Node: This refers to the number of edges from the root to the node.

- Depth of A = 0, B = 1, C = 1, E = 2

Height of a Node: This is the number of edges on the longest path from a given node to a leaf.

- Height of A = 2 (to reach F, G, or H)
- Height of B = 1 (to D or E)

Subtree: This refers to a tree formed by a node and all its descendants.

- The subtree rooted at B includes B, D, E, I, J, and K.

Therefore, trees are not just theoretical constructs; they are widely used in real-world systems because of their hierarchical nature and efficient organization of data. One of the most common applications is in **Binary Search Trees (BSTs)**, which enable fast searching, insertion, and deletion operations. These features make them a cornerstone for efficient data handling. Similarly, **heaps** play a vital role in implementing priority queues, where elements are processed based on their priority rather than arrival order. Another practical use is seen in **tries**, which are specialized trees designed for string operations. They are particularly useful for tasks such as autocomplete and fast prefix matching in dictionaries or search engines. In the field of programming languages, **Abstract Syntax Trees (ASTs)** form the backbone of compilers and represent the structure of source code during parsing and interpretation. Beyond these, tree structures are also the foundation of **file systems, XML parsers, and decision trees in Artificial Intelligence (AI)**, where hierarchical relationships are critical for decision-making and organizing complex data.

Tree Representations

A tree can be represented in multiple ways depending on how its nodes and relationships are stored. The three commonly used representations are:

- List Representation
- Left Child-Right Sibling Representation
- Degree-Two Tree Representation

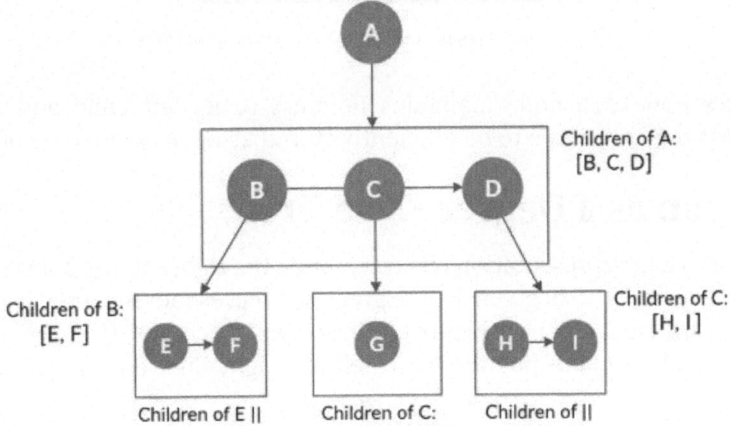

Figure 6.3: *Tree Representation*

List Representation

In this approach, two types of nodes are employed: one to hold the actual data and another to manage references to child nodes. The representation starts at the root node, which contains data. Each node is connected to its children via reference nodes. This linking continues recursively until all nodes in the tree are captured in the structure.

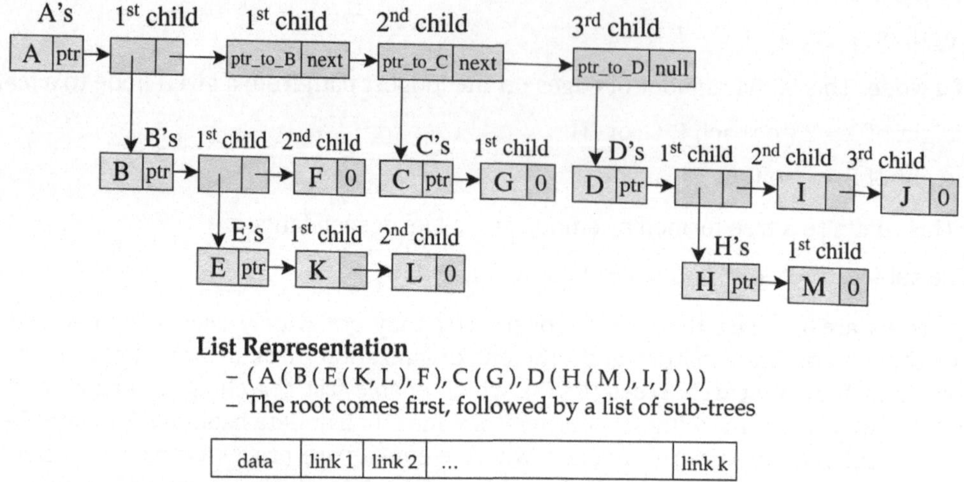

Figure 6.4: *Possible Node Structure for a Tree of Degree K*

Figure 6.4 shows how a tree can be organized using the list representation, with reference nodes that connect each data node to its children.

Left Child–Right Sibling Representation

This approach uses a single type of node with three fields:

- **Data Field:** Stores the actual value of the node
- **Left Child Field:** Points to the leftmost child of the node, or NULL if there is no left child
- **Right Sibling Field:** Points to the node's next sibling, or NULL if there is no sibling

Figure 6.5: *Graphical Representation of a Node*

Figure 6.5 illustrates how each node maintains pointers to its left child and right sibling. This representation allows the entire tree to be efficiently stored using only one type of node.

Representation as a Degree–Two Tree

To obtain a degree-two tree representation of a tree, rotate the right-sibling pointers in the left child-right sibling tree clockwise by 45 degrees. In a degree-two representation, the two children of anode are referred to as left and right children. *Figure* 6.6 illustrates the degree-two representation of a tree, and shows how each node contains pointers to its left and right children to structure a binary tree.

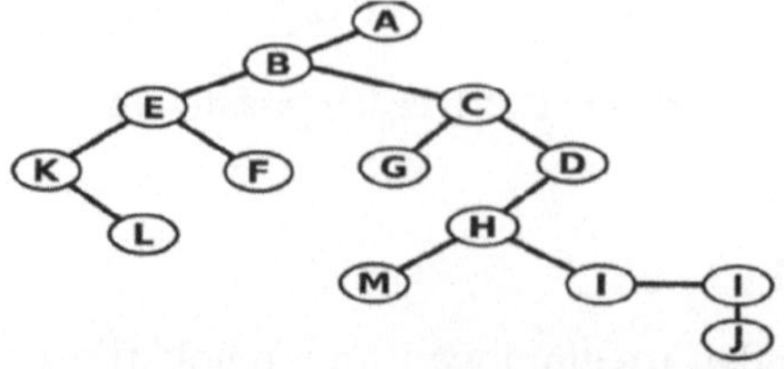

Figure 6.6: *Degree Two Tree Representation for the Tree*

Array and Linked Representation

Binary trees can be represented in two common ways: **linked representation** and **array representation**. Each representation has its own advantages and is chosen based on memory constraints and problem requirements.

Linked Representation

In linked representation, a binary tree is implemented using **nodes** connected through pointers (in C++) or object references (in Python). Each node contains the following **three fields**:

- **data/info** → Stores the actual value of the node
- **left/llink** → Stores the reference (or pointer) to the left subtree
- **right/rlink** → Stores the reference (or pointer) to the right subtree

Therefore, this representation is efficient for dynamic memory allocation, as nodes are created only when needed.

C++ Implementation:

```
#include <iostream>
using namespace std;

struct Node {
    int data;
    Node* left;   // Pointer to left subtree
    Node* right;  // Pointer to right subtree

    // Constructor
    Node(int value) {
        data = value;
        left = right = nullptr;
    }
};

// Example: Creating a root node
int main() {
    Node* root = new Node(10);
    root->left = new Node(20);
    root->right = new Node(30);

    cout << "Root Node: " << root->data << endl;
    cout << "Left Child: " << root->left->data << endl;
    cout << "Right Child: " << root->right->data << endl;

    return 0;
}
```

Python Implementation:

```
class Node:
    def __init__(self, data):
        self.data = data      # Store node value
        self.left = None      # Pointer to left child
        self.right = None     # Pointer to right child

# Example: Creating a root node
root = Node(10)
root.left = Node(20)
```

```
root.right = Node(30)

print("Root Node:", root.data)
print("Left Child:", root.left.data)
print("Right Child:", root.right.data)
```

Figure 6.7(*a*) shows the memory representation of a tree node with left and right pointers (**`llink`** and **`rlink`**), and a data field (**`info`**).

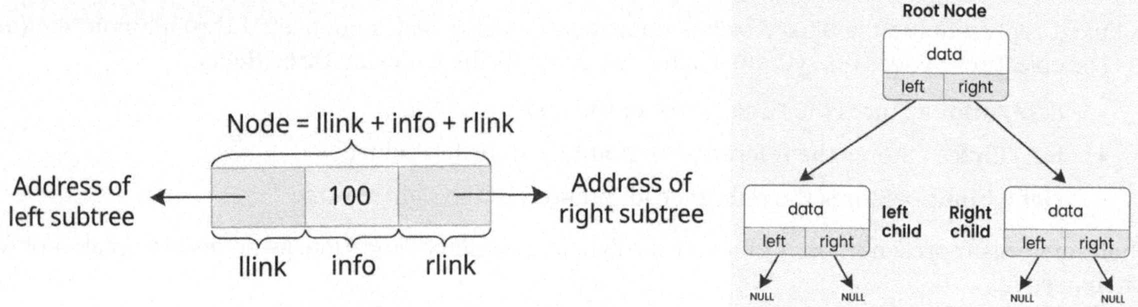

Figure 6.7: *(a) Structure of a Tree Node Using Left and Right Links; (b) Graphical Representation of a Binary Tree Node*

Figure 6.7(*b*) illustrates a tree node in a binary tree, while showing the root node and its left and right children with **`NULL`** pointers for absent children.

Array Representation

The **array representation** (also called **sequential representation**) stores the tree in a **1D array** where each node is mapped to a specific index. This is **efficient** when working with **complete binary trees,** as there are **no gaps** between nodes.

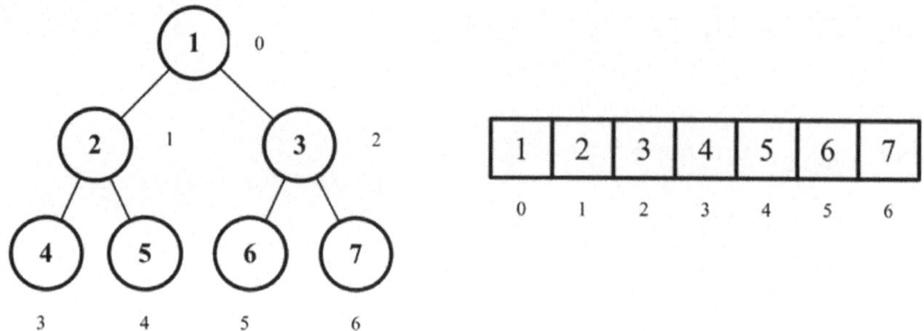

Figure 6.8: *Array Representation*

In *Figure* 6.8, the binary tree is represented using an array, where each node is assigned a unique position starting from 0. Therefore, this representation allows us to determine the parent and child relationships that are entirely based on node indices. From this array-based structure, we can make the following observations:

- The **root** of the tree is always the node at position 0.
- For a node at position i:

  Its **left child** is located at position 2i + 1.

  Its **right child** is located at position 2i + 2.
- If a node is a left child, its **right sibling** is at position i + 1. Similarly, if a node is a right child, its **left sibling** is at position i - 1.

- The **parent** of a node at position i can be found using (i - 1) / 2.

  If i is odd, the node is the left child of its parent.

  If i is even, the node is the right child of its parent.

This simple array-based indexing makes it easy to navigate a binary tree without using explicit pointers, and is particularly useful for implementing complete binary trees efficiently. Hence, a node can be represented using a structure as follows:

C++ Implementation:

```
#include <iostream>
using namespace std;

const int MAX_SIZE = 100;

struct Node {
    int data;
    bool used;  // To check if the node position is occupied
};

int main() {
    Node tree[MAX_SIZE];

    // Initialize all nodes as unused
    for (int i = 0; i < MAX_SIZE; i++) {
        tree[i].used = false;
    }

    // Insert root node
    tree[0].data = 10;
    tree[0].used = true;

    // Insert left and right children
    tree[1].data = 20; tree[1].used = true;  // Left child of root
    tree[2].data = 30; tree[2].used = true;  // Right child of root

    cout << "Root Node: " << tree[0].data << endl;
    cout << "Left Child: " << tree[1].data << endl;
    cout << "Right Child: " << tree[2].data << endl;

    return 0;
}
```

Python Implementation:

```
MAX_SIZE = 100

# Initialize an empty array for tree representation
tree = [None] * MAX_SIZE

# Insert root node
tree[0] = 10

# Insert left and right children
tree[1] = 20  # Left child of root
tree[2] = 30  # Right child of root

print("Root Node:", tree[0])
print("Left Child:", tree[1])
print("Right Child:", tree[2])
```

Binary Trees

A **binary tree** is a hierarchical data structure consisting of a finite set of nodes. Each binary tree is either empty or comprises a **root node** along with two subtrees that are known as the **left subtree** and **right subtree**. Conceptually, a binary tree can be divided into three components: the root, the left subtree, and the right subtree.

- **Root**: The topmost node of the tree, which is present when the tree is not empty, is called the root node.
- **Left Subtree**: This is the subtree attached to the left of the root. Since it grows towards the left, it is referred to as the left subtree.
- **Right Subtree**: This is the subtree attached to the right of the root. As it extends towards the right, it is called the right subtree.

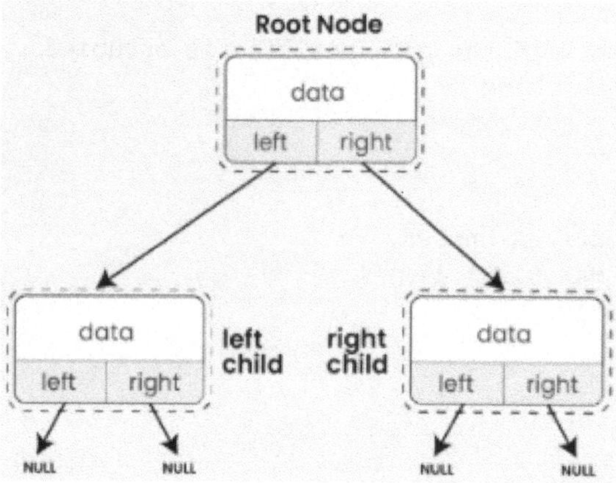

***Figure 6.9**: Structure of a Binary Tree Node*

C++ Implementation

In C++, a binary tree node can be represented using a **struct** or a **class**. Each node typically contains a data field to store the value and pointers (or references) to its left and right children.

```
#include <iostream>
using namespace std;

// Structure of a binary tree node
struct Node {
    int data;       // Stores node value
    Node* left;     // Pointer to left child
    Node* right;    // Pointer to right child

    // Constructor to initialize a node
    Node(int value) {
        data = value;
        left = nullptr;
        right = nullptr;
    }
};

int main() {
    // Creating the root node
    Node* root = new Node(10);
```

```
    // Adding child nodes
    root->left = new Node(20);
    root->right = new Node(30);

    cout << "Root Node: " << root->data << endl;
    cout << "Left Child: " << root->left->data << endl;
    cout << "Right Child: " << root->right->data << endl;

    return 0;
}
```

Each node stores **three parts**:

- Data → Holds the value
- Left → Pointer to the left child
- Right → Pointer to the right child

From this example, we can surmise that the node constructor ensures **easy initialization**.

Moreover, dynamic memory allocation (new) is used to create nodes.

Python Implementation

Python does not have pointers like C++ but uses **object references** to link nodes, which is shown here:

```
# Structure of a binary tree node
class Node:
    def __init__(self, data):
        self.data = data        # Stores node value
        self.left = None        # Reference to left child
        self.right = None       # Reference to right child

# Creating the root node
root = Node(10)

# Adding child nodes
root.left = Node(20)
root.right = Node(30)

# Displaying the tree nodes
print("Root Node:", root.data)
print("Left Child:", root.left.data)
print("Right Child:", root.right.data)
```

Properties of Binary Trees

A **binary tree** is a hierarchical data structure in which each node can have at most two children, which are commonly referred to as the *left child* and the *right child*. Thus, understanding its structural properties helps in analyzing and optimizing operations such as insertion, deletion, and traversal.

Maximum Number of Nodes at a Given Level

In a binary tree, the **maximum number of nodes at level *i*** is given by maximum nodes at level $i=2^i$, where $i \geq 0$. This means:

- Level 0 can have 1 node ($2^0=1$).
- Level 1 can have 2 nodes ($2^1=2$).

- Level 2 can have 4 nodes (2^2=4).
- Level 3 can have 8 nodes (2^3=8), and so on.

Maximum Number of Nodes in a Binary Tree of Depth *k*

If the tree has a depth (or height) of *k*, then the **maximum number of nodes** that can exist in such a tree is represented by:

$n_t=2^k-1$

This represents a *full binary tree*, where all possible nodes are filled at each level.

Example: For a tree of depth 4,

$n_t= 2^4 - 1 =15$

Hence, a full binary tree of depth 4 has 15 nodes in total.

Relationship between Leaf Nodes and Nodes with Two Children

In a binary tree:

$n_0=n_2+1$

Where:

- n_0 = Number of Leaf Nodes (Degree 0)
- n_2 = Number of Nodes with Two Children (Degree 2)

Hence, this property states that the number of leaf nodes is always **one more** than the number of nodes with two children.

Proof of the Relationship

Let:

- n_0 = Number of Nodes with Degree 0
- n_1 = Number of Nodes with Degree 1
- n_2 = Number of Nodes with Degree 2

Therefore, the total number of nodes in the tree is:

$n=n_0 + n_1 + n_2$

The total number of **branches (edges)** in the tree is one less than the total number of nodes, which is represented by:

$B=n-1$

Each node contributes to branches based on its degree:

$B=n_1+2n_2$

Substituting the value of B:

$n-1=n_1+2n_2$

Finally, we will rearrange the terms:

$n_0=n_2+1$

Thus, in any binary tree, the number of leaf nodes is always one more than the number of nodes having two children.

Relationship between Tree Depth and Levels

If a binary tree has a maximum level iii, then its depth kkk is given by:

```
k=i+1
```

This helps in relating the height or depth of the tree to the number of levels it contains. Figure 6.10 depicts a **complete binary tree** with **four levels** (levels 0 to 3). Each node can be labeled numerically to show its position and hierarchy clearly. The structure can be represented as follows:

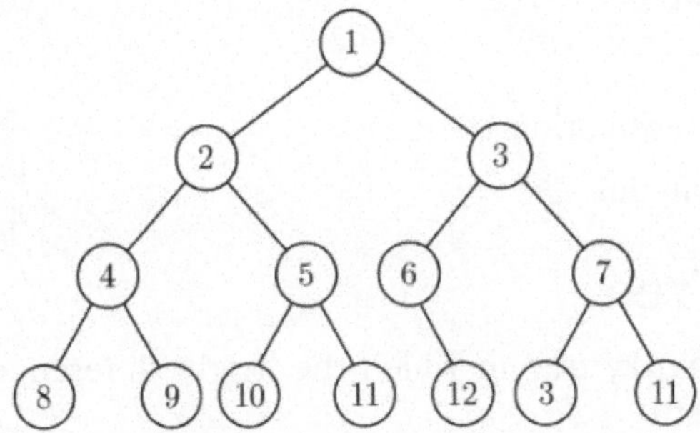

***Figure* 6.10:** *A Complete Binary Tree*

The figure illustrates a **nearly complete binary tree** that demonstrates how nodes are arranged level by level. In this structure, each level is filled from **left to right**. All levels, except the last, are completely filled.

At the **topmost level (Level 0)**, there is a **single root node (1)**. Each node in the upper levels connects to its child nodes in the lower levels, maintaining the binary property—that is, every node can have **at most two children**. The arrangement continues as follows:

- **Level 0** → Node **1** (Root)
- **Level 1** → Nodes **2** and **3**
- **Level 2** → Nodes **4, 5, 6, and 7**
- **Level 3** → Nodes **8, 9, 10, 11, 12, 13, and 14**

As seen here, the tree contains a total of **14 nodes**, with all levels completely filled except the last one, which is partially filled but follows the left-to-right insertion order. Thus, this structure visually conveys how binary trees maintain their hierarchical nature—balancing node placement efficiently, while adhering to the binary constraint of two children per node.

Types of Binary Trees

A binary tree is a tree data structure in which each node has at most two children, that are usually referred to as the left child and the right child. Based on their structure and properties, binary trees can be classified into several types:

Full Binary Tree

A full binary tree is a binary tree in which every node, other than the leaves, has exactly two children.

Properties:

- Every non-leaf node has two children.
- Number of Nodes at Level `i = 2^i`.

Perfect Binary Tree

A perfect binary tree is a full binary tree in which all leaf nodes are at the same level.

Properties:

- Total Number of Nodes = `2^(h+1) - 1`, where h is the height of the tree.
- Height h `= log2(n+1) - 1`.

Complete Binary Tree

A complete binary tree is a binary tree in which all levels are completely filled except for the last, which is filled from left to right.

Properties:

- Efficient for array representation
- Keeps tree height minimum

Balanced Binary Tree

A balanced binary tree is a binary tree in which the height difference between the left and right subtrees of any node is at most 1.

Properties: Improves search, insertion, and deletion efficiency (O(log n) in AVL trees)

Degenerate (or Pathological) Tree

A degenerate tree is a binary tree where each parent node has only one child, which essentially makes it a linked list.

Properties:

Height = Number of nodes

Therefore, operations like search, insert, delete become **`O(n)`**.

Skewed Binary Tree

A skewed binary tree is a special case of a degenerate tree where all nodes are either left skewed (all nodes have only left child), or right skewed (all nodes have only right child).

Properties: Operations have `O(n)` complexity.

Binary Search Tree (BST)

Though not strictly structural, a BST is a binary tree with the following property:

Left Subtree Nodes ≤ Parent Node ≤ Right Subtree Nodes.

Properties: The most apparent properties include efficient searching, insertion, deletion (average `O(log n)`). It can be balanced or skewed.

Abstract Data Type (ADT) of a Binary Tree

The **ADT of a binary tree** defines the **operations** that can be performed on the tree without specifying the actual implementation details. The following table summarizes the **main functions** used in a binary tree.

Function	Definition	Description / Purpose
`Create()`	`BinTree Create()`	Creates and returns an **empty binary tree**
`IsEmpty(bt)`	`Boolean IsEmpty(bt)`	Checks if the given binary tree, **bt,** is empty. Returns **TRUE** if empty, else **FALSE**
`MakeBT(bt1, item, bt2)`	`BinTree MakeBT(bt1, item, bt2)`	Creates a **new binary tree** with **item** as the root, **bt1** as the left subtree, and **bt2** as the right subtree
`Lchild(bt)`	`BinTree Lchild(bt)`	Returns the **left subtree** of **bt**. If **bt** is empty, it returns an **error**
`Rchild(bt)`	`BinTree Rchild(bt)`	Returns the **right subtree** of **bt**. If **bt** is empty, it returns an **error**
`Data(bt)`	`Element Data(bt)`	Returns the **data value** stored in the **root node** of **bt**. It also returns an **error** if the tree is empty.

Table 6.1: *Abstract Data Type (ADT) Functions for Binary Trees*

Binary Tree Construction

Construct a binary tree for the following elements: 1, 2, 3, 4, 5, 6, 7, 8, 9.

Step 1: Understand the Rules of Construction.

a. For a **complete binary tree**, the first element becomes the **root**.
b. The next two elements become the **left** and **right** children of the root.
c. The next four elements become the children of the preceding nodes, and so on.
d. Formula to find children of a node at index i (1-based index):
   i. **Left Child = 2 × I**
   ii. **Right Child = 2 × i + 1**

Step 2: Insert the Elements.

- **Level 1 (Root)**
  - Take the **first element** → 1 → **Root Node**.
- **Level 2**
  - Next two elements → 2 and 3
    - 2 → **Left child** of 1
    - 3 → **Right child** of 1
- **Level 3**
  - Next four elements → 4, 5, 6, 7
    - 4 → **Left child** of 2
    - 5 → **Right child** of 2
    - 6 → **Left child** of 3
    - 7 → **Right child** of 3
- **Level 4**
  - Remaining elements → 8, 9
    - 8 → **Left child** of 4
    - 9 → **Right child** of 4

The binary tree shown in Figure 6.11 is constructed by sequentially inserting the elements **1, 2, 3, 4, 5, 6, 7, 8, 9**. Each element is added following the standard rules of binary tree insertion, where each new node is positioned relative to its parent based on the insertion order. This representation clearly demonstrates the hierarchical arrangement of nodes and the parent-child relationships in a binary tree.

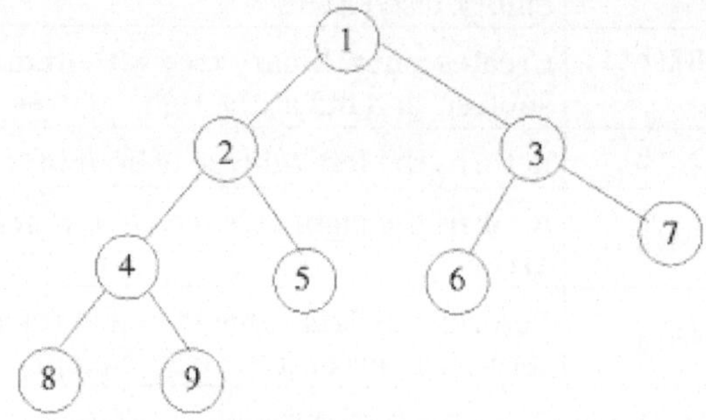

Figure 6.11: *Binary for the Sequence of Elements* 1, 2, 3, 4, 5, 6, 7, 8, 9

Binary Tree Traversal

Traversing a binary tree implies systematically visiting all its nodes to process the information they hold. The order of traversal depends on the problem at hand: sometimes we need sorted data; sometimes we need to replicate the structure of a tree; and sometimes we need to process all nodes level by level. There are four widely used traversal strategies: **inorder, preorder, postorder, and level-order**. Each one serves a unique purpose in problem-solving.

Inorder Traversal

In an **inorder traversal**, the algorithm visits the **left subtree first**, then processes the **root node**, and finally visits the **right subtree**. If the tree is a **Binary Search Tree (BST)**, inorder traversal naturally produces nodes in **sorted order**, which makes it extremely useful in searching and sorting contexts.

Steps:

a. Traverse the left subtree.

b. Visit the root.

c. Traverse the right subtree.

C++ Example:

```
#include <iostream>
using namespace std;

struct Node {
    int data;
    Node* left;
    Node* right;
    Node(int val) : data(val), left(nullptr), right(nullptr) {}
};

void inorder(Node* root) {
    if (root == nullptr) return;
    inorder(root->left);          // L
    cout << root->data << " ";    // N
    inorder(root->right);         // R
}

int main() {
```

```
    Node* root = new Node(6);
    root->left = new Node(4);
    root->right = new Node(8);
    root->left->left = new Node(3);
    root->left->right = new Node(5);
    cout << "Inorder Traversal: ";
    inorder(root);
    return 0;
}
```

Python Example:

```
class Node:
    def __init__(self, val):
        self.data = val
        self.left = None
        self.right = None

def inorder(root):
    if root is None:
        return
    inorder(root.left)              # L
    print(root.data, end=" ")       # N
    inorder(root.right)             # R

root = Node(6)
root.left = Node(4)
root.right = Node(8)
root.left.left = Node(3)
root.left.right = Node(5)

print("Inorder Traversal:", end=" ")
inorder(root)
```

Example

Inorder: A, B, C, D, E, F, G, H, I.

Preorder Traversal

In a **Preorder traversal**, the algorithm processes the **root node first**, then the **left subtree**, followed by the **right subtree**. This order is commonly used to **copy or serialize a tree**, as it preserves the structure from the root downwards.

Steps:

a. Visit the root.

b. Traverse the left subtree.

c. Traverse the right subtree.

C++ Example:

```
void preorder(Node* root) {
    if (root == nullptr) return;
    cout << root->data << " ";   // N
    preorder(root->left);        // L
    preorder(root->right);       // R
}
```

Python Example:

```
def preorder(root):
    if root is None:
        return
    print(root.data, end=" ")    # N
    preorder(root.left)          # L
    preorder(root.right)         # R
```

Example

Preorder: F, B, A, D, C, E, G, I, H.

Postorder Traversal

In **postorder traversal**, the algorithm visits the **left subtree first**, then the **right subtree**, and finally the **root node**. Hence, this approach is particularly useful when we need to **delete a tree safely**, since it ensures that child nodes are processed before their parent.

Steps:

a. Traverse the left subtree.

b. Traverse the right subtree.

c. Visit the root.

C++ Example:

```
void postorder(Node* root) {
    if (root == nullptr) return;
    postorder(root->left);        // L
    postorder(root->right);       // R
    cout << root->data << " ";    // N
}
```

Python Example:

```
void postorder(Node* root) {
    if (root == nullptr) return;
    postorder(root->left);        // L
    postorder(root->right);       // R
    cout << root->data << " ";    // N
}
```

Example

Postorder: A, C, E, D, B, H, I, G, F.

Level Order Traversal

Unlike the previous three, **level-order traversal** does not follow a recursive pattern. Instead, it uses a **queue** to visit nodes level by level from **left to right**. This strategy is fundamental to **Breadth-First Search (BFS),** and is widely applied in **shortest path algorithms**, **task scheduling**, and **tree visualization**.

Steps:

a. Enqueue the root node.

b. Dequeue a node, visit it, and then enqueue its children.

c. Repeat until the queue is empty.

C++ Example:

```
#include <queue>

void levelOrder(Node* root) {
    if (root == nullptr) return;
    queue<Node*> q;
    q.push(root);

    while (!q.empty()) {
        Node* current = q.front();
        q.pop();

        cout << current->data << " ";

        if (current->left) q.push(current->left);
        if (current->right) q.push(current->right);
    }
}
```

Python Example:

```
from collections import deque

def level_order(root):
    if root is None:
        return
    q = deque([root])
    while q:
        current = q.popleft()
        print(current.data, end=" ")
        if current.left:
            q.append(current.left)
        if current.right:
            q.append(current.right)
```

Example

Level-Order: F, B, G, A, D, I, C, E, H

Here, while analyzing tree traversals, the time complexity for level-order, pre-order, and post-order traversals will be O(n), where n is the number of nodes in the tree, as each node is visited exactly once during the traversal. The space complexity, however, depends on the type of traversal. For level-order traversal, a queue is used to store the nodes of each level as they are visited. In the worst case, all nodes may be present in the queue at the same time, which leads to a space complexity of O(n). On the contrary, pre-order and post-order traversals typically use recursion or an explicit stack to keep track of nodes that still need to be visited. The maximum number of nodes stored at any point corresponds to the height of the tree, denoted as h. Therefore, the space complexity for these traversals is O(h). For a balanced tree, the height h will roughly be log n, whereas in a skewed tree, it can be as large as n.

Binary Search Tree

A **Binary Search Tree (BST)** is a type of binary tree that follows an ordering property: for any node x in the tree, all the values stored in its **left subtree** are smaller than the value of x, while all the values in its **right subtree** are greater than the value of x. A BST maintains elements in a **sorted hierarchical structure**. For any given node:

- All values in the **left subtree** are **less than** the node's value.

- All values in the **right subtree** are **greater than** the node's value.

Both left and right subtrees are also BSTs.

Due to this property, BSTs are widely used for **efficient searching, insertion, deletion, and ordered traversal** in applications such as databases, compilers, and search engines. The process of constructing a BST organizes elements in such a way that, for every node, the values in the left subtree are smaller, while the values in the right subtree are larger. The resultant tree structure is illustrated in *Figure* 6.12.

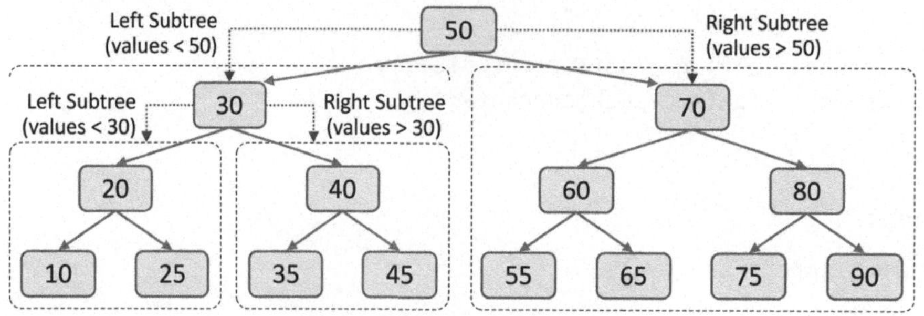

***Figure 6.12:** Binary Search Tree*

Binary Search Tree Construction

Construct a binary search tree for the following elements: 25, 20, 36, 10, 22, 30, 40, 5, 12, 28, 38, 48

Step 1 → Insert 25.

Tree is empty → Therefore, **25** becomes the **root**

Step 2 → Insert 20.

20 < 25 → Go **left** → Insert as left child.

Step 3 → Insert 36.

36 > 25 → Go **right** → Insert as right child.

Step 4 → Insert 10.

9 < 25 → Go **left** → 10 < 20 → Go **left** → Insert here.

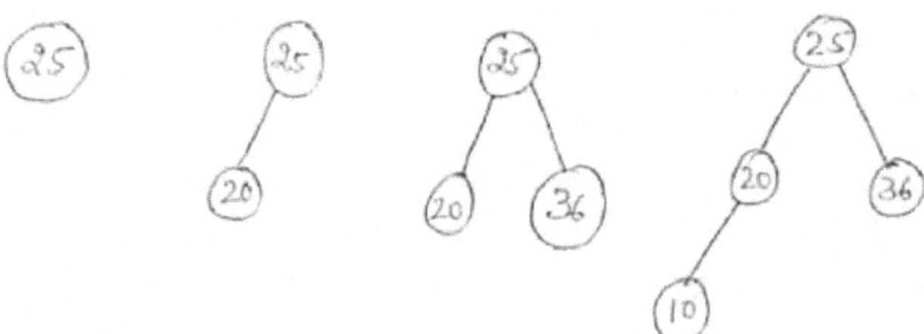

***Figure 6.12(a):** Binary Search Tree Showing the First Four Insertions*

Step 5 → Insert 22.

22 < 25 → Go **left** → 22 > 20 → Go **right** → Insert here.

Step 6 → Insert 30.

30 > 25 → Go **right** → 30 < 36 → Go **left** → Insert here.

Step 7 → Insert 40.

40 > 25 → Go **right** → 40 > 36 → Go **right** → Insert here.

Step 8 → Insert 5.

5 < 25 → Go **left** → 5 < 20 → Go **left** → 5 < 10 → Go **left** → Insert here.

Step 9 → Insert 12.

12 < 25 → Go **left** → 12 < 20 → Go **left** → 12 > 10 → Go **right** → Insert here.

Step 10 → Insert 28.

28 > 25 → Go **right** → 28 < 36 → Go **left** → 28 < 30 → Go **left** → Insert here.

Step 11 → Insert 38.

38 > 25 → Go **right** → 38 > 36 → Go **right** → 38 < 40 → Go **left** → Insert here.

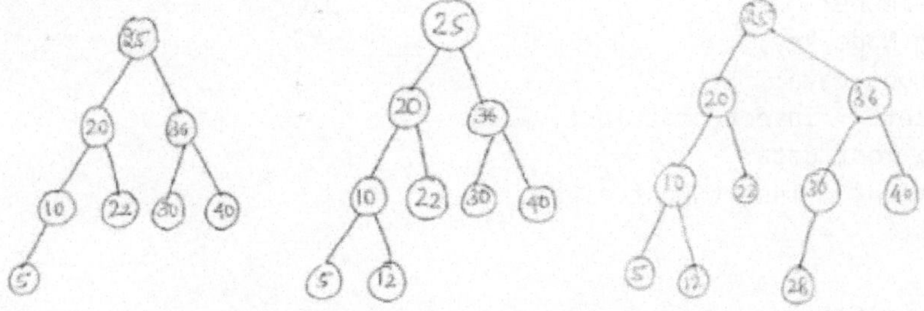

Figure 6.12(b): *Binary Search Tree after Steps 8–11*

Step 12 → Insert 48.

48 > 25 → Go **right** → 48 > 36 → Go **right** → 48 > 40 → Go **right** → Insert here.

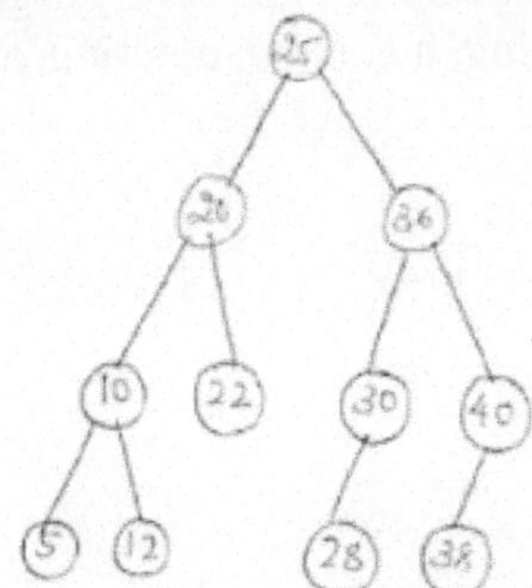

Figure 6.12(c): *Completed Binary Search Tree after Step 12*

Final BST Structure:

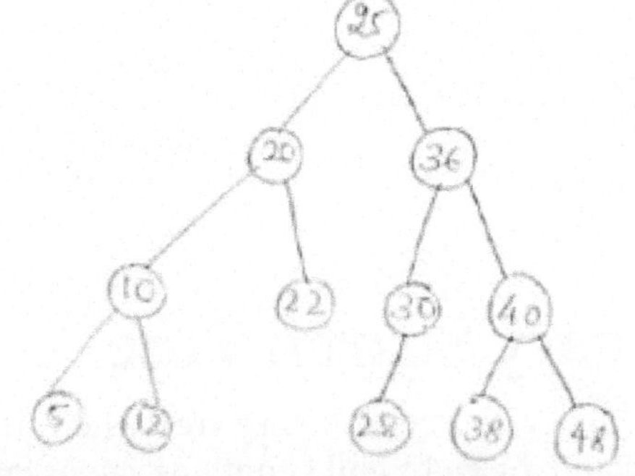

Figure 6.12(d): *Final Binary Search Tree Structure*

C++ Implementation:

```
Node* insert(Node* root, int key) {
    if (root == nullptr) {
        return new Node(key);
    }
    if (key < root->data)
        root->left = insert(root->left, key);
    else if (key > root->data)
        root->right = insert(root->right, key);
    return root;
}
```

Python Implementation:

```
def insert(root, key):
    if root is None:
        return Node(key)
    if key < root.data:
        root.left = insert(root.left, key)
    elif key > root.data:
        root.right = insert(root.right, key)
    return root
```

Node Representation

In a binary tree or binary search tree, **nodes** are the fundamental building blocks that store data and establish relationships between elements. Each node typically contains **three components**: the **data field** that holds the actual value, a **pointer/reference to the left child**, and a **pointer/reference to the right child**. Therefore, this structure allows us to efficiently organize and traverse hierarchical data. It also enables operations such as searching, inserting, deleting, and traversing nodes in a tree.

C++ Implementation:

```
    struct Node {
        int data;
        Node* left;
        Node* right;

        Node(int value) {
            data = value;
            left = right = nullptr;
        }
};
```

Python Implementation:

```
    class Node:
        def __init__(self, data):
            self.data = data
            self.left = None
     self.right = None
```

Operations on Binary Search Tree

A **Binary Search Tree (BST)** is a special type of binary tree where the **left child** of a node contains values **less than** the node's data, and the **right child** contains values **greater than** the node's data. This property facilitates efficient searching, insertion, deletion, and traversal.

Insertion in a BST

Insertion in a BST places a new node in its correct position while maintaining the BST property. You might observe either of these possibilities:

- If the new value is **less than** the current node → Move to the **left** subtree.
- If the new value is **greater than** the current node → Move to the **right** subtree.
- If the tree is empty, the new node becomes the **root**.

Function to Insert an Item into a Binary Search Tree:

C++ Implementation:

```
#include <iostream>
using namespace std;

struct Node {
    int data;
    Node* left;
    Node* right;
};

Node* createNode(int value) {
    Node* newNode = new Node();
    newNode->data = value;
    newNode->left = newNode->right = nullptr;
    return newNode;
}

Node* insert(Node* root, int value) {
    if (root == nullptr) {
        return createNode(value);
    }
    if (value < root->data)
        root->left = insert(root->left, value);
    else if (value > root->data)
        root->right = insert(root->right, value);
    return root;
}
```

Python Implementation:

```
class Node:
    def __init__(self, data):
        self.data = data
        self.left = None
        self.right = None

def insert(root, value):
    if root is None:
        return Node(value)
    if value < root.data:
        root.left = insert(root.left, value)
    elif value > root.data:
        root.right = insert(root.right, value)
    return root
```

The algorithm recursively compares the new value with the current node which shows up as follows:

- If **smaller**, it moves to the **left**.
- If **larger**, it moves to the **right**.

It ultimately stops when the correct spot is found, and then inserts the new node.

Deletion in a BST

Deletion in a BST has **three possible cases**:

- **Node Has No Children**: Simply delete the node.
- **Node Has One Child**: Replace the node with its child.
- **Node Has Two Children**: Find the **inorder successor** (the smallest value in the right subtree), replace the node's value, and delete the successor.

Function to Delete a Node from the Binary Search Tree:

C++ Implementation:

```
Node* findMin(Node* root) {
    while (root && root->left != nullptr)
        root = root->left;
    return root;
}

Node* deleteNode(Node* root, int key) {
    if (root == nullptr) return root;

    if (key < root->data)
        root->left = deleteNode(root->left, key);
    else if (key > root->data)
        root->right = deleteNode(root->right, key);
    else {
        if (root->left == nullptr) {
            Node* temp = root->right;
            delete root;
            return temp;
        }
        else if (root->right == nullptr) {
            Node* temp = root->left;
            delete root;
            return temp;
        }
        Node* temp = findMin(root->right);
        root->data = temp->data;
        root->right = deleteNode(root->right, temp->data);
    }
    return root;
}
```

Python Implementation:

```
def find_min(root):
    while root.left:
        root = root.left
    return root
```

```
def delete_node(root, key):
    if root is None:
        return root

    if key < root.data:
        root.left = delete_node(root.left, key)
    elif key > root.data:
        root.right = delete_node(root.right, key)
    else:
        if root.left is None:
            return root.right
        elif root.right is None:
            return root.left
        temp = find_min(root.right)
        root.data = temp.data
        root.right = delete_node(root.right, temp.data)
    return root
```

Searching in a BST

Searching in a BST is efficient because we exploit its ordering property:

- If the target value equals the current node → **found**.
- If the target is smaller → search **left**.

If larger → search **right**.

Function to Search a Node from the Binary Search Tree

C++ Implementation:

```
Node* search(Node* root, int key) {
    if (root == nullptr || root->data == key)
        return root;
    if (key < root->data)
        return search(root->left, key);
    return search(root->right, key);
}
```

Python Implementation:

```
def search(root, key):
    if root is None or root.data == key:
        return root
    if key < root.data:
        return search(root.left, key)
    return search(root.right, key)
```

The search process moves down the tree in **O(log n)** time on average, but can be **O(n)** in the worst case for unbalanced trees.

Traversals in a Binary Search Tree (BST)

A **Binary Search Tree (BST)** is a tree data structure where:

The **left child** of a node contains values **less than** the node.

The **right child** of a node contains values **greater than** the node.

Traversal is the process of **visiting every node of the tree exactly once** in a systematic order. Traversals help in searching, sorting, copying, or deleting trees. There are **three primary depth-first traversal methods**, which are explained as follows:

Inorder Traversal

In **inorder traversal**, we first visit the **left subtree**, then the **root**, and finally the **right subtree** (Left → Root → Right). This produces nodes in **ascending order**, which is particularly useful for retrieving sorted data. **Therefore, the consequent use cases are** sorting, searching, and validating BST properties.

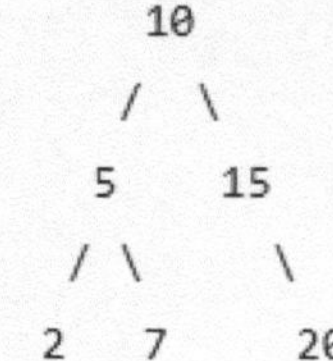

Figure 6.13: *Example BST*

Inorder Output, for Example, BST: 2 5 7 10 15 20

C++ Code – Inorder Traversal:

```
#include <iostream>
using namespace std;

struct Node {
    int data;
    Node* left;
    Node* right;
    Node(int val) { data = val; left = right = nullptr; }
};

void inorder(Node* root) {
    if (root != nullptr) {
        inorder(root->left);      // Visit left subtree
        cout << root->data << " "; // Visit root
        inorder(root->right);     // Visit right subtree
    }
}

int main() {
    Node* root = new Node(10);
    root->left = new Node(5);
    root->right = new Node(15);
    root->left->left = new Node(2);
    root->left->right = new Node(7);
    root->right->right = new Node(20);

    cout << "Inorder Traversal: ";
    inorder(root);
    return 0;
}
```

Python Code – Inorder Traversal:

```
class Node:
    def __init__(self, data):
```

```
        self.data = data
        self.left = None
        self.right = None

def inorder(root):
    if root:
        inorder(root.left)        # Visit left subtree
        print(root.data, end=" ") # Visit root
        inorder(root.right)       # Visit right subtree

# Create the BST
root = Node(10)
root.left = Node(5)
root.right = Node(15)
root.left.left = Node(2)
root.left.right = Node(7)
root.right.right = Node(20)
print("Inorder Traversal:", end=" ")
inorder(root)
```

Preorder Traversal

Visit the root first, then traverse the left subtree, followed by the right subtree (Root → Left → Right).

Use case: To **copy or serialize** the tree; helps in saving the tree structure.

Preorder Output for Example BST: 10 5 2 7 15 20

C++ Code – Preorder Traversal:

```
void preorder(Node* root) {
    if (root != nullptr) {
        cout << root->data << " "; // Visit root
        preorder(root->left);      // Visit left subtree
        preorder(root->right);     // Visit right subtree
    }
}
```

Python Code – Preorder Traversal:

```
def preorder(root):
    if root:
        print(root.data, end=" ") # Visit root
        preorder(root.left)       # Visit left subtree
        preorder(root.right)      # Visit right subtree
```

Postorder Traversal

First, traverse the left subtree, then the right subtree, and finally visit the root (Left → Right → Root).

Use case: Safely **delete or free** the tree. It is useful in evaluating **postfix expressions**.

Postorder Output for Example BST: 2 7 5 20 15 10

C++ Code – Postorder Traversal:

```
void postorder(Node* root) {
    if (root != nullptr) {
```

```
        postorder(root->left);     // Visit left subtree
        postorder(root->right);    // Visit right subtree
        cout << root->data << " "; // Visit root
    }
}
```

Python Code – Postorder Traversal:

```
def postorder(root):
    if root:
        postorder(root.left)      # Visit left subtree
        postorder(root.right)     # Visit right subtree
        print(root.data, end=" ") # Visit root
```

Balanced and Unbalanced BSTs

A **Binary Search Tree (BST)** can have different shapes depending on the order in which nodes are inserted. The shape of a BST has a direct impact on the **efficiency of operations** such as search, insertion, and deletion.

Balanced BST: A BST is **balanced** if the height of the tree is minimized, meaning that the left and right subtrees of every node have heights that differ by at most one. In a balanced BST, the operations of search, insertion, and deletion take **O(log n) time** on average because the tree's height is proportional to **log n**. **Example:** A perfectly balanced BST with 7 nodes looks like:

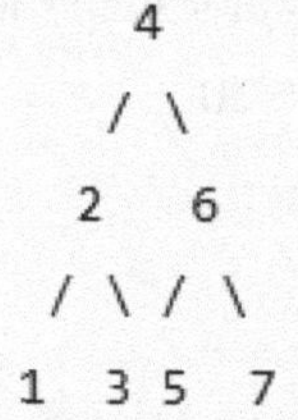

Figure 6.14: *Example Balanced BST*

Unbalanced BST: A BST becomes **unbalanced** when nodes are inserted in a sorted or nearly sorted order. In such cases, the tree degenerates into a structure similar to a linked list, while operations can take **O(n) time** in the worst case. **Example:** Inserting nodes in ascending order: 1, 2, 3, 4, 5 may look like:

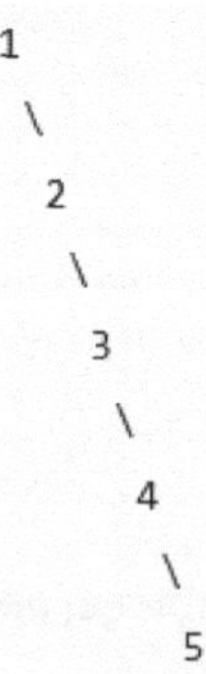

Figure 6.15: *Example Unbalanced BST*

Note: *Keeping a BST balanced is crucial for maintaining optimal performance. Techniques such as* **AVL trees** *and* **Red-Black trees** *are designed to automatically maintain balance.*

Other Operations on Binary Search Tree

Beyond traversal, a BST supports several important operations such as:

Find Maximum Element in BST

The maximum element is found by following the **right child** pointers until you arrive at the rightmost node.

Function to Find the Maximum Element in a BST:

C++ Example:

```
Node* findMaximum(Node* root) {
    if (root == nullptr) return nullptr;
    Node* cur = root;
    while (cur->right != nullptr) cur = cur->right;
    return cur;
}
```

Python Example:

```
def find_maximum(root):
    if root is None:
        return None
    cur = root
    while cur.right:
        cur = cur.right
    return cur
```

Find Minimum Element in BST

The minimum element is found by following the **left child** pointers until you arrive at the leftmost node.

Function to Find the Minimum Element in a BST:

C++ Example:

```
Node* findMinimum(Node* root) {
    if (root == nullptr) return nullptr;
    Node* cur = root;
    while (cur->left != nullptr) cur = cur->left;
    return cur;
}
```

Python Example:

```
def find_minimum(root):
    if root is None:
        return None
    cur = root
    while cur.left:
        cur = cur.left
    return cur
```

Count Leaf Nodes

A **leaf node** is a node with no left or right child. Recursively count all leaf nodes.

Function to Count Leaves in a Tree:

C++ Example:

```
int countLeaves(Node* root) {
    if (root == nullptr) return 0;
    if (root->left == nullptr && root->right == nullptr) return 1;
    return countLeaves(root->left) + countLeaves(root->right);
}
```

Python Example:

```
def count_leaves(root):
    if root is None:
        return 0
    if root.left is None and root.right is None:
        return 1
    return count_leaves(root.left) + count_leaves(root.right)
```

Copy a BST

To copy a tree, recursively create new nodes with the same data.

Function to Copy a Tree:

C++ Example:

```
Node* copyTree(Node* root) {
    if (!root) return nullptr;
    Node* newNode = new Node(root->data);
    newNode->left = copyTree(root->left);
    newNode->right = copyTree(root->right);
    return newNode;
}
```

Python Example:

```
def copy_tree(root):
    if root is None:
        return None
    new_node = Node(root.data)
    new_node.left = copy_tree(root.left)
    new_node.right = copy_tree(root.right)
    return new_node
```

Check if Two Trees are Equal:

Two trees are equal if:

- Their roots contain the same data.
- Their left and right subtrees are equal.

Function to Check Whether Two Trees are Equal or Not:

C++ Example:

```
bool isEqual(Node* r1, Node* r2) {
    if (!r1 && !r2) return true;
```

```
    if (!r1 || !r2) return false;
    return (r1->data == r2->data) &&
           isEqual(r1->left, r2->left) &&
           isEqual(r1->right, r2->right);
}
```

Python Example:

```
def is_equal(r1, r2):
    if r1 is None and r2 is None:
        return True
    if r1 is None or r2 is None:
        return False
    return (r1.data == r2.data and
            is_equal(r1.left, r2.left) and
            is_equal(r1.right, r2.right))
```

Find the Height of a Tree

The **height** is the number of nodes along the longest path from the root to a leaf.

Function to Find the Height of a Tree:

C++ Example:

```
int height(Node* root) {
    if (!root) return 0;
    int leftHeight = height(root->left);
    int rightHeight = height(root->right);
    return 1 + max(leftHeight, rightHeight);
}
```

Python Example:

```
def height(root):
    if root is None:
        return 0
    return 1 + max(height(root.left), height(root.right))
```

The following table summarizes the key operations on a binary tree, along with their purpose and average time complexity:

Operation	Purpose	Time Complexity (Avg)
Traversal	Visit all nodes in order.	O(n)
Insertion	Add a node.	O(log n) to O(n)
Deletion	Remove a node.	O(log n) to O(n)
Search	Find a value.	O(log n) to O(n)
Height	Compute tree depth.	O(n)
Count Nodes	Total number of nodes.	O(n)
Count Leaves	Total leaf nodes.	O(n)

Table 6.2: *Binary Tree Operations*

Expression Trees

An **expression tree** is a specialized form of a binary tree used to represent arithmetic expressions. It follows these properties:

- Every **leaf node** corresponds to an operand (such as a constant or variable).
- Every **internal node**, including the root, represents an operator.
- Each **subtree** represents a subexpression, with its root node acting as the operator for that subexpression.

The expression tree for the following infix expression is as follows:

```
( ( 6 + ( 3 - 2 ) * 5 ) ^ 2 + 3 )
```

The process of constructing a binary tree from a postfix expression ultimately results in a special type of binary tree known as an **expression tree**, where operators form the internal nodes and operands occupy the leaf nodes. This is illustrated in *Figure 6.16*.

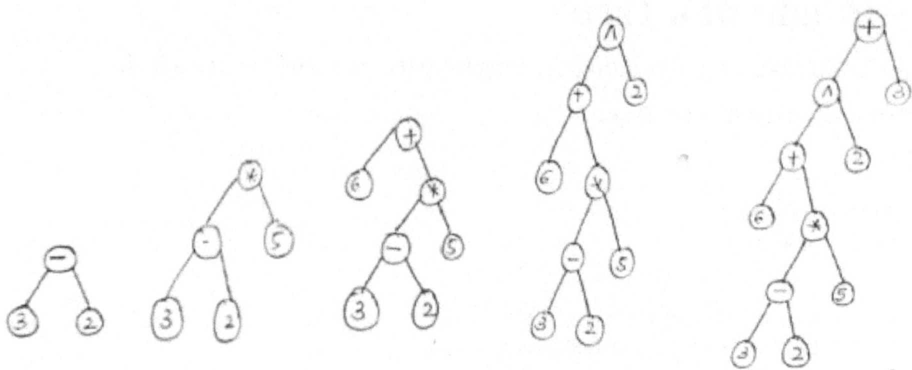

Figure 6.16: *An Expression Tree*

Conversion:

Postfix: 632-5*+2^3+

Prefix: +^+6#-32523

Algorithm: Constructing a Binary Tree from a Postfix Expression

Read the postfix expression from **left to right**, while scanning one symbol at a time. For each symbol encountered, create a **new node**.

1. If the symbol is an **operand**, push its node onto the stack.
2. If the symbol is an **operator**:
   a. Pop the first node from the stack and make it the **right child** of the operator node (since in postfix, the first popped element is the right operand).
   b. Pop the second node from the stack and make it the **left child** of the operator node.
   c. Push this operator node (now linked with its left and right subtrees) back onto the stack.

Repeat this process until the entire postfix expression is scanned. Once all the symbols have been processed, the node remaining at the **top of the stack** will represent the **root of the expression tree**.

C++ Implementation – Expression Tree:

```
#include <iostream>
#include <stack>
#include <cmath>
#include <cctype>
using namespace std;

struct Node {
    char data;
    Node* left;
    Node* right;
    Node(char val) : data(val), left(nullptr), right(nullptr) {}
};

// Create expression tree from postfix
Node* createExpressionTree(string postfix) {
    stack<Node*> st;
    for (char ch : postfix) {
        Node* node = new Node(ch);
        if (isalnum(ch)) {
            st.push(node);
        } else {
            node->right = st.top(); st.pop();
            node->left = st.top(); st.pop();
            st.push(node);
        }
    }
    return st.top();
}

// Evaluate expression tree
float evaluate(Node* root) {
    if (!root) return 0;
    char ch = root->data;
    if (isdigit(ch)) return ch - '0';
    float leftVal = evaluate(root->left);
    float rightVal = evaluate(root->right);
    switch(ch) {
        case '+': return leftVal + rightVal;
        case '-': return leftVal - rightVal;
        case '*': return leftVal * rightVal;
        case '/': return leftVal / rightVal;
        case '^': return pow(leftVal, rightVal);
    }
    return 0;
}

// Display tree
void display(Node* root, int level=0) {
    if (!root) return;
    display(root->right, level + 1);
    for (int i = 0; i < level; i++) cout << "    ";
```

```
    cout << root->data << "\n";
    display(root->left, level + 1);
}

int main() {
    string postfix;
    cout << "Enter postfix expression: ";
    cin >> postfix;
    Node* root = createExpressionTree(postfix);
    cout << "Expression Tree:\n";
    display(root);
    cout << "Result = " << evaluate(root) << "\n";
    return 0;
}
```

Python Implementation – Expression Tree:

```
class Node:
    def __init__(self, data):
        self.data = data
        self.left = None
        self.right = None

def create_expression_tree(postfix):
    stack = []
    for ch in postfix:
        node = Node(ch)
        if ch.isalnum():
            stack.append(node)
        else:
            node.right = stack.pop()
            node.left = stack.pop()
            stack.append(node)
    return stack[0]

def evaluate(root):
    if root.data.isdigit():
        return int(root.data)
    left = evaluate(root.left)
    right = evaluate(root.right)
    if root.data == '+': return left + right
    if root.data == '-': return left - right
    if root.data == '*': return left * right
    if root.data == '/': return left / right
    if root.data == '^': return left ** right

def display(root, level=0):
    if root is None:
        return
    display(root.right, level + 1)
    print('    ' * level + root.data)
    display(root.left, level + 1)

postfix = input("Enter postfix expression: ")
root = create_expression_tree(postfix)
```

```
print("Expression Tree:")
display(root)
print("Result =", evaluate(root))
```

Validate a BST

Given a binary tree, check if it satisfies the **BST property**:

Recursive Method:

a. Keep track of the **allowed value range** for each node.

b. Initially, the root node can take any value.

c. For the left child, update the **maximum allowed value** to the parent's value.

d. For the right child, update the **minimum allowed value** to the parent's value.

e. If any node violates the allowed range, the tree is **not a BST**.

C++ Example:

```
bool isBST(Node* root, int minVal, int maxVal) {
    if (!root) return true;
    if (root->data < minVal || root->data > maxVal) return false;
    return isBST(root->left, minVal, root->data - 1) &&
           isBST(root->right, root->data + 1, maxVal);
}

// Usage
bool result = isBST(root, INT_MIN, INT_MAX);
```

Python Example:

```
def isBST(root, min_val=float('-inf'), max_val=float('inf')):
    if not root:
        return True
    if root.data < min_val or root.data > max_val:
        return False
    return (isBST(root.left, min_val, root.data - 1) and
            isBST(root.right, root.data + 1, max_val))

# Usage
result = isBST(root)
```

This method efficiently validates the BST property by ensuring that all nodes follow the ordering rules recursively.

Lowest Common Ancestor

The **Lowest Common Ancestor (LCA)** of two nodes n1 and n2 in a BST is defined as the **deepest node that has both n1 and n2 as descendants** (a node can be a descendant of itself).

If both n1 and n2 are smaller than the current node, LCA lies in the **left subtree**.

If both are larger, LCA lies in the **right subtree**.

Otherwise, the current node is the **LCA**.

Given a BST and two nodes n1 and n2, find the **lowest common ancestor**, which is the deepest node that has both n1 and n2 as descendants.

Example: In a binary tree, the Lowest Common Ancestor (LCA) of two given nodes is the deepest node that has both nodes as its descendants. This concept is illustrated in *Figure 6.17*.

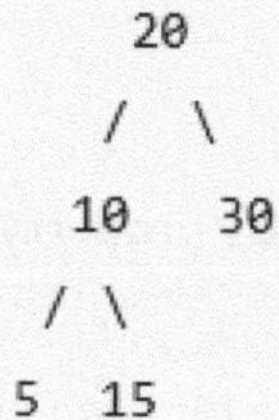

***Figure 6.17:** Lowest Common Ancestor*

LCA of 5 and 15 is 10, and LCA of 5 and 30 is 20.

C++ Example:

```
Node* LCA(Node* root, int n1, int n2) {
    if (!root) return nullptr;

    if (root->data > n1 && root->data > n2)
        return LCA(root->left, n1, n2);
    if (root->data < n1 && root->data < n2)
        return LCA(root->right, n1, n2);

    return root; // This is the split point
}
```

Python Example:

```
def LCA(root, n1, n2):
    if not root:
        return None

    if root.data > n1 and root.data > n2:
        return LCA(root.left, n1, n2)
    if root.data < n1 and root.data < n2:
        return LCA(root.right, n1, n2)

    return root  # This is the split point
```

In a BST, the **search path naturally guides us to the LCA** by comparing node values. This approach works in **`O(h)` time**, where h is the height of the tree.

Conclusion

In this chapter, we explored **trees and Binary Search Trees (BSTs)**, learning how hierarchical data can be efficiently represented, traversed, and manipulated. You now understand **tree terminology, binary tree construction, various traversal techniques**, and key **BST operations** such as insertion, deletion, search, and height calculation. We also discussed **balanced versus unbalanced BSTs**, their impact on performance, and practical applications, including **expression trees, BST validation, and finding the Lowest Common Ancestor (LCA)**. These concepts provide a strong foundation for solving problems involving hierarchical and recursive data. Building on the knowledge of trees, the next chapter will introduce the concept of **heaps**, which is a specialized tree structure used to implement **priority queues efficiently**. You will learn also about **min-heaps and max-heaps, heap operations** such as insertion, deletion, and heapify, as well as **heap construction from arrays**. The chapter will cover **heapsort** and real-world applications such as **scheduling, top-K problems, and real-time processing**. Mastering heaps will enable you to handle scenarios where **priority and quick access to extreme**

elements are crucial, while bridging the concepts of hierarchical trees to efficient, priority-driven data management.

Points to Remember

- A **tree** is a hierarchical data structure consisting of nodes connected by edges.
- The **height** of a tree is the length of the longest path from the root to a leaf.
- **Binary Tree:** Each node has at most two children (left and right).
- **Binary Search Tree (BST):** Left subtree contains smaller elements; right subtree contains larger elements.
- **Balanced BST:** Height is minimized; operations are `O(log n)` on average.
- **Unbalanced BST:** May degenerate into a linear structure; worst-case operations `O(n)`
- **Tree Traversals:**
    - **Inorder:** Left → Root → Right (sorted order in BST)
    - **Preorder:** Root → Left → Right (useful for copying or serializing the tree)
    - **Postorder:** Left → Right → Root (useful for deleting nodes)
    - **Level-order:** Visit nodes level by level using a queue.
- Other BST operations include finding max/min, counting nodes/leaves, copying, checking equality, and computing height.
- **Expression Trees:** Leaf nodes are operands, while internal nodes are operators; they are used to evaluate arithmetic expressions.

Multiple Choice Questions

1. Which of the following traversal of a BST produces elements in **sorted order**?
    a. Preorder
    b. Inorder
    c. Postorder
    d. Level-Order
2. In a BST, the **maximum element** is found by following:
    a. Left Child Pointers
    b. Right Child Pointers
    c. Both Left and Right Child Pointers
    d. None of the Above
3. What is the **time complexity of search** in a **balanced BST** with n nodes?
    a. `O(n)`
    b. `O(log n)`
    c. `O(n log n)`
    d. `O(1)`

4. Which traversal is used to **delete a tree** safely?
   a. Inorder
   b. Preorder
   c. Postorder
   d. Level-order
5. The **height of a perfectly balanced BST** with 7 nodes is:
   a. 2
   b. 3
   c. 4
   d. 7
6. What is the **space complexity** of recursive inorder traversal for a tree of height h?
   a. `O(1)`
   b. `O(log n)`
   c. `O(h)`
   d. `O(n²)`
7. Which traversal method uses a **queue** data structure?
   a. Preorder
   b. Postorder
   c. Inorder
   d. Level-order
8. What is the **minimum number of nodes** in a binary tree of height h?
   a. `h`
   b. `2^h - 1`
   c. `h + 1`
   d. `2^(h-1)`
9. In an **unbalanced BST** with n nodes inserted in ascending order, the **time complexity of search** is:
   a. `O(log n)`
   b. `O(n)`
   c. `O(1)`
   d. `O(n log n)`
10. Which of the following is **true for a leaf node**?
    a. It has one child.
    b. It has no children.
    c. It is always the root.
    d. It always has two children.
11. Which of the following is **not a property of a BST**?
    a. Left subtree contains nodes smaller than the root.
    b. Right subtree contains nodes greater than the root.

   c. Duplicate nodes are always allowed in the right subtree.
   d. Both left and right subtrees are BSTs.

12. An **expression tree** is primarily used for:
   a. Searching elements efficiently
   b. Evaluating arithmetic expressions
   c. Counting nodes
   d. Traversing trees in level-order

13. Which of the following statements about **balanced BSTs** is correct?
   a. Height is minimal for the given number of nodes.
   b. Height equals to the number of nodes.
   c. Only preorder traversal is efficient.
   d. Search operation always takes O(n).

14. What is the **Lowest Common Ancestor (LCA)** of two nodes in a BST?
   a. The root of the tree.
   b. The smallest node, which is greater than both nodes.
   c. The deepest node that has both nodes as descendants.
   d. The parent of the first node only.

Answers

1. b.
2. b.
3. b.
4. c.
5. b.
6. c.
7. d.
8. a.
9. b.
10. b.
11. c.
12. b.
13. a.
14. c.

Questions

1. Explain the difference between a **binary tree** and a **Binary Search Tree (BST)**.
2. Write recursive functions for **inorder, preorder, and postorder traversals** of a binary tree.
3. Implement a function to **count the number of leaf nodes** in a BST.
4. How does a **level-order traversal** differ from depth-first traversals?

5. Write an algorithm to **find the Lowest Common Ancestor (LCA)** of two nodes in a BST.
6. Given the **preorder and inorder traversal arrays** of a BST, reconstruct the tree.
7. Explain the difference between a **balanced** and an **unbalanced BST**, and how it affects operation complexity.
8. What is an **expression tree**, and how is it used to evaluate arithmetic expressions?
9. Write a function to **validate whether a given binary tree is a BST**.
10. Discuss the **time and space complexity** of different tree traversal methods (recursive and iterative).

Key Terms

- **Tree:** A hierarchical data structure with nodes connected by edges
- **Node:** An element of a tree that contains data and references to its children
- **Root:** The topmost node of a tree
- **Leaf Node:** A node with no children
- **Height:** The number of nodes along the longest path from the root to a leaf
- **Binary Tree:** A tree where each node has at most two children
- **Binary Search Tree (BST):** A binary tree where left child < root < right child
- **Balanced BST:** A BST with minimal height for efficient operations
- **Unbalanced BST:** A BST that may degenerate into a linear structure
- **Traversal:** Visiting all nodes of a tree in a specific order
- **Inorder Traversal:** Left → Root → Right
- **Preorder Traversal:** Root → Left → Right
- **Postorder Traversal:** Left → Right → Root
- **Level-order Traversal:** Visiting nodes level by level using a queue.
- **Expression Tree:** A binary tree where leaf nodes are operands and internal nodes are operators
- **Lowest Common Ancestor (LCA):** The deepest node that has both given nodes as descendants

CHAPTER 7

Heaps and Priority Queues

Introduction

In many real-life situations, we often need to process tasks or data based on priority, rather than the order they arrive in. For example, in a hospital emergency room, patients with more severe conditions are treated before those with minor issues. In a computer system, certain processes or tasks may need to run before others depending on their urgency or importance. When managing events, the next event to happen is the one with the earliest time. A heap is a specialized data structure designed to solve this efficiently: It maintains the order of elements so that the highest (or lowest) priority is always easy to access at the root. It allows inserting new items and removing the highest priority item quickly (in logarithmic time). This makes heaps perfect for implementing priority queues, which are essential in scheduling, simulations, and many algorithms. In short, heaps and priority queues help us manage and process prioritized data efficiently and dynamically. This is important for both everyday applications and complex computer algorithms. Therefore, throughout this chapter, we will explore the fundamental concepts, operations, step-by-step implementations, and practical applications of these data structures. Additionally, we will cover their C and Python implementations and solve a collection of common coding patterns and interview-focused problems to strengthen your conceptual understanding and programming skills.

Structure

In this chapter, we will cover the following topics:

- Heap
- Heapsort
- Priority Queue

Heap

A heap is a specialized tree-based data structure that satisfies the heap property. It is typically implemented as a complete binary tree, which means that all levels of the tree are fully filled except possibly the last level. The last level is filled from left to right. The most important thing about a heap is that it takes O(1) time to find the largest element in the heap. Furthermore, it takes O(log n) time to extract the largest element from the heap (finding and removing it). These properties make heaps very useful for implementing a priority queue.

Heap Property

The **heap property** defines the fundamental ordering rule that distinguishes heaps from other tree-based data structures. It dictates a consistent relationship between each parent node and its child nodes, while ensuring that a parent's key is either always greater than or equal to (in a Max heap) or always less than or equal to (in a Min heap) the keys of its children. Therefore, this property preserves the hierarchical order required for efficient priority-based operations such as insertion, deletion, and retrieval of the root element.

Min Heap Property

A min heap is a binary heap data structure that satisfies the following property:

For every node i, the value of i is less than or equal to the values of its children.

Key Properties of a Min Heap

- Heap Order Property:
  - Parent ≤ Left Child
  - Parent ≤ Right Child
  - This ensures that the smallest element is always at the root.
- Complete Binary Tree:
  - All levels are fully filled except possibly the last, which is filled from left to right.

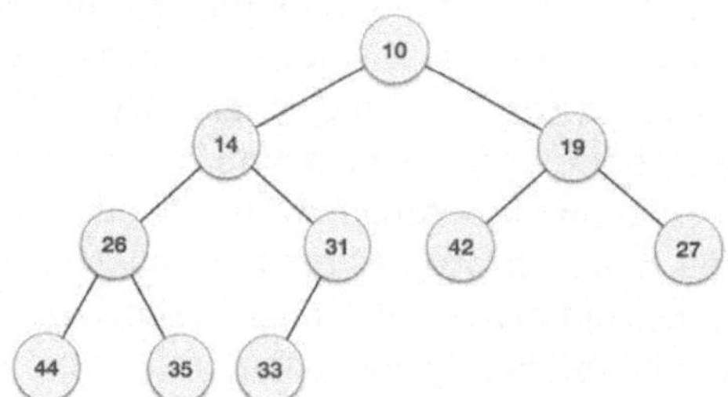

Figure 7.1: *Min Heap*

Min Heap in Array Form

Min heaps are often implemented using arrays, where for a node at index i:

- Left Child = 2*i + 1
- Right Child = 2*i + 2
- Parent = (i - 1) // 2

Here is an array representation of the previous example:

0	1	2	3	4	5	6	7	8	9	**Array index**
10	14	19	26	31	42	27	44	35	33	**Node value**

Table 7.1: *Array Representation for Min Heap Shown in Figure 7.1*

Max Heap Property

A max heap is a binary heap where:

For every node i, the value of i is greater than or equal to the values of its children.

Key Properties of a Max Heap

Heap Order Property:

- Parent ≥ Left Child
- Parent ≥ Right Child
- Ensures the largest element is always at the root

Complete Binary Tree:

a. All levels are completely filled except possibly the last, which is filled left to right.

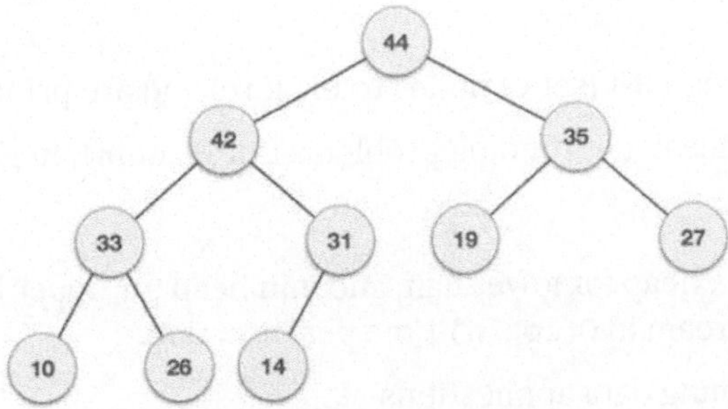

Figure 7.2: *Max Heap*

Max Heap in Array Form

Max heaps are often implemented using arrays, where for a node at index i:

- Left Child = 2*i + 1
- Right Child = 2*i + 2
- Parent = (i - 1) // 2

Here is an array representation of the previous example:

0	1	2	3	4	5	6	7	8	9	Array index
44	42	35	33	31	19	27	10	26	14	Node value

Table 7.2: *Array Representation for Max Heap Shown in Figure 7.2*

Applications of Heaps

Heaps (especially min heaps and max heaps) are used in many algorithmic and real-world applications due to their efficient insert and extract (min/max) operations. Here are their key applications:

Priority Queues

- Most common use-case of heaps
- A heap efficiently implements a priority queue where elements are inserted with priorities and the highest (or lowest) priority item is always removed first.
- Min Heap → Lowest priority first
- Max Heap → Highest priority first

Heap Sort

- Sorting algorithm that uses a heap
- Steps:
  1. Build a Max Heap from the array.

2. Repeatedly extract the max and move it to the end.
3. Time Complexity: `O(n log n)`
4. In-place and non-stable

Dijkstra's Algorithm (for the Shortest Paths)

- Uses a min Heap (priority queue) to efficiently pick the next vertex with the smallest distance
- Reduces time complexity from `O(V²)` to `O((V + E) log V)` when using a heap-based priority queue

Search Algorithm

- Heaps manage the open list (set of nodes to explore) and are prioritized by cost estimate.
- Improves performance in pathfinding problems (for example, in games and robotics)

Median Maintenance

- Use two heaps (a max heap for lower half, and min heap for upper half) to maintain the median of a dynamic data stream in `O(log n)` time per insertion.
- Very useful in streaming data applications

Job Scheduling in Operating Systems

- Heaps are used to schedule jobs based on priority (for example, CPU task scheduling).
- Ensures that high-priority jobs are executed first

Kth Largest / Smallest Element

- Use min heap (for kth largest) or max heap (for kth smallest) to find the kth element in an array in `O(n log k)` time.

Merging K Sorted Lists / Arrays

- Use a min heap to efficiently merge k sorted lists in `O(n log k)` time (used in external sorting, big data apps).

Bandwidth Management / Load Balancing

- Use min heap to always assign new tasks to the least loaded server.

Real-time Event Simulation / Gaming

- Heaps help manage events by priority (for example, in simulations or game engines, where events must be triggered in order).

Building a Heap

All nodes in a heap are subjected to **`MaxHeapify`** by the **`BuildMaxHeap`** process, which begins at the nodes directly above the leaves and works its way down to the root. Since we need the subtrees of a node to already be heaps in order to perform **`MaxHeapify`** on it, we will begin from the bottom. Remember that the nodes indexed by bn=2c+1 are the heap's leaves. Thus, when we utilize our array implementation, we simply begin at the index **`bA:length=2c`**, and then go towards 1.

`Build_max_heap(A)`

1. `A.heap_size = A.length`
2. `for i = ⌊A>length/2⌋downto 1`
3. `Max_heapify(A,i)`

Max_heapify(A,i)

1. `L = Left(i)`
2. `R = Right(i)`
3. `If L ≤ A.heap_size and A[L] > A[i]`
4. `Largest = L`
5. `Else largest = i`
6. `If R ≤ A.heap_size and A[r] > A[largest]`
7. `Largest = R`
8. `if Largest ≠ i`
9. `Exchange A[i] with A[largest]`
10. `Max_heapify(A, largest)`

C++ Implementation:

```
#include <iostream>
using namespace std;

// Function to heapify a subtree rooted with node i
// n is size of heap
void heapify(int arr[], int n, int i) {
    int largest = i;          // Initialize largest as root
    int left = 2 * i + 1;     // Left child index
    int right = 2 * i + 2;    // Right child index

    // If left child is larger than root
    if (left < n && arr[left] > arr[largest])
        largest = left;

    // If right child is larger than largest so far
    if (right < n && arr[right] > arr[largest])
        largest = right;

    // If largest is not root
    if (largest != i) {
        swap(arr[i], arr[largest]);

        // Recursively heapify the affected subtree
        heapify(arr, n, largest);
    }
}

// Function to build a Max Heap
void buildHeap(int arr[], int n) {
    // Index of last non-leaf node
    int startIdx = (n / 2) - 1;

    // Perform reverse level order traversal
    // from last non-leaf node and heapify each node
    for (int i = startIdx; i >= 0; i--) {
        heapify(arr, n, i);
    }
}

// Utility function to print the heap
void printHeap(int arr[], int n) {
    for (int i = 0; i < n; i++)
```

```
        cout << arr[i] << " ";
    cout << endl;
}
int main() {
    int arr[] = {4, 10, 3, 5, 1};
    int n = sizeof(arr) / sizeof(arr[0]);

    cout << "Original array:" << endl;
    printHeap(arr, n);

    buildHeap(arr, n);

    cout << "Array represented as Max Heap:" << endl;
    printHeap(arr, n);

    return 0;
}
```

Python Implementation:

```
def heapify(arr, n, i):
    largest = i         # Initialize largest as root
    left = 2 * i + 1    # left child
    right = 2 * i + 2   # right child

    # If left child is larger than root
    if left < n and arr[left] > arr[largest]:
        largest = left

    # If right child is larger than largest so far
    if right < n and arr[right] > arr[largest]:
        largest = right

    # If largest is not root
    if largest != i:
        arr[i], arr[largest] = arr[largest], arr[i]  # swap
        heapify(arr, n, largest)


def buildHeap(arr):
    n = len(arr)
    # Index of last non-leaf node
    startIdx = (n // 2) - 1

    # Perform reverse level order traversal
    for i in range(startIdx, -1, -1):
        heapify(arr, n, i)


def printHeap(arr):
    print(" ".join(map(str, arr)))


# Driver code
if __name__ == "__main__":
    arr = [4, 10, 3, 5, 1]

    print("Original array:")
    printHeap(arr)

    buildHeap(arr)
```

```
print("Array represented as Max-Heap:")
    printHeap(arr)
```

Figure 7.3 shows the Data Structure Before the Call to **Max_heapify** in Line 3 of **Build_max_heap**. *(a)* A 10-Element Input Array A and the Binary Tree It Represents. The Figure Shows the Loop Index i Refers to Node 5 before the Call **Max_heapify(A,i)**. *(b)* The Data Structure That Results. The Loop Index i for *The Next Iteration* Refers to **Node 4**. (c) – (e) Subsequent Iterations of the for Loop in **Build_max_heap**. Observe That Whenever **Max_heapify** is Called on a Node, the Two Subtrees of That Node are Both Max-Heaps. *(f)* The Max-Heap after **Build_max_heap** Finishes:

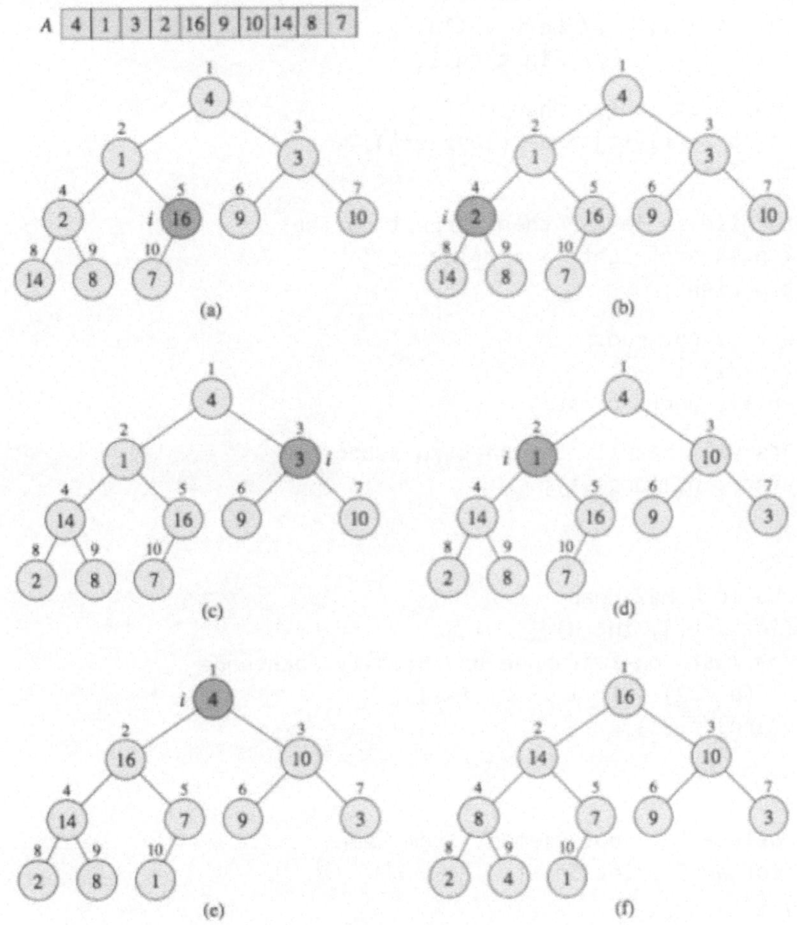

Figure 7.3: The Operation of *Build_max_heap*

Runtime:

- **Basic Upper Bound:** There are **O(n)** calls to **MaxHeapify**, each of which takes **O(log n)** time. Therefore, the running time is **O(n log n)**.
- **Better Upper Bound:** Recall that an n-element heap has height log **n** ⌊**log n** ⌋. Additionally, an n element heap has at most ⌊**n/ 2 h+1**⌋ nodes of any height h.

Delete Element from Max Heap

In a max heap, deletion usually means removing the root element (the maximum).

Steps to Delete from a Heap

1. Swap the root with the last element.

2. Remove the last element (which was the root).
3. Call **heapify()** on the root to restore the heap property.

C++ Implementation:

```
#include <iostream>
using namespace std;
// Function to heapify a subtree rooted with node i
void heapify(int arr[], int n, int i) {
    int largest = i;        // Initialize largest as root
    int left = 2 * i + 1;   // Left child
    int right = 2 * i + 2;  // Right child

    // If left child is larger than root
    if (left < n && arr[left] > arr[largest])
        largest = left;

    // If right child is larger than largest so far
    if (right < n && arr[right] > arr[largest])
        largest = right;

    // If largest is not root
    if (largest != i) {
        swap(arr[i], arr[largest]);

        // Recursively heapify the affected subtree
        heapify(arr, n, largest);
    }
}

// Function to build a Max-Heap
void buildHeap(int arr[], int n) {
    // Start from last non-leaf node and heapify each node
    for (int i = (n / 2) - 1; i >= 0; i--) {
        heapify(arr, n, i);
    }
}

// Function to delete the root element from heap
int deleteRoot(int arr[], int &n) {
    if (n <= 0) {
        cout << "Heap is empty!" << endl;
        return -1;
    }

    // Root element to be deleted
    int root = arr[0];

    // Step 1: Replace root with last element
    arr[0] = arr[n - 1];

    // Step 2: Reduce heap size
    n--;

    // Step 3: Heapify root to maintain heap property
    heapify(arr, n, 0);

    return root;
}
```

```
// Utility function to print heap
void printHeap(int arr[], int n) {
    for (int i = 0; i < n; i++)
        cout << arr[i] << " ";
    cout << endl;
}

// Driver code
int main() {
    int arr[] = {4, 10, 3, 5, 1};
    int n = sizeof(arr) / sizeof(arr[0]);

    cout << "Original array:" << endl;
    printHeap(arr, n);

    buildHeap(arr, n);
    cout << "Max-Heap:" << endl;
    printHeap(arr, n);

    int deleted = deleteRoot(arr, n);
    cout << "Deleted root element: " << deleted << endl;

    cout << "Heap after deletion:" << endl;
    printHeap(arr, n);

    return 0;
}
```

Python Implementation:

```
def heapify(arr, n, i):
    largest = i
    left = 2 * i + 1
    right = 2 * i + 2

    if left < n and arr[left] > arr[largest]:
        largest = left

    if right < n and arr[right] > arr[largest]:
        largest = right

    if largest != i:
        arr[i], arr[largest] = arr[largest], arr[i]
        heapify(arr, n, largest)

def buildHeap(arr):
    n = len(arr)
    for i in range((n // 2) - 1, -1, -1):
        heapify(arr, n, i)

def deleteRoot(arr, n):
    # Step 1: Replace root with last element
    arr[0], arr[n - 1] = arr[n - 1], arr[0]

    # Step 2: Remove last element
    root = arr.pop()

    # Step 3: Heapify root to maintain heap property
```

```
    heapify(arr, len(arr), 0)

    return root   # return deleted root value

def printHeap(arr):
    print(" ".join(map(str, arr)))

# Driver code
if __name__ == "__main__":
    arr = [4, 10, 3, 5, 1]
    print("Original array:")
    printHeap(arr)

    buildHeap(arr)
    print("Max-Heap:")
    printHeap(arr)

    deleted = deleteRoot(arr, len(arr))
    print(f"Deleted root element: {deleted}")
    print("Heap after deletion:")
    printHeap(arr)
```

Other Operations on Max Heap

A max heap supports several useful operations besides just building and deleting.

Hence, the common operations enacted on a max heap are:

1. **Insertion**
    a. Insert the new element at the end.
    b. "*Bubble up*" (**heapify-up**) until heap property is restored.

C++ Implementation:

```
void insert(int arr[], int &n, int value) {
    n++;
    int i = n - 1;
    arr[i] = value;    // Place new element at the end

    // Heapify-up (percolate up)
    while (i != 0 && arr[(i - 1) / 2] < arr[i]) {
        swap(arr[i], arr[(i - 1) / 2]);
        i = (i - 1) / 2;
    }
}
```

2. **Get Maximum (Peek):** The maximum element is always at index 0 (root).

C Implementation:

```
int getMax(int arr[], int n) {
    if (n <= 0) {
        printf("Heap is empty!\n");
        return -1;
    }
    return arr[0];
}
```

3. **Increase/Decrease Key**
   a. Increase key: Replace a value with a larger one → Bubble-up.
   b. Decrease key: Replace a value with a smaller one → Heapify-down.

C++ Implementation:

```
// Function to increase the key value at index i
void increaseKey(int arr[], int i, int newValue) {
    arr[i] = newValue;

    // Heapify-up (percolate up) to maintain Max-Heap property
    while (i != 0 && arr[(i - 1) / 2] < arr[i]) {
        swap(arr[i], arr[(i - 1) / 2]);
        i = (i - 1) / 2;
    }
}
```

Python Implementation:

```
class MaxHeap:
    def __init__(self):
        self.heap = []

    # Utility function to swap elements
    def swap(self, i, j):
        self.heap[i], self.heap[j] = self.heap[j], self.heap[i]

    # Heapify-down (used in deleteRoot and heapSort)
    def heapify(self, n, i):
        largest = i
        left = 2 * i + 1
        right = 2 * i + 2

        if left < n and self.heap[left] > self.heap[largest]:
            largest = left

        if right < n and self.heap[right] > self.heap[largest]:
            largest = right

        if largest != i:
            self.swap(i, largest)
            self.heapify(n, largest)

    # Build heap from existing array
    def buildHeap(self, arr):
        self.heap = arr[:]
        n = len(self.heap)
        for i in range((n // 2) - 1, -1, -1):
            self.heapify(n, i)

    # Insert new element
    def insert(self, value):
        self.heap.append(value)
        i = len(self.heap) - 1
        # Bubble up
        while i > 0 and self.heap[(i - 1) // 2] < self.heap[i]:
            self.swap(i, (i - 1) // 2)
```

```
            i = (i - 1) // 2

    # Get maximum element
    def getMax(self):
        if not self.heap:
            return None
        return self.heap[0]

    # Delete root (maximum element)
    def deleteRoot(self):
        if not self.heap:
            return None
        n = len(self.heap)
        root = self.heap[0]
        self.heap[0] = self.heap[n - 1]
        self.heap.pop()
        self.heapify(len(self.heap), 0)
        return root

    # Increase key at index i
    def increaseKey(self, i, newValue):
        if i < 0 or i >= len(self.heap):
            return
        self.heap[i] = newValue
        # Bubble up
        while i > 0 and self.heap[(i - 1) // 2] < self.heap[i]:
            self.swap(i, (i - 1) // 2)
            i = (i - 1) // 2

    # Heap Sort
    def heapSort(self):
        n = len(self.heap)
        arr = self.heap[:]
        for i in range(n - 1, 0, -1):
            arr[0], arr[i] = arr[i], arr[0]
            self._heapify_static(arr, i, 0)
        return arr

    # Static heapify (for heapSort only)
    def _heapify_static(self, arr, n, i):
        largest = i
        left = 2 * i + 1
        right = 2 * i + 2

        if left < n and arr[left] > arr[largest]:
            largest = left
        if right < n and arr[right] > arr[largest]:
            largest = right
        if largest != i:
            arr[i], arr[largest] = arr[largest], arr[i]
            self._heapify_static(arr, n, largest)

    # Print heap
    def printHeap(self):
        print(self.heap)
```

Heapsort

Heapsort is a method in which a binary tree is used. In this method first the heap is created using a binary tree, and then the heap is sorted using a priority queue. Heapsort is a way of sorting arrays. First, we use **`BuildMaxHeap`** to turn the array into a max-heap. Now, we can extract the maximum (that is, the root) from the heap, while swapping it with the last element in the array, and then shrinking the size of the heap, so that we never operate on the max element again. At this point, the heap property is violated because the root may be smaller than other elements. Therefore, we call **`MaxHeapify`** on the root, which restores the max heap property. Now, we can keep repeating this until the whole array is sorted.

Heapsort(A)

1. `Build_max_heap(a)`
2. `For i = A.length downto 2`
3. `Exchange A[1] with A[i]`
4. `A.heapsize = A.heap_size-1`
5. `Max_heapify(A,i)`

Example:

25 57 48 38 10 91 84 33

In the heapsort method, we first take all these elements in the array "A":

A[0]	A[1]	A[2]	A[3]	A[4]	A[5]	A[6]	A[7]
25	57	48	38	10	91	84	33

Now, start building the heap structure. The key point while forming the heap is building it in such a way that the highest value in the array will always be a root.

Insert 25:

Figure 7.4: *Heap after Inserting 25*

Insert 57:

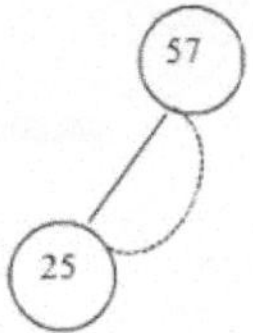

Figure 7.5: *Heap after Inserting 57 (57 Becomes the Root, 25 as Left Child)*

Since 25<57, 57 is the root, and 25 is the left child.

Insert 48:

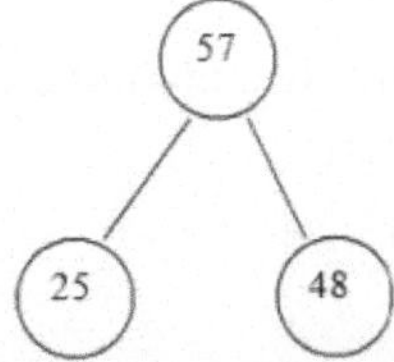

Figure 7.6: *Heap after Inserting 48 (48 as Right Child of 57)*

Now, since 48 is less than 57, it cannot be a root. Therefore, the root is 57. However, 48>25, so it cannot be the left child of 25. Attach 48 as a right child of 57.

Insert 38:

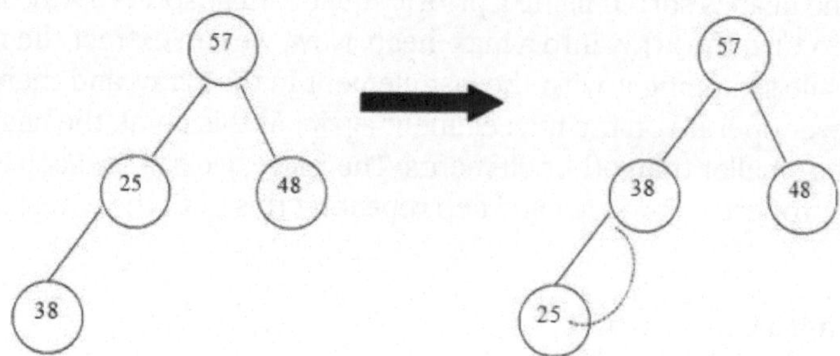

***Figure 7.7**: Heap after Inserting 38 (38 Replaces 25 as Parent)*

As 38>25, so 38 becomes the parent of 25.

Insert 10:

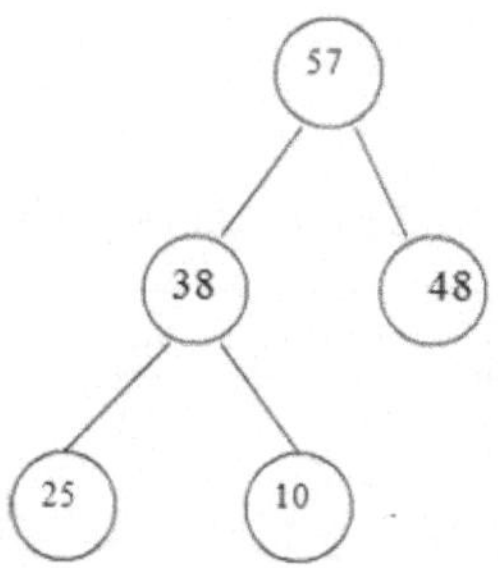

***Figure 7.8**: Heap after Inserting 10 (10 Added as Right Child of 38)*

The element 10 is attached in the left sub tree of 57, that is, as a right child of 38. The element 10 can be attached as a left child of 25, or it can be attached as a left child of 25, or it can be attached as a left child of 48. However, we will always assume to complete the left sub tree having both left and right children. Thus, for the sake of completion, the node 10 is attached to the right of 38.

Insert 91:

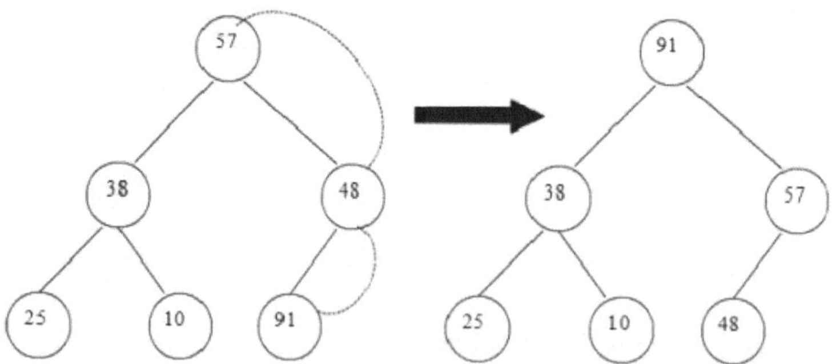

***Figure 7.9**: Heap after Inserting 91 (91 Becomes the New Root)*

As 91 is the largest element compared to all other elements, it will be the root node.

Insert 84:

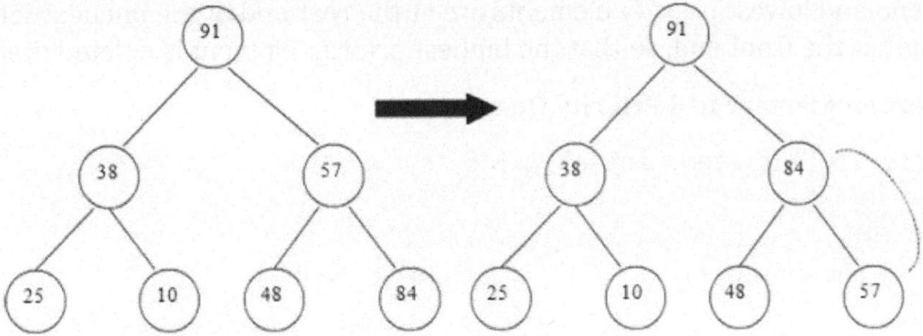

Figure 7.10: *Heap after Inserting 84 (84 as Left Child of 91)*

The next element is 84, now 91>84>57. Therefore, 84 will be the parent of 57. To make the complete binary tree, 57 will be attached to the right of 84.

Insert 33:

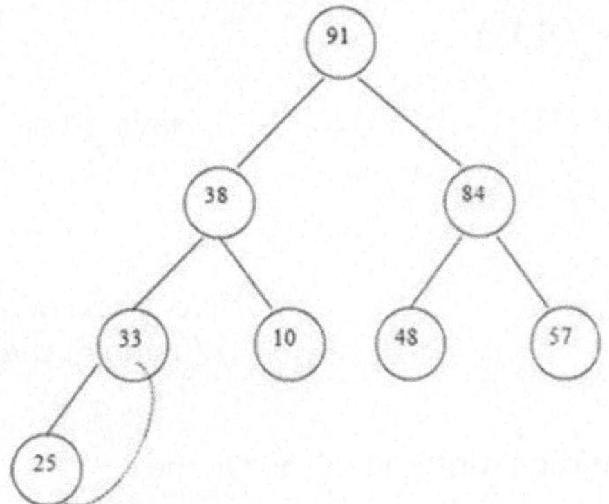

Figure 7.11: *Heap after Inserting 33 (33 Added between 38 and 25)*

The next element is 33, 38>33>25. This makes 33 a parent of 25, but a child of 38.

Priority Queues

A queue in which we are able to insert items or remove items from any position based on priority is called a priority queue. An element with higher priority is always processed before any lower priority element. If the elements in the queue are of the same priority, then the element which is inserted first into the queue is processed. Priority queues are used in job scheduling algorithms in the design of an operating system, where the jobs with the highest priority have to be processed first.

The priority queues are classified into the following groups:

1. **Ascending Priority Queue**: In an ascending priority queue elements can be inserted in any order. However, while deleting an element from the queue, only the smaller element is deleted first.
2. **Descending Priority Queue**: In a descending priority queue elements can be inserted in any order. However, while deleting an element from the queue, only the largest element is deleted first.

Implementation of Priority Queue

In this technique, we will assume that the item to be inserted itself denotes the priority. So, the items with the least value will be considered as higher priority and items with highest value will be considered as the items with least priority. To implement the priority queue, we will insert items in such a way that they are always in increasing order. With this technique, the highest priority elements are at the front end and lowest priority elements are at the rear end of the queue. While deleting, we delete the element at the front end, so that the highest priority element is deleted first.

Function to Insert an Element in a Priority Queue

```
void insert_priority(int item, int q[], int *r)
{
        int j;
        if(*r == queuesize-1)           //check overflow
                {
                printf("Queue is full");
                return;
                }
        j=*r;                                    //compare from initial rear
point

        /*make room for inserting element in appropriate position based on priority*/
        while(j>=0 && item < q[j])
                {
                 q[j+1] = q[j];              //move element from q[j] position to
its next position
                  j--;
                 }
          q[j+1] = item;                //insert element at appropriate position
          *r = *r+1;                       //update the rear pointer
}
```

Function to Delete Element from the Front End of the Queue

```
int delete_front()
         {
         if(front>rear)
                 return -1;
         return q[front++];
         }
```

Applications of Priority Queue

Priority queues are widely used in computer science, operating systems, AI, networking, and real-world applications.

Operating Systems

- **CPU Scheduling**: Processes are scheduled based on priority (for example, highest priority process executed first).
- **Interrupt Handling**: Higher-priority interrupts (for example, emergency signals) are serviced before lower-priority ones.
- **Disk Scheduling**: Requests with higher priority (like system processes) are serviced first.

Graph Algorithms

- **Dijkstra's Shortest Path Algorithm**: Uses a priority queue to always process the next closest vertex
- **Prim's Minimum Spanning Tree Algorithm**: Chooses the next edge with minimum weight using a priority queue

- **A* Search Algorithm**: Uses priority queue (min-heap) to explore nodes with the lowest estimated cost

Networking

- **Packet Scheduling in Routers**: High-priority packets (like voice/video) are transmitted first.
- **Load Balancing**: Tasks with higher importance are scheduled before others.

Data Compression and Encoding

- **Huffman Coding**: Uses priority queue (min-heap) to build an optimal prefix code tree

Event-Driven Simulations

- **Discrete Event Simulation**: Events are stored in a priority queue (ordered by timestamp) and processed in chronological order.

Artificial Intelligence

- **Best-First Search, A* Algorithm**: Nodes are expanded in order of priority (heuristic + cost).
- **Game AI**: Priority queues help decide the most important actions first.

Real-Life Applications

- **Emergency Room in Hospitals**: Patients with more critical conditions are treated first.
- **Job Scheduling in Companies**: Important tasks are executed first.
- **Airline Boarding System**: Priority boarding for business class, elderly, or special needs passengers.
- **Printer Queue**: Urgent documents can be printed first.

In real-world **banking, supply chain, and manufacturing systems**, priority queues implemented using **heaps** are extensively used to manage intelligent decision-making workflows. In banking, AI-driven fraud detection systems prioritize suspicious transactions, so that high-risk activities are investigated before regular transactions. In supply chain management, priority queues help AI systems schedule shipments and warehouse operations based on delivery deadlines, demand urgency, and resource availability. In manufacturing, smart production systems use priority queues to decide which jobs should be processed first based on machine availability, production deadlines, or failure risk. Therefore, heap-based implementation ensures fast insertion and removal of tasks as well as allows these systems to dynamically adapt priorities in real time, while maintaining high efficiency.

Conclusion

In this chapter, we explored the concept of heaps, which are specialized tree-based data structures that efficiently manage data based on priority. We understood how the heap property maintains order in both min and max heaps, while enabling quick access to the smallest or the largest element. Through examples and code illustrations, we learned how to build, insert, and delete elements in a heap, along with additional operations, such as retrieving the maximum element, and modifying key values. The **Heapsort** algorithm demonstrated how heaps form the basis of one of the most efficient sorting techniques, while the discussion on priority queues highlighted their significance in real-world applications like scheduling and graph-based computations. Having mastered heaps, we will now move to **the next chapter**, which introduces **Graph Fundamentals**—a powerful way to model complex relationships using vertices and edges. The upcoming chapter will help you understand different graph types, representations, and traversal techniques such as BFS and DFS, which form the backbone of many advanced algorithms and problem-solving strategies.

Multiple Choice Questions

1. Descending priority queue can be implemented using ______
   a. Max Heap
   b. Min Heap
   c. Min-Max Heap
   d. Tree
2. The ascending heap property is ___________
   a. `A[Parent(i)] =A[i]`
   b. `A[Parent(i)] <= A[i]`
   c. `A[Parent(i)] >= A[i]`
   d. `A[Parent(i)] > 2 * A[i]`
3. Which one of the following array elements represents a binary min heap?
   a. 12 10 8 25 14 17
   b. 8 10 12 25 14 17
   c. 25 17 14 12 10 8
   d. 14 17 25 10 12 8
4. Which of the following data structures is most commonly used to implement a priority queue efficiently?
   a. Linked List
   b. Array
   c. Binary Search Tree
   d. Heap
5. In a Max-Heap, where is the largest element always located?
   a. At a leaf node
   b. At the root node
   c. At the rightmost node
   d. Anywhere in the heap
6. What is the time complexity to insert an element into a binary heap of N elements?
   a. `O(1)`
   b. `O(N)`
   c. `O(log N)`
   d. `O(N log N)`
7. Which of the following is NOT a valid property of a min heap?
   a. The value of each node is less than or equal to the value of its children.
   b. The smallest element is at the root.
   c. It is a complete binary tree.
   d. The value of each node is greater than or equal to the value of its children.

8. A priority queue can be used for which of the following applications?
    a. Implementing an Undo operation in a text editor
    b. Managing print jobs in an operating system
    c. Simulating recursion
    d. Implementing a FIFO queue
9. What is the time complexity to extract the maximum element from a Max-Heap of N elements?
    a. `O(1)`
    b. `O(N)`
    c. `O(log N)`
    d. `O(N log N)`
10. Which of the following algorithms uses a heap data structure?
    a. Bubble Sort
    b. Merge Sort
    c. Heap Sort
    d. Quick Sort

Answers

1. a
2. b
3. b
4. d
5. b
6. c
7. d
8. b
9. c
10. d

Questions

1. Explain different types of heaps with examples for each.
2. Explain applications of heap.
3. Write a function to build a max heap.
4. Write function to delete an element from max heap.
5. Explain the following operation on max heap (i) Insertion (ii) Find maximum (iii) Increase or decrease key.
6. Define heapsort. Write an algorithm to arrange elements using heapsort.
7. Sort the given elements using heapsort: 67, 84, 35, 92, 16, 27, 48, 54, 72.
8. Explain priority queues, their importance, and real-world use cases.

9. Write functions to insert and delete elements in the priority queue.
10. Explain applications of the priority queue.

Key Terms

- **Heap:** A specialized tree-based data structure where parent nodes are either greater than or equal to (max heap) or less than or equal to (min heap) their child nodes.
- **Max Heap:** Parent nodes are either greater than or equal to their child nodes.
- **Min Heap:** Parent nodes are either less than or equal to their child nodes.
- **Heapsort:** An efficient sorting technique based on the heap data structure.
- **Priority Queue:** A priority queue is a type of queue in which elements are served based on their priority rather than their insertion order. This means that the highest or lowest priority element is always processed first.

Chapter 8
Graph Fundamentals

Introduction

Graphs are one of the most versatile and widely used structures in computer science, as they provide a natural way to model relationships and connections between different entities. At their core, graphs consist of **vertices** (also called nodes) and **edges** that link these vertices. They form networks that can represent anything from social connections and transportation routes, to computer networks and organizational hierarchies.

Therefore, understanding graphs is essential because many real-world problems can be mapped onto them. This allows for efficient analysis and solution design. Key characteristics of graphs, such as the **degree of a vertex**, **paths**, and **cycles**, describe their structure and behavior. Graphs can vary in type – they may be **directed or undirected**, **weighted or unweighted**, **connected or disconnected**. Every type has specific applications and algorithmic considerations.

Hence, in this chapter, we will explore how graphs are represented in memory using adjacency matrices and adjacency lists, examine traversal techniques like **Breadth-First Search (BFS)** and **Depth-First Search (DFS)**, and learn how these traversals are applied in practical scenarios, including **cycle detection**, **finding connected components**, and **path finding**. Through examples in **C++ and Python**, as well as visual illustrations of graph structures and traversal processes, learners will be able to develop a strong foundation to solve both academic and real-world graph problems efficiently.

Thus, by the end of this chapter, you will not only understand the fundamentals of graph structures but also be able to implement and apply traversal algorithms to solve practical problems. This will prepare you for more advanced graph algorithms in the following chapters.

Structure

In this chapter, we will cover the following topics:

- Introduction to Graphs
- Types of Graphs
- Graph Representations
- Graph Traversal Techniques

- Applications of Graph Traversal
- Practice Problems

Introduction to Graphs

Graphs are powerful data structures that allow us to represent relationships between objects in a structured and flexible way. They consist of **vertices** (also called nodes), which represent entities; and **edges**, which connect pairs of vertices. This simple combination can model a wide variety of real-world systems, from social networks and transportation maps, to communication networks and organizational hierarchies.

Significance of Graphs in Computer Science

Graphs are among the most powerful and widely used structures in computer science because they provide a natural way to represent relationships between objects. Unlike linear data structures such as arrays or linked lists, graphs can capture **complex, non-linear connections**. This makes them ideal for modeling networks, dependencies, and hierarchies.

One key reason graphs are significant is their **ability to model real-world problems efficiently**. For example:

- **Social Networks:** Users are represented as vertices, and friendships or followers as edges. Algorithms on these graphs help suggest friends, identify communities, and analyze influence.
- **Transportation and Logistics:** Cities or stations are vertices, and roads, railways, or flight routes are edges. Graph algorithms like shortest-path computation optimize routes and travel planning.
- **Computer Networks:** Devices and servers are vertices, while connections between them are edges. Graph traversal and connectivity analysis ensure efficient data routing and fault detection.
- **Web Page Linking:** Web pages are vertices, and hyperlinks are edges. Search engines use graph algorithms to rank pages and determine relevance.

Graphs also serve as the **foundation for advanced algorithms** in areas such as scheduling, compiler design, Artificial Intelligence (AI), and operations research. By learning graph structures and algorithms, students and developers gain the tools to tackle problems that involve interconnections, dependencies, and network dynamics.

Terminology: Vertices, Edges, Degree, Paths, and Cycles

To work effectively with graphs, it is essential to understand the basic components that define their structure. These terms provide a vocabulary for describing and analyzing graphs in both theory and applications.

- **Vertices (Nodes):** Vertices are the fundamental units of a graph, representing entities or objects. For example, in a **transportation network**, each city is a vertex, while in a **social network**, each user is a vertex.
- **Edges:** Edges connect pairs of vertices, representing the relationships or interactions between them. Edges can be **directed**, which indicates a one-way relationship (like a follower on social media); or **undirected**, which indicates a mutual connection (like a friendship). Edges may also carry **weights**, representing distance, cost, or time, which is crucial in applications like routing or logistics.

- **Degree:** The degree of a vertex is the number of edges connected to it. In directed graphs, there are two types:
  - **In-Degree:** Number of edges coming into a vertex
  - **Out-Degree:** Number of edges leaving a vertex

  For example, in a social network, the number of followers of a user corresponds to in-degree and the number of people the user follows corresponds to out-degree.
- **Paths:** A path is a sequence of vertices connected by edges. Paths determine **reachability** between vertices. For instance, in a road network, a path represents a possible route from one city to another.
- **Cycles:** A cycle is a path that starts and ends at the same vertex without repeating any edge. Therefore, detecting cycles is important in **task scheduling**, **deadlock detection**, and analyzing **network loops**.

Types of Graphs

Graphs can take several forms depending on the nature of their edges, connectivity, and structure. Hence, understanding these types is crucial for applying the right algorithms and modeling real-world systems effectively.

Directed and Undirected Graphs: In a **directed graph (digraph)**, edges have a specific direction, which indicate a one-way relationship between vertices. For example, in a social media platform, if user A follows user B, it does not necessarily mean that B follows A; this relationship is directed. In an **undirected graph**, edges have no direction, representing mutual relationships. Friendship networks, road maps between cities, or collaboration networks are common examples where connections are bidirectional.

Weighted and Unweighted Graphs:

- A **weighted graph** assigns numerical values to edges, often representing **cost, distance, or time**. For instance, in a GPS navigation system, weights can indicate travel time between locations. Moreover, weighted graphs are crucial in shortest-path calculations, logistics, and network optimization.
- **Unweighted graphs** treat all edges equally. The focus is solely on whether a connection exists. Some examples of unweighted graphs include basic social networks or simple network topologies, where connectivity matters more than cost or distance.

Connected and Disconnected Graphs: A **connected graph** ensures there is a path between every pair of vertices. This is important in scenarios like transportation networks or fully operational communication systems. A **disconnected graph** contains vertices that cannot reach each other. This occurs in fragmented road networks, isolated computer networks, or partially connected social systems. Thus, handling disconnected graphs often requires applying traversal algorithms to each component individually.

Special Categories (Cyclic, Acyclic, Complete Graphs, Bipartite Graphs)

- **Cyclic versus Acyclic:** Cyclic graphs contain loops, while acyclic graphs do not. Task scheduling or dependency graphs are typically acyclic to prevent circular dependencies.
- **Complete Graphs:** Every vertex is connected to every other vertex, like a fully connected office communication network.
- **Bipartite Graphs:** Vertices are divided into two sets, and edges only connect vertices from different sets. Examples include student-course enrollment systems or job assignment problems.

Python Example (Directed, Weighted Graph Using Adjacency List):

```python
graph = {
    'A': [('B', 5), ('C', 3)],
    'B': [('C', 2)],
    'C': [('A', 1)],
    'D': [('C', 4)]
}
print("Graph adjacency list with weights:", graph)
```

C++ Example (Directed, Weighted Graph Using Adjacency List):

```cpp
#include <iostream>
#include <vector>
using namespace std;

int main() {
    vector<pair<int,int>> graph[4];
    graph[0].push_back({1,5}); // A -> B with weight 5
    graph[0].push_back({2,3}); // A -> C with weight 3
    graph[1].push_back({2,2}); // B -> C with weight 2
    graph[3].push_back({2,4}); // D -> C with weight 4

    for(int i = 0; i < 4; i++) {
        cout << "Vertex " << i << " -> ";
        for(auto &p : graph[i])
            cout << "(" << p.first << "," << p.second << ") ";
        cout << endl;
    }
}
```

Graph Representations

Graphs can be stored in computer memory in several ways, depending on how frequently operations such as traversal, edge look-up, or modification are performed. The two most common representations are the **adjacency matrix** and the **adjacency list**. Each approach offers unique advantages in terms of **speed, memory usage, and ease of implementation**, and is thus explained in more detail.

Adjacency Matrix Representation

An **adjacency matrix** uses a two-dimensional array (or matrix) to represent connections between vertices. If a graph has n vertices, an `n × n` matrix `M` is used, where:

`M[i][j]= 1`, if there is an edge from vertex i to j.

`M[i][j]= 0`, otherwise

For **weighted graphs**, the entry may store the **edge weight**, instead of just 1 or 0.

Consider a directed graph with edges A → B, A → C, and B → C. Its adjacency matrix looks like this:

	A	B	C
A	0	1	1
B	0	0	1
C	0	0	0

Table 8.1: *Adjacency Matrix Example*

Here, each row represents the outgoing edges from a vertex.

Advantages

It is easy to implement and check if an edge exists between two vertices—constant time **`O(1)`** lookup. This works well for **dense graphs** (many edges).

Disadvantages

This requires **$O(V^2)$** space even if only a few edges exist.

Inserting or removing vertices may involve reconstructing the entire matrix.

C++ Example (Adjacency Matrix):

```
#include <iostream>
#include <vector>
using namespace std;

int main() {
    int vertices = 3;
    vector<vector<int>> adjMatrix(vertices, vector<int>(vertices, 0));

    adjMatrix[0][1] = 1; // A -> B
    adjMatrix[0][2] = 1; // A -> C
    adjMatrix[1][2] = 1; // B -> C

    cout << "Adjacency Matrix:\n";
    for (auto &row : adjMatrix) {
        for (int val : row)
            cout << val << " ";
        cout << endl;
    }
}
```

Python Example (Adjacency Matrix):

```
vertices = 3
adj_matrix = [[0]*vertices for _ in range(vertices)]

adj_matrix[0][1] = 1  # A -> B
adj_matrix[0][2] = 1  # A -> C
adj_matrix[1][2] = 1  # B -> C

print("Adjacency Matrix:")
for row in adj_matrix:
    print(row)
```

Adjacency List Representation

An **adjacency list** represents a graph as a collection of **lists**, where each vertex stores its **neighbors**. This method is more **space-efficient** for sparse graphs. For example, the same graph (A → B, A → C, B → C) would be represented as:

```
A → B, C
B → C
C →
```

Advantages

- This requires `O(V + E)` space (much smaller for sparse graphs.
- It is easy to add or remove edges dynamically.

Disadvantages

- Edge lookup between two specific vertices takes `O(V)` time in the worst case.
- This is a slightly more complex implementation.

C++ Example (Adjacency List):

```
#include <iostream>
#include <vector>
using namespace std;

int main() {
    int vertices = 3;
    vector<vector<int>> adjList(vertices);

    adjList[0].push_back(1); // A -> B
    adjList[0].push_back(2); // A -> C
    adjList[1].push_back(2); // B -> C

    cout << "Adjacency List:\n";
    for (int i = 0; i < vertices; i++) {
        cout << i << " -> ";
        for (int v : adjList[i]) cout << v << " ";
        cout << endl;
    }
}
```

Python Example (Adjacency List):

```
graph = {
    'A': ['B', 'C'],
    'B': ['C'],
    'C': []
}

print("Adjacency List:")
for vertex, neighbors in graph.items():
    print(f"{vertex} -> {neighbors}")
```

Comparative Analysis of Matrix vs. List

Before diving into the details of traversal or algorithms, it is important to understand how the choice of **graph representation** impacts performance. The **adjacency matrix** and **adjacency list** are the two most common methods, each with its own advantages and trade-offs in terms of **time complexity**, **space efficiency**, and **ease of implementation**. Thus, the following table compares these two approaches to help you choose the most suitable representation based on the problem's requirements:

Operation	Adjacency Matrix	Adjacency List
Space Complexity	$O(V^2)$	O(V + E)
Check if edge exists	O(1)	O(V)
Add an edge	O(1)	O(1)

Operation	Adjacency Matrix	Adjacency List
Remove an edge	O(1)	O(V)
Iterate over neighbors	O(V)	O(degree of vertex)
Best suited for	Dense graphs	Sparse graphs

Table 8.2: *Comparative Analysis of Matrix vs. List*

Graph Traversal Techniques

Graph traversal is a fundamental operation that allows us to explore and process all vertices and edges in a graph. It plays a crucial role in understanding graph structure, discovering paths, detecting connectivity, and solving real-world problems such as network routing and social network analysis. Two of the most widely used traversal strategies are **Breadth-First Search (BFS)** and **Depth-First Search (DFS)**, with each offering a unique way of navigating through graphs.

Breadth-First Search: Iterative Implementation

Breadth-First Search (BFS) is one of the most fundamental graph traversal algorithms. It explores a graph **level by level**, starting from a source vertex, and visits all of its direct neighbors before moving on to the next level of vertices. This approach ensures that the algorithm always visits the **shortest possible path first** in an unweighted graph. BFS uses a **queue** data structure to keep track of the vertices to be visited.

a. Start by adding the **source vertex** to the queue, and then mark it as **visited.**
b. Remove the front element from the queue, explore all of its **unvisited neighbors**, and add them to the queue.
c. Repeat the process until the queue becomes empty.

This ensures that nodes are explored in the order of their **distance from the source vertex.**

Consider a **social network**, where each person is represented as a node and friendships as edges. If you want to find the shortest chain of introductions between two people, BFS can efficiently determine the **minimum number of connections** required.

C++ Implementation (Iterative BFS Using STL):

```
#include <iostream>
#include <queue>
#include <vector>
using namespace std;

void bfs(int start, vector<vector<int>>& adj) {
    vector<bool> visited(adj.size(), false);
    queue<int> q;
    visited[start] = true;
    q.push(start);

    cout << "BFS Traversal: ";
    while (!q.empty()) {
        int node = q.front();
        q.pop();
        cout << node << " ";

        for (int neighbor : adj[node]) {
```

```
                if (!visited[neighbor]) {
                    visited[neighbor] = true;
                    q.push(neighbor);
                }
            }
        }
    }

int main() {
    int vertices = 5;
    vector<vector<int>> adj = {
        {}, {2, 3}, {1, 4}, {1, 5}, {2}, {3}
    };

    bfs(1, adj);
    return 0;
}
```

Python Implementation (Iterative BFS Using Queue)

```
from collections import deque

def bfs(start, adj):
    visited = [False] * len(adj)
    queue = deque([start])
    visited[start] = True

    print("BFS Traversal:", end=" ")
    while queue:
        node = queue.popleft()
        print(node, end=" ")
        for neighbor in adj[node]:
            if not visited[neighbor]:
                visited[neighbor] = True
                queue.append(neighbor)

adj = [
    [], [2, 3], [1, 4], [1, 5], [2], [3]
]
bfs(1, adj)
```

- **Time Complexity:** `O(V+E)`, where **V** is the number of vertices, and **E** is the number of edges. Each vertex and edge is processed once.
- **Space Complexity:** `O(V)`, due to the storage of the **visited array** and **queue.**

Depth-First Search: Recursive and Iterative Approaches

Depth-First Search (DFS) is a fundamental graph traversal algorithm that explores as far as possible, along each branch before backtracking. In contrast to **Breadth-First Search (BFS)**, which explores level by level, DFS dives deep into a path and explores each branch to its fullest depth, before it returns to explore other branches. DFS can be implemented in two primary ways: **recursive** (using function calls) and **iterative** (using an explicit stack). The core idea of DFS is **backtracking**.

1. Start from a **source vertex** and mark it as **visited**.
2. Explore one of its unvisited neighbors.
3. Continue this process, until you reach a vertex that has no unvisited neighbors.
4. Backtrack to the previous vertex and explore other unvisited neighbors.
5. Repeat until all reachable vertices are visited.

This makes DFS ideal for exploring **deeply nested** structures such as **file systems, mazes**, or **dependency graphs**. For instance, consider a **file system directory** where folders contain subfolders and files. Here, DFS can be used to list all files in a directory by exploring each folder completely, before moving on to the next one.

C++ Implementation (Recursive DFS):

```
#include <iostream>
#include <vector>
using namespace std;

void dfs(int node, vector<vector<int>>& adj, vector<bool>& visited) {
    visited[node] = true;
    cout << node << " ";

    for (int neighbor : adj[node]) {
        if (!visited[neighbor])
            dfs(neighbor, adj, visited);
    }
}

int main() {
    int vertices = 5;
    vector<vector<int>> adj = {
        {}, {2, 3}, {1, 4}, {1, 5}, {2}, {3}
    };

    vector<bool> visited(vertices + 1, false);
    cout << "DFS Traversal (Recursive): ";
    dfs(1, adj, visited);

    return 0;
}
```

Python Implementation (Recursive DFS):

```
def dfs(node, adj, visited):
    visited[node] = True
    print(node, end=" ")
    for neighbor in adj[node]:
        if not visited[neighbor]:
            dfs(neighbor, adj, visited)

adj = [
    [], [2, 3], [1, 4], [1, 5], [2], [3]
]
visited = [False] * len(adj)

print("DFS Traversal (Recursive):", end=" ")
dfs(1, adj, visited)
```

Iterative Implementation Using Stack

While recursion provides a clean and elegant DFS, it can lead to **stack overflow** for very deep graphs. Hence, an **iterative approach** using an explicit stack is often preferred in such cases.

C++ Implementation (Iterative DFS):

```
#include <iostream>
#include <stack>
#include <vector>
using namespace std;

void dfsIterative(int start, vector<vector<int>>& adj) {
    vector<bool> visited(adj.size(), false);
    stack<int> s;
    s.push(start);

    cout << "DFS Traversal (Iterative): ";
    while (!s.empty()) {
        int node = s.top();
        s.pop();

        if (!visited[node]) {
            visited[node] = true;
            cout << node << " ";

            for (int i = adj[node].size() - 1; i >= 0; i--) {
                int neighbor = adj[node][i];
                if (!visited[neighbor])
                    s.push(neighbor);
            }
        }
    }
}

int main() {
    int vertices = 5;
    vector<vector<int>> adj = {
        {}, {2, 3}, {1, 4}, {1, 5}, {2}, {3}
    };

    dfsIterative(1, adj);
    return 0;
}
```

Python Implementation (Iterative DFS):

```
def dfs_iterative(start, adj):
    visited = [False] * len(adj)
    stack = [start]

    print("DFS Traversal (Iterative):", end=" ")
    while stack:
        node = stack.pop()
        if not visited[node]:
            visited[node] = True
            print(node, end=" ")
            for neighbor in reversed(adj[node]):
```

```
                if not visited[neighbor]:
                    stack.append(neighbor)

adj = [
    [], [2, 3], [1, 4], [1, 5], [2], [3]
]
dfs_iterative(1, adj)
```

- **Time Complexity:** O(V+E), where **V** = number of vertices, **E** = number of edges. Each vertex and edge is visited once.
- **Space Complexity: Recursive DFS: `O(V)`** (due to call stack) **Iterative DFS: `O(V)`** (due to explicit stack).

Comparing BFS and DFS

Both **Breadth-First Search (BFS)** and **Depth-First Search (DFS)** are foundational graph traversal algorithms used to explore or search through graph structures. However, while they aim to visit all vertices of a graph, they differ in **the order of traversal, data structures used, and practical applications**. Thus, understanding their differences helps in choosing the right approach for specific problems.

Aspect	Breadth-First Search (BFS)	Depth-First Search (DFS)
Traversal Approach	Explores nodes **level by level**, while visiting all immediate neighbors first	Explores nodes **deeply**, while going as far as possible along one branch before backtracking
Data Structure Used	**Queue (FIFO)** – Ensures nodes are visited in the order in which they are discovered	**Stack (LIFO)** or **Recursion** – Ensures depth-oriented exploration
Path Discovery	Guarantees **shortest path** in unweighted graphs	Does **not guarantee** the shortest path
Memory Usage	Can consume **more memory** for wide graphs since all neighbors at a level are stored	Typically uses **less memory** for narrow or deep graphs
Completeness	**Complete** – Always finds a solution if one exists	**May not find** the shallowest solution without backtracking
Time Complexity	(`O(V + E)`)	(`O(V + E)`)
Space Complexity	(`O(V)`) (due to queue storage)	(`O(V)`) (due to stack or recursion)
Traversal Pattern	Level-Wise Exploration – Suitable for shallow graphs	Depth-Wise Exploration – Suitable for deep graphs
Applications	Shortest path finding, network broadcasting, social graph traversal, AI level search	Cycle detection, topological sorting, maze solving, backtracking problems
Example Use Case	Finding the minimum number of hops in a network	Solving Sudoku or exploring all paths in a maze
Implementation Style	**Iterative**, typically using a queue	Can be **iterative or recursive**, using a stack
Performance	Better for **broad and shallow** graphs	Better for **deep and narrow** graphs

Table 8.3: *Key Differences between BFS and DFS*

Applications of Graph Traversal

Graph traversal algorithms such as **Breadth-First Search (BFS)** and **Depth-First Search (DFS)** are not just theoretical concepts; they form the backbone of many practical and real-world applications. Traversing a graph helps uncover relationships between nodes, detect structures or patterns, and solve complex computational problems efficiently. Here are some key applications that highlight the versatility of graph traversal techniques:

Cycle Detection in Graphs

One of the most common uses of DFS is to determine whether a graph contains a **cycle**, which refers to a path that starts and ends at the same vertex. In **directed graphs**, cycles indicate potential issues such as **deadlocks** in operating systems, or **circular dependencies** in task scheduling. In **undirected graphs**, cycle detection is essential for identifying redundant connections in networks. Thus, via DFS, a cycle can be detected by tracking the recursion stack, or by marking visited and currently exploring nodes. Detecting deadlocks in process scheduling or circular references in dependency graphs.

Connected Components Identification

Graph traversal helps determine **connected components**, which are subsets of nodes where each vertex is reachable from any other vertex in the same subset. In **undirected graphs**, connected components represent isolated clusters, whereas in **directed graphs**, they are referred to as **strongly connected components (SCCs)**. This concept is widely used in social network analysis to identify groups of interconnected users, or in network reliability testing to find isolated nodes. Identifying communities in social networks like Facebook, or detecting disconnected subnetworks in communication systems can be considered as strong examples of path finding.

Path Finding in Graphs

Both BFS and DFS play crucial roles in discovering **paths between nodes**.

- **BFS** is ideal for finding the **shortest path** in an **unweighted graph**, since it explores nodes level by level.
- **DFS**, while not guaranteeing the shortest path, is useful for **exploring all possible paths. It can also be** modified for applications like backtracking.

GPS navigation systems, network routing, and AI movement planning, all rely on efficient pathfinding algorithms built upon traversal principles.

Handling Disconnected Graphs

In many real-world graphs, not all nodes are connected. For example, a social media platform may have users who are not connected to anyone. To ensure that all vertices are processed, traversal algorithms must account for **disconnected graphs** by repeatedly initiating traversal from **unvisited vertices** until every node is explored. This approach guarantees complete coverage of the graph, regardless of its connectivity. Ensuring data integrity during web crawling or analyzing isolated components in power grid systems.

Real-World Applications of Graph Traversal

Graph traversal algorithms are widely embedded in real-world systems in the following ways:

- **Search Engines:** Web crawlers use BFS to systematically explore and index pages across the internet.

- **Social Networks:** Platforms like LinkedIn or Facebook use traversal to suggest mutual connections (friends-of-friends).
- **AI and Game Development:** Pathfinding algorithms like BFS, DFS, and A* are essential for navigation and movement logic.
- **Networking:** BFS helps determine the shortest route for data packets in communication networks.
- **Compilers and Dependency Analysis:** DFS assists in ordering tasks (topological sorting) and identifying dependencies among modules.

In **AI systems**, graph traversal enables intelligent decision-making by exploring state spaces efficiently. Recommendation engines, knowledge graphs, and reasoning systems rely on BFS and DFS to discover relationships between entities and infer meaningful connections. Moreover, in **gamification and game design**, traversal algorithms enable level navigation, quest dependency tracking, Non-Player Character (NPC) movement, and reward unlocking mechanisms for smooth progression and balanced gameplay. Similarly, in **social media networks**, graph traversal is fundamental for analyzing user interactions, detecting communities, ranking influencers, recommending content, and identifying information spread patterns. Thus, by traversing user graphs, platforms can efficiently model engagement, predict trends, and personalize user experiences at scale.

Practice Problems

Graph traversal and representation form the core of solving many computational problems. The following exercises will help you consolidate your understanding of graphs and their practical applications:

Number of Islands Problem

The **Number of Islands Problem** involves a 2D grid representing land and water, where:

`'1'` represents **land.**

`'0'` represents **water.**

An **island** is formed by connecting adjacent lands **horizontally or vertically**. The task is to **count the number of distinct islands** in the grid. Imagine a satellite image where water and land patches are marked. Consequently, counting the separate landmasses (islands) can help in geographical analysis, urban planning, or environmental studies.

Python Implementation (DFS Approach):

```
def num_islands(grid):
    if not grid:
        return 0

    rows, cols = len(grid), len(grid[0])

    def dfs(r, c):
        if r < 0 or r >= rows or c < 0 or c >= cols or grid[r][c] == '0':
            return
        grid[r][c] = '0'  # Mark visited
        dfs(r+1, c)
        dfs(r-1, c)
        dfs(r, c+1)
        dfs(r, c-1)

    count = 0
```

```
    for r in range(rows):
        for c in range(cols):
            if grid[r][c] == '1':
                dfs(r, c)
                count += 1
    return count

# Example Usage
grid = [
    ['1','1','0','0','0'],
    ['1','1','0','0','0'],
    ['0','0','1','0','0'],
    ['0','0','0','1','1']
]
print("Number of islands:", num_islands(grid))  # Output: 3
```

Each '1' triggers a DFS to **visit all connected land cells.**

Every completed DFS corresponds to **one distinct island.**

C++ Implementation (DFS Approach):

```
#include <iostream>
#include <vector>
using namespace std;

void dfs(vector<vector<char>>& grid, int r, int c) {
    int rows = grid.size();
    int cols = grid[0].size();
    if (r < 0 || r >= rows || c < 0 || c >= cols || grid[r][c] == '0')
        return;

    grid[r][c] = '0';  // Mark visited

    dfs(grid, r+1, c);
    dfs(grid, r-1, c);
    dfs(grid, r, c+1);
    dfs(grid, r, c-1);
}

int numIslands(vector<vector<char>>& grid) {
    int count = 0;
    int rows = grid.size();
    int cols = grid[0].size();
    for (int r = 0; r < rows; r++) {
        for (int c = 0; c < cols; c++) {
            if (grid[r][c] == '1') {
                dfs(grid, r, c);
                count++;
            }
        }
    }
    return count;
}

int main() {
    vector<vector<char>> grid = {
        {'1','1','0','0','0'},
```

```
        {'1','1','0','0','0'},
        {'0','0','1','0','0'},
        {'0','0','0','1','1'}
    };
    cout << "Number of islands: " << numIslands(grid) << endl;  // Output: 3
}
```

The DFS recursively marks all connected land cells for each starting with '1'. After traversing an island completely, the island counter is incremented. This ensures that **each distinct island is counted exactly once.**

Bipartite Graph Check

A bipartite graph is a graph whose vertices can be divided into two disjoint sets such that no two vertices within the same set are adjacent. In simpler terms, the graph can be colored using two colors so that no connected vertices share the same color.

Common real-world examples include:

- assigning students to two project groups where collaboration occurs only across groups, and
- matching jobs with applicants, where connections exist only between the two sets.

Python Implementation (BFS Approach):

```
from collections import deque

def is_bipartite(graph):
    n = len(graph)
    color = [-1] * n  # -1 indicates uncolored

    for i in range(n):
        if color[i] == -1:
            queue = deque([i])
            color[i] = 0  # Start with color 0
            while queue:
                node = queue.popleft()
                for neighbor in graph[node]:
                    if color[neighbor] == -1:
                        color[neighbor] = 1 - color[node]  # Assign opposite color
                        queue.append(neighbor)
                    elif color[neighbor] == color[node]:
                        return False
    return True

# Example graph represented as adjacency list
graph = [
    [1, 3],
    [0, 2],
    [1, 3],
    [0, 2]
]

print("Is bipartite:", is_bipartite(graph))  # Output: True
```

The algorithm determines whether a graph is bipartite by performing a Breadth-First Search (BFS) and applying the following coloring steps:

- Start BFS from an uncolored node.

- Color its neighbors with the opposite color.
- If a neighbor already has the same color as the current node, the graph cannot be bipartite.

C++ Implementation (BFS Approach):

```
#include <iostream>
#include <vector>
#include <queue>
using namespace std;

bool isBipartite(vector<vector<int>>& graph) {
    int n = graph.size();
    vector<int> color(n, -1); // -1 indicates uncolored

    for (int i = 0; i < n; i++) {
        if (color[i] == -1) {
            queue<int> q;
            q.push(i);
            color[i] = 0;

            while (!q.empty()) {
                int node = q.front();
                q.pop();

                for (int neighbor : graph[node]) {
                    if (color[neighbor] == -1) {
                        color[neighbor] = 1 - color[node];
                        q.push(neighbor);
                    } else if (color[neighbor] == color[node]) {
                        return false;
                    }
                }
            }
        }
    }
    return true;
}

int main() {
    vector<vector<int>> graph = {
        {1, 3},
        {0, 2},
        {1, 3},
        {0, 2}
    };
    cout << "Is bipartite: " << (isBipartite(graph) ? "True" : "False") << endl; //
Output: True
}
```

The BFS approach ensures that **neighboring vertices receive opposite colors**. Therefore, by checking each node and its neighbors, we can verify if the graph satisfies bipartite conditions. This method works for **both connected and disconnected graphs**.

Graph Cloning

Graph cloning involves creating a **deep copy** of a given graph such that **all nodes and edges are duplicated** without modifying the original graph. Each node in the new graph should have the same value and connections as in the original graph, but the memory references must be different. Graph cloning involves creating a **deep copy** of a given graph such that **all nodes and edges are duplicated** without modifying the original graph. Therefore, each node in the new graph should have the same value and connections as in the original graph, but the memory references must be different.

Python Implementation (DFS Approach):

```
class Node:
    def __init__(self, val):
        self.val = val
        self.neighbors = []

def clone_graph(node):
    if not node:
        return None

    visited = {}

    def dfs(n):
        if n in visited:
            return visited[n]

        clone = Node(n.val)
        visited[n] = clone
        for neighbor in n.neighbors:
            clone.neighbors.append(dfs(neighbor))
        return clone

    return dfs(node)

# Example Usage
node1 = Node(1)
node2 = Node(2)
node3 = Node(3)
node1.neighbors = [node2, node3]
node2.neighbors = [node1, node3]
node3.neighbors = [node1, node2]

cloned_node = clone_graph(node1)
print(cloned_node.val)  # Output: 1
```

In this example:

- The visited dictionary maps original nodes to their clones.
- DFS ensures that every node is visited and cloned exactly once.
- Edges are recreated by appending cloned neighbors.

C++ Implementation (DFS Approach):

```
#include <iostream>
#include <vector>
#include <unordered_map>
using namespace std;

class Node {
public:
    int val;
    vector<Node*> neighbors;
    Node(int _val) : val(_val) {}
```

```
};

Node* cloneGraph(Node* node, unordered_map<Node*, Node*>& visited) {
    if (!node) return nullptr;
    if (visited.find(node) != visited.end()) return visited[node];

    Node* clone = new Node(node->val);
    visited[node] = clone;

    for (Node* neighbor : node->neighbors) {
        clone->neighbors.push_back(cloneGraph(neighbor, visited));
    }
    return clone;
}

Node* cloneGraph(Node* node) {
    unordered_map<Node*, Node*> visited;
    return cloneGraph(node, visited);
}

// Example Usage
int main() {
    Node* node1 = new Node(1);
    Node* node2 = new Node(2);
    Node* node3 = new Node(3);
    node1->neighbors = {node2, node3};
    node2->neighbors = {node1, node3};
    node3->neighbors = {node1, node2};

    Node* cloned_node = cloneGraph(node1);
    cout << cloned_node->val << endl; // Output: 1
}
```

In this example:

a. The **visited** map ensures that each original node is cloned only once.

b. DFS traversal creates clones and reconnects neighbors correctly.

c. This approach handles **cyclic graphs** and prevents the creation of infinite loops.

Conclusion

This chapter has established a strong foundation in **graph fundamentals**, while addressing essential concepts, types, and representations of graphs, along with key traversal techniques like BFS and DFS. Through practical problems such as the **number of islands**, **bipartite graph check**, and **graph cloning**, learners have gained experience in applying graph theory to real-world scenarios, besides understanding how hierarchical and networked data can be modeled efficiently. By mastering these traversal strategies and representations, readers will be now well-equipped to handle more advanced graph computations. Moving forward, **the next chapter** will build on this foundation by introducing critical algorithms for solving problems on weighted graphs, including **shortest path determination with Dijkstra's and Bellman-Ford algorithms**, and constructing **minimum spanning trees with Prim's and Kruskal's approaches**. Learners will also explore algorithm design, optimization strategies, and practical coding implementations that are central to applications like **GPS navigation, network design, and resource optimization**. Hence, mastering these concepts will prepare them to tackle both real-world problem-solving and technical interviews.

Points to Remember

- A graph G(V, E) consists of a set of vertices (V), and edges (E) that connect pairs of vertices.
- Graphs can be directed or undirected, weighted or unweighted, and connected or disconnected.
- Important categories include cyclic, acyclic (trees, DAGs), complete, and bipartite graphs.
- Uses a 2D array; space complexity is $O(V^2)$; efficient for dense graphs
- Uses linked lists or arrays; space complexity is O(V + E); efficient for sparse graphs
- Traverses level by level using a queue; ideal for finding the shortest path in unweighted graphs
- Traverses depth-wise using recursion or stack; useful for cycle detection and topological sorting
- BFS → explores broadly (level order), DFS → explores deeply (path-wise)
- Used for cycle detection, connected components, path finding, and graph cloning

Multiple Choice Questions

1. The space complexity of an adjacency matrix for a graph with V vertices is:
   a. `O(V)`
   b. `O(E)`
   c. $O(V^2)$
   d. `O(V + E)`
2. BFS uses which data structure?
   a. Stack
   b. Queue
   c. Recursion
   d. Priority Queue
3. A graph that has no cycles is called:
   a. Complete Graph
   b. Bipartite Graph
   c. Acyclic Graph
   d. Weighted Graph
4. DFS is best implemented using:
   a. Queue
   b. Stack
   c. Priority Queue
   d. Array
5. A bipartite graph does not contain:
   a. Odd-Length Cycles
   b. Even-Length Cycles
   c. Parallel Edges
   d. Self-Loops

6. In an unweigh3ted graph, the shortest path can be found using:
   a. DFS
   b. Dijkstra's Algorithm
   c. BFS
   d. Bellman-Ford Algorithm
7. A graph with every vertex connected to every other vertex is called:
   a. Cyclic Graph
   b. Complete Graph
   c. Connected Graph
   d. Tree
8. Adjacency list representation is most suitable for:
   a. Dense Graphs
   b. Sparse Graphs
   c. Complete Graphs
   d. Weighted Graphs
9. Which of the following is true for DFS?
   a. Explores level by level
   b. Uses queue
   c. Uses stack or recursion
   d. Always finds the shortest path
10. The number of edges in a complete graph with *n* vertices is:
   a. `n`
   b. `n²`
   c. `n(n - 1)/2`
   d. `n(n + 1)/2`

Answers

1. c
2. b
3. c
4. b
5. a
6. c
7. b
8. b
9. c
10. c

Questions

1. Explain BFS algorithm with an example and pseudocode.
2. Explain DFS algorithm (both recursive and iterative).
3. Compare adjacency matrix and adjacency list representations.
4. Describe different types of graphs and provide suitable diagrams.
5. Discuss the applications of graph traversal algorithms in real-world scenarios.
6. How can you detect cycles in a graph using DFS?
7. Explain connected and disconnected graphs with examples.
8. Describe how graphs are used in network routing and social networks.

Key Terms

- **Graph:** A set of vertices connected by edges
- **Vertex (Node):** A fundamental unit of a graph representing an entity
- **Edge:** A connection between two vertices
- **Degree of a Vertex:** Number of edges connected to a vertex
- **Path:** Sequence of vertices connected by edges
- **Cycle:** A path that starts and ends at the same vertex
- **Directed Graph (Digraph):** Graph with edges having a direction
- **Weighted Graph:** Graph where edges carry weights (cost, distance, and so on)
- **Adjacency Matrix:** 2D array representing connections between vertices
- **Adjacency List:** List structure storing neighbors of each vertex
- **Breadth-First Search (BFS):** Traversal exploring level by level
- **Depth-First Search (DFS):** Traversal exploring as deep as possible along each branch
- **Bipartite Graph:** Graph whose vertices can be divided into two sets with edges only between sets
- **Connected Component:** Subset of vertices where every pair is connected

Chapter 9
Graph Algorithm

Introduction

Graphs are powerful structures used to model real-world systems. They are like cities connected by roads, computers linked in a network, or even social connections between people. While the previous chapter introduced how graphs are represented and traversed, this chapter focuses on solving deeper, practical problems that arise within these networks. How do we find the shortest route between two points? How can we connect every location using the least possible cost? And how do we detect if a network contains unnecessary or problematic loops?

To answer these questions, we explore a set of foundational algorithms: **Dijkstra's and Bellman-Ford** for shortest paths; and **Prim's and Kruskal's** for constructing minimum spanning trees. We will also study the **Union-Find data structure**, a powerful tool for handling connectivity and cycle detection efficiently. Through explanations, real-world applications, and coding examples, this chapter will build the intuition required to solve network routing, logistics, clustering, and infrastructure optimization problems. Thus, by the end, you will not only be able to understand how these algorithms work, but also when and why to use them in practical scenarios.

Structure

In this chapter, we will cover the following topics:

- Introduction to Weighted Graphs
- Shortest Path Algorithms
- Minimum Spanning Tree (MST) Algorithms
- Graph Cycles and Union-Find Basics
- Applications of MST and Shortest Path Algorithms
- Performance Analysis and Edge Case Handling
- Common Pitfalls and Edge Case Handling Practice Problems

Introduction to Weighted Graphs

Not all connections in a graph are equal—some paths may be longer, costlier, or more efficient than others. In such cases, assigning numerical values to edges helps quantify these differences. **Weighted**

graphs bring this concept to life by associating a *weight* or *cost* with every edge, while allowing us to create precise models of real-world systems such as road networks, communication links, and resource flows.

Definition and Characteristics of Weighted Graphs

In many real-world problems, simply knowing whether two entities are connected is not enough; we also need to understand the strength, cost, distance, or time associated with that connection. A **weighted graph** is a type of graph where each edge carries a **numerical value** known as a **weight**. This weight represents the cost or importance of traversing that edge.

Formally, a weighted graph **G(V, E, W)** consists of:

- **V (Vertices)**: The set of nodes or points
- **E (Edges)**: The connections between the vertices
- **W (Weights)**: The numerical values assigned to each edge

The weight can represent various real-world quantities, such as:

- The distance between two locations
- The time taken to travel between nodes
- The cost of communication or data transfer
- The capacity or bandwidth of a network

These numerical weights help algorithms decide **the best or most efficient path** through the graph, such as finding the shortest route or minimum cost connection.

Edge Weight Representation

In a weighted graph, every edge is represented along with its associated weight. For example, if an edge connects vertex **A** to vertex **B** with a weight of **5**, it can be represented as (A, B, 5)

Depending on the type of graph, we have the following considerations:

In **directed weighted graphs**, the edge (A → B) may have a different weight than (B → A). In **undirected weighted graphs**, the weight between two nodes is the same in both directions. Weighted edges can be **positive**, **zero**, or even **negative** (in certain algorithms like Bellman-Ford). However, negative weights must be handled carefully, as they can complicate the shortest path calculations and lead to cycles of decreasing cost.

Let us consider five cities—A, B, C, D, and E— that are connected via roads. The number on each road represents the distance (in kilometers).

Here, the numbers (5, 3, 2, 4, 1) are **edge weights**, which help us compute the shortest or the least costly path between cities.

Importance of Weighted Graphs in Problem-Solving

Weighted graphs are among the most practical data structures used in **optimization and decision-making problems**. They allow us to model and solve challenges where different paths have varying costs or priorities. Some common real-world applications include:

- **Navigation Systems:** GPS applications like Google Maps use weighted graphs to represent road networks, where edge weights denote distance or travel time. Algorithms like **Dijkstra's** help find the fastest route between two points.

- **Network Routing:** In computer networks, routers use weighted graphs to determine the **least congested or least costly** path for data transmission, while optimizing speed and resource usage.
- **Airline and Logistics Planning:** Weighted graphs are used to plan optimal flight routes or delivery schedules, where weights may represent **fuel cost**, **distance**, or **time**.
- **Social and Recommendation Networks:** Edge weights can represent the **strength of relationships**, **interaction frequency**, or **similarity scores** in social graphs or recommender systems.
- **AI and Game Design:** Weighted graphs are used in **pathfinding algorithms** (like A* search) for game characters, robots, or autonomous vehicles navigating complex environments.

In essence, **weighted graphs form the backbone of optimization in computational systems**. Thus, by quantifying relationships through weights, they enable algorithms to make smarter, data-driven decisions. This becomes a foundation for many intelligent systems we rely on today.

Shortest Path Algorithms

In many real-world networks—such as road maps, communication systems, or airline routes—finding the most efficient way to travel from one point to another is a common challenge. **Shortest path algorithms** provide systematic methods to determine the minimum cost or the distance between nodes in a graph.

These algorithms differ in how they handle edge weights and negative values, but they share the same core idea: **iteratively improving path estimates, until the shortest route is identified**. The two most fundamental techniques used here are **Dijkstra's algorithm**, which efficiently handles graphs with non-negative weights using a greedy approach; and the **Bellman-Ford algorithm**, which extends this capability to graphs that may contain negative edge weights. Together, they form the foundation for modern routing, navigation, and optimization systems.

Dijkstra's Algorithm

When navigating through a network of roads, you often want to find the shortest route between two locations. Similarly, in graph-based problems, we aim to determine the **minimum distance from a source vertex to all other vertices**.

Dijkstra's algorithm, introduced by *Edsger Dijkstra* in 1956, is a **greedy algorithm** that solves this problem efficiently for graphs with **non-negative edge weights**. It builds the shortest path tree step by step by **always choosing the vertex with the smallest known distance** at each iteration and updating the distances to its neighbors.

The core idea is simple yet powerful:

"*At every step, choose the next node with the smallest known distance and relax its neighbors.*"

This approach ensures that once a vertex's shortest distance is finalized, it never changes. This property makes the algorithm both elegant and efficient.

Priority Queue-Based Approach

The core mechanism of Dijkstra's algorithm is a **priority queue (or min-heap)**, which helps efficiently pick the next vertex with the smallest tentative distance. The algorithm follows this workflow:

1. Assign a tentative distance of **0** to the source vertex and **∞** (infinity) to all others. Insert the source vertex into the priority queue.

2. While the queue is not empty:
   a. Extract the vertex u with the smallest distance.
   b. For each neighbor v of u, calculate the new distance **`dist[u]`** + **`weight(u, v)`**.
   c. If this new distance is smaller than **`dist[v]`**, update it and push v into the queue.
3. Repeat until all vertices are processed.

Step-by-Step Working Example

Consider the following weighted graph:

```
A ---4--- B
| \       |
2  5      1
|    \    |
C ---3--  D
```

Let **A** be the source vertex.

1. Start with **`dist[A] = 0`**, and all others as ∞.
2. From **A**, the shortest edges go to **C (2)** and **B (4)**.
3. Next, visit **C**, which leads to **D (2 + 3 = 5)**.
4. Now **B** can reach **D** in **4 + 1 = 5**.

The algorithm finalizes the shortest distances:

```
A → A = 0
A → B = 4
A → C = 2
A → D = 5
```

Pseudocode: Dijkstra's Algorithm

```
Dijkstra(Graph, source):
    for each vertex v in Graph:
        dist[v] = ∞
        prev[v] = None
    dist[source] = 0
    PQ = priority queue with (0, source)

    while PQ is not empty:
        (d, u) = PQ.extract_min()
        for each neighbor v of u:
            alt = d + weight(u, v)
            if alt < dist[v]:
                dist[v] = alt
                prev[v] = u
                PQ.insert((dist[v], v))
```

The pseudocode works as follows:

- **Initialization**
  - Every vertex is assigned an initial distance of infinity (∞) since initially, we do not know how to reach them.
  - The distance to the source node is set to 0 as it is the starting point.

- **Priority Queue Setup**
  - A **priority queue (min-heap)** stores vertices along with their current shortest distances.
  - This ensures that we are always processing the vertex with the smallest distance first.
- **Relaxation Step**
  - For each neighbor v of the current node u, we will calculate a new possible distance: `alt = dist[u] + weight(u, v).`
  - If this new distance is shorter, we will update **`dist[v]`** and record u as its predecessor (**`prev[v] = u`**).
- **Termination:** The algorithm stops when all vertices have been visited. This means that we have found the shortest distance to all reachable nodes.

C++ Implementation:

```
#include <iostream>
#include <vector>
#include <queue>
#include <climits>
using namespace std;

void dijkstra(int n, vector<vector<pair<int,int>>>& adj, int src) {
    vector<int> dist(n, INT_MAX);
    dist[src] = 0;

    priority_queue<pair<int,int>, vector<pair<int,int>>, greater<pair<int,int>>> pq;
    pq.push({0, src});

    while (!pq.empty()) {
        int d = pq.top().first;
        int u = pq.top().second;
        pq.pop();

        if (d > dist[u]) continue;

        for (auto [v, w] : adj[u]) {
            if (dist[v] > dist[u] + w) {
                dist[v] = dist[u] + w;
                pq.push({dist[v], v});
            }
        }
    }

    cout << "Vertex  Distance from Source\n";
    for (int i = 0; i < n; i++)
        cout << i << "\t" << dist[i] << "\n";
}

int main() {
    int n = 5;
    vector<vector<pair<int,int>>> adj(n);
    adj[0] = {{1, 10}, {2, 3}};
    adj[1] = {{2, 1}, {3, 2}};
    adj[2] = {{1, 4}, {3, 8}, {4, 2}};
    adj[3] = {{4, 7}};
    adj[4] = {{3, 9}};
```

```
    dijkstra(n, adj, 0);
    return 0;
}
```

Python Implementation:

```
import heapq

def dijkstra(graph, source):
    dist = {node: float('inf') for node in graph}
    dist[source] = 0
    pq = [(0, source)]

    while pq:
        d, u = heapq.heappop(pq)
        if d > dist[u]:
            continue
        for v, w in graph[u]:
            if dist[v] > d + w:
                dist[v] = d + w
                heapq.heappush(pq, (dist[v], v))

    print("Vertex\tDistance from Source")
    for node in graph:
        print(f"{node}\t{dist[node]}")

graph = {
    0: [(1, 10), (2, 3)],
    1: [(2, 1), (3, 2)],
    2: [(1, 4), (3, 8), (4, 2)],
    3: [(4, 7)],
    4: [(3, 9)]
}
dijkstra(graph, 0)
```

Applications in GPS and Network Routing

Dijkstra's algorithm is the foundation of many **real-world applications** such as:

- **GPS Navigation Systems:** Finding the fastest driving route between two locations
- **Network Routing Protocols**: Algorithms like Open Shortest Path First (OSPF) use Dijkstra's algorithm for computing optimal data transmission paths.
- **Robotics and AI Pathfinding**: Used to plan efficient movement in grid-based environments

Bellman–Ford Algorithm

Although Dijkstra's algorithm is efficient, it fails when the graph contains **negative edge weights**, which is a commonly occurring situation in real-world cost networks or credit systems.

The **Bellman–Ford algorithm** fills this gap. It is designed to handle graphs where edges may have negative weights and can also **detect negative weight cycles**, which is something Dijkstra's algorithm cannot do.

The core difference lies in the **edge relaxation strategy, which plays out as follows**:

- Dijkstra's algorithm always picks the next vertex with the smallest tentative distance (greedy approach).

- Bellman-Ford, instead, repeatedly relaxes **all edges** to ensure that every vertex's shortest path is correctly updated, even when negative weights are present.

Hence, Bellman-Ford trades speed for versatility; it is slightly slower, but more robust in handling complex weighted graphs.

The relaxation process is central to Bellman-Ford. It works on the following rule:

> If the path through vertex u to v is shorter than the currently known distance to v, then update it.

Algorithm Steps:

1. Initialize distances from the source to all vertices as infinity (∞), except for the source itself, which is `0`.
2. Repeat the following **(V – 1)** times (where V is the number of vertices):

   For every edge (u, v) with weight w, if **`dist[u] + w < dist[v]`**, update **`dist[v] = dist[u] + w`**.
3. After all relaxations, perform one more iteration over all edges. If any distance still improves, it indicates a **negative weight cycle** in the graph.

Pseudocode:

```
BellmanFord(Graph, source):
    for each vertex v in Graph:
        dist[v] = ∞
    dist[source] = 0

    for i from 1 to |V| - 1:
        for each edge (u, v, w) in Graph:
            if dist[u] + w < dist[v]:
                dist[v] = dist[u] + w

    for each edge (u, v, w) in Graph:
        if dist[u] + w < dist[v]:
            print("Graph contains a negative weight cycle")
```

C++ Implementation:

```cpp
#include <iostream>
#include <vector>
#include <climits>
using namespace std;

struct Edge {
    int u, v, w;
};

void bellmanFord(int n, vector<Edge>& edges, int src) {
    vector<int> dist(n, INT_MAX);
    dist[src] = 0;

    // Relax edges |V| - 1 times
    for (int i = 1; i < n; i++) {
        for (auto &e : edges) {
            if (dist[e.u] != INT_MAX && dist[e.u] + e.w < dist[e.v]) {
                dist[e.v] = dist[e.u] + e.w;
            }
```

```
        }
    }

    // Check for negative weight cycle
    for (auto &e : edges) {
        if (dist[e.u] != INT_MAX && dist[e.u] + e.w < dist[e.v]) {
            cout << "Graph contains a negative weight cycle\n";
            return;
        }
    }

    cout << "Vertex\tDistance from Source\n";
    for (int i = 0; i < n; i++)
        cout << i << "\t" << dist[i] << "\n";
}

int main() {
    int n = 5;
    vector<Edge> edges = {
        {0, 1, 6}, {0, 2, 7}, {1, 2, 8}, {1, 3, 5},
        {1, 4, -4}, {2, 3, -3}, {2, 4, 9},
        {3, 1, -2}, {4, 0, 2}, {4, 3, 7}
    };
    bellmanFord(n, edges, 0);
    return 0;
}
```

Python Implementation:

```
def bellman_ford(graph, vertices, source):
    dist = {v: float('inf') for v in vertices}
    dist[source] = 0

    # Relax edges |V| - 1 times
    for _ in range(len(vertices) - 1):
        for u, v, w in graph:
            if dist[u] + w < dist[v]:
                dist[v] = dist[u] + w

    # Check for negative weight cycle
    for u, v, w in graph:
        if dist[u] + w < dist[v]:
            print("Graph contains a negative weight cycle")
            return

    print("Vertex\tDistance from Source")
    for v in vertices:
        print(f"{v}\t{dist[v]}")

edges = [
    (0, 1, 6), (0, 2, 7), (1, 2, 8), (1, 3, 5),
    (1, 4, -4), (2, 3, -3), (2, 4, 9),
    (3, 1, -2), (4, 0, 2), (4, 3, 7)
]
bellman_ford(edges, [0, 1, 2, 3, 4], 0)
```

Some real-world use cases of this algorithm include:

- **Currency Exchange Systems**: Detecting arbitrage (negative cycles)
- **Telecommunication Networks**: Optimizing routes with mixed link weights
- **Credit and Risk Modeling**: Handling negative and positive cost scenarios
- **Distributed Systems**: Calculating time delays or propagation costs

Minimum Spanning Tree Algorithms

In many real-world applications, such as designing road networks, electrical circuits, or communication systems, we often face the challenge of connecting multiple points (nodes) with the **minimum total cost,** while ensuring **all nodes remain connected**. However, unlike shortest path problems that focus on one source vertex, **Minimum Spanning Tree (MST) algorithms** aim to connect **all vertices in a weighted graph** with the smallest possible total edge weight without forming cycles.

Thus, MST algorithms play a crucial role in optimizing resource usage, minimizing costs, and ensuring efficient connectivity. The two most widely used algorithms for constructing MSTs are **Prim's algorithm** and **Kruskal's algorithm**, which are based on the **greedy approach**, but differ in their strategy of edge selection.

Understanding Minimum Spanning Trees

A **Minimum Spanning Tree (MST)** of a connected, weighted, undirected graph is a subset of edges that connects all vertices **without forming any cycle** and with the **minimum possible total edge weight**. Formally, if `G=(V,E)G = (V, E)G=(V,E)` is a connected weighted graph, then MST is a tree T⊆ET **`\subseteq`** ET⊆E that:

- Spans all vertices of GGG and has no cycles
- Has the minimum possible sum of edge weights

Key Properties:

- For a connected graph with VVV vertices, the MST always contains exactly V−1V - 1V−1 edges.
- The MST is **not necessarily unique**; multiple MSTs can exist if some edges have equal weights.
- Removing any edge from the MST will **disconnect** the graph.

Real-World Significance (Network and Circuit Design)

MSTs have practical importance in various fields such as:

- **Telecommunication Networks:** To connect multiple communication towers using cables of minimum length
- **Electrical Circuit Design:** To connect multiple components with minimal wiring
- **Transportation Systems:** To build road or railway networks connecting cities at the lowest cost
- **Clustering in Machine Learning**: To detect structure in data by connecting points in minimal distance order

Comparison with Shortest Path Problems

While both MST and shortest path algorithms operate on **weighted graphs**, their goals differ:

Feature	Shortest Path Problem	Minimum Spanning Tree
Objective	Find the minimum distance from a **single source** to all other vertices.	Connect **all vertices** with the minimum total edge weight.
Output	Path tree rooted at one source	A tree spanning all nodes
Can Contain Cycles	No	No
Example Algorithms	Dijkstra's, Bellman–Ford	Prim's, Kruskal's

Table 9.1: *Comparison with the Shortest Path Problems*

Prim's Algorithm

Prim's algorithm is one of the most widely used methods for finding a **Minimum Spanning Tree (MST)** in a connected, weighted, undirected graph. It follows a **greedy strategy**—at each step, it selects the **smallest edge** that connects a vertex already included in the MST to a vertex that is not yet included.

The algorithm starts with any arbitrary vertex and grows the MST one edge at a time until all vertices are connected. By always choosing the minimum available edge that does not form a cycle, Prim's algorithm ensures that the final spanning tree has the **minimum total edge weight**.

In simple terms, Prim's algorithm says:

"*Keep expanding the tree by choosing the least costly edge that connects the tree to a new vertex.*"

Let us consider a simple weighted graph:

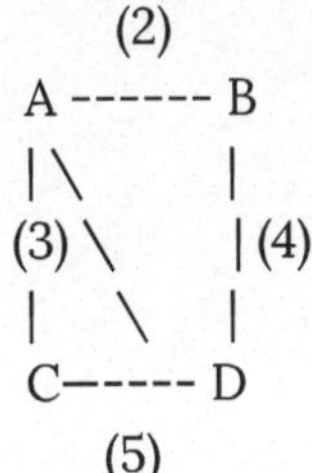

Steps to find the MST using Prim's algorithm:

1. **Start with any vertex** (say, A).

   Add vertex A to the MST set.

2. **Pick the smallest edge** connected to A.

   Among edges (A–B:2), (A–C:3), (A–D:4), choose **A–B** (weight 2).

3. **Add the vertex B** to the MST and include its edges.

   Now, consider edges (A–C:3), (A–D:4), and (B–D:4).

   The smallest edge among these is **A–C (3)**.

4. **Add vertex C**, and continue.

   The only remaining vertex not yet in the MST is D.

   The smallest connecting edge is **A–D (4)**.

5. **Stop when all vertices are included.**

Resulting MST Edges: A–B (2), A–C (3), A–D (4)

Total Weight = 2 + 3 + 4 = 9

Implementation Using Priority Queue

To efficiently pick the smallest weighted edge at every step, we use a **priority queue (min-heap)**. This ensures that edge selection takes logarithmic time, while improving the overall performance.

The algorithm maintains:

- A list of **visited vertices** (those already included in MST).
- A **min heap (priority queue)** that stores edges by increasing weight, and the **total MST cost** as we pick edges.

C++ Implementation:

```
#include <iostream>
#include <vector>
#include <queue>
#include <climits>
using namespace std;

void primMST(int n, vector<vector<pair<int,int>>>& adj) {
    vector<int> key(n, INT_MAX);  // Minimum weight to connect each vertex
    vector<bool> inMST(n, false); // Whether vertex is included in MST
    key[0] = 0;

    // Min-heap to pick smallest key vertex
    priority_queue<pair<int,int>, vector<pair<int,int>>, greater<pair<int,int>>> pq;
    pq.push({0, 0});

    int totalWeight = 0;

    while (!pq.empty()) {
        int u = pq.top().second;
        pq.pop();

        if (inMST[u]) continue;
        inMST[u] = true;
        totalWeight += key[u];

        for (auto [v, w] : adj[u]) {
            if (!inMST[v] && w < key[v]) {
                key[v] = w;
                pq.push({key[v], v});
            }
        }
    }

    cout << "Total weight of MST: " << totalWeight << endl;
}

int main() {
    int n = 5;
    vector<vector<pair<int,int>>> adj(n);

    adj[0] = {{1, 2}, {3, 6}};
    adj[1] = {{0, 2}, {2, 3}, {3, 8}, {4, 5}};
    adj[2] = {{1, 3}, {4, 7}};
```

```
    adj[3] = {{0, 6}, {1, 8}, {4, 9}};
    adj[4] = {{1, 5}, {2, 7}, {3, 9}};

    primMST(n, adj);
    return 0;
}
```

- **Initialization:** Each vertex's key value (minimum connection weight) is initialized to **`INT_MAX`**. The first vertex (0) is given a key of `0` to start the MST.
- **Priority Queue:** A min heap is used to always extract the vertex with the smallest key value.
- **Building the MST:** For each vertex **`u`** selected, all its adjacent vertices `v` are checked. If vertex `v` is not in the MST and edge weight `w` is smaller than its current key value, we will update it.
- **Total Weight:** As vertices are added, their corresponding edge weights will contribute to the MST's total weight.

Python Implementation:

```
import heapq

def prim_mst(graph):
    visited = set()
    total_weight = 0
    start = 0
    pq = [(0, start)]

    while pq:
        weight, u = heapq.heappop(pq)
        if u in visited:
            continue
        visited.add(u)
        total_weight += weight

        for v, w in graph[u]:
            if v not in visited:
                heapq.heappush(pq, (w, v))

    print("Total weight of MST:", total_weight)

graph = {
    0: [(1, 2), (3, 6)],
    1: [(0, 2), (2, 3), (3, 8), (4, 5)],
    2: [(1, 3), (4, 7)],
    3: [(0, 6), (1, 8), (4, 9)],
    4: [(1, 5), (2, 7), (3, 9)]
}

prim_mst(graph)
```

The **graph** is stored as a dictionary where each vertex maps to a list of (**`neighbor`**, **`weight`**) pairs.

A **min-heap (priority queue)** helps in efficiently selecting the smallest edge at every step.

- The algorithm keeps track of **visited vertices** to prevent cycles.
- The **total MST weight** accumulates as edges are added.
- The process stops when all the vertices have been visited.

Kruskal's Algorithm

Kruskal's algorithm is another **Greedy algorithm** used to find the **Minimum Spanning Tree (MST)** of a connected, weighted, and undirected graph. Unlike Prim's algorithm, which grows the MST **one vertex at a time**, Kruskal's algorithm builds it **one edge at a time.**

The main idea is simple: you must pick the smallest edge that does not form a cycle with the edges that are already chosen for the MST. Initially, every vertex is treated as a separate component. The algorithm then repeatedly selects the shortest edge that connects two different components, while merging them into one. This process continues until all vertices belong to a single connected component—the MST.

To prevent forming cycles, Kruskal's algorithm uses a **cycle detection mechanism** based on the **Disjoint Set Union (DSU)** or **Union-Find** data structure.

Role of Disjoint Set (Union-Find)

The **Disjoint Set Union (DSU)**, also known as **Union-Find**, is a data structure that efficiently keeps track of elements divided into multiple disjoint (non-overlapping) sets. It supports two primary operations:

- **`Find(x)`:** Determines the representative (parent) of the set containing element x. It is used to check whether two vertices belong to the same component.
- **`Union(x, y)`:** DSU merges the sets containing **`x`** and **`y`**. If they are already in the same set, adding an edge between them would form a **cycle.**

In Kruskal's algorithm, before including an edge, the **`Find`** operation checks if the two vertices are in the same set. If they are not, the edge is safe to add, and the **`Union`** operation merges them into one set. Let us take a simple weighted graph as an example:

```
  (1)
A-------B
| \     |
(4) (3) (2)
|     \ |
C-------D
   (5)
```

Step 1: Sort all edges in increasing order of their weights.

Edge	Weight
A-B	1
B-D	2
A-D	3
A-C	4
C-D	5

Table 9.2: *Sorting Weights*

Step 2: Start with an empty MST.

Step 3: Pick edges in order of increasing weight and add them if they do not form a cycle.

a. Pick **A-B (1)** → No cycle → Add to MST.

b. Pick **B-D (2)** → No cycle → Add to MST.

c. Pick **A–D (3)** → Forms a cycle (A–B–D–A) → Skip.

d. Pick **A–C (4)** → No cycle → Add to MST.

Resulting MST Edges: A–B (1), B–D (2), A–C (4)

Total Weight = 7

C++ Implementation:

```
#include <iostream>
#include <vector>
#include <algorithm>
using namespace std;

// Disjoint Set Union (Union-Find)
struct DSU {
    vector<int> parent, rank;
    DSU(int n) {
        parent.resize(n);
        rank.resize(n, 0);
        for (int i = 0; i < n; i++) parent[i] = i;
    }
    int find(int x) {
        if (parent[x] != x)
            parent[x] = find(parent[x]); // Path compression
        return parent[x];
    }
    void unite(int x, int y) {
        int rootX = find(x);
        int rootY = find(y);
        if (rootX != rootY) {
            if (rank[rootX] < rank[rootY]) swap(rootX, rootY);
            parent[rootY] = rootX;
            if (rank[rootX] == rank[rootY]) rank[rootX]++;
        }
    }
};

struct Edge {
    int u, v, w;
};

bool compare(Edge a, Edge b) {
    return a.w < b.w;
}

void kruskalMST(int n, vector<Edge>& edges) {
    sort(edges.begin(), edges.end(), compare);
    DSU dsu(n);
    int totalWeight = 0;

    cout << "Edges in MST:\n";
    for (auto &edge : edges) {
        if (dsu.find(edge.u) != dsu.find(edge.v)) {
            cout << edge.u << " - " << edge.v << " : " << edge.w << endl;
            totalWeight += edge.w;
```

```
            dsu.unite(edge.u, edge.v);
        }
    }

    cout << "Total weight of MST: " << totalWeight << endl;
}

int main() {
    int n = 4;
    vector<Edge> edges = {
        {0, 1, 1}, {1, 3, 2}, {0, 3, 3}, {0, 2, 4}, {2, 3, 5}
    };

    kruskalMST(n, edges);
    return 0;
}
```

- **Graph Representation:** The graph is represented as an **edge list** where each edge contains **`(u, v, w)`**, which denote source, destination, and weight, respectively.
- **Sorting Edges:** All edges are sorted in ascending order of weights using the **`sort()`** function.
- **Union-Find Structure:** The DSU structure manages vertex groups. **`find()`** identifies which component a vertex belongs to. **`unite()`** merges two components, if they are not already connected.
- **Building the MST:** For every edge in sorted order, if its endpoints belong to different sets, include it in the MST and merge them.
- **Cycle Prevention:** The DSU ensures that adding an edge connecting two vertices already in the same set will be skipped, and avoids cycles automatically.

Python Implementation:

```
class DSU:
    def __init__(self, n):
        self.parent = list(range(n))
        self.rank = [0] * n

    def find(self, x):
        if self.parent[x] != x:
            self.parent[x] = self.find(self.parent[x])  # Path compression
        return self.parent[x]

    def union(self, x, y):
        rootX, rootY = self.find(x), self.find(y)
        if rootX != rootY:
            if self.rank[rootX] < self.rank[rootY]:
                rootX, rootY = rootY, rootX
            self.parent[rootY] = rootX
            if self.rank[rootX] == self.rank[rootY]:
                self.rank[rootX] += 1

def kruskal(n, edges):
    edges.sort(key=lambda x: x[2])
    dsu = DSU(n)
    total_weight = 0

    print("Edges in MST:")
    for u, v, w in edges:
```

```
        if dsu.find(u) != dsu.find(v):
            print(f"{u} - {v} : {w}")
            total_weight += w
            dsu.union(u, v)

    print("Total weight of MST:", total_weight)

edges = [(0, 1, 1), (1, 3, 2), (0, 3, 3), (0, 2, 4), (2, 3, 5)]
kruskal(4, edges)
```

- **Edge List Representation:** The graph is represented as a list of tuples **`(u, v, w)`**.
- **Sorting Edges:** The edges are sorted by weight using the **`sort()`** method with a custom key.
- **Union-Find Implementation:** The `DSU` class handles connected components efficiently using path compression and union by rank.
- **MST Construction:** Edges are processed in increasing order, and only those that connect distinct components are added to the MST.
- **Cycle Avoidance:** As in the C++ version, cycles are automatically avoided through the DSU structure.

Time Complexity and Comparison with Prim's Algorithm

Table 9.2 presents a comparison of the time complexity and key characteristics of **Kruskal's algorithm** and **Prim's algorithm**, while highlighting their efficiency and suitable use cases. The comparison of Kruskal's algorithm with Prim's algorithm is as follows:

Aspect	Prim's Algorithm	Kruskal's Algorithm
Graph Representation	Adjacency list	Edge list
Edge Sorting	Not required	Required (O(E log E))
Best for	Dense graphs	Sparse graphs
Cycle Prevention	Implicit (visited array)	Explicit (Union-Find)
Time Complexity	(O(E \log V))	(O(E \log E))
Space Complexity	(O(V + E))	(O(V + E))

Table 9.3: *Time Complexity and Comparison with Prim's Algorithm*

Kruskal's algorithm is ideal when the graph has **fewer edges (sparse graphs)**, whereas, Prim's algorithm performs better on **dense graphs** with many edges. Both guarantee the construction of a **minimum-cost spanning tree**.

Graph Cycles and Union-Find Basics

In complex networks and graph-based systems, **cycles** often determine the structure's behavior and whether a network remains efficient, redundant, or unstable. Detecting and managing these cycles is essential for ensuring correctness in algorithms such as **Minimum Spanning Trees (MSTs)** and **connectivity analysis**. To efficiently perform this task, computer scientists rely on a specialized data structure called the **Disjoint Set Union (DSU)** or **Union-Find**, which provides a systematic way to group connected components and detect cycles with minimal computational overhead.

Therefore, this section explores the concept of graph cycles, their role in network and algorithmic design, and how the Union-Find structure allows for **fast and elegant cycle detection** in large-scale graphs.

Understanding Graph Cycles

A **cycle** in a graph is a path that starts and ends at the same vertex. Cycles can occur in both **directed** and **undirected** graphs, but their interpretation differs slightly in the following ways:

- **Undirected Graphs:** A cycle occurs if, while traversing edges, we revisit a vertex that is not the immediate parent.

  For example, in an undirected graph with edges (A–B), (B–C), and (C–A), a cycle exists because we can return to **A** starting from **A**.

- **Directed Graphs:** A cycle occurs when there exists a sequence of directed edges that leads back to the starting vertex.

  For instance, A → B → C → A forms a directed cycle.

Detecting cycles is crucial because certain algorithms (like Kruskal's and topological sorting) rely on **acyclic properties** for correctness.

Role of Cycle Detection in MST and Connectivity Problems

In **Minimum Spanning Tree (MST)** algorithms, cycles are undesirable since a spanning tree must connect all vertices with **no cycles** and **minimum total weight**.

Kruskal's algorithm, for example, checks for cycles before adding an edge to ensure that the resulting structure remains a tree.

Union–Find (or **Disjoint Set Union**, DSU) is the most efficient tool for this cycle detection in undirected graphs.

Cycle detection is also key in:

- **Network Reliability Testing**: To ensure that no redundant loops remain
- **Graph Connectivity Problems**: To check if adding an edge connects two previously separate components or not

Disjoint Set Union or Union–Find Data Structure

The **Disjoint Set Union (DSU)**, or **Union–Find**, is a powerful data structure used to efficiently manage partitions of elements into disjoint sets. It helps determine whether two elements belong to the same set (that is, they are connected) and merges sets efficiently.

Core Operations:

- **Find(x)**: Determines the representative (or parent) of the set containing element x
- **Union(x, y)**: Merges the sets containing elements, x and y
- **Path Compression (Optimization):** While performing `Find`, we directly connect each node to its root to flatten the structure to reduce future lookup times.
- **Union by Rank (Optimization):** This ensures that smaller trees are always attached under larger trees, while keeping the overall height minimal.

These optimizations bring the time complexity per operation close to $O(\alpha(n))$, where α is the *inverse Ackermann function*. It is an extremely slow-growing function, and is effectively constant for all practical purposes.

C++ Implementation:

```
#include <iostream>
#include <vector>
using namespace std;

class DSU {
    vector<int> parent, rank;
public:
    DSU(int n) {
        parent.resize(n);
        rank.resize(n, 0);
        for (int i = 0; i < n; i++)
            parent[i] = i;
    }

    int find(int x) {
        if (parent[x] != x)
            parent[x] = find(parent[x]); // Path Compression
        return parent[x];
    }

    void unionSet(int x, int y) {
        int rootX = find(x);
        int rootY = find(y);

        if (rootX != rootY) {
            if (rank[rootX] < rank[rootY])
                parent[rootX] = rootY;
            else if (rank[rootX] > rank[rootY])
                parent[rootY] = rootX;
            else {
                parent[rootY] = rootX;
                rank[rootX]++;
            }
        }
    }
};

// Cycle detection using DSU
bool hasCycle(int n, vector<pair<int, int>>& edges) {
    DSU dsu(n);
    for (auto edge : edges) {
        int u = edge.first, v = edge.second;
        if (dsu.find(u) == dsu.find(v))
            return true; // Cycle detected
        dsu.unionSet(u, v);
    }
    return false;
}

int main() {
    vector<pair<int, int>> edges = {{0, 1}, {1, 2}, {2, 0}};
    cout << (hasCycle(3, edges) ? "Cycle Detected" : "No Cycle");
    return 0;
}
```

Python Implementation:

```
class DSU:
    def __init__(self, n):
        self.parent = [i for i in range(n)]
        self.rank = [0] * n

    def find(self, x):
        if self.parent[x] != x:
            self.parent[x] = self.find(self.parent[x])  # Path Compression
        return self.parent[x]

    def union(self, x, y):
        rootX = self.find(x)
        rootY = self.find(y)

        if rootX != rootY:
            if self.rank[rootX] < self.rank[rootY]:
                self.parent[rootX] = rootY
            elif self.rank[rootX] > self.rank[rootY]:
                self.parent[rootY] = rootX
            else:
                self.parent[rootY] = rootX
                self.rank[rootX] += 1

def has_cycle(n, edges):
    dsu = DSU(n)
    for u, v in edges:
        if dsu.find(u) == dsu.find(v):
            return True  # Cycle detected
        dsu.union(u, v)
    return False

# Example usage
edges = [(0, 1), (1, 2), (2, 0)]
print("Cycle Detected" if has_cycle(3, edges) else "No Cycle")
```

Each vertex starts as its **own parent**, which results in the formation of disjoint sets.

Therefore, when an edge connects two vertices, you must keep the following in consideration:

- If they belong to **different sets**, the algorithm merges (unites) them.
- If they already share the same parent (that is, same set), adding that edge would form a **cycle**.
- **Path compression** and **rank optimization** ensure that the operations are almost constant time.

Thus, the **Union-Find structure** efficiently handles **connectivity** and **cycle detection** tasks. It is a critical component in algorithms like **Kruskal's MST** and **network connectivity analysis**. Through **path compression** and **union by rank**, it achieves near-constant efficiency for large graphs.

Cycle Detection Using Union-Find Structure

In an **undirected graph**, a *cycle* occurs when we can start at one vertex and return to it by traversing edges without repeating any edge. Therefore, detecting such cycles is crucial in many algorithms, particularly while building a **Minimum Spanning Tree (MST)**, since adding an edge that forms a cycle will violate the tree's property.

The **Union-Find (Disjoint Set Union, DSU)** data structure provides an efficient way to detect cycles during edge processing. The idea is based on grouping vertices into disjoint sets, and checking if two vertices belong to the same set before connecting them.

Concept:

- **Initialization**: Every vertex starts as its own parent (that is, a separate component).
- **Union Operation**: When an edge connects two different sets, we *merge* those sets.
- **Find Operation:** Before merging, we should check if both vertices of an edge already belong to the same set.

  If yes → A **cycle** exists (since connecting them again forms a loop).

  If no → Safely connect them by performing the union operation.

Thus, this approach ensures that no redundant edges (that would create loops) are added.

Pseudocode:

```
function detectCycle(edges, V):
    parent = [i for i in range(V)]

    function find(x):
        if parent[x] != x:
            parent[x] = find(parent[x])    # Path compression
        return parent[x]

    function union(x, y):
        parent[find(x)] = find(y)

    for (u, v) in edges:
        x = find(u)
        y = find(v)
        if x == y:
            return True    # Cycle detected
        union(x, y)

    return False  # No cycle found
```

- **Find** helps trace the *representative parent* of a node (the root of its set).
- **Union** connects two sets, while ensuring that components gradually merge without overlap.

If two vertices of an edge share the *same parent*, it means they are already connected; adding another edge would complete a loop, thereby indicating a **cycle**.

Example: Consider an undirected graph with edges: (0,1), (1,2), (2,3), (3,0).

After processing (0,1), (1,2), (2,3), all are connected without cycles. When (3,0) is checked, both vertices belong to the same parent set, hence, a **cycle is detected**.

Applications include:

- Constructing a Minimum Spanning Tree (Kruskal's Algorithm)
- Conducting network connectivity checks
- Avoiding redundant links in communication systems
- Cluster analysis and union-based graph problems

Applications of MST and the Shortest Path Algorithms

Graph algorithms such as **Dijkstra's**, **Bellman–Ford**, **Prim's**, and **Kruskal's** extend far beyond theoretical study; they are the foundation of numerous real-world systems that require optimal connectivity, efficiency, and cost minimization.

Now, let us explore some of their most impactful applications which are explained as follows:

Network Design

In telecommunications, electrical grids, and computer networks, it is essential to connect all nodes (like routers or substations) while minimizing the total wiring or transmission cost.

MST algorithms (Prim's and Kruskal's) are ideal for designing **least-cost networks**, and ensuring that every node is connected without redundancy.

Example: Designing an optimal **fiber-optic network** layout connecting multiple cities.

Route Planning and Logistics

Navigation systems, public transport planners, and delivery networks use the **shortest path algorithms** to determine the most efficient routes.

- **Dijkstra's algorithm** powers GPS navigation by finding the quickest or shortest path between locations.
- **Bellman-Ford algorithm** is used when routes may include **negative edge weights**, such as routes with varying tolls or rewards. For example, determining the **minimum-time route** for a delivery truck across multiple destinations.

Bandwidth Optimization in Data Networks

In large-scale data transmission networks, bandwidth must be distributed efficiently across paths to prevent congestion.

Thus, the shortest path algorithms help determine **low-latency routes** for data packets, **while MST algorithms** minimize the **backbone cost** of network cabling and wireless connections.

Clustering and Segmentation in AI/ML Systems

In data science and machine learning, graphs are widely used to represent relationships between data points.

Minimum Spanning Trees (MSTs) are applied in hierarchical clustering methods, such as the Single-Linkage algorithm, to form natural data clusters.

Shortest-path algorithms, in contrast, help identify similarity-based neighborhoods and are useful in graph-based semi-supervised learning and image segmentation.

Performance Analysis and Edge Case Handling

Understanding how each graph algorithm performs under various conditions is crucial for selecting the right one. Factors such as graph density, edge weights, and network size significantly affect performance.

Comparative Efficiency of Algorithms

Algorithm	Approach	Handles Negative Weights	Time Complexity	Space Complexity	Best Use Case	Benefits
Dijkstra's	Greedy	No	O((V + E) log V) using min-heap	O(V + E)	Fast route computation with non-negative weights	Very fast in practice, optimal for real-time shortest path problems, widely supported in libraries
Bellman-Ford	Dynamic Programming	Yes	O(V × E)	O(V)	Graphs with possible negative edges	Detects negative weight cycles, simple logic, reliable for correctness in constrained graphs
Prim's	Greedy	No	O(E log V) using min-heap	O(V + E)	Dense graph MST construction	Efficient for dense graphs, incremental MST growth, easy integration with adjacency lists
Kruskal's	Greedy (Union-Find)	No	O(E log E)	O(V + E)	Sparse graph MST construction	Simple implementation, works well with sparse graphs, highly efficient using DSU with path compression

Table 9.4: *Comparative Efficiency of Algorithms*

Although multiple graph algorithms can solve similar problems, their performance can vary significantly depending on the size of the graph, the number of edges, and the nature of edge weights. Therefore, to make informed decisions in real applications, it is important to compare how efficiently each algorithm works in terms of time and memory usage. The following list summarizes the strengths, limitations, and ideal scenarios for Dijkstra's, Bellman-Ford, Prim's, and Kruskal's algorithms, so that you can choose the right one for a given problem.

Handling Special Cases:

- **Negative Weight Edges:**
  - Use Bellman-Ford instead of Dijkstra's algorithm to avoid incorrect results.
- **Disconnected Graphs:**
  - For MST problems, handle each connected component separately.
  - For shortest paths, mark unreachable nodes with ∞ (infinity).
- **Dense Graphs:**
  - Prefer Prim's algorithm, as it performs efficiently when the number of edges is close to V^2.
- **Sparse Graphs:**
  - Kruskal's algorithm is often faster and simpler for graphs with fewer edges.
- **Large-Scale Datasets:**
  - Optimize with adjacency lists instead of matrices.

  - Use priority queues (heaps) and efficient Disjoint Set Union (DSU) structures with path compression.

Optimization Techniques for Large Datasets:

- **Use Lazy Evaluation**: Avoid unnecessary relaxation steps in Dijkstra's algorithm or Bellman-Ford.
- **Parallelize MST Construction**: For massive networks, divide and merge subtrees in parallel.
- **Leverage Graph Libraries**: Use optimized implementations like NetworkX (Python) or Boost Graph Library (C++).
- **Memory Optimization**: Compress adjacency lists and avoid redundant edge storage.

Practice Problems

To reinforce the concepts learned in this chapter, the following problems offer hands-on experience with shortest path computation, MST construction, and cycle detection. These problems are commonly asked in coding interviews and competitive programming, which makes them valuable for skill-building and revision.

- **Shortest Path in a Grid:** You are given a 2D grid where each cell has a movement cost. Starting from the top-left cell, find the minimum cost path to reach the bottom-right cell. This problem can be solved using **Dijkstra's Algorithm** by treating each cell as a graph node, and allowing movements as edges.
- **Network Delay Time:** You are given a directed, weighted graph representing signal transmission times between network nodes. If a signal is sent from a particular source, determine how long it will take for all nodes to receive the signal. This problem models **single-source shortest paths,** and is typically solved using Dijkstra's or Bellman-Ford, depending on edge weights.
- **Connecting Cities with Minimum Cost:** Several cities are connected by possible roads, each with a construction cost. Your task is to connect all cities with the **minimum total cost,** while ensuring the network has no cycles. This is a direct application of **MST** algorithms such as **Prim's** or **Kruskal's**.
- **Detecting Cycle Using Union-Find:** Given an undirected graph described by a list of edges, determine whether the graph contains a cycle. Use the **Union-Find (Disjoint Set Union)** structure to efficiently check if any edge connects two vertices already in the same set.

Additional Practice Challenges

For more practice, you can attempt the following challenges:

- Shortest path with negative weights
- Minimum cost to connect points in a plane (Euclidean MST)
- Cheapest flight route with limited stops
- Shortest alternating path in colored edge graphs
- Redundant connection detection in networks

These exercises help build intuition and fluency with graph algorithms. They will also prepare you for real-world development and competitive programming environments.

Conclusion

In this chapter, we explored essential graph algorithms that power real-world systems, from navigation and routing, to network design and clustering. We understood how algorithms like Dijkstra's and Bellman-Ford can compute shortest paths, and how Prim's and Kruskal's algorithms build MSTs. Additionally, we also learned how the Union-Find structure can efficiently detect cycles in large graphs. Through performance comparisons, optimization techniques, and practical problems, this chapter provided both theoretical clarity and hands-on intuition needed to solve graph-based challenges effectively. As we move ahead to *Chapter 10: Sorting and Searching*, we will shift our attention to two of the most fundamental pillars of computer science. We will begin by understanding why sorting matters. We will also explore classical comparison-based algorithms, aside from studying efficient techniques such as Merge Sort, Quick Sort, and Heap Sort, and introducing non-comparison methods such as Counting Sort and Radix Sort. We will also build a strong foundation in binary search and its practical variations, while learning when to choose each algorithm in real-world scenarios.

Points to Remember

- Graph algorithms are used in routing, logistics, clustering, network design, GPS navigation, and bandwidth optimization.
- Dijkstra's algorithm finds shortest paths in graphs with non-negative edge weights using a greedy approach.
- Bellman-Ford algorithm supports negative edge weights and detects negative weight cycles.
- A Minimum Spanning Tree (MST) connects all vertices using exactly V – 1 edges with minimum total weight.
- Prim's algorithm expands the MST from a starting vertex by repeatedly selecting the minimum-weight connecting edge.
- Kruskal's algorithm builds the MST by sorting edges by weight and adding them while avoiding cycles.
- Union-Find efficiently manages connected components and supports cycle detection in undirected graphs.
- Cycle detection in MST construction is efficiently handled using Union-Find.
- Graph density affects algorithm choice: Prim's is preferred for dense graphs, while Kruskal's suits sparse graphs.
- Dijkstra's algorithm has time complexity **O((V + E) log V)** when implemented using a min-heap.
- Bellman-Ford algorithm has time complexity **O(VE)**.
- Dijkstra's algorithm must not be used on graphs with negative edge weights.
- MST algorithms do not apply to directed graphs or graphs containing negative cycles.
- Multiple valid MSTs may exist when edges have equal weights.
- Efficient implementations rely on adjacency lists, priority queues, and optimized Union-Find operations.

Multiple Choice Questions

1. Which algorithm is used to find the shortest paths in graphs without negative weights?
   a. Prim's
   b. Dijkstra's
   c. Kruskal's
   d. BFS
2. Bellman–Ford differs from Dijkstra's because Bellman–Ford:
   a. Uses a priority queue.
   b. Works only on trees.
   c. Supports negative weights.
   d. Requires sorted edges.
3. A Minimum Spanning Tree of a connected graph with V vertices contains:
   a. V edges
   b. V–1 edges
   c. E edges
   d. Variable number of edges
4. Kruskal's Algorithm requires sorting of:
   a. Vertices
   b. Edges
   c. Paths
   d. Components
5. Union–Find is mainly used to:
   a. Sort elements.
   b. Perform graph traversal.
   c. Detect cycles and manage components.
   d. Count edges.
6. Path compression is used to optimize:
   a. DFS
   b. BFS
   c. Union–Find
   d. Bellman–Ford
7. If a graph has negative cycles, which algorithm can detect it?
   a. Dijkstra's
   b. Kruskal's
   c. Bellman–Ford
   d. Floyd-Warshall only

8. Prim's Algorithm selects:
   a. The smallest weight edge in the entire graph.
   b. The smallest outgoing edge from the current MST.
   c. The largest edge.
   d. A random edge.
9. The time complexity of Kruskal's Algorithm is approximately:
   a. `O(V2)O(V^2)O(V2)`
   b. `O(ElogE)O(E \log E)O(ElogE)`
   c. `O(E)O(E)O(E)`
   d. `O(V+E)O(V + E)O(V+E)`
10. Dijkstra's algorithm fails when:
    a. The graph is undirected.
    b. The graph has many edges.
    c. The graph has negative edge weights.
    d. The graph is sparse.
11. The Bellman–Ford algorithm relaxes edges:
    a. Exactly once
    b. V–1 times
    c. E^2 times
    d. Until cycles disappear
12. MST algorithms apply to:
    a. Directed Graphs
    b. Undirected Weighted Graphs
    c. Only Trees
    d. Graphs with Negative Cycles
13. The priority queue in Dijkstra's algorithm stores:
    a. Components
    b. Sorted Edges
    c. (Distance, Vertex) Pairs
    d. Adjacency Matrix
14. Cycle detection using Union–Find happens when:
    a. Two vertices already have the same root.
    b. Distance becomes negative.
    c. Graph has no weights.
    d. Adjacency list is full.
15. Kruskal's algorithm is preferred over Prim's when:
    a. The graph is dense.
    b. The graph has many edges.

c. The graph is sparse.

d. The graph has negative edges.

Answers

1. b
2. c
3. b
4. b
5. c
6. c
7. c
8. b
9. b
10. c
11. b
12. b
13. c
14. a
15. c

Questions

1. Explain the working of Dijkstra's algorithm with an example. Discuss how the priority queue improves efficiency.
2. Describe the Bellman–Ford algorithm. How does it detect negative weight cycles?
3. What is a Minimum Spanning Tree? Also compare Prim's and Kruskal's algorithms in detail.
4. Explain the Union–Find (Disjoint Set Union) data structure. How do path compression and union by rank improve performance?
5. Discuss real-world applications of the shortest path algorithms in routing, logistics, and navigation systems.
6. Why is Kruskal's algorithm efficient for sparse graphs? Illustrate with a sample graph.
7. Write the differences between the shortest path computation and MST construction.
8. Describe performance trade-offs among algorithms like Dijkstra's, Bellman–Ford, Prim's, and Kruskal's. Also explain the occasions when each of them should be used.

Key Terms

- **Shortest Path**: The minimum total edge weight required to travel from one vertex to another in a weighted graph
- **Relaxation**: The process of updating the shortest known distance to a vertex when a shorter path is found

- **Minimum Spanning Tree (MST):** A set of edges that connects all vertices of a graph with minimum total weight and without forming cycles
- **Greedy Algorithm:** An algorithmic strategy that makes the locally optimal choice at each step to build a solution
- **Priority Queue / Min-Heap:** A data structure that allows efficient retrieval of the element with the smallest key value
- **Union-Find (Disjoint Set Union):** A data structure used to maintain disjoint sets and efficiently perform union and connectivity checks
- **Path Compression:** A Union-Find optimization that flattens the tree structure during Find operations to improve performance
- **Union by Rank:** A Union-Find optimization that attaches the smaller tree under the root of the larger tree
- **Negative Weight Cycle:** A cycle in a graph whose total edge weight is negative, causing shortest path computations to be undefined
- **Connected Components:** Subsets of vertices in a graph where each vertex is reachable from every other vertex in the same subset
- **Dense Graph:** A graph in which the number of edges is close to the maximum possible number of edges
- **Sparse Graph:** A graph in which the number of edges is much smaller than the maximum possible
- **Cycle Detection:** The process of determining whether a graph contains a cycle
- **Edge List:** A graph representation that stores all edges as pairs (or triples) of connected vertices and weights
- **Adjacency List:** A graph representation where each vertex stores a list of its neighboring vertices and associated edge weights
- **Graph Optimization:** Techniques used to improve the time and space efficiency of graph algorithms

CHAPTER 10
Sorting and Searching

Introduction

In every computing system, data is more than just stored information; it is something we constantly **organize, access, analyze, and retrieve**. Whether it is searching for a contact on a smartphone, arranging student records by marks, filtering messages by date, or recommending content on social platforms, the efficiency of these operations largely depends on how fast data can be sorted and searched. **Therefore, sorting** is the process of arranging data in a specific order, usually ascending or descending. Although it sounds simple, sorting is an immensely powerful tool. Once data is sorted, it becomes easier to process, merge, compare, search, and optimize. Many higher-level algorithms such as binary search, greedy strategies, and certain graph algorithms depend heavily on sorted data. **Therefore, searching** is the task of locating a specific element from a collection of data. An efficient searching technique ensures quick access to required information even when the dataset is extremely large. For example, a database cannot scan millions of records one by one every time; instead, it relies on intelligent searching techniques to answer queries in milliseconds. Sorting and searching together form the backbone of algorithmic problem-solving. They are used in operating systems, databases, networking, Machine Learning (ML) pipelines, e-commerce applications, cybersecurity tools, and virtually every modern software system. Understanding these operations is not only essential for mastering Data Structures and Algorithms (DSA), but also for writing programs that are fast, scalable, and reliable. Hence, in this chapter, we will explore a wide range of sorting and searching algorithms from simple, intuitive methods, to more advanced and highly efficient techniques. Along with working principles, we will analyze their time and space complexity, stability, use-cases, limitations, and real-world relevance. Thus, by the end of the chapter, learners will be well-equipped to choose the right algorithm based on problem requirements and implement practical solutions confidently.

Structure

In this chapter, we will cover the following topics:

- Introduction to Sorting and Searching
- Fundamentals of Sorting
- Basic Comparison-Based Sorting Techniques
- Efficient Comparison-Based Sorting Techniques

- Non-Comparison Sorting Techniques
- Searching Techniques
- Binary Search
- Variants of Binary Search
- Practical Applications of Binary Search
- Problem-Solving Patterns Based on Binary Search
- Algorithm Selection Guidelines
- Frequent Mistakes in Sorting and Searching

Introduction to Sorting and Searching

Sorting and searching are two of the most fundamental operations in computer science. Whether a system is managing a small list of numbers or a massive database, the way data is organized and accessed directly affects performance. Hence, every modern application from mobile phones to cloud servers—relies on sorting to arrange information and on searching to retrieve it efficiently. Thus, before diving into the techniques and algorithms that make these operations fast and reliable, this section will build the foundation by understanding why sorting and searching matter and how deeply they influence real-world computing.

Role of Sorting in Computing

Sorting refers to arranging data in a systematic order, most commonly in ascending or descending sequence. While the idea is simple, sorting plays a crucial role in improving the efficiency of almost every data-related operation. When data is sorted:

- Searching becomes faster.
- Duplicate values can be detected easily.
- Records can be compared, merged, and analyzed efficiently.
- Many advanced algorithms, such as binary search or greedy techniques, rely on sorted input.

For example, student scores arranged from the highest to lowest make ranking straightforward. In networking, packets are often ordered by time to reconstruct messages correctly. Even everyday apps such as photo galleries use sorting silently in the background to sort images by date.

In short, sorting helps to convert raw, unorganized data into a structured form that is easier to process and understand.

Role of Searching in Computing

Searching is the process of locating a specific piece of data from a collection. As the size of data increases, the importance of fast searching grows. Without efficient search methods, a system would need to check every item one by one, which becomes slow and impractical for large datasets.

Searching algorithms are designed to reduce the time needed to find results. For example:

- Messaging apps search through thousands of conversations instantly.
- Search engines look for keywords in millions of pages.
- E-commerce platforms locate a product among thousands of items within seconds.

Efficient searching ensures quick access, accurate retrieval, and better performance in almost every software system. In fact, without powerful search techniques, modern computing would feel slow and unresponsive.

Real-World Applications of Sorting and Searching

Sorting and searching are deeply integrated into real-life digital systems in the following ways:

- **Databases** sort and search records for faster queries.
- **Operating systems** sort files by name, size, or date.
- **E-commerce platforms** sort products by price, rating, or relevance and search items in milliseconds.
- **Streaming services** search content by genre and sort recommendations based on user interest.
- **Navigation apps** search locations and sort routes by distance or time.

Even simple daily tasks such as scrolling through contacts, filtering emails, or organizing photos are powered by sorting and searching algorithms.

Fundamentals of Sorting

Sorting is one of the most commonly used operations in computing. It refers to arranging data in a specific order, usually in ascending or descending form. Although the idea sounds simple, sorting serves as a foundation for many advanced tasks. Well-sorted data makes searching faster, supports data analysis, and improves the performance of several algorithms and software systems.

Definition of Sorting

Sorting is the process of organizing a collection of items based on a defined rule or comparison. For example:

- Arranging integers from the smallest to the largest
- Sorting student records by marks
- Ordering names alphabetically

Once the data is sorted, it becomes easier to search, compare, merge, and process. Many algorithms assume that the input is already sorted, which makes sorting a crucial preparatory step in numerous applications.

Comparison-Based Sorting and Non-Comparison Sorting

Sorting techniques fall into two broad categories:

- **Comparison-Based Sorting:** In these algorithms, decisions are made by comparing elements with each other.

  Examples: Bubble Sort, Insertion Sort, Merge Sort, Quick Sort

These algorithms typically have time complexities like $O(n^2)$ or $O(n \log n)$.

- **Non-Comparison Sorting:** These methods do not compare elements directly. Instead, they use properties such as value range or digit structure.

  Examples: Counting Sort, Bucket Sort, Radix Sort.

They can achieve faster performance like $O(n)$, but only under specific conditions.

Key Properties of Sorting Algorithms

Every sorting technique has certain characteristics that affect how it behaves in different situations. Some algorithms preserve the order of equal elements, some use extra memory, while others perform better when the data is nearly sorted. These characteristics are known as the key properties of sorting algorithms, and they help in understanding when and where a particular method is most suitable.

- **Stability:** A sorting algorithm is said to be stable if it maintains the relative order of elements with equal keys.

  Example: If two students have the same marks, a stable sort keeps them in the order they originally appeared.

  - **Stable Examples**: Bubble Sort, Merge Sort, Counting Sort
  - **Unstable Examples**: Selection Sort, Quick Sort, Heap Sort

Therefore, stability is important in real-world scenarios like sorting records on multiple attributes (for example, first by marks, and then by name).

- **In-Place Sorting:** The algorithm rearranges elements within the original data structure, using a constant or minimal extra memory. **Example**: Quick Sort, Insertion Sort
- **Out-of-Place Sorting:** The algorithm requires extra memory to store temporary results. **Example**: Merge Sort, Counting Sort

Therefore, in-place algorithms are preferred when memory is limited, while out-of-place ones offer cleaner logic or better stability.

- **Adaptive Sorting:** Performance improves when the input is already partially sorted. **Example**: Insertion Sort works rapidly on nearly sorted data.

Adaptive algorithms are useful in real-time systems where data is frequently updated rather than rearranged from scratch.

- **Non-Adaptive Sorting:** The algorithm takes the same time regardless of input order. **Example**: Selection Sort, Quick Sort.

Parameters for Evaluating Sorting Algorithms

Before choosing a sorting algorithm for a problem, it is important to understand how to measure its efficiency. Sorting techniques may produce correct results, but they differ in speed, memory usage, and the amount of work done on the data. To compare different algorithms fairly, we use several evaluation parameters such as:

Time Complexity indicates how the running time of the algorithm grows as the size of the data increases. Most sorting algorithms fall into categories such as:

- `O(n²)`: Slow for large datasets (Bubble Sort, Selection Sort)
- `O(n log n)`: Efficient for large datasets (Merge Sort, Quick Sort, Heap Sort)
- `O(n)`: Special cases using non-comparison sorting (Counting Sort)

Space Complexity measures additional memory used by the algorithm

- **In-Place Sorts**: O(1) extra space
- **Out-of-Place Sorts**: O(n) extra space

Efficient systems prefer algorithms with low memory usage, especially while handling large input sizes.

Basic Comparison-Based Sorting Techniques

Comparison-based sorting algorithms arrange data by comparing elements with each other. These methods help build a strong foundational understanding of how sorting works internally. Although they may not always be the fastest for large datasets, their logic is easy to visualize, which makes them excellent for learning and for small-scale applications.

Bubble Sort

Bubble Sort repeatedly scans through the list and compares adjacent elements. If a pair is out of order, the elements are swapped. Hence, with each pass, the largest element "bubbles up" to its correct position at the end of the list. This process continues until no more swaps are needed.

Step-by-Step Illustration

Consider the array: `[5, 3, 2, 4]`. Now, follow these steps:

```
Compare 5 and 3 → Swap → [3, 5, 2, 4].
Compare 5 and 2 → Swap → [3, 2, 5, 4].
Compare 5 and 4 → Swap → [3, 2, 4, 5].
```

After one full pass, 5 is in its correct position. The next pass arranges the remaining elements and the list becomes sorted.

This simple process makes Bubble Sort easy to visualize, but works slowly for large inputs.

C++ Implementation:

```
void bubbleSort(int arr[], int n) {
    bool swapped;
    for (int i = 0; i < n - 1; i++) {
        swapped = false;
        for (int j = 0; j < n - i - 1; j++) {
            if (arr[j] > arr[j + 1]) {
                // Swap
                int temp = arr[j];
                arr[j] = arr[j + 1];
                arr[j + 1] = temp;
                swapped = true;
            }
        }
        // If no swaps occurred, the list is already sorted
        if (!swapped)
            break;
    }
}
```

Python Implementation:

```
def bubble_sort(arr):
    n = len(arr)
    for i in range(n - 1):
        swapped = False
        for j in range(n - i - 1):
            if arr[j] > arr[j + 1]:
                arr[j], arr[j + 1] = arr[j + 1], arr[j]
```

```
            swapped = True
        if not swapped:
            break
```

Complexity Analysis

- **Best Case**: `O(n)` (when the list is already sorted)
- **Average Case**: `O(n²)`
- **Worst Case**: `O(n²)`
- **Space Complexity**: `O(1)`, as sorting happens in-place

Therefore, we can conclude that Bubble Sort is stable, but is not efficient for large-scale applications.

Selection Sort

Selection Sort divides the array into two parts: a sorted portion at the beginning and an unsorted portion after it. During each pass, it finds the smallest element in the unsorted part and swaps it with the first unsorted element. Therefore, as passes continue, the sorted portion grows until the entire array is sorted.

Unlike Bubble Sort, Selection Sort performs fewer swaps, but the number of comparisons remains high.

For the array **[4, 1, 3, 2]:**

```
The smallest element is 1 → Swap with 4 → [1, 4, 3, 2].
The next smallest is 2 → Swap with 4 → [1, 2, 3, 4].
```

As you can see, the remaining elements are already sorted.

After two passes, the list becomes fully sorted.

C++ Implementation:

```
void selectionSort(int arr[], int n) {
    for (int i = 0; i < n - 1; i++) {
        int minIndex = i;
        for (int j = i + 1; j < n; j++) {
            if (arr[j] < arr[minIndex])
                minIndex = j;
        }
        int temp = arr[minIndex];
        arr[minIndex] = arr[i];
        arr[i] = temp;
    }
}
```

Python Implementation:

```
def selection_sort(arr):
    n = len(arr)
    for i in range(n - 1):
        min_index = i
        for j in range(i + 1, n):
            if arr[j] < arr[min_index]:
                min_index = j
        arr[i], arr[min_index] = arr[min_index], arr[i]
```

Complexity Analysis

- **Best Case:** $O(n^2)$
- **Average Case:** $O(n^2)$
- **Worst Case:** $O(n^2)$
- **Space Complexity:** O(1) (in-place)
- **Stability:** Not stable (equal elements may change order)

Selection Sort is simple and predictable, but is usually inefficient for large input sizes.

Insertion Sort

Insertion Sort builds a sorted list one element at a time. It picks the next element (called the key) and inserts it into its correct position inside the already-sorted portion of the array. Elements are shifted until the correct location is found. This method is efficient when the list is nearly sorted or very small.

A common example is arranging playing cards in hand. Players pick up one card at a time and insert it where it belongs among the previously arranged cards.

C++ Implementation:

```
void insertionSort(int arr[], int n) {
    for (int i = 1; i < n; i++) {
        int key = arr[i];
        int j = i - 1;

        while (j >= 0 && arr[j] > key) {
            arr[j + 1] = arr[j];
            j--;
        }

        arr[j + 1] = key;
    }
}
```

Python Implementation:

```
def insertion_sort(arr):
    for i in range(1, len(arr)):
        key = arr[i]
        j = i - 1

        while j >= 0 and arr[j] > key:
            arr[j + 1] = arr[j]
            j -= 1

        arr[j + 1] = key
```

Complexity Analysis

- **Best Case:** `O(n)` – When the list is already almost sorted
- **Average Case:** $O(n^2)$
- **Worst Case:** $O(n^2)$
- **Space Complexity:** `O(1)` (in-place)
- **Stability:** Stable

Behavior on Nearly Sorted Data

Insertion Sort performs extremely well when the input is already close to sorted. Thus, in such cases, the inner shifting happens very few times, which makes it significantly faster than Bubble Sort and Selection Sort. Due to this, real-world systems often use Insertion Sort as a final optimization step after other algorithms partially sort data.

Efficient Comparison-Based Sorting Techniques

The sorting methods studied earlier (Bubble, Selection, and Insertion Sort) are simple and easy to visualize, but their performance is limited for large input sizes. As data grows into thousands, millions, or even billions of elements, these basic techniques become too slow. Therefore, efficient comparison-based sorting algorithms can overcome this limitation by reducing the number of comparisons and operations needed to sort data. They commonly achieve time complexity close to **O(n log n)**, which makes them suitable for real-world applications and performance-critical systems. The three most widely used efficient sorting techniques are **Merge Sort, Quick Sort, and Heap Sort**.

Merge Sort

Sorting large datasets efficiently can be challenging, especially when simple methods become slow as the input size grows. Merge Sort overcomes this limitation using a powerful strategy that breaks the problem into smaller parts, and solves them independently. It guarantees fast performance even in the worst case, making it one of the most trusted and widely used sorting algorithms in both theory and real-world applications.

Divide-and-Conquer Strategy

Merge Sort follows a powerful technique known as **Divide-and-Conquer**. Instead of trying to sort the entire array at once, it breaks the problem into smaller and easier parts. This technique is composed of the following steps:

a. **Divide:** Split the array into two equal halves.

b. **Conquer:** Recursively sort both halves.

c. **Combine:** Merge the two sorted halves into a single sorted array.

Thus, by breaking the data into smaller pieces and sorting them independently, Merge Sort avoids long, repeated comparisons on the full list. The merge step is the heart of the algorithm, where two sorted lists are combined efficiently into a new sorted list.

Consider the array [8, 3, 5, 2] and follow these steps:

Step 1: Divide

`Split → [8, 3]` and `[5, 2].`

`Split again → [8] [3]` and `[5] [2].`

The single-element lists are already sorted.

Step 2: Conquer (Merge)

Merge `[8]` and `[3] → [3, 8].`

Merge `[5]` and `[2] → [2, 5].`

Step 3: Final Merge

Merge `[3, 8]` and `[2, 5] → [2, 3, 5, 8].`

The array is now sorted.

C++ Implementation:

```
void merge(int arr[], int left, int mid, int right) {
    int n1 = mid - left + 1;
    int n2 = right - mid;

    int L[n1], R[n2];

    for (int i = 0; i < n1; i++)
        L[i] = arr[left + i];

    for (int i = 0; i < n2; i++)
        R[i] = arr[mid + 1 + i];

    int i = 0, j = 0, k = left;

    while (i < n1 && j < n2) {
        if (L[i] <= R[j])
            arr[k++] = L[i++];
        else
            arr[k++] = R[j++];
    }

    while (i < n1)
        arr[k++] = L[i++];

    while (j < n2)
        arr[k++] = R[j++];
}

void mergeSort(int arr[], int left, int right) {
    if (left >= right)
        return;

    int mid = (left + right) / 2;

    mergeSort(arr, left, mid);
    mergeSort(arr, mid + 1, right);

    merge(arr, left, mid, right);
}
```

Python Implementation:

```
def merge_sort(arr):
    if len(arr) <= 1:
        return arr

    mid = len(arr) // 2
    left = merge_sort(arr[:mid])
    right = merge_sort(arr[mid:])

    return merge(left, right)

def merge(left, right):
    result = []
    i = j = 0

    while i < len(left) and j < len(right):
        if left[i] <= right[j]:
            result.append(left[i])
```

```
        i += 1
    else:
        result.append(right[j])
        j += 1

result.extend(left[i:])
result.extend(right[j:])
return result
```

Stability and Applications

Merge Sort is a **stable sorting algorithm**. Thus, if two elements have the same value, they will maintain their original order in the output.

Merge Sort is useful in these cases:

- Large datasets, where a consistent O(n log n) performance is required
- Linked lists (easy merging without extra memory)
- External sorting (for example, sorting data stored on disk in chunks)
- When stability is important, such as sorting records by marks and then by name

Merge Sort may use extra memory, but it remains one of the most reliable and widely used sorting algorithms in both academic and professional systems.

Quick Sort

Quick Sort is one of the most efficient and widely used sorting algorithms in practice. It follows the divide-and-conquer approach but takes a different path compared to Merge Sort. Instead of splitting the array into equal halves, Quick Sort rearranges elements around a pivot so that smaller elements move to one side and larger elements move to the other. This process is called **partitioning** and makes Quick Sort fast and memory-efficient.

Partitioning Technique

The heart of Quick Sort is the **partition** step.

Choose an element as the **pivot**. Rearrange the array so that:

- All elements smaller than the pivot appear on its left.
- All elements greater than the pivot appear on its right.

After partitioning, the pivot occupies its correct position in the sorted array.

Recursively apply Quick Sort on the left and right partitions.

This approach avoids extra merging steps and works directly on the original array, making Quick Sort an **in-place** sorting technique.

Pivot Selection Strategies

Performance depends heavily on how the pivot is chosen. Common methods include:

- **Last Element as Pivot (simple and popular)**
- **First Element as Pivot**
- **Middle Element as Pivot**
- **Random Pivot**: Reduces risk of worst-case behavior.

- **Median-of-Three Pivot**:
  - Choose the median of the first, middle, and last elements to improve balance
  - A good pivot ensures the partitions are roughly equal in size, which keeps the algorithm fast.

Sort the array [7, 4, 9, 2] and follow these steps:

```
Choose pivot = 7
Partition:
       Smaller than 7 → [4, 2]
       Greater than 7 → [9] → [4, 2, 7, 9]
Now repeat on [4, 2]:
       Pivot = 2
       Partition → [2, 4]
```

The final result is [2, 4, 7, 9].

Thus, Quick Sort recursively organizes each section until the whole list becomes sorted.

C++ Implementation:

```
int partition(int arr[], int low, int high) {
    int pivot = arr[high];
    int i = low - 1;

    for (int j = low; j < high; j++) {
        if (arr[j] < pivot) {
            i++;
            int temp = arr[i];
            arr[i] = arr[j];
            arr[j] = temp;
        }
    }

    int temp = arr[i + 1];
    arr[i + 1] = arr[high];
    arr[high] = temp;

    return i + 1;
}

void quickSort(int arr[], int low, int high) {
    if (low < high) {
        int pi = partition(arr, low, high);

        quickSort(arr, low, pi - 1);
        quickSort(arr, pi + 1, high);
    }
}
```

Python Implementation:

```
def partition(arr, low, high):
    pivot = arr[high]
    i = low - 1

    for j in range(low, high):
        if arr[j] < pivot:
            i += 1
```

```
            arr[i], arr[j] = arr[j], arr[i]

    arr[i + 1], arr[high] = arr[high], arr[i + 1]
    return i + 1

def quick_sort(arr, low, high):
    if low < high:
        pi = partition(arr, low, high)
        quick_sort(arr, low, pi - 1)
        quick_sort(arr, pi + 1, high)
```

Optimizations

To avoid worst-case performance and improve efficiency, several optimizations are used such as:

- **Randomized Pivot:** Choosing a random pivot reduces the chance of bad partitions
- **Median-of-Three:** Taking the median of the first, middle, and last elements as pivot often produces balanced partitions
- **Tail Recursion Elimination:** Reduces recursion depth
- **Hybrid Approach:** Switch to Insertion Sort when the array becomes very small to improve speed on partially sorted data.

Heap Sort

Heap Sort is another efficient comparison-based sorting technique that guarantees **O(n log n)** performance in all cases. Unlike Merge Sort, it works **in-place** without requiring extra memory; and unlike Quick Sort, it does not suffer from worst-case slowdowns caused by poor pivot choices. Moreover, Heap Sort is built on a special tree-based structure known as a **heap**, which makes extracting the largest (or smallest) element very efficient.

Using the Heap Data Structure

A **heap** is a complete binary tree where each parent node follows a specific ordering rule, which is:

- In a **max heap**, every parent node is greater than or equal to its children.
- In a **min heap**, every parent node is smaller than or equal to its children.

Heap Sort typically uses a **max heap,** so the largest element moves to the root. Once the largest value is at the top, it can be swapped to the end of the array. By shrinking the heap size and repeating this step, the list becomes sorted.

Heap Construction and Heapify

Heap Sort has two major phases:

1. **Build a Heap**
    a. Convert the input array into a valid max-heap.
    b. This ensures the largest element is always at the root.
2. **Heapify**
    a. After placing the largest element at the end, the heap property may break.
    b. The `heapify` procedure restores the heap structure by moving elements to their correct positions.
    c. This repeated process of extracting the maximum. Thereafter, heapifying gradually sorts the array.

C++ Implementation:

```
void heapify(int arr[], int n, int i) {
    int largest = i;
    int left = 2 * i + 1;
    int right = 2 * i + 2;

    if (left < n && arr[left] > arr[largest])
        largest = left;

    if (right < n && arr[right] > arr[largest])
        largest = right;

    if (largest != i) {
        int temp = arr[i];
        arr[i] = arr[largest];
        arr[largest] = temp;

        heapify(arr, n, largest);
    }
}
void heapSort(int arr[], int n) {
    // Build max-heap
    for (int i = n / 2 - 1; i >= 0; i--)
        heapify(arr, n, i);

    // Extract elements from heap
    for (int i = n - 1; i > 0; i--) {
        int temp = arr[0];
        arr[0] = arr[i];
        arr[i] = temp;

        heapify(arr, i, 0);
    }
}
```

Python Implementation:

```
def heapify(arr, n, i):
    largest = i
    left = 2 * i + 1
    right = 2 * i + 2

    if left < n and arr[left] > arr[largest]:
        largest = left

    if right < n and arr[right] > arr[largest]:
        largest = right

    if largest != i:
        arr[i], arr[largest] = arr[largest], arr[i]
        heapify(arr, n, largest)

def heap_sort(arr):
    n = len(arr)

    for i in range(n // 2 - 1, -1, -1):
        heapify(arr, n, i)
```

```
    for i in range(n - 1, 0, -1):
        arr[0], arr[i] = arr[i], arr[0]
        heapify(arr, i, 0)
```

Non-Comparison Sorting Techniques

Most sorting algorithms work by comparing one element with another. However, there are special cases where data can be sorted **without comparisons**. These techniques use the mathematical properties of the data itself, like value ranges or digits, to achieve performance faster than O(n log n). In this section, we will learn about Counting Sort and Radix Sort, which are the most popular non-comparison-based methods used in competitive programming, data indexing, and real-time systems.

Counting Sort

Counting Sort works by counting how many times each value appears in the input. Instead of comparing elements, it uses an auxiliary array to store the frequency of each number. By converting these frequencies into positions, Counting Sort places elements directly into their correct sorted location. Hence, this feature makes the algorithm extremely fast when:

- The input values are integers.
- The range of values (0 to k) is not very large.

Sort the array [4, 2, 2, 8, 3, 3, 1] and follow the instructions:

Count the number of times each value appears.

```
1 → 1 time
2 → 2 times
3 → 2 times
4 → 1 time
8 → 1 time
```

Build cumulative counts to determine correct positions.

Place each element into a new output array in the sorted order.

The final sorted result will be [1, 2, 2, 3, 3, 4, 8].

Therefore, as you can see in the example, no comparisons were required between numbers.

C++ Implementation:

```
void countingSort(int arr[], int n, int maxVal) {
    int count[maxVal + 1] = {0};

    for (int i = 0; i < n; i++)
        count[arr[i]]++;

    int index = 0;
    for (int i = 0; i <= maxVal; i++) {
        while (count[i] > 0) {
            arr[index++] = i;
            count[i]--;
        }
    }
}
```

Python Implementation:

```
def counting_sort(arr):
    max_val = max(arr)
    count = [0] * (max_val + 1)

    for num in arr:
        count[num] += 1

    index = 0
    for i in range(len(count)):
        while count[i] > 0:
            arr[index] = i
            index += 1
            count[i] -= 1
```

Time and Space Complexity

Time Complexity: O(n + k)

Where n = number of elements and k = range of values.

Space Complexity: O(k) for the count array

Stability: Stable (when implemented using cumulative counts and output array)

Hence, Counting Sort becomes extremely fast for datasets where the value range is small compared to n.

Applications

Counting Sort is used when:

- Input consists of integers within a limited range.
- Speed is more important than memory usage.
- Stability is required (for example, sorting records by age, while preserving the order of names).

Real-World Uses:

- Statistical Counting
- Frequency Tables
- Sorting Exam Scores or Voting Counts
- Pre-Processing Steps for Radix Sort

Radix Sort

Sorting large numbers efficiently becomes easier when we look at them digit by digit instead of treating the whole value at once. Radix Sort uses this idea by processing numbers one digit at a time and gradually arranging them into a fully sorted list. Hence, it avoids direct comparisons between elements, which makes it faster than many traditional methods when the input size is large, and the number of digits is limited.

Digit-Wise Processing

Radix Sort processes numbers **digit by digit**, from least significant digit to most significant digit (LSD-first). Instead of comparing values, it groups numbers based on their digits and sorts each digit position using a stable algorithm like Counting Sort.

Example (LSD-first):

Sort [170, 45, 75, 90, 802, 24, 2, 66] and follow these instructions:

- Sort by 1st digit → 170, 90, 802, 2, 24, 45, 75, 66.
- Sort by 10s digit.
- Sort by 100s digit.

The final output will become fully sorted.

Use of Stable Sorting: Radix Sort works correctly **only if the sorting performed at each digit level is stable.** For this reason, Counting Sort is commonly used as the internal step, as it does not disturb the order of equal digits.

Suitable Applications

Radix Sort is useful when:

- Values have a fixed number of digits (for example, phone numbers, IDs, IP addresses).
- The data range is large, but the digit length is small.
- Faster-than-O(n log n) sorting is required.

Typical real-world applications include:

- Sorting large numeric datasets
- Database indexing
- Processing integers, strings, or fixed-length keys

Radix Sort can achieve `O(d × (n + k))`, where d is the number of digits and k is the range per digit, which makes it faster than comparison-based algorithms in many practical cases.

Searching Techniques

Searching refers to the process of finding a required element inside a given collection of data. It is one of the most common operations performed in programming, from checking whether a value exists in a list, to locating a record inside a database. As the data size becomes larger, choosing an efficient searching method becomes crucial to ensure good performance.

Definition of Searching

Searching is the task of locating a specific value (called the *key*) within a dataset. If the key is present, the algorithm returns its position; otherwise, it indicates that the value does not exist. Therefore, the effectiveness of searching depends on how the data is organized, and how intelligently the search is performed.

Linear Search

Linear Search is the simplest method of searching for an element in a list. It begins at the first element, and checks items one by one until the required value is found, or the end of the list is reached. Since no assumptions are made about ordering, Linear Search works on both **sorted and unsorted** data.

It is easy to understand, easy to implement, and useful for small datasets. However, as the size of the data grows, searching becomes slower because every element might need to be examined.

Example:

Search for **7** in the array [4, 9, 1, 7, 5].

Steps:

```
Check 4 → Not a match.
Check 9 → Not a match.
Check 1 → Not a match.
Check 7 → Match found at index 3.
```

If the element does not exist, the algorithm reaches the end of the list and reports "not found."

C++ Implementation:

```
int linearSearch(int arr[], int n, int key) {
    for (int i = 0; i < n; i++) {
        if (arr[i] == key)
            return i;  // Key found
    }
    return -1; // Key not found
}
```

Python Implementation:

```
def linear_search(arr, key):
    for i in range(len(arr)):
        if arr[i] == key:
            return i  # Key found
    return -1  # Key not found
```

Time and Space Complexity

- **Best Case - `O(1)`**: First element matches
- **Worst Case - `O(n)`**: Last element matches or is not present
- **Average - `O(n)`**
- **Space Complexity - `O(1)`**: as no extra memory is used

Use Cases

Linear Search is preferred when:

- The dataset is small.
- Elements are unsorted.
- Simplicity is more important than speed.
- When dealing with large or repeatedly accessed data, faster methods like Binary Search are usually chosen.

Importance of Efficient Searching

In modern computing, searching is one of the most frequently performed operations. Applications constantly look up data, whether it is searching for a contact in a phone, fetching a customer record from a database, or locating a file on a computer. As the amount of stored information grows, the time taken to search becomes a critical factor.

For small inputs, even a simple method like Linear Search works well. However, when the number of elements increases to millions or billions, checking each item one by one becomes slow and inefficient. This delay affects responsiveness, processing cost, and overall user experience.

Efficient searching algorithms improve performance by reducing the number of comparisons required to find a result. Binary Search, for example, eliminates half of the search space at every step, allowing results to be found in a fraction of a second, even in very large datasets. Fast searching is especially important in:

- **Databases and servers** that handle large volumes of queries.
- **Search engines** that retrieve relevant results.
- **E-commerce platforms** that filter products quickly.
- **Mobile and web applications** that need real-time responses.

In short, efficient searching saves time, reduces computational load, and allows systems to scale smoothly as data grows. It is a key requirement for building high-performance software and intelligent data-driven applications.

Binary Search

Binary Search is one of the most efficient methods to search for an element in a **sorted** list. Unlike Linear Search, which checks every element one by one, Binary Search divides the search space into halves at each step, allowing the algorithm to quickly eliminate large portions of the data. This makes it extremely fast, especially for large datasets.

Working Principle

Binary Search follows these steps:

1. Identify the middle element of the list.
2. Compare it with the target key.

   `If equal → Search is successful.`

   `If the key is smaller → Search only the left half.`

   `If the key is larger → Search only the right half.`

3. Repeat the process by halving the search space until:

   The key is found.

   Or, the range becomes empty.

Since the search area gets reduced exponentially, Binary Search is significantly faster than Linear Search.

Iterative Implementation

Binary Search can be implemented using a loop, where the search space is adjusted step by step without using recursion. This approach requires less memory, and is often preferred in practical applications.

Python Implementation:

```
def binary_search_iterative(arr, key):
    low, high = 0, len(arr) - 1

    while low <= high:
        mid = (low + high) // 2

        if arr[mid] == key:
            return mid
        elif arr[mid] < key:
            low = mid + 1
```

```
        else:
            high = mid - 1

    return -1  # Key not found
```

C++ Implementation:

```
int binarySearchIterative(int arr[], int n, int key) {
    int low = 0, high = n - 1;

    while (low <= high) {
        int mid = low + (high - low) / 2; // safer mid calculation

        if (arr[mid] == key)
            return mid;
        else if (arr[mid] < key)
            low = mid + 1;
        else
            high = mid - 1;
    }

    return -1; // Key not found
}
```

Recursive Implementation

Binary Search can also be expressed in a recursive form, where the function repeatedly calls itself on smaller subarrays until the element is found, or the range becomes empty. This version closely follows the logical Divide-and-Conquer idea of the algorithm.

Python Implementation:

```
def binary_search_recursive(arr, low, high, key):
    if low > high:
        return -1

    mid = (low + high) // 2

    if arr[mid] == key:
        return mid
    elif arr[mid] < key:
        return binary_search_recursive(arr, mid + 1, high, key)
    else:
        return binary_search_recursive(arr, low, mid - 1, key)
```

C++ Implementation:

```
int binarySearchRecursive(int arr[], int low, int high, int key) {
    if (low > high)
        return -1;

    int mid = low + (high - low) / 2;

    if (arr[mid] == key)
        return mid;
    else if (arr[mid] < key)
        return binarySearchRecursive(arr, mid + 1, high, key);
    else
        return binarySearchRecursive(arr, low, mid - 1, key);
}
```

Time and Space Complexity

The efficiency of an algorithm is usually evaluated by how much time it takes to run and how much memory it needs. Binary Search is considered highly efficient because it reduces the search space by half during each step. Hence, this behavior gives it a logarithmic running time, which is significantly faster than checking every element one by one.

Time Complexity

- **Best Case - `O(1)`:** The middle element matches the key in the first comparison.
- **Average Case - `O(log n)`:** The array is repeatedly divided into halves until the key is found.
- **Worst Case - `O(log n)`:** The key may be in the last remaining portion and requires multiple halving steps.

This logarithmic complexity makes Binary Search scalable. Even for extremely large datasets, the number of steps needed is very small.

For example:

- Searching 1,000,000 elements needs only about **20 comparisons.**
- Searching 1,000,000,000 needs only about **30 comparisons.**

This shows how efficient Binary Search is compared to Linear Search, as the latter needs to check every element.

Space Complexity

- **Iterative Implementation - `O(1)`:** The algorithm only uses a few variables (low, high, mid), so extra memory is constant regardless of input size.
- **Recursive Implementation - `O(log n)`:** Each recursive call stores function information on the stack, which results in memory usage equal to the depth of recursion.

Common Logical Errors in Binary Search

Even though the idea is simple, Binary Search is often implemented incorrectly. Common mistakes include:

- **Incorrect loop conditions** (for example, using **`low < high`** instead of **`low <= high`**)
- **Not updating low/high properly**, which leads to infinite loops
- **Integer overflow** when calculating mid as **`(low + high) / 2`** in languages like C++

  Safer formula:

  ```
  mid = low + (high - low) / 2;
  ```

- **Applying to unsorted data**, which produces incorrect results
- **Ignoring duplicates** when looking for first or last occurrences

  Therefore, careful boundary handling ensures a correct and efficient implementation.

Variants of Binary Search

Binary Search is not limited to simply checking whether an element exists in a sorted array. With small modifications, it can solve a wide variety of practical problems. These variants are thus frequently used in competitive programming, interviews, and real-world applications where efficiency is a priority.

Locating First Occurrence

In a sorted array containing duplicate values, the standard Binary Search may return any valid position, not necessarily the first one.

To find the first occurrence:

- Continue searching on the **left side,** when a match is found.
- Stop when either the element is at index 0 or the previous element is different.

Hence, this ensures that the earliest position of the value is returned.

Locating Last Occurrence

Similarly, to find the last position of a key in a sorted array:

- When a match is found, continue searching on the **right side.**
- Stop when either the element is at the last index or the next element is different. This helps in counting duplicates and locating boundaries.

Counting Total Occurrences

Once the first and last positions are known, follow this method:

Total occurrences = (last index – first index + 1)

Hence, this method avoids scanning the entire array and works efficiently in `O(log n)` time.

Determining Insertion Position

Binary Search can also find where a new element should be placed to keep the array sorted. Even if the element does not exist in the array:

- The position where the search ends indicates where it should be inserted.
- It is useful in dynamic data structures, auto-sorted lists, and suggestion systems.
- This concept leads to `lower_bound` and `upper_bound` operations that are used in many libraries.

Lower Bound:

- It returns the first index where the element is **greater than or equal to** the key.
- If the key exists, it gives its first occurrence. If not, it gives the position to insert it.

Upper Bound:

- Returns the first index where the element is **strictly greater than** the key
- Useful for placing elements after all duplicates

Both operations use binary search internally and run in `O(log n)` time. They are widely available in C++ STL, Java, and Python modules.

Practical Applications of Binary Search

Beyond locating elements in a sorted array, Binary Search is widely used for solving problems that involve finding a boundary, threshold, or optimal value within an ordered or monotonic search space. In many practical scenarios, the data may not appear explicitly sorted, yet the problem can still be transformed into a form where Binary Search efficiently narrows the solution range. This approach is commonly applied in scheduling, resource allocation, numerical optimization, and competitive programming tasks that require minimizing or maximizing a feasible answer.

Searching in a Rotated Sorted Array

A rotated sorted array is an array that was originally sorted, but then shifted from some pivot position.

Example:

Original: [1, 2, 3, 4, 5, 6]

Rotated: [4, 5, 6, 1, 2, 3]

Even though the entire array is not sorted, **one of the halves is always sorted.**

Binary Search first detects which half is sorted, and then decides where to continue the search.

The key idea is to:

- Check the mid element.
- Identify if the left half is sorted or the right half is sorted.
- Search only in the sorted half where the key could exist. This allows efficient searching in `O(log n)` even in rotated arrays used in system logs, circular buffers, and time-based data.

Locating a Peak Element

A *peak* is an element that is not smaller than its immediate neighbors. Example peaks include:

- In `[1, 3, 2]`, peak = 3
- In `[5, 4, 6, 3]`, peaks = 5 and 6

Binary Search can locate a peak without scanning the entire array:

- If `mid` is smaller than `mid + 1`, the peak lies on the right.
- Otherwise, it lies on the left or at the middle.

This works because at least one peak always exists in any array. Due to its versatile functions, Binary Search is often used in audio signal processing, mountain array problems, and optimization tasks.

Binary Search on a Sorted Matrix

In row-wise and column-wise sorted matrices, Binary Search can be applied in two ways:

1. **Treat the Entire Matrix as a Single Sorted List.**
   a. Convert 2D indices to 1D.
   b. Apply standard binary search:
      i. `mid = (low + high) // 2`
      ii. `(row = mid / columns, col = mid % columns)`
2. **Staircase Search**
   a. Start at top-right or bottom-left.
   b. Move left or down depending on the comparison.
   c. Runs in `O(n + m)`

We can thus conclude that conducting binary search in this way is useful in databases, search engines, geographic heatmaps, and AI grid-pattern search.

Problem-Solving Patterns Based on Binary Search

Binary Search is not only a searching tool; it is also used to find answers in **optimization** and **decision-making problems.**

This pattern is called **Binary Search on answers** or **Binary Search on the solution space**.

It works when:

- The answer lies in a numeric range.
- A function can check if a guess is valid.

Examples:

- Minimum time required to complete tasks
- Smallest capacity needed to store items
- Maximum possible height, distance, or speed
- Scheduling and allocation problems

Instead of searching in an array, Binary Search searches among all possible answers and narrows them step by step.

Therefore, when Binary Search is combined with logical conditions, it becomes a powerful tool that can solve many advanced problems far beyond simple array lookups. Hence, understanding these patterns helps in competitive programming, technical interviews, and real-world system optimization.

Algorithm Selection Guidelines

Sorting and searching do not follow a single "best" method. The right algorithm depends on the nature of the input, system constraints, and expected performance. Thus, choosing wisely can reduce processing time, save memory, and improve the efficiency of the overall program.

Based on Input Size:

- For **small datasets**, simpler algorithms like Insertion Sort or Linear Search may be sufficient. They require little overhead and can even outperform complex algorithms on small inputs due to low constant operations.
- For **large datasets**, efficient algorithms such as Merge Sort, Quick Sort, Heap Sort, or Binary Search should be preferred. Their logarithmic or n log n complexity scales much better than `O(n²)` or `O(n)`.

Example: Sorting 10 numbers with Bubble Sort is fine, but sorting 1 million numbers requires Merge Sort, Quick Sort, or Heap Sort.

Based on Memory Constraints:

- If available memory is limited, **in-place algorithms** like Quick Sort (in practice), Heap Sort, Insertion Sort, and Selection Sort are preferred.
- When extra memory is available and consistent performance is needed, Merge Sort is a good choice because it offers predictable `O(n log n)` time.

Example: Embedded systems or mobile devices often avoid memory-heavy algorithms.

Based on Stability Requirements:

- If equal elements must preserve their original order, choose a **stable sorting algorithm like**:
    - Merge Sort
    - Insertion Sort
    - Counting Sort
- If stability does not matter, algorithms like Heap Sort and Quick Sort are acceptable.

Example: Sorting student records first by marks, then by name, requires stability to maintain order among equal-mark students.

Based on Data Distribution:

- If the data is **nearly sorted**, Insertion Sort performs extremely well with O(n) time.
- If the data contains **integer keys within a small range**, Counting Sort or Radix Sort may be faster than comparison-based algorithms.
- If the dataset is **random and large**, Quick Sort often gives the fastest practical performance.
- If the dataset is stored on external memory (like disks), Merge Sort is preferred because it handles block-based processing efficiently.

Making an informed choice ensures reliable performance, and avoids unnecessary computation. By analyzing input conditions before choosing an algorithm, programs become faster, more scalable, and more resource-aware.

In **banking systems**, algorithm selection plays a critical role in handling large volumes of transactional data. For example, during end-of-day settlement, millions of transaction records must be sorted and searched efficiently. If transactions are streamed in near-sorted order, **Insertion Sort** or indexed **Binary Search** on sorted data can be highly effective. For large historical datasets used in fraud analysis or audit reporting, **Merge Sort** is preferred due to its predictable performance and stability, as it ensures accurate ordering of records with identical values.

In **manufacturing systems**, production scheduling and inventory management often involve sorting tasks based on priority, deadlines, or resource availability. When data is continuously updated and memory is constrained, **Heap Sort** or **in-place Quick Sort** is commonly used. For scenarios involving product IDs within a limited range, such as batch processing in assembly lines, **Counting Sort** provides faster processing. Thus, selecting the appropriate algorithm based on data size, memory limits, and data distribution helps manufacturing systems remain scalable, reliable, and cost-efficient.

Frequent Mistakes in Sorting and Searching

Even though sorting and searching algorithms are conceptually simple, many errors occur during implementation. These mistakes can lead to incorrect results, unexpected behavior, or infinite loops. Hence, understanding these common pitfalls helps avoid bugs and write more reliable codes.

Logical Issues in Sorting

Some mistakes often seen in sorting implementations include:

Incorrect swapping of elements, which results in lost values or disrupted order

Not handling equal elements properly, which may break stability.

Improper use of temporary arrays in algorithms like Merge Sort

Incorrect loop boundaries, such as stopping too early or repeating unnecessary passes

These errors may produce partially sorted output or make the algorithm run slower than expected.

Boundary Errors in Searching

Searching logic becomes tricky when handling indices, especially when we do the following:

- Forgetting to update low and high correctly may lead to infinite loops.
- Using low < high instead of low <= high may skip comparison of the last element.
- Returning the wrong index when multiple occurrences exist (first or last occurrence tasks).

- Applying Binary Search on **unsorted data** produces meaningless output.

Therefore, careful attention to boundary checks is necessary to get accurate results.

Mid-Calculation and Overflow Errors

In languages like C and C++, calculating the middle index using:

mid = (low + high) / 2;

It can cause **integer overflow** when `low` and `high` hold large values.

A safer approach is:

mid = low + (high - low) / 2;

This avoids overflow and makes the implementation more robust. Hence, programmers can avoid bugs and handle edge cases confidently by being aware of these common mistakes. Also, correct logic, proper boundary handling, and safe mid calculations ensure that sorting and searching algorithms perform as expected in all situations.

Conclusion

Sorting and searching are fundamental operations that shape how data is organized, accessed, and processed in modern computing. This chapter introduced various techniques ranging from basic comparison-based methods such as Bubble Sort, Selection Sort, and Insertion Sort, to highly efficient algorithms like Merge Sort, Quick Sort, Heap Sort, and Binary Search. Along the way, learners explored important concepts such as algorithm stability, in-place processing, time and space trade-offs, and practical scenarios where each method performs best. We also saw how Binary Search extends beyond simple lookups to solve real-world problems, including rotated array search, peak finding, and matrix search. With this understanding, students are now equipped to choose the right technique based on input size, memory constraints, stability needs, and data characteristics, which will enable them to build faster and more reliable programs. In **the next chapter, learners strengthen their problem-solving skills by exploring two powerful algorithmic paradigms.** The chapter focuses on greedy techniques through applications such as Activity Selection, Fractional Knapsack, Huffman Coding, and Job Scheduling, while also revisiting Divide-and-Conquer ideas for problems like Binary Search, Maximum Subarray, and fast multiplication. Therefore, by the end of this chapter, students will be able to develop a clear understanding of when these strategies succeed, when they fail, and how to analyze their efficiency using recurrence relations.

Points to Remember

- Sorting arranges data into a specific order (ascending or descending).
- Searching locates a target value inside a dataset.
- Comparison-based sorting includes Bubble Sort, Selection Sort, Insertion Sort, Merge Sort, Quick Sort, and Heap Sort.
- Non-comparison sorting includes Counting Sort and Radix Sort.
- Bubble Sort and Insertion Sort are stable; Selection Sort and Heap Sort are not.
- Merge Sort always gives O(n log n) time but needs extra memory.
- Quick Sort is fast in practice but has a worst case of $O(n^2)$ with poor pivot choices.
- Heap Sort is in-place and always O(n log n), but not stable.
- Counting Sort and Radix Sort are very fast when the data range/digits are small.
- Linear Search works on any dataset but is slow for large inputs.

- Binary Search works only on sorted data and takes O(log n) time.
- Variants of Binary Search can find the first/last occurrence, insertion position, and bounds.
- Binary Search forms the base of rotated array search, peak element finding, and matrix search.
- Algorithm choice depends on input size, memory, stability, and data distribution.
- Common mistakes include wrong boundaries, incorrect mid calculation, and ignoring stability.

Multiple Choice Questions

1. Which sorting algorithm works best on nearly sorted data?
    a. Selection Sort
    b. Insertion Sort
    c. Heap Sort
    d. Quick Sort
2. Merge Sort follows which technique?
    a. Greedy
    b. Divide and Conquer
    c. Dynamic Programming
    d. Backtracking
3. Worst-case time complexity of Quick Sort is:
    a. `O(n)`
    b. `O(n log n)`
    c. `O(n²)`
    d. `O(log n)`
4. Which sorting algorithm is NOT stable?
    a. Bubble Sort
    b. Insertion Sort
    c. Heap Sort
    d. Counting Sort
5. Counting Sort works efficiently when:
    a. Data is sorted.
    b. Range of values is small.
    c. Values are strings.
    d. Data is linked.
6. Binary Search requires:
    a. Random Access
    b. Sorted Data
    c. Hashing
    d. Tree Traversal

7. What is the time complexity of Binary Search?
   a. `O(n)`
   b. `O(n²)`
   c. `O(log n)`
   d. `O(1)`
8. Which sorting uses a heap data structure?
   a. Quick Sort
   b. Merge Sort
   c. Heap Sort
   d. Insertion Sort
9. Lower Bound operation returns:
   a. The last occurrence
   b. The first element greater than key
   c. The first occurrence of element ≥ key
   d. The index of the smallest element
10. Which algorithm always takes O(n log n) time?
    a. Bubble Sort
    b. Merge Sort
    c. Quick Sort (Average Case)
    d. Insertion Sort
11. Rotated array searching uses:
    a. Linear Search only
    b. Modified Binary Search
    c. BFS
    d. Hashing
12. Space complexity of iterative Binary Search is:
    a. `O(1)`
    b. `O(log n)`
    c. `O(n)`
    d. `O(n log n)`
13. Which algorithm is in-place and always O(n log n)?
    a. Merge Sort
    b. Heap Sort
    c. Counting Sort
    d. Radix Sort
14. Mid calculation error occurs mainly in:
    a. Python
    b. Java

c. C / C++

d. SQL

15. Stability of sorting ensures that:

    a. Extra memory is used.

    b. Order of equal elements is preserved.

    c. Sorting becomes faster.

    d. Recursion is used.

Answers

1. b
2. b
3. c
4. c
5. b
6. b
7. c
8. c
9. c
10. b
11. b
12. a
13. b
14. c
15. b

Questions

1. Explain the differences between comparison-based and non-comparison-based sorting algorithms with examples.
2. Describe the working principle of Merge Sort. Explain how the Divide-and-Conquer strategy is used.
3. Show how Quick Sort partitions data using a pivot. Include a step-by-step trace.
4. What is stability in sorting? Which algorithms are stable, and why is stability useful?
5. Compare Bubble Sort, Selection Sort, and Insertion Sort based on time complexities and use cases.
6. Explain Counting Sort with an example. When is it preferable over comparison sorting?
7. Give the iterative and recursive implementations of Binary Search and compare them.
8. How can Binary Search be used to find the first and last occurrences of an element?
9. Explain how to search for an element in a rotated sorted array using Binary Search logic.
10. Discuss the common mistakes in Binary Search implementation, including mid overflow and boundary errors.

11. Write short notes on the lower bound and upper bound.
12. Compare Merge Sort, Quick Sort, and Heap Sort in terms of time, space, and stability.

Key Terms

- **Sorting:** Arranging elements in ascending or descending order
- **Searching:** Finding a target value within a dataset
- **Stable Sorting:** Maintains the relative order of equal elements
- **In-Place Sorting:** Sorting done using constant extra memory
- **Divide and Conquer:** Breaking a problem into smaller subproblems and combining their solutions
- **Pivot:** Element used to partition data in Quick Sort
- **Heap:** A complete binary tree used in Heap Sort
- **Heapify:** Process of restoring the heap property after modification
- **Counting Array:** Auxiliary array used in Counting Sort to store frequencies
- **Binary Search:** An Efficient search that halves the search range at each step
- **Lower Bound:** First index where value is ≥ key
- **Upper Bound:** First index where value is > key
- **Rotated Array:** A sorted array shifted from a pivot point
- **Peak Element:** Element not smaller than its neighbors
- **Time Complexity:** Measure of how fast an algorithm runs as the input grows

CHAPTER 11

Greedy and Divide-and-Conquer Strategies

Introduction

Algorithm design often goes beyond writing the correct code; it is about choosing the most suitable strategy to solve a problem efficiently. Different problems demand different approaches, and two of the most influential strategies in Computer Science are the Greedy method and the Divide-and-Conquer approach. Although they aim to solve problems efficiently, their motivating logics are very different. The Greedy strategy works by making the best possible decision at each step with the hope that these local decisions will eventually lead to a globally optimal solution. It is fast, intuitive, and often produces elegant solutions. Many real-life tasks naturally follow this pattern, such as selecting the maximum number of non-overlapping activities, compressing data using Huffman coding, or scheduling jobs to maximize profit. However, the Greedy method does not work for every problem. Sometimes a series of locally optimal decisions leads to a poor final outcome. Understanding when the greedy approach succeeds and when it fails is one of the key goals of this chapter. The Divide-and-Conquer strategy uses a very different thought process. Instead of solving the full problem at once, it breaks the problem into smaller subproblems, solves each part independently, and then combines the results to form the final answer. Some of the most famous algorithms in Computer Science such as Merge Sort, Quick Sort, and Binary Search are built using this strategy. Divide-and-Conquer even helps speed up mathematical computations like multiplication and provides solutions to problems like the maximum subarray. It also gives us a structured way to analyze algorithm efficiency using recurrence relations and the Master Theorem. This chapter explores both strategies in depth, while showing how they are applied, where they fit, and what makes them powerful. By studying these ideas, learners can develop stronger problem-solving intuition and prepare for more advanced concepts such as dynamic programming, optimization, and competitive programming challenges.

Structure

In this chapter, we will cover the following topics:

- Greedy Strategy
- Standard Greedy Applications
- Limitations of Greedy Algorithms
- Comparison with Dynamic Programming and Backtracking

- Divide and Conquer Strategy
- Maximum Subarray Problem
- Time Complexity Analysis Using Recurrences
- Practice and Application Exercises
- Common Implementation Challenges

Greedy Strategy

The greedy strategy is one of the most intuitive ways to solve optimization problems. Instead of analyzing every possible option, a greedy algorithm makes the best choice at each step and moves forward without revisiting previous decisions. This "take the best now" mindset often leads to fast and elegant solutions, especially in tasks involving scheduling, resource allocation, and compression. However, it works only when local choices naturally lead to the best global outcome, which is why you should understand its behavior before applying it.

Fundamentals of the Greedy Approach

The greedy approach is a problem-solving strategy where decisions are made step by step, while choosing the best possible option at that moment without reconsidering earlier choices. Instead of exploring every possible path or evaluating future consequences, the greedy method focuses on the most promising local decision and hopes that this sequence of local optimizations leads to the best overall solution. This strategy works beautifully in many real-world-inspired problems. For example, if you want to schedule as many non-overlapping events as possible in a day, a simple greedy idea will be to always pick the activity that finishes earliest, which turns out to be optimal. Similarly, if you want to fill a bag with items to maximize profit in the fractional knapsack problem, choosing items with the highest value-to-weight ratio first will grant the best result. The main advantage of the greedy strategy is its simplicity and speed. Since it avoids exhaustive searching or complex dynamic programming, greedy algorithms usually run efficiently and are easy to implement. However, not all problems support greedy solutions. Sometimes the best short-term choice can lead to a poor overall result, and a more complex strategy may be required. For this reason, it is important to understand why the greedy strategy works in certain cases, rather than assuming it works everywhere.

Greedy Choice Property

The greedy choice property is the key condition that allows the greedy approach to produce an optimal solution. It states that if a problem can be solved optimally by making a local best choice at each step without needing to look back or revise earlier decisions, then a greedy algorithm is suitable.

In simple terms, if choosing the best option at the current moment never prevents achieving the best final answer, the problem has the greedy choice property.

This property is what allows problems like activity selection or fractional knapsack to be solved greedily. Each choice directly contributes to the final optimal outcome, and no later decision forces us to undo or modify a previous one. When the greedy choice property fails, a greedy solution might only provide a good answer, but not the best one. Therefore, before applying a greedy algorithm, it is essential to check whether selecting a local optimum can safely lead to a global optimum.

Optimal Substructure in Greedy Algorithms

Optimal substructure means that the solution to a problem can be built from optimal solutions to smaller subproblems. This feature is common in many algorithmic strategies, including Divide-and-Conquer and Dynamic Programming, but it is also required for greedy solutions.

For greedy algorithms, an optimal substructure ensures that once a greedy decision is made, the remaining part of the problem still has an optimal solution. In other words, after choosing the best immediate option, the smaller remaining problem behaves just like the original one, and solving it optimally contributes to the overall optimal result.

For example, in the activity selection problem, once we choose the activity that ends first, the remaining time interval forms a smaller version of the same problem; select the next compatible activity that finishes earliest. The structure repeats, making the greedy approach correct.

When a problem lacks optimal substructure, a greedy step may ruin the chances of getting the best answer. In such cases, more advanced techniques like dynamic programming or backtracking are required.

Standard Greedy Applications

Many optimization problems can be solved efficiently using a greedy approach when the problem guarantees that a locally optimal choice leads to a globally optimal result. Therefore, instead of exploring every possibility, a greedy algorithm gradually builds a solution step by step, making the best choice available at each moment. Several classic computer science problems demonstrate the power of this strategy in scheduling, compression, and resource allocation.

Activity Selection Technique

The activity selection technique focuses on choosing the maximum number of non-overlapping activities from a list where each activity has a start time and a finish time. The greedy idea behind this problem is beautifully simple: always pick the activity that finishes the earliest. This is because finishing sooner leaves the maximum remaining time for upcoming activities.

After selecting the earliest finishing activity, the next step is to skip every activity that overlaps with it and then choose the next earliest finishing one from the remaining list. By repeating this process, the set of chosen activities grows, while still maintaining the condition that no two activities overlap. This method guarantees the optimal number of activities, even though the algorithm makes decisions locally at every step.

The activity selection technique appears in real-world scenarios such as scheduling meetings in a conference room, allocating bandwidth slots, or assigning CPU time to tasks that must not overlap.

Fractional Knapsack Approach

The Fractional Knapsack problem requires filling a bag of limited capacity with items of different weights and values in such a way that the total value is maximized. The greedy strategy used here selects items based on the highest value-to-weight ratio first. If the bag cannot hold the entire item, a fractional part of it is taken.

The reason this greedy choice works is that the value increases at the fastest rate per unit of weight when choosing the item with the best ratio. By repeatedly selecting items in this order, the bag reaches its maximum possible total value. This behavior is what makes the Fractional Knapsack problem perfectly suited for greedy logic, unlike the 0/1 Knapsack problem, where items cannot be broken and greedy choices can fail.

Examples of the Fractional Knapsack logic appear in resource allocation situations such as stock investments, cargo loading, or bandwidth sharing where partial distribution is allowed.

Huffman Coding

Huffman coding is a greedy-based compression technique used to reduce the size of data by assigning shorter codes to frequent characters and longer codes to less frequent ones. It constructs an optimal prefix-free code by repeatedly combining the two least frequent symbols into a new node and then continuing the process until only one node remains. The resulting binary tree encodes letters in such a way that no code becomes a prefix of another, while ensuring lossless compression.

Although the complete construction involves priority queues and binary trees, the greedy nature lies in always choosing the smallest two frequency nodes at each step. This repeated local choice leads to globally optimal compression. Huffman coding remains widely used in file compression formats, multimedia encoding, and network transmission.

Job Scheduling with Deadlines

In job scheduling with deadlines, each job has a profit and a deadline, and only one job can be performed at a time. The objective is to schedule jobs so that total profit is maximized. The greedy solution sorts the jobs in decreasing order of profit and then schedules each one in the closest available time slot before its deadline. By placing highly profitable jobs first and filling earlier deadlines with them, the final set of scheduled jobs yields the maximum possible profit.

This problem resembles real-world decision-making situations such as advertisement slot booking, processor scheduling, and event planning where time is limited and tasks compete for space.

Limitations of Greedy Algorithms

Although greedy algorithms are elegant and efficient, they do not always guarantee the best solution. Their strategy is based on making the best decision at each individual step without considering how that choice affects the future. When a problem does not support this behavior, the greedy approach can lead to a suboptimal or completely incorrect result. Therefore, understanding the limitations of greedy algorithms is just as important as knowing where they succeed.

Situations Where Greedy Algorithm Fails

Greedy algorithms fail whenever a locally optimal choice does not lead to a globally optimal result. In such situations, looking only at what seems best right now blocks access to a better solution later. Many problems require exploring multiple possibilities, using dynamic programming, or performing backtracking to guarantee the best answer.

For example, in the **0/1 Knapsack problem**, choosing the item with the highest value-to-weight ratio is not always optimal because items must be taken whole. A greedy choice strategy might consume capacity quickly with high-ratio items, but it will prevent a combination of smaller items that would provide a greater total value. Here, the greedy path looks promising at the start but fails to reach the true optimum.

A classic counterexample is the coin change problem. If a currency system uses denominations like 1, 5, 10, 25, the greedy strategy works well; choosing the largest possible coin at each step leads to the fewest coins. However, if the currency set is 1, 3, and 4, the strategy will no longer hold.

To make **6**, the greedy strategy would choose 4, then 1, then 1 → **3 coins**. However, the optimal solution is 3 + 3 → **2 coins**.

The greedy choice of 4 seemed best locally, but it blocked access to the truly optimal answer.

Another example is scheduling jobs for minimum waiting time in a queue. Choosing the job with the longest time first might seem useful in some contexts, but it leads to high total waiting time.

The correct strategy is the opposite—shortest job first—which greedy strategies might not consider without careful formulation.

Hence, these examples show that greedy behavior is not universally reliable and must be justified rather than assumed.

Identifying Unsuitable Cases

A problem is unsuitable for a greedy approach when:

- Choosing the best local option can block a better global outcome.
- Future decisions depend heavily on earlier ones.
- A partial solution cannot be extended greedily without backtracking.
- The problem requires exploring combinations, not single-step choices.
- Optimal substructure exists, but the greedy choice property does not.

In such cases, dynamic programming or exhaustive search often provides the correct direction because they evaluate broader possibilities, instead of committing too early. Thus, before applying a greedy algorithm, it is important to reason about the structure of the problem, and verify that every local decision safely leads to the optimal final result.

Comparison with Dynamic Programming and Backtracking

While greedy algorithms are appealing because of their speed and simplicity, they are not always the right tool for every problem. Before applying a greedy strategy, it is important to understand how it compares with other powerful approaches like Dynamic Programming and Backtracking, which sometimes provide better accuracy or flexibility.

Fundamental Differences

Greedy algorithms build a solution one step at a time by choosing the option that looks best at the current moment. They never revise earlier choices, which makes the process fast and straightforward. This approach succeeds only when local decisions naturally lead to a globally optimal result.

Dynamic programming uses a more careful strategy. Instead of committing to a decision immediately, it explores different possibilities by breaking the problem into smaller overlapping subproblems and storing their results. This prevents repeated work and guarantees optimal outcomes even when greedy choices fail.

Backtracking goes further by exploring all possible combinations if needed. It tries a path, and if that path becomes invalid or inefficient, it reverses and tries a different branch. This makes backtracking a complete but often slower search strategy, especially for problems with many possible configurations.

Efficiency and Memory Considerations

Greedy algorithms are usually the most efficient in terms of both time and memory. They only follow one decision path, require no extra data structures, and work quickly even for large inputs. Their major limitation is correctness; if the greedy criteria do not guarantee optimality, the solution may be wrong.

Dynamic programming trades speed and memory for accuracy. By storing results of subproblems, it avoids recomputation and ensures the best solution is found. However, this storage increases memory usage, and its time complexity is often higher than that of greedy methods.

Backtracking focuses on correctness rather than efficiency. Since it may explore many possible solutions, it can take significant time and memory in the worst case. However, it becomes the preferred method when constraints must be respected or when no simpler shortcut exists.

Typical Scenarios Where Each Strategy is Preferred

Greedy algorithms are preferred when the problem supports the greedy choice property. This means that every optimal decision made locally leads to the global optimum. Examples include activity selection, fractional knapsack, job scheduling with deadlines, and building Huffman codes.

Dynamic programming is ideal when decisions depend on previously computed values or when multiple solutions must be compared. Problems like 0/1 knapsack, longest common subsequence, coin change for minimum coins, and shortest path in weighted graphs fall into this category.

Backtracking is used when the solution must satisfy strict constraints or when every possibility must be explored. Classic examples include solving N-Queens, Sudoku, generating permutations, or finding all valid subsets. In these cases, greediness would miss solutions, and dynamic programming may not apply.

Divide and Conquer Strategy

Divide-and-Conquer is a powerful problem-solving paradigm that works by breaking a complex problem into smaller subproblems, solving each of them independently, and then combining their results to form a complete solution. Instead of handling a large dataset or task all at once, the algorithm repeatedly divides it into pieces until the parts become simple enough to solve directly. Because of this structured breakdown, Divide-and-Conquer often leads to clean recursive algorithms and significant improvements in performance.

This strategy forms the backbone of many efficient algorithms used in searching, sorting, numerical computation, and optimization. When used correctly, it not only simplifies logic, but also reduces time complexity dramatically.

Core Concept of Divide and Conquer

The core idea behind Divide-and-Conquer can be understood through three clear steps:

- **Divide**: The original problem is split into two or more smaller, simpler subproblems.
- **Conquer**: Each subproblem is solved independently, often using recursion.
- **Combine**: The solutions of the subproblems are merged to form the final answer.

This structure works especially well when the subproblems are similar in nature to the original problem. With each division, the input becomes smaller and easier to handle, and once the individual pieces are solved, the combination produces the overall result. Many famous algorithms such as sorting methods, fast multiplication, and search techniques use this approach because of its clarity and efficiency.

Recurrence Relations

As Divide-and-Conquer algorithms repeatedly break down problems into smaller parts, their running time is often expressed using recurrence relations. A recurrence relation describes how the total running time depends on the running time of its subproblems.

For example, if an input of size **n** is divided into two subproblems of size **n/2**, and the merging step takes **O(n)** time, the recurrence can be written as:

```
T(n) = 2T(n/2) + O(n)
```

Solving recurrence relations helps determine how fast a Divide-and-Conquer algorithm grows as input size increases. Later in this chapter, methods such as the substitution approach, recursion tree analysis, and the master theorem will be used to interpret these recurrences and fully understand the time complexities of different algorithms.

Merge Sort

Merge Sort is a classical example of the Divide-and-Conquer strategy. It divides an array into two halves, recursively sorts each half, and merges them into a single sorted array. No matter how the elements are arranged, Merge Sort always maintains a time complexity of `O(n log n)` and guarantees stability—making it ideal for large datasets and external sorting. *The complete explanation, step-by-step illustration, pseudocode, and implementation are provided in Chapter 10, Sorting and Searching.*

Quick Sort

Quick Sort also follows Divide-and-Conquer, but instead of merging sorted halves, it partitions the array around a pivot element. The smaller elements move to one side of the pivot, while the larger ones move to the other side. The two partitions are then sorted recursively. On average, Quick Sort performs extremely well, and since it sorts in-place, it uses minimal additional memory. *For the detailed working principle, partitioning logic, pivot strategies, example traces, and full code, refer to Chapter 10, Sorting and Searching.*

Applications of Divide-and-Conquer

Divide-and-Conquer extends far beyond sorting. Several important algorithms rely on it to achieve high efficiency.

- **Binary Search:** Binary Search divides a sorted array into halves repeatedly to determine whether a target element exists. Each step removes half of the remaining search space, which is why it runs in **O(log n)** time. When seen through a Divide-and-Conquer lens, every recursive call becomes a smaller instance of the same search problem. *The full explanation, iterative and recursive versions, and real-world problem variations are covered in Chapter 10, Sorting and Searching.*
- **Karatsuba Multiplication:** Traditional multiplication of large numbers takes a long time because it multiplies every digit with every other digit. Karatsuba's algorithm reduces this workload by dividing numbers into parts and combining results smartly. It performs fewer multiplications, which makes it faster than the standard approach. Even though the complete arithmetic can be complex, the high-level idea shows how dividing numbers cleverly leads to efficiency.
- **Maximum Subarray Problem:** The task is to find a contiguous subarray with the highest possible sum. A Divide-and-Conquer solution splits the array into two halves, finds the best subarray on the left, the best on the right, and the best subarray that crosses the middle. The final answer is the maximum among these three. Although Kadane's algorithm solves the same problem in linear time, the Divide-and-Conquer method provides a strong theoretical understanding of how complex problems can be broken into manageable pieces.

Maximum Subarray Problem

The Maximum Subarray problem involves finding a contiguous portion of an array that has the highest possible sum. This problem appears in areas like stock price analysis, signal processing, and performance measurements, where detecting the most profitable or strongest continuous segment is important. There are multiple ways to solve it and Divide-and-Conquer provides one of the most insightful solutions to this problem.

The Divide-and-Conquer Technique

The Divide-and-Conquer approach splits the array into two halves and considers three possibilities:

- The maximum subarray lies entirely in the **left half.**
- The maximum subarray lies entirely in the **right half.**
- The maximum subarray **crosses the midpoint**, containing elements from both halves.

For the first two parts, the problem is simply solved recursively on smaller portions of the array. For the third case, the algorithm expands outward from the middle, while collecting the best possible sum on the left side and the best possible sum on the right side. Once these three values are known, the largest of them becomes the answer for that level of recursion.

Eventually, the partial solutions are combined until the final maximum subarray sum is determined for the whole array. Although this approach is more involved than simpler methods, it clearly demonstrates how breaking a large problem into smaller ones and merging their results can produce a correct global solution. The Divide-and-Conquer version typically runs in **`O(n log n)`** time.

Contrast with Kadane's Linear Solution

Kadane's Algorithm provides a faster, simpler solution by scanning the array in a single pass and keeping track of the current running sum and the best sum found so far. It never divides the array or inspects multiple combinations. Instead, it uses a clever update rule to decide whether to extend the current subarray or start fresh from the current element. This makes Kadane's algorithm an **`O(n)`** time linear solution, which is more efficient than the Divide-and-Conquer approach.

However, the Divide-and-Conquer method remains valuable from a theoretical perspective. It explains the structure of the problem more deeply and shows how optimal subarrays can be constructed from smaller segments. Understanding both methods helps learners appreciate not only performance differences, but also the role of problem decomposition in algorithm design.

Time Complexity Analysis Using Recurrences

Many Divide-and-Conquer algorithms split a problem into smaller pieces and then combine the results. Due to this, their running time cannot be described with a simple expression. Instead, the total time depends on the time required to solve the smaller subproblems plus the time spent combining them. This behavior is captured using **recurrence relations.** A recurrence expresses time complexity in terms of the time needed for smaller inputs, which allows us to reason mathematically about how fast the algorithm grows as the input size increases.

Substitution Idea

The substitution method is an intuitive way to solve a recurrence by repeatedly expanding it. The idea is to write the recurrence several times and observe how the pattern evolves. Each substitution reveals how the problem keeps shrinking until it reaches a basic constant-time case.

For example, consider:

```
T(n) = 2T(n/2) + n
```

After substituting once:

```
T(n) = 2[2T(n/4) + n/2] + n
```

Expanding again:

```
T(n) = 4T(n/4) + 2n
```

Repeating this pattern shows that the total work eventually becomes `n log n`, which matches the known running time of algorithms like Merge Sort. Even though the method may take several steps, substitution builds a clear understanding of how recursive calls contribute to the final complexity.

Recursion Tree Interpretation

The recursion tree method visualizes the cost of each recursive level. Every level of the tree represents work done during that step of the recursion, and the total running time is the sum of all levels.

For the same recurrence:

```
T(n) = 2T(n/2) + n
```

- Level 0 performs **n** work.
- Level 1 performs **n/2 + n/2 = n.**
- Level 2 performs **n/4 + n/4 + n/4 + n/4 = n.**

This continues until the problem reduces to a constant size. If every level contributes **n** work and the height of the tree is **log n**, the total time becomes **n × log n**. Recursion trees help learners see the cost distribution clearly instead of handling algebra alone.

Master Theorem

The master theorem is a powerful tool that directly gives the time complexity of many Divide-and-Conquer algorithms without long expansion. It applies to recurrences of the form:

```
T(n) = aT(n/b) + f(n)
```

Where:

a = Number of subproblems

n/b = Size of each subproblem

f(n) = Work required to divide and combine

The master theorem compares **f(n)** with **n^(log_b a)** and determines whether the final complexity is dominated by dividing, conquering, or combining:

- If combining work is smaller, the recursive work dominates.
- If combining work is larger, the merging dominates.
- If they are roughly equal, both contribute together.

For example, Merge Sort fits perfectly into this model:

```
T(n) = 2T(n/2) + n
```

Here:

```
a = 2
b = 2
f(n) = n
n^(log_b a) = n^(log_2 2) = n¹ = n
```

Since **f(n)** matches `n^(log_b a)`, the master theorem gives:

```
T(n) = Θ(n log n)
```

This allows us to conclude the running time instantly, without substitution or recursion tree expansion. The Master Theorem is widely used for analyzing Divide-and-Conquer approaches such as Binary Search, Merge Sort, Quick Sort (average case), and many other mathematical algorithms.

This analysis framework gives a deeper appreciation of why Divide-and-Conquer algorithms are efficient and how their running time scales with input size. By understanding substitution, recursion trees, and the master theorem, learners can gain the tools needed to evaluate complex recursive algorithms with confidence.

Practice and Application Exercises

To reinforce the concepts learned in this chapter, the following exercises encourage hands-on application of both Greedy and Divide-and-Conquer strategies. Each problem highlights where the respective technique offers a clear advantage and helps in building problem-solving intuition.

Greedy-Based Problem Exercises

- **Activity Selection Scheduling:** Given a list of activities with start and finish times, select the maximum number of non-overlapping activities that can be performed in a single room.
- **Fractional Knapsack Optimization:** A thief is allowed to take fractional quantities of items. Each item has a value and a weight. Determine the maximum profit that can be obtained for a given knapsack capacity.
- **Job Scheduling with Deadlines and Profit:** Each job requires one time slot, has a deadline, and yields profit if completed. Schedule jobs so that profit is maximized.
- **Minimum Number of Platforms (Train Scheduling):** Given the arrival and departure times of trains at a station, find the minimum number of platforms required so that no train waits.
- **Huffman Coding Table Construction:** Given character frequencies, build a Huffman tree and generate binary codes for each character.
- **Minimum Cost to Connect Ropes:** You are given ropes with different lengths. Connect all ropes into a single rope with minimum cost, where the cost of joining two ropes equals their combined length.
- **Optimal Page Replacement (Greedy Approximation):** Given a sequence of memory requests and a cache size, use a greedy approach to minimize the number of page faults.

Divide-and-Conquer Practice Problems

- **Binary Search Implementation and Testing:** Implement Binary Search recursively and iteratively. Test it on sorted data of different sizes and compare running time.
- **Counting Inversions in an Array:** Using Divide-and-Conquer logic similar to Merge Sort, count how many pairs `(i, j)` exist such that `i < j` and `arr[i] > arr[j]`.
- **Maximum Subarray Sum:** Implement the Divide-and-Conquer method to find the maximum subarray sum and compare results with Kadane's algorithm.
- **Karatsuba Multiplication (Conceptual Implementation):** Simulate multiplication of large integers using the Karatsuba strategy to observe reduction in operations.
- **Closest Pair of Points (2-D Plane):** Use Divide-and-Conquer to find the pair of points with the minimum Euclidean distance in a set of coordinates.
- **Merge Sort Performance Comparison:** Sort datasets of increasing sizes using Merge Sort and compare performance with an $O(n^2)$ algorithm like Insertion Sort.
- **Peak Element in an Array:** Use Divide-and-Conquer logic to find any peak element in an array (an element not smaller than its neighbors).

These exercises are designed to build confidence in choosing the correct strategy, applying it correctly, and understanding the impact of algorithmic efficiency in real scenarios. Working through them encourages deeper problem-solving ability and prepares learners for advanced competitive programming and interview-level challenges.

Common Implementation Challenges

Even though Greedy and Divide-and-Conquer algorithms are powerful, beginners often make mistakes while translating the logic into actual code. These challenges usually arise not from the idea itself, but from small details in logic, base cases, and complexity analysis. Understanding these common pitfalls helps avoid bugs and ensures correct and efficient implementations.

Incorrect Greedy Decisions

One of the most frequent problems with greedy solutions occurs when the "best local decision" is chosen without verifying that it leads toward the global optimum. If the Greedy Choice property does not hold for the problem, the algorithm might work for a few test cases but produce wrong results in others.

For example, selecting items solely based on profit instead of value-to-weight ratio in the fractional knapsack problem leads to a lower overall value. Similarly, sorting activities by start time rather than finish time breaks the activity selection solution. These issues often appear when the greedy rule is assumed rather than proven.

To avoid such mistakes, the greedy decision should always be justified—either through a proof, a known theorem, or reliable reasoning.

Recursion Base Case Errors

Divide-and-Conquer solutions rely heavily on recursion. A common mistake is forgetting or mishandling the base case, which is the condition at which recursion stops. If the base case is missing or incorrect, the program may run indefinitely or produce wrong intermediate results.

For instance, in Merge Sort or Binary Search, failing to stop when the subarray size reaches one element leads to unnecessary recursion or out-of-bounds errors. Similarly, in the Maximum Subarray Divide-and-Conquer approach, the midpoint logic must return correct results for very small segments.

Clearly defining and testing base cases prevents stack overflow and incorrect answers.

Misapplication of Master Theorem

The master theorem is extremely useful for analyzing recurrence relations, but it applies only when the recurrence matches the standard form shown here:

```
T(n) = aT(n/b) + f(n)
```

Beginners sometimes apply the theorem even when the recurrence does not fit this structure. For example, when:

- The number of subproblems is not fixed.
- The split sizes are irregular.
- The work done is not polynomially comparable to `n^(log_b a)`.

Using the master theorem in such cases leads to incorrect time complexity conclusions. In those situations, substitution or recursion tree expansion is more appropriate. Understanding when the theorem applies and when it does not is essential for accurate analysis.

By keeping track of these challenges, learners can implement the Greedy and Divide-and-Conquer algorithms confidently and correctly. Careful reasoning, well-chosen base cases, and proper complexity analysis will lead to clean, reliable solutions in both academic and real-world environments.

In real-world **banking and large-scale enterprise systems**, implementation challenges in greedy and Divide-and-Conquer algorithms can have serious consequences if not handled carefully. For instance, in a **fraud detection system**, a greedy rule that prioritizes transactions only by amount instead of risk score may overlook smaller but highly suspicious transactions, which can lead to security breaches. Similarly, in **manufacturing scheduling systems**, incorrect greedy decisions when assigning jobs to machines can cause delays, underutilization of resources, or missed production deadlines.

Divide-and-conquer errors are equally critical in industry. In **search and analytics platforms**, incorrect recursion base cases in binary search or indexing modules can result in infinite loops or missed records, impacting system reliability. In **financial analytics or cloud services**, misapplying the master theorem while estimating system scalability may lead to underestimating resource requirements, causing performance bottlenecks during peak loads. These examples highlight why careful validation of greedy decisions, correct handling of recursion base cases, and accurate complexity analysis are essential for building robust, production-ready systems.

Conclusion

In this chapter, learners explored two of the most influential problem-solving strategies in Computer Science: Greedy algorithms and Divide-and-Conquer. The Greedy approach showed how choosing the best option at each step can produce elegant and efficient solutions in areas like Activity Selection, Fractional Knapsack, Huffman Coding, and Job Scheduling, while also emphasizing that greedy decisions must be validated because local choices do not always guarantee a global optimum. Divide-and-Conquer offered a different kind of efficiency by breaking a complex problem into smaller pieces, solving them independently, and combining the results. Through examples such as Merge Sort, Quick Sort, Binary Search, Karatsuba Multiplication, and the Maximum Subarray Problem, students understood how recursion and structured decomposition lead to powerful algorithms. The chapter also introduced recurrence relations and the Master Theorem to help analyze the time complexity of recursive solutions. Together, these strategies strengthened algorithmic thinking, highlighting when fast local decisions are enough and when deeper analysis is needed. In the upcoming ***chapter***, learners move further into optimization by studying how overlapping subproblems can be solved efficiently using memoization and tabulation. Classic problems such as Fibonacci, Climbing Stairs, House Robber, Longest Common Subsequence, Edit Distance, and 0/1 Knapsack will guide learners toward recognizing DP patterns, formulating states and transitions, and building solutions that outperform naive recursion and brute-force methods.

Points to Remember

- Greedy algorithms make the best local choice at every step with the hope of reaching a global optimum.
- A greedy solution works only when the **Greedy Choice property** and **optimal substructure** both hold.
- Standard greedy applications include Activity Selection, Fractional Knapsack, Huffman Coding, and Job Scheduling.
- Greedy solutions are usually fast and simple, often running in `O(n log n)` or `O(n)`.
- Greedy fails when a local optimum blocks access to a better global solution, such as in 0/1 Knapsack or some coin systems.
- Divide-and-Conquer breaks a problem into subproblems, solves them recursively, and combines results.

- Merge Sort and Quick Sort are classic examples of Divide-and-Conquer.
- Binary Search repeatedly halves the search space, giving `O(log n)` complexity.
- Recurrence relations express the time complexity of Divide-and-Conquer algorithms.
- The **Master Theorem** helps solve recurrences of the form `T(n) = aT(n/b) + f(n)`.
- Karatsuba multiplication reduces the total number of multiplications using Divide-and-Conquer.
- The Maximum Subarray problem can be solved using Divide-and-Conquer in `O(n log n)`.
- Greedy vs. DP vs. Backtracking: Greedy takes local decisions, DP stores past results, and backtracking explores possibilities.
- Recursion errors, incorrect greedy rules, and misuse of the master theorem are common implementation mistakes.
- Choosing between Greedy and Divide-and-Conquer strategies depends on input size, correctness guarantees, and problem structure.

Multiple Choice Questions

1. Greedy algorithms make decisions based on:
   a. Future outcomes
   b. Current best choice
   c. Full search of all possibilities
   d. Random choice
2. The greedy method is correct only when:
   a. The data is sorted.
   b. Local optimum leads to global optimum.
   c. We use recursion.
   d. We use dynamic memory.
3. Activity Selection works correctly when activities are sorted by:
   a. Start time
   b. Finish time
   c. Duration
   d. Profit
4. Fractional Knapsack is best solved by choosing:
   a. Highest profit
   b. Lowest weight
   c. Highest value/weight ratio
   d. Largest item
5. Huffman Coding assigns:
   a. Equal length codes
   b. Shorter codes to frequent characters

    c. Longer codes to frequent characters
    d. Random codes

6. Job Scheduling (profit maximization) uses:
    a. BFS
    b. Sorting jobs by profit
    c. Sorting jobs by weight
    d. Backtracking only
7. Divide-and-Conquer consists of:
    a. Guessing and checking
    b. Divide, Conquer, Combine
    c. Predicting outcomes
    d. Using a queue
8. Merge Sort has time complexity:
    a. $O(n^2)$
    b. O(log n)
    c. O(n log n)
    d. O(n!)
9. Binary Search requires the input to be:
    a. Random
    b. Sorted
    c. Rotated
    d. Reverse sorted
10. Recursion tree method is useful for:
    a. Memory leaks
    b. Solving recurrences
    c. Hashing
    d. Pointer arithmetic
11. In Karatsuba multiplication, the improvement comes from:
    a. Faster input reading
    b. Fewer multiplications
    c. Sorting digits
    d. Using floating numbers
12. Kadane's Algorithm solves Maximum Subarray in:
    a. `O(log n)`
    b. `O(n)`
    c. `O(n log n)`
    d. `O(n²)`

13. Quick Sort worst-case time:
    a. `O(n log n)`
    b. `O(1)`
    c. `O(n²)`
    d. `O(n³)`
14. Greedy fails in:
    a. Fractional Knapsack
    b. 0/1 Knapsack
    c. Activity Selection
    d. Huffman Coding
15. Master theorem helps compute:
    a. Hash collisions
    b. Recurrence time complexity
    c. Linked list length
    d. Page faults

Answers

1. b
2. b
3. b
4. c
5. b
6. b
7. b
8. c
9. b
10. b
11. b
12. b
13. c
14. b
15. b

Questions

- Explain the greedy choice property. Why is it important? Provide an example where it works and an example where it fails.
- Describe Activity Selection and explain why the earliest-finish-time rule guarantees an optimal solution.
- Compare the Fractional Knapsack problem and the 0/1 Knapsack problem. Why is the Greedy approach correct for one and incorrect for the other?

- Explain Huffman Coding with a small example of character frequencies.
- Describe Divide-and-Conquer with the steps "divide, conquer, combine" and give two example algorithms.
- Explain how Binary Search achieves `O(log n)` performance. Provide the divide-and-conquer view.
- Describe the Divide-and-Conquer approach for the Maximum Subarray Problem and contrast it with Kadane's algorithm.
- What is a recurrence relation? Explain how the master theorem is used to find time complexity.

Key Terms

- **Greedy Algorithm:** A strategy that picks the best immediate choice at each step to build a final solution
- **Greedy Choice Property:** Condition where a local optimum leads to a global optimum
- **Optimal Substructure:** A problem whose solution can be built from optimal solutions of subproblems
- **Activity Selection:** A greedy method that schedules the maximum number of non-overlapping tasks
- **Fractional Knapsack:** A knapsack variant where items can be taken in fractions, solved by value/weight ratio
- **Huffman Coding:** A compression algorithm that assigns shorter codes to frequent symbols
- **Job Scheduling:** Selecting profitable jobs before deadlines to maximize total profit
- **Divide-and-Conquer:** Algorithmic technique that divides problems, solves parts recursively, and combines results
- **Binary Search:** Searching by repeatedly halving sorted data, achieving `O(log n)` time
- **Recurrence Relation:** An equation expressing `T(n)` using smaller `T(n/b)`
- **Master Theorem:** A formula to directly compute time complexity of many divide-and-conquer recurrences
- **Recursion Tree:** A visual model showing cost distribution across recursive levels
- **Karatsuba Multiplication:** Faster integer multiplication using fewer recursive multiplications
- **Maximum Subarray:** Finding a contiguous portion of an array with maximum sum
- **Kadane's Algorithm:** Linear-time algorithm to solve Maximum Subarray using running sum update

CHAPTER 12
Dynamic Programming

Introduction

Dynamic Programming (DP) is one of the most powerful techniques in algorithm design. It is used to solve complex problems efficiently by breaking them into smaller overlapping subproblems and storing their solutions so they do not need to be recomputed. Instead of repeatedly solving the same subproblem, DP saves the result and reuses it, which transforms exponential-time solutions into polynomial-time ones. This ability makes DP essential in competitive programming, optimization tasks, and advanced computer science topics.

Many problems that appear too slow or impossible using straightforward recursion become manageable with DP. Classic examples include computing Fibonacci numbers, finding the shortest path in a grid, determining the minimum cost to reach the top of a staircase, or identifying the longest common subsequence between two strings. Although the problems vary widely, they share a common structure: their solutions depend on solutions to smaller versions of the same problem.

This chapter takes a step-by-step approach to building DP intuition. Students will learn how to recognize overlapping subproblems and optimal substructure, convert slow recursive algorithms into efficient top-down or bottom-up solutions, and construct states and transitions that model the logic of a problem. Through 1-D and 2-D examples, performance comparisons, and optimization techniques, learners will gain the ability to design DP solutions confidently, as it is a skill that is highly valued in technical interviews and real-world applications.

Structure

In this chapter, we will cover the following topics:

- Introduction to Dynamic Programming
- Fundamentals of Dynamic Programming
- Classic One-Dimensional DP Problems
- Two-Dimensional DP and Grid-Based Problems
- DP Optimization Techniques
- Problem-Solving Patterns in Dynamic Programming

- Common Implementation Challenges
- Practice Exercises

Introduction to Dynamic Programming

Dynamic Programming (DP) is a problem-solving strategy used to handle complex tasks efficiently by breaking them into smaller subproblems, solving each subproblem once, and storing the results for future use. Many computational problems appear difficult at first glance because they involve repeated decisions, multiple paths, or exponential combinations. However, closer inspection often reveals that these problems reuse the same smaller subproblems many times. DP takes advantage of this repetition. Instead of recalculating answers again and again, it saves previously computed results and reuses them whenever needed.

Dynamic programming might sound intimidating at first, but the core idea is simple: **do not repeat work**. A problem that takes exponential time using plain recursion because it recomputes the same values repeatedly, can often be solved in polynomial time with DP, simply by storing and reusing results. Famous examples include the Fibonacci sequence, minimum cost path calculations, longest common subsequence, and the 0/1 Knapsack problem. Although these problems appear unrelated, they share two important characteristics: their solutions depend on solutions to subproblems and those subproblems repeat many times during computation.

DP also improves how we think about algorithms. Instead of focusing only on the final answer, DP encourages the development of step-by-step logic through **state representation**, where each state describes a smaller piece of the problem. Once the transition between states is clear, solving the problem becomes systematic rather than trial-and-error.

This chapter builds DP intuition gradually. We will start with the difference between simple recursion, memoization, and bottom-up tabulation. This way, learners will be able to understand when DP is useful and how to apply it. Through well-known 1-D and 2-D problems, performance comparisons, and optimization techniques, students will learn to convert slow recursive approaches into fast, efficient solutions. By the end of this chapter, DP will no longer feel like a mysterious trick, but a dependable tool for designing algorithms that run efficiently, even on large inputs.

Fundamentals of Dynamic Programming

Dynamic programming (DP) becomes valuable when a problem can be broken into smaller parts that repeat during computation. Instead of solving the same subproblem many times, DP solves it once and stores the result. This idea transforms slow algorithms into fast and reliable ones. To know when DP is applicable, it is important to understand two key properties: overlapping subproblems and optimal substructure.

Overlapping Subproblems and Optimal Substructure

A problem has **overlapping subproblems** when the same smaller tasks appear multiple times during computation. For example, computing the Fibonacci sequence with plain recursion repeatedly recalculates values like F(3), F(4), and F(5). These repeated calls waste time. DP avoids this by saving answers and reusing them whenever required.

A problem shows **optimal substructure** when an optimal answer can be built from optimal answers to smaller subproblems. In other words, solving the big problem depends on solving smaller versions of the same problem correctly. For example, the shortest path in a grid is formed by the shortest partial paths leading into it. This property ensures that combining smaller optimal results leads to a globally optimal solution.

When both properties are present, Dynamic Programming is usually the most efficient method available.

Recursion, Memoization, and Dynamic Programming

Many DP solutions begin as simple recursive solutions. Recursion expresses a problem naturally by defining it in terms of smaller versions of itself. However, naive recursion can be extremely slow when subproblems repeat many times.

- **Memoization (Top-Down DP):** Memoization improves recursion by storing the result of each subproblem the first time it is computed. If the same subproblem appears again, the stored value is returned immediately instead of recalculating it. This preserves the clarity of recursion and eliminates repeated work.
- **Dynamic Programming (Tabulation or Bottom-Up):** Instead of starting from the top and recursing down, the bottom-up method fills a table iteratively from the simplest subproblems upward. Each entry holds a sub-result, and larger results are built using previously filled values. This removes recursion entirely and often improves performance and memory predictability.

Both approaches achieve the same goal: using previous results to avoid recomputation, but they differ in implementation style and memory usage.

Top-Down Approach

In the top-down approach, the algorithm begins with the original problem and breaks it down through recursive calls. Each time a subproblem is solved, its result is stored in a cache (often an array, list, or dictionary). If the same subproblem is required again, the cached result is returned instantly.

This method is intuitive, easy to write, and ideal for beginners. It works particularly well when only a few subproblems are actually needed, since unvisited subproblems are never computed.

Bottom-Up Approach

The bottom-up approach avoids recursion altogether. Instead of solving big problems first, it starts with the smallest subproblems and works upward, while filling a DP table. Once simpler results are known, they are combined step by step until the final answer is reached.

Tabulation often provides better control over memory and avoids recursion depth issues. It is preferred in competitive programming or when recursion limits may be a concern.

State Representation and Transition Formulation

At the heart of every DP problem is the idea of defining a **state**, which is a symbolic representation of a subproblem. A state answers the question: *what subproblem does this value represent?*

For example:

- `dp[i]` might represent the best answer for the first i elements.
- `dp[i][j]` might represent a result involving two indices or dimensions.

Once the state is defined, the next step is to establish the **transition**, which shows how one state depends on others.

For example:

- `dp[i] = dp[i-1] + dp[i-2]` (Fibonacci Transition)
- `dp[i][j] = dp[i-1][j] + dp[i][j-1]` (Unique Paths Transition)

Good DP design depends on choosing the right states and writing clear transitions.

Time and Space Complexity Considerations

A major advantage of DP is that it converts exponential or high-complexity problems into polynomial-time solutions. By storing results of subproblems, DP eliminates repeated computations and allows most solutions to run in **O(n)** or **O(n²)** time, depending on the state size.

However, storing results also requires memory.

- 1-D DP usually needs **O(n)** space.
- 2-D DP often needs **O(n × m)** space.

To reduce memory usage, optimization techniques such as storing only necessary previous states, using rolling arrays, or compressing states can significantly lower space requirements. This foundation prepares you for the practical DP problems that follow—we will begin from simple 1-D examples and then progress to 2-D grid problems and optimization-focused techniques.

Classic One-Dimensional DP Problems

Many DP problems begin with a one-dimensional state, where each state represents the best answer up to a certain position. These problems are ideal for learning DP basics because the transitions are simple, the patterns are easy to observe, and the results clearly show how memoization or tabulation eliminates repeated computation. The following examples demonstrate how recursive solutions can be gradually transformed into efficient DP approaches:

Fibonacci Sequence

The Fibonacci sequence is one of the most common introductory DP problems. Although the mathematical definition is simple, the naive recursive approach becomes extremely slow as numbers grow.

Recursive Insight

The Fibonacci sequence is defined as:

```
F(0) = 0
F(1) = 1
F(n) = F(n-1) + F(n-2) for n ≥ 2
```

A direct recursive implementation follows this formula naturally: to compute F(n), we compute the two smaller values **F(n-1)** and **F(n-2)**. However, this creates exponential time complexity because the same subproblems are recomputed many times. For example, F(5) requires F(4) and F(3), and F(4) again needs F(3) and F(2), therefore, F(3) gets calculated repeatedly.

This repetition makes the naive recursion inefficient and highlights the need for DP.

Memoized Implementation

With memoization, the recursion remains the same, but every computed value is stored. Once F(k) is computed, the result is saved in an array or dictionary. If F(k) is requested again later, the stored answer is returned instantly without recomputation.

This reduces time complexity from **O(2ⁿ)** to **O(n)** and shows how DP removes duplicate work, while keeping the algorithm easy to understand.

Tabulation Method

In the bottom-up version, we start from the smallest values and build the solution iteratively, as shown here:

store **dp[0] = 0** and **dp[1] = 1**
use **dp[i] = dp[i-1] + dp[i-2]** to fill **dp[2]**, **dp[3]**, ... up to **dp[n]**

This avoids recursion entirely, uses a simple loop, and also runs in **O(n)** time. With a small optimization, even the DP array can be removed, while keeping only two variables to track the last two computed values.

The Fibonacci sequence is valuable not for the answer itself, but for the insight; problems with repeated subcomputations benefit enormously from DP.

Climbing Stairs

In the Climbing Stairs problem, a person can climb either 1 or 2 steps at a time. The task is to find how many distinct ways there are to reach the top of an n-step staircase.

If you think about reaching step **n**, the last move must have come from either step n-1 (taking 1 step) or from step **n-2** (taking 2 steps).

Therefore:

```
ways[n] = ways[n-1] + ways[n-2]
```

This is the same recurrence as Fibonacci, making it a simple 1-D DP problem.

A table or two rolling variables can produce the result efficiently.

Minimum Cost Climbing Stairs

In this problem, each stair has a cost. From stair i, you can move to i+1 or i+2, and the total cost is the sum of the stairs you step on.

The goal is to reach the top with minimum cost.

If **dp[i]** represents the minimum cost to reach stair i, then:

```
dp[i] = cost[i] + min(dp[i-1], dp[i-2])
```

The answer is the minimum of reaching the last or second-last stair, because either move can reach the top.

This problem demonstrates how DP optimizes decision-making by comparing the best choices from previous states.

House Robber Concept

In the House Robber problem, a robber wants to steal from houses on a street, but cannot rob two adjacent houses because security systems are connected.

If **dp[i]** represents the maximum money collectible up to house **i**, we have two choices:

- Rob the current house → Add its value to **dp[i-2]**.
- Skip it → Keep **dp[i-1]**.

Therefore:

```
dp[i] = max(dp[i-1], dp[i-2] + house[i])
```

This pattern shows how DP helps in problems involving non-adjacent choices. With just one loop and a small table, the optimal solution becomes clear and efficient.

Jump Game Approach

In Jump Game, each index contains a number representing how far you can jump. The task is to check whether you can reach the end of the array. A DP-style thinking helps track the farthest reachable index:

- Let **`reach`** store how far we can go at any moment.
- As we move through the array, if the current index is within reach, we will update **`reach`** as **`max(reach, i + nums[i])`**.

If **`reach`** eventually passes the last index, the end is reachable. Although sometimes solved greedily, the insight is similar to DP: decisions at each step depend on results from previous steps. These one-dimensional problems form the foundation of DP. They teach how to define a state, build transitions, and compare recursive, memoized, and tabulated solutions. With this base, learners are ready to extend DP ideas to 2-dimensional grid and string problems.

Two-Dimensional DP and Grid-Based Problems

Some problems require examining two dimensions instead of one, such as movement on a grid or comparing sequences. In these cases, the DP state is often represented using a 2-D table, where each cell stores the result of a subproblem formed by combining smaller segments of input. These problems appear frequently in interviews and competitive programming because they reveal a learner's ability to model complex logic using states and transitions. Common examples include path counting, minimum-cost travel, sequence matching, and optimization under constraints.

Unique Paths

Consider a robot standing at the top-left of an $m \times n$ grid, allowed to move only right or down. The task is to count how many distinct paths lead to the bottom-right corner.

Each cell **`(i, j)`** can be reached either from the cell above **`(i - 1, j)`** or from the cell to the left **`(i, j - 1)`**.

Therefore, the number of ways to reach it is:

```
dp[i][j] = dp[i-1][j] + dp[i][j-1]
```

The first row and first column have only one possible path because movement is restricted to right or down. Filling the DP table row by row yields the total number of unique paths. This problem demonstrates how 2-D DP models movement on a grid and counts possibilities efficiently, while avoiding slow recursive branching.

Minimum Path Sum

Here, each cell of the grid contains a cost. The goal is to reach the bottom-right cell with the minimum total cost, while moving only right or down.

Define **`dp[i][j]`** as the minimum cost required to reach cell **`(i, j)`**.

Since the robot must come from left or above:

```
dp[i][j] = cost[i][j] + min(dp[i-1][j], dp[i][j-1])
```

The base case is **`dp[0][0] = grid[0][0]`**.

Just like Unique Paths, the first cell starts the table, and borders can be filled using only one direction. This problem shows how DP handles optimization instead of counting. A brute-force recursive solution has exponential complexity, while DP solves it in linear time over the grid.

Longest Common Subsequence (LCS)

The **Longest Common Subsequence (LCS)** problem is a foundational DP problem in string processing. Given two strings, the task is to find the length of the longest sequence that appears in both strings (not necessarily contiguous).

Let the two strings be X and Y of lengths `m` and `n`.

Define `dp[i][j]` as the length of the LCS between the first i characters of X and the first j characters of Y.

The recurrence is:

- If `X[i-1] == Y[j-1]`, then `dp[i][j] = 1 + dp[i-1][j-1]`.
- Otherwise, `dp[i][j] = max(dp[i-1][j], dp[i][j-1])`.

The base cases are when either string is empty (`dp[i][0] = dp[0][j] = 0`). LCS is widely used in version control systems, DNA sequence analysis, and document comparison tools.

Edit Distance

The **Edit Distance** (or **Levenshtein Distance**) problem measures how different two strings are by counting the minimum number of operations required to transform one string into another. The allowed operations are **insert**, **delete**, and **replace** a character.

Let `dp[i][j]` represent the minimum edit distance between the first i characters of string A and the first j characters of string B. The recurrence is:

If `A[i-1] == B[j-1]`, then `dp[i][j] = dp[i-1][j-1]`.

Otherwise:

```
dp[i][j] = 1 + min(
    dp[i-1][j],     // deletion
    dp[i][j-1],     // insertion
    dp[i-1][j-1]    // replacement
)
```

The base cases are when one of the strings is empty:

`dp[i][0] = i` and `dp[0][j] = j`

This DP problem is vital in applications like spell checkers, plagiarism detectors, and DNA sequence alignment.

0/1 Knapsack Problem

The **0/1 Knapsack Problem** is one of the most famous DP problems in optimization. Given n items, each with a weight and a value, and a knapsack of capacity W, the goal is to maximize the total value without exceeding the weight limit. Each item can either be taken (1) or not taken (0).

Let `dp[i][w]` represent the maximum value attainable using the first i items and a knapsack capacity `w`.

The transition will be:

```
If weight[i-1] <= w:
    dp[i][w] = max(value[i-1] + dp[i-1][w - weight[i-1]], dp[i-1][w])
Else:
    dp[i][w] = dp[i-1][w]
```

The base case is **`dp[0][w] = 0`** for all `w`.

The final answer is **`dp[n][W]`**.

The 0/1 Knapsack problem teaches how DP manages trade-offs between choices and efficiently explores all valid combinations.

Two-dimensional DP extends the same core logic as 1-D problems but adds a second layer of dependency.

By using matrices or tables, DP captures relationships between two variables, such as coordinates or string indices.

These problems form the foundation for many advanced algorithms in Artificial Intelligence (AI), Natural Language Processing (NLP), and bioinformatics.

DP Optimization Techniques

DP can greatly improve time efficiency, but sometimes it requires significant memory to store intermediate results. As problem sizes increase, storing large DP tables becomes expensive. To handle memory limits while keeping the algorithm efficient, several optimization techniques are used. These techniques preserve correctness while reducing space, simplifying transitions, or eliminating unnecessary states.

Space Optimization in DP

Many DP problems only depend on a small portion of previous states. For example, the Fibonacci sequence does not require storing the entire DP array; only the last two values are needed to compute the next one.

Instead of using **`dp[n]`**, we can use two variables:

```
prev2 = 0
prev1 = 1
current = prev1 + prev2
```

This reduces space from **`O(n)`** to **`O(1)`**.

Other DP problems such as **Climbing Stairs**, **Minimum Path Sum**, and even **Longest Common Subsequence** can also be optimized by storing only one row or one column of the DP table at a time.

Space optimization is useful when the DP matrix is large and only the previous state is required for the next calculation.

Prefix Sums Used in DP

Prefix sums are a technique that speeds up repeated range calculations.

Instead of recalculating a sum from scratch, prefix sums store cumulative totals so that any range can be answered in O(1) time.

For example, if **`prefix[i]`** represents the sum of the first **`i`** elements, then the sum from index l to r can be computed as:

```
range_sum = prefix[r] - prefix[l-1]
```

Prefix sums are especially helpful in DP problems involving cost accumulation, subarray scoring, or cumulative minimization. By precomputing prefix values, transitions become faster, and unnecessary inner loops are avoided, which reduces overall time complexity.

State Compression Concepts

When a DP state includes many dimensions or complex conditions, memory usage may become extremely high. **State compression** reduces the amount of memory by packing multiple pieces of information into a smaller representation, often using bit manipulation.

A common example is solving subset-related problems. Instead of storing full DP tables, the subset can be represented as a binary mask.

If the binary number `1011` represents a subset, it means elements at positions 0, 1, and 3 are included. This allows a DP table of size `2^n` to represent all subsets efficiently without storing multi-dimensional data.

State compression is widely used in bitmask DP, traveling salesman problems, scheduling tasks, and game theory problems. Although more advanced than basic DP, it makes otherwise impossible solutions feasible within memory limits.

Optimizing DP is not about changing the result; it is about computing it in a smarter way.

- **Space optimization** reduces DP tables to minimal memory.
- **Prefix sums** simplify repeated calculations.
- **State compression** shrinks large state spaces using compact representations.

These techniques help DP scale to larger input sizes. They make solutions faster, lighter, and suitable for real-world applications.

Problem-Solving Patterns in Dynamic Programming

DP becomes much easier to recognize once common problem patterns are understood. Even though DP problems appear different on the surface, many follow similar logical structures. By learning these patterns, students can quickly identify when DP should be used and formulate states and transitions more confidently. The three most frequent patterns in DP are decision-making, subset/partitioning, and sequence alignment.

Decision-Making Pattern

Many optimization problems require choosing actions step-by-step while maximizing or minimizing some result. At every step, the algorithm must decide between two or more choices, such as taking or skipping an element, moving forward or backward, selecting or ignoring an option.

The key idea is that **the best decision for the current step depends on the best decisions for smaller substeps**, which fits directly into the DP model of building answers from prior states.

Examples:

- **House Robber**: Choose to rob or skip each house.
- **Jump Game**: Decide which jump leads to the farthest progress.
- **Minimum Cost Climbing Stairs**: Decide from which previous step the optimal path will come.

In these problems:

- The **state** often represents the best result up to position `i`.
- The **transition** compares choices (take vs skip, jump vs wait, and so on).

This pattern teaches learners to frame real-world decision processes into efficient DP choices, rather than brute-force exploration.

Subset and Partitioning Pattern

Some problems involve splitting elements into groups or selecting a subset that satisfies certain conditions, such as reaching a target sum, balancing weights, or choosing items for optimal reward. These problems typically involve two varying factors: **element index** and **remaining capacity / target / cost**. As a result, they naturally fit into 2-D DP tables.

Examples:

- **0/1 Knapsack Problem**: Choose which items to include without exceeding weight.
- **Subset Sum / Partition Equal Subset**: Determine if a set can be divided evenly.
- **Coin Change (Ways or Minimum Coins)**: Count how many ways to form a total.

In these cases:

- `dp[i][j]` often implies if by using the first i elements, can we achieve or maximize something with value j?
- Transitions involve deciding whether to include an element in the subset or leave it out.

This pattern is widely used in finance, scheduling, and combinatorial optimization.

Sequence Alignment Pattern

This pattern appears in problems involving comparisons between two sequences, often as characters, numbers, or tokens. Rather than working along one dimension, the algorithm gradually aligns prefixes of both sequences and builds the answer using 2-D states.

Examples:

Longest Common Subsequence (LCS)

Edit Distance

String Matching and DNA Alignment

Typical state definition: `dp[i][j] = Result` based on first i characters of sequence A and first `j` characters of sequence B

Transitions are based on whether characters match and if they follow these conditions:

- If characters align, add a match or zero cost.
- If not, consider insert/delete/replace operations or skip characters appropriately.

This pattern is fundamental in text processing, spell checking, plagiarism detection, version control, and bioinformatics.

Even though DP problems may look different, many follow predictable structures such as:

- The **decision-making pattern** compares choices at each step.
- The **subset and partitioning pattern** evaluates combinations of elements.
- The **sequence alignment pattern** aligns two sequences through 2-D states.

Recognizing these patterns helps students convert complex logic into structured DP solutions with clear states and transitions.

In real-world industry applications, Dynamic Programming plays a critical role in solving complex optimization problems efficiently by avoiding redundant computations. In **finance and banking**, DP is used for portfolio optimization, credit risk assessment, and transaction scheduling, where decision-making patterns help select optimal actions under constraints. In **logistics and supply chain systems**, subset and partitioning patterns are applied to load optimization, warehouse resource allocation, and shipment batching to minimize cost and time. Similarly, in **software engineering and data platforms**, sequence alignment patterns power text comparison tools, version control systems, and recommendation engines by efficiently analyzing similarities between large datasets. By breaking problems into overlapping subproblems and reusing computed results, Dynamic Programming enables these systems to scale effectively while delivering accurate and optimal solutions under real-world constraints.

Common Implementation Challenges

DP provides efficient solutions to many complex problems, but beginners often face difficulties while converting an idea into a correct DP implementation. Most mistakes arise not from the algorithm itself, but from small flaws in state design, transitions, or boundary handling. Understanding these common challenges helps avoid logical errors and ensures that DP solutions are both correct and optimal.

Incorrect State Formulation

The most frequent DP mistake is defining the wrong state. If the state does not represent the correct subproblem, then the final DP table will not contain the right answer. For example, in 0/1 Knapsack, tracking only the total weight is not enough; you must also track how many items have been considered. If the state ignores an important dimension, the solution will lose its meaning. A well-defined state answers a precise question, such as:

- *What is the best answer up to index `i`?*
- *What is the cost for a subgrid ending at `(i, j)`?*

You must think carefully before writing code, as correct state representation is the foundation of every DP solution.

Missing Base Conditions

Every DP table needs base cases to define the smallest subproblems. If these are missing or incorrect, the transition rules apply on uninitialized or invalid values. Examples:

Failing to set **`dp[0]`** and **`dp[1]`** in Fibonacci

Forgetting **`dp[0][j] = j`** and **`dp[i][0] = i`** in Edit Distance

Not initializing **`dp[0][*] = 0`** for Knapsack

Base conditions act like the starting block of a building. Without them, the structure collapses as soon as transitions begin.

Inefficient Transitions

Even when the logic is correct, DP can become slow if transitions repeat unnecessary computations.

For example, a nested DP that recalculates a sum or cost from scratch in each iteration will lead to quadratic or cubic overhead. Prefix sums, rolling arrays, and pre-computed values help remove redundant work.

Efficient transitions keep the algorithm inside expected time limits and are particularly important for competitive programming and large inputs.

Overuse of Recursion without Memoization

Beginners often write recursive solutions without memoizing results, especially in problems like Fibonacci, climbing stairs, or LCS. Without memoization, recursion performs repeated work and becomes exponential in time. Memoization stores every result the first time it is computed and returns it instantly on the next request, thereby converting slow recursion into an efficient top-down DP.

In larger problems, recursion without memoization can also cause stack overflow or exceed time limits. When recursion depth becomes too large, the bottom-up tabulation approach is often safer.

Practice Exercises

To strengthen our understanding of DP, it is important to solve a variety of problems that reinforce state formulation, transitions, and edge-case handling. The following exercises are selected to cover different difficulty levels and patterns discussed in this chapter:

1-D DP Practice Problems

- **Fibonacci Number (Top-Down and Bottom-Up):** Compute the nth Fibonacci number efficiently using memoization and tabulation.
- **Climbing Stairs:** Find the number of distinct ways to reach step n when one or two steps can be taken at a time.
- **Minimum Cost Climbing Stairs:** Given an array of step costs, determine the minimum total cost to reach the top.
- **House Robber:** Given a list of non-negative integers representing money in houses, find the maximum sum without robbing two adjacent houses.
- **Jump Game:** Determine whether it is possible to reach the last index when each element represents the maximum jump length from that position.

2-D DP Practice Problems

- **Unique Paths:** Count how many ways a robot can travel from the top-left to the bottom-right of a grid, moving only right or down.
- **Minimum Path Sum:** Given a grid with non-negative values, compute the minimum cost to reach the bottom-right cell.
- **Longest Common Subsequence (LCS):** Find the length of the longest subsequence common to two given strings.
- **Edit Distance:** Determine the minimum number of insertions, deletions, and replacements to convert one string into another.
- **0/1 Knapsack:** Given weights and values of items and a capacity limit, maximize total value without exceeding capacity.

Optimization-Based DP Problems

- **Space-Optimized Fibonacci:** Compute Fibonacci numbers using only two variables, instead of a full DP array.

- **Longest Common Subsequence with Space Reduction:** Reduce the LCS DP from `O(m×n)` space to `O(min(m, n))` by storing only necessary rows.
- **Knapsack with 1-D DP Array:** Implement 0/1 Knapsack using a single-dimension DP array to optimize memory.
- **Prefix-Sum Enhanced Subarray Problem:** If you are given an array, efficiently compute the minimum or maximum subarray score using prefix sums combined with DP transitions.
- **Bitmask-Based Subset DP (Conceptual):** Represent subsets of a small set using bitmasks and find the subset having the maximum total value under certain constraints.

These exercises provide a balanced mix of theoretical understanding and practical implementation. Solving them will strengthen the ability to design DP states, reason about transitions, and optimize memory usage where needed.

Conclusion

DP is one of the most powerful tools in algorithm design, and this chapter transformed it from an intimidating concept into a practical, step-by-step strategy for solving problems efficiently. Through the ideas of overlapping subproblems and optimal substructure, learners discovered how storing intermediate results eliminates redundant work and converts slow, exponential solutions into fast, polynomial ones. Starting with intuitive 1-D problems like Fibonacci, Climbing Stairs, House Robber, and Jump Game, the chapter demonstrated how simple recursive thinking evolves into memoization and tabulation. It then expanded into 2-D DP and grid-based models, covering essential problems such as Unique Paths, Minimum Path Sum, Longest Common Subsequence, Edit Distance, and 0/1 Knapsack, each highlighting how states and transitions are carefully constructed. Advanced topics like space optimization, prefix sums, and state compression showed that even large DP solutions can be made memory-efficient. By practicing common patterns such as decision-making, subset/partitioning, and sequence alignment, students gained the skill to recognize DP problems in new situations and build correct, efficient solutions from the ground up.

In the upcoming chapter, the journey continues with algorithms that explore solution spaces more flexibly. While DP avoids recomputation, backtracking systematically explores possibilities by undoing choices when they lead to dead ends, and Branch-and-Bound improves efficiency by pruning unpromising search paths. Learners will see how these strategies apply to puzzles, combinatorial problems, constraint satisfaction, and optimization scenarios. By connecting this chapter's optimization mindset with the search-based strategies elaborated in the next chapter, students will be able to deepen their understanding of problem-solving techniques used in advanced programming and competitive environments.

Points to Remember

- Dynamic Programming solves problems by breaking them into overlapping subproblems and storing results to avoid repeated computation.
- Two properties must exist for DP to work: **overlapping subproblems** and **optimal substructure**.
- DP can be implemented using **top-down (memoization)** or **bottom-up (tabulation)**.
- Memoization uses recursion and caching, while tabulation uses iterative computation and a DP table.
- State representation defines what each DP cell means; transitions describe how results flow from smaller states to larger ones.
- Classic 1-D problems include Fibonacci, Climbing Stairs, Minimum Cost Climbing Stairs, House Robber, and Jump Game.

- Two-dimensional DP is widely used in grid problems and string matching tasks such as Unique Paths, Minimum Path Sum, LCS, Edit Distance, and 0/1 Knapsack.
- DP can drastically reduce time complexity—from exponential to polynomial.
- Space optimization techniques allow DP to run using only a few variables instead of full tables.
- Prefix sums eliminate repeated range calculations and improve performance.
- State compression reduces memory by representing complex states using bits.
- Common DP patterns include decision-making, subset/partitioning, and sequence alignment.
- Many implementation errors come from incorrect states, missing base cases, and lack of memoization.
- DP is heavily used in optimization, pathfinding, scheduling, string analysis, and combinatorics.
- Strong DP skill comes from practicing how to convert recurrence logic into code.

Multiple Choice Questions

1. Dynamic Programming works best when a problem has:
    a. Unique subproblems
    b. Overlapping subproblems
    c. Random processing
    d. No recursion
2. Optimal Substructure means that:
    a. A problem cannot be divided.
    b. Optimal solution contains optimal solutions to subproblems.
    c. Only greedy solutions work.
    d. Brute force must be used.
3. Memoization is typically implemented using:
    a. Loops only
    b. Recursion + caching
    c. Greedy sorting
    d. BFS traversal
4. Tabulation builds the solution:
    a. From the biggest case to smallest
    b. From smallest cases upward
    c. Randomly
    d. Using binary search
5. Fibonacci using naive recursion has time complexity:
    a. `O(n)`
    b. `O(log n)`
    c. $O(2^n)$
    d. `O(1)`

6. In Climbing Stairs, the recurrence relation resembles:
   a. Sorting
   b. Fibonacci sequence
   c. Binary search
   d. Graph traversal
7. Unique Paths uses DP by:
   a. Counting number of BFS paths
   b. Storing number of ways to reach each grid cell
   c. Greedy choice
   d. Trying all permutations
8. In Minimum Path Sum, transitions take the minimum of:
   a. Left or right
   b. Top or bottom
   c. Top or left
   d. Two diagonals
9. LCS compares two strings using:
   a. Binary tree
   b. Hashing
   c. 2-D DP table
   d. Priority queue
10. Edit Distance counts minimum:
    a. Rotations
    b. Insertions, deletions, replacements
    c. Substrings
    d. Lexicographic swaps
11. 0/1 Knapsack restricts each item to be:
    a. Taken multiple times
    b. Fractionally divided
    c. Either taken or not taken
    d. Ignored always
12. Space optimization works by:
    a. Removing input
    b. Storing only necessary rows or variables
    c. Increasing table size
    d. Removing transitions
13. Prefix sums help by:
    a. Slowing down range queries
    b. Avoiding repeated summation

   c. Sorting numbers
   d. Eliminating DP
14. State compression is commonly implemented using:
   a. Strings
   b. Floating numbers
   c. Bitmasks
   d. Linked lists
15. A common mistake in DP is:
   a. Writing transitions
   b. Using base cases correctly
   c. Missing memoization and repeating work
   d. Using arrays to store results

Answers

1. b
2. b
3. b
4. b
5. c
6. b
7. b
8. c
9. c
10. b
11. c
12. b
13. b
14. c
15. c

Questions

1. Explain the difference between recursion, memoization, and tabulation with examples.
2. Describe overlapping subproblems and optimal substructure. Why are they important for DP?
3. Write the DP logic for Fibonacci using both memoization and tabulation.
4. Discuss how DP is used to solve the Unique Paths problem. Include state and transitions.
5. Explain the Edit Distance problem and derive the DP recurrence.
6. Describe the 0/1 Knapsack problem and its DP table formulation.
7. What is space optimization in DP? Provide examples where it removes the need for full DP arrays.
8. Compare decision-making, subset, and sequence-alignment DP patterns with examples.

Key Terms

- **Dynamic Programming:** Technique that solves complex problems by storing results of overlapping subproblems
- **Overlapping Subproblems:** Same smaller task appears repeatedly during computation.
- **Optimal Substructure:** Optimal solution can be formed from optimal solutions of subproblems.
- **Memoization:** Top-down DP where recursion stores solved subproblems
- **Tabulation:** Bottom-up DP using iterative table filling
- **State Representation:** Meaning assigned to each DP entry (for example, `dp[i]`, `dp[i][j]`)
- **Transition:** Rule showing how states depend on previous states
- **Unique Paths:** DP problem counting ways to reach grid cells from top-left to bottom-right
- **Minimum Path Sum:** DP that finds lowest cost path in a grid
- **LCS (Longest Common Subsequence):** Longest sequence appearing in same order in two strings
- **Edit Distance:** Minimum edits to convert one string into another
- **0/1 Knapsack:** Maximize value with weight capacity where each item is taken once or not at all
- **Space Optimization:** Technique that reduces memory by storing only necessary DP states
- **Prefix Sum:** Array storing cumulative totals to answer range queries efficiently
- **State Compression:** Reducing memory by packing states (often with bitmasking)

Chapter 13
Backtracking and Recursion Patterns

Introduction

Recursion and backtracking are fundamental techniques that form the backbone of many complex problem-solving strategies in computer science. While recursion provides a natural way to break large problems into smaller, manageable pieces, backtracking builds on this idea by exploring all possible solutions step by step, and abandoning those paths that fail to satisfy given constraints. Together, these techniques enable programmers to solve a wide range of problems that involve decision making, combinations, arrangements, and constraint satisfaction. Recursion works by allowing a function to call itself to solve smaller versions of the same problem until a simple base case is reached. This approach closely mirrors human logical thinking and is widely used in tree traversal, **Divide-and-Conquer algorithms, and mathematical computations.** However, when recursion is combined with systematic trial-and-error and intelligent pruning of wrong paths, it transforms into the powerful strategy known as backtracking. Backtracking is especially useful when a problem has multiple possible choices at each step and requires finding all valid solutions rather than just one. Instead of blindly trying every possible combination, backtracking builds solutions incrementally and immediately rejects partial solutions that cannot lead to a valid final answer. This makes it highly efficient for problems such as generating subsets and permutations, solving puzzles such as Sudoku, placing queens on a chessboard in the N-Queens problem, and partitioning strings into palindromes. This chapter strengthens the learner's understanding of recursion from the ground up and then introduces backtracking as a natural extension of recursive thinking. Through structured patterns, classic problems, visual recursion trees, and systematic tracing techniques, students will learn not only how these algorithms work, but also how to design, debug, and optimize recursive and backtracking solutions effectively. By the end of this chapter, learners will be well-equipped with the confidence to tackle complex combinatorial and constraint-based problems using structured recursion and intelligent backtracking strategies.

Structure

In this chapter, we will cover the following topics:

- Recursion Fundamentals
- Backtracking Essentials
- Classic Backtracking Problems
- Techniques and Problem-Solving Patterns

- Visualization and Debugging in Backtracking
- Common Implementation Challenges
- Practice Exercises

Recursion Fundamentals

Recursion is a powerful programming technique in which a function solves a problem by calling itself to solve smaller versions of the same problem. It closely follows the natural way humans think about repetitive tasks by breaking a large task into simpler sub-tasks until the simplest case is reached. Although recursion often makes code shorter and easier to understand, it must be used with care to avoid infinite calls and memory issues. Understanding its core components is essential before moving to advanced backtracking problems.

Recursion versus Iteration

Both recursion and iteration are used to repeat a set of instructions, but they differ in how repetition is handled.

Iteration uses loops such as for, while, or do-while to repeatedly execute statements. It is generally memory-efficient because it does not create additional function calls. Iteration is commonly used when the number of repetitions is known or when performance and memory usage are critical.

Recursion, on the other hand, uses function calls to repeat operations. Each recursive call creates a new entry on the call stack. Recursion is especially useful for problems that naturally have a recursive structure, such as:

- Tree Traversal
- Divide-and-Conquer algorithms
- Generating subsets, permutations, and combinations

While recursive programs are often more elegant and easier to reason about, they may consume more memory and can be slower than iterative solutions, if not carefully designed.

While practicing, use **iteration** for simple repetitive tasks and **recursion** when the problem naturally breaks into smaller identical subproblems.

Base Case and Recursive Step

Every correct recursive function consists of **two essential parts**:

Base Case: The base case is the stopping condition of recursion. It defines the simplest version of the problem that can be solved directly without making further recursive calls. Without a base case, the function would keep calling itself endlessly, causing a stack overflow.

In factorial calculation, **`factorial(0) = 1`** is the base case.

Recursive Step: The recursive step reduces the problem into a smaller version of itself and calls the function again with this reduced input.

`factorial(n) = n × factorial(n - 1)` is the recursive step.

For a recursive solution to work correctly:

The recursive step **must always move toward the base case**. The base case **must be reachable for all valid inputs.**

Together, the base case and recursive step ensure correctness, termination, and logical flow of recursion.

Stack Behavior in Recursion

Recursion relies heavily on the **call stack**, which is a memory structure that keeps track of active function calls. Each time a function is called, a stack frame is created to store:

- Local Variables
- Function Parameters
- Return Address

When a recursive function calls itself:

A new stack frame is pushed onto the stack. This continues until the base case is reached.

Once the base case returns a value, stack frames are removed one by one in **Last-In-First-Out (LIFO)** order.

This behavior explains why:

- Deep recursion can cause a **stack overflow.**
- Recursion uses **more memory than iteration.**

Debugging recursive programs often involves understanding the order of stack expansion and collapse.

Visualizing stack behavior using recursion trees or trace tables greatly improves comprehension and debugging accuracy.

Tail Recursion and Its Optimization

A recursion is called **tail recursion** when the recursive call is the **last operation** performed in the function. This means no further computation is required after the recursive call returns.

In tail recursion, the result of the recursive call is immediately returned. There is no pending operation waiting after the recursive call.

Because of this special structure, some compilers can apply **Tail Call Optimization (TCO)**, which converts recursive calls into iterative loops internally. This eliminates the need for additional stack frames and makes tail-recursive functions as memory-efficient as iterative ones.

Benefits of Tail Recursion:

- Prevents stack overflow for large inputs
- Improves performance
- Retains the clarity of recursive logic

Not all programming languages perform tail-call optimization automatically. Therefore, programmers must still be cautious when using deep recursion.

Backtracking Essentials

Backtracking is a powerful algorithmic technique used to explore all possible solutions to a problem in a **systematic and controlled manner**. It works by building a solution step by step and abandoning a path immediately when it becomes clear that the current partial solution cannot lead to a valid final answer. Instead of blindly trying every possibility, backtracking "goes back" (backtracks) as soon as it detects a violation of constraints. This smart trial-and-error approach makes it highly effective for combinatorial and constraint-based problems.

Concept and Working of Backtracking

Backtracking is a systematic problem-solving technique that explores **all possible solutions by building them one step at a time** and then abandoning those paths that fail to satisfy the problem's constraints. Instead of trying every combination blindly, backtracking makes intelligent decisions by checking conditions at each step and **reversing choices immediately when they lead to an invalid state**. This ability to move forward, detect failure early, and then "go back" to try the next option is what gives backtracking its name.

At its core, backtracking is based on **recursive decision-making**. At every stage of the problem, the algorithm:

- Selects one possible option from the available choices
- Proceeds with that choice to the next level
- Checks whether the current partial solution is valid

If it is invalid, the choice is undone, and the algorithm tries a different option.

This process continues until either a complete, valid solution is formed or all possibilities have been exhausted.

Backtracking works in a **Depth-First Search (DFS) manner**. The algorithm explores one complete path as deeply as possible before switching to another path. This allows it to quickly detect failures and backtrack early, instead of exploring unnecessary branches.

For example:

While placing queens in the **N-Queens problem**, a queen is only placed if it does not attack previously placed queens.

In **Sudoku**, a number is placed only if it satisfies row, column, and sub-grid constraints.

During **permutation generation**, a number is chosen only if it has not been used earlier in the current arrangement.

In each of these cases, the algorithm moves forward when the choice is valid and immediately backtracks when a constraint is violated.

The real strength of backtracking lies in its ability to **avoid useless computation**. By rejecting partial solutions that cannot lead to a valid answer, it significantly reduces the search space compared to brute-force methods. Although backtracking still has exponential worst-case complexity, intelligent constraint checking makes it efficient enough for many real-world and competitive programming applications.

Recursion Tree and Decision Branching

The behavior of a backtracking algorithm can be best understood using a **recursion tree**. A recursion tree is a visual representation that shows how a recursive or backtracking solution explores different possibilities step by step. Each node in the tree represents a **state of the partial solution**, and each edge represents a **decision or choice** made at that point.

The **root of the recursion tree** represents the initial state where no choices have been made. As the algorithm moves forward, every decision creates a new branch. Each level of the tree corresponds to one step or depth of the decision-making process. When a complete and valid solution is formed, the path ends at a **leaf node**. If a choice leads to a violation of constraints, the branch is terminated early, and the algorithm moves back to explore the next branch.

This process is known as **decision branching**. At each step, the algorithm:

- Examines all possible choices for the current position
- Selects one choice and moves to the next level
- Continues branching until a solution is found or rejected

For example:

- In **subsets generation**, each element creates two branches: include or exclude.
- In **permutations**, each unused element creates a new branch.
- In **N-Queens**, every column placement creates a branch for the next row.

Thus, the recursion tree grows wider as the number of choices increases and deeper as more decisions are fixed.

Backtracking explores this tree using a **Depth-First Search (DFS) strategy**. The algorithm fully explores one branch from root to leaf before moving to another branch. This is why it is able to detect failures early and return quickly to try alternative paths.

Recursion trees also play an important role in **analysis and debugging**:

- They help visualize how many recursive calls are made.
- They show exactly where branches fail.
- They explain why time complexity often becomes exponential in backtracking problems.

The recursion tree provides a clear picture of how a backtracking algorithm navigates through all possible choices, while decision branching explains how different options lead to different solution paths. Understanding this structure makes it much easier to trace, debug, and optimize backtracking programs.

Pruning Branches and Constraint Checks

One of the most important factors that makes backtracking practical and efficient is **pruning**. Pruning refers to the process of **eliminating a branch of the recursion tree as soon as it is clear that it cannot lead to a valid solution**. Instead of continuing deeper into an invalid path and wasting time, the algorithm immediately stops exploring that branch and backtracks to try another option.

Pruning works hand-in-hand with **constraint checks**. At every step of a backtracking algorithm, the current partial solution is tested against a set of conditions defined by the problem. These conditions are called constraints. If a constraint is violated, the current path is considered invalid and is pruned.

For example:

In the **N-Queens problem**, a queen placement is rejected immediately if it attacks another queen in the same row, column, or diagonal. In the **Sudoku**, a number is discarded if it already exists in the same row, column, or 3×3 subgrid. In **Palindrome Partitioning**, a substring is accepted only if it forms a valid palindrome. In **Combination Sum problems**, a branch is pruned if the current sum exceeds the target value.

In each case, constraint checking prevents the algorithm from exploring combinations that are guaranteed to fail.

Pruning significantly **reduces the size of the recursion tree**. Without pruning, a backtracking algorithm behaves like brute force and explores every possible combination.

With proper pruning, large portions of the tree are cut off early, which:

- Saves computation time

- Reduces memory usage
- Makes otherwise infeasible problems solvable in practice

Effective pruning depends on how early constraints can be checked. The sooner a violation is detected, the more work is saved. That is why backtracking algorithms are usually designed to check constraints **immediately after making a choice**, not after completing all decisions.

Branching generates possibilities, **constraint checks validate choices**, and **pruning eliminates failures early**. Together, these three components make backtracking a powerful and efficient strategy for solving complex combinatorial and constraint-based problems.

General Template for Backtracking Problems

Although backtracking problems may look different on the surface, most of them follow a **common logical structure**. Once this structure is understood, it becomes much easier to design correct and efficient solutions. The backtracking process always follows the same idea: **make a choice, explore further, and undo the choice if it leads to failure**. This repeated pattern forms the general template used in almost all backtracking algorithms.

At a high level, a backtracking algorithm works, as shown here:

1. **Check Completion Condition.**

   First, check whether the current partial solution satisfies the condition for a complete solution.

   If yes, store or display the solution.

   If no, continue making further choices.

2. **Try All Possible Choices.**

   For the current position or state, iterate over all possible choices available.

3. **Check Validity (Constraints).**

   Before proceeding with a choice, verify whether it satisfies the problem's constraints.

   If the choice is invalid, skip it.

   If valid, proceed to the next step.

4. **Make the Choice.**

   Add the chosen option to the current solution.

5. **Recur to the Next Level.**

   Call the backtracking function recursively to process the next position.

6. **Undo the Choice (Backtrack).**

   After returning from the recursive call, remove the last choice to restore the previous state. This allows the algorithm to try the next option.

   This sequence of steps repeats at every level of recursion until all the possible valid solutions are explored.

Conceptual Backtracking Structure

In simple terms, every backtracking algorithm follows this flow:

If the solution is complete → **record it.**

Otherwise →For each possible valid option:

a. **Choose** the option.

b. `Explore` further using recursion.

c. `Unchoose` the option (backtrack).

This is often summarized as the `Choose - Explore - Unchoose` pattern.

This general template ensures that:

- All possible valid solutions are explored.
- Invalid paths are rejected early using constraint checks.
- Memory usage remains under control by undoing changes after each recursive call.
- The algorithm remains systematic and avoids random trial-and-error.

This same template is used in:

- Subsets and Permutations Generation
- Combination Sum Problems
- Palindrome Partitioning
- N-Queens and Sudoku Solvers

Once students master this template, they can easily map most backtracking problems into a structured and reliable solution.

Classic Backtracking Problems

Classic backtracking problems illustrate how recursive decision-making, constraint checks, and pruning work together to explore large solution spaces efficiently. These problems appear frequently in interviews and real-world applications because they involve generating combinations, arrangements, or satisfying constraints under strict rules. Each of the following problems highlights a common backtracking pattern:

Subsets (Power Set Generation)

The **Subsets** problem, also known as power set generation, requires finding all possible subsets of a given set of elements, including the empty set and the full set.

At each step, the algorithm faces a **binary decision** for every element:

- Include the current element.
- Exclude the current element.

The recursion tree, therefore, branches into two paths at each level. Backtracking systematically explores both choices, adds valid subsets to the result, and then removes the last choice before moving on to the next possibility.

This problem demonstrates the **inclusion–exclusion pattern**, where every element independently decides its presence in a subset.

Subsets II (Handling Duplicates)

In **Subsets II**, the input set may contain duplicate elements. The goal is to generate all **unique subsets** without repetition.

The main challenge here is **duplicate handling**. If the same value appears multiple times, naive backtracking may generate identical subsets. To avoid this:

- The input is usually **sorted first**.

- During branching, identical elements at the same recursion level are skipped.

This problem teaches the importance of **sorting + controlled branching** for producing only unique combinations.

Permutations (Order-Based Generation)

The **Permutations** problem requires generating all possible orderings of a given set of distinct elements. Unlike subsets, the **order of elements matters** here.

At each level of recursion:

- One unused element is chosen.
- It is marked as used.
- The algorithm proceeds to fill the next position.

After returning from recursion, the element is unmarked (backtracked), while making it available for other permutations.

This problem illustrates:

- Fixing one position at a time
- Tracking used elements with a visited array
- Exploring all factorial-level arrangements systematically

Permutations II (Duplicate Handling)

Permutations II extends the basic permutation problem by allowing duplicate elements in the input. The challenge is to ensure that **duplicate permutations are not generated**.

To solve this:

- The array is first **sorted**.
- A duplicate element is used only if its earlier identical occurrence has already been used at the same recursion level.

This careful control avoids repetition and enforces **lexicographic uniqueness**. It highlights the importance of **both sorting and visited-state tracking** in duplicate-sensitive problems.

Combination Sum Variants

The **Combination Sum** family of problems focuses on finding combinations of numbers that add up to a target value. Backtracking is ideal here because it explores combinations incrementally while pruning paths whose sum already exceeds the target.

Combination Sum I

In **Combination Sum I**, each number may be used **multiple times**. The algorithm chooses a number, reduces the target, and reuses the same number at the next recursion level if needed.

Pruning happens when the remaining target becomes negative. This variant demonstrates **repetition-based branching**.

Combination Sum II

In **Combination Sum II**, each number may be used **only once** and the input may contain duplicates.

To ensure uniqueness:

- The array is sorted.
- Duplicate numbers at the same level are skipped.
- The recursion index is advanced after each choice.

This version blends **subset-style traversal with duplicate handling**.

Palindrome Partitioning

In **Palindrome Partitioning**, a string is divided into substrings such that **every substring in the partition is a palindrome**.

At each position, the algorithm tries every possible prefix. If the prefix is a palindrome, it is added to the current partition. The algorithm then recurses on the remaining string.

If a prefix is not a palindrome, that branch is immediately pruned. This problem highlights how **string validation and backtracking work together** to solve partitioning problems efficiently.

N-Queens Problem

The **N-Queens Problem** asks how to place N queens on an N × N chessboard such that no two queens attack each other.

The algorithm places one queen per row:

- At each row, all columns are tested.
- A queen is placed only if the column and both diagonals are safe.
- If no valid column exists, the algorithm backtracks.

This is a classic example of:

- **Constraint Satisfaction**
- **Heavy Use of Pruning**
- **One Decision per Recursion Level**

The N-Queens problem demonstrates how backtracking scales to large, highly constrained search spaces.

Sudoku Solver

The **Sudoku Solver** fills a 9 × 9 board while respecting three constraints: numbers 1–9 must appear once per row, once per column, and once per 3×3 subgrid.

The algorithm finds an empty cell, tries digits from 1 to 9, checks if placement is valid, recurses to the next empty cell, and backtracks if a conflict occurs.

Sudoku is a real-world example of **depth-first search with constraint propagation**. It shows how backtracking solves practical puzzles efficiently by eliminating invalid paths early.

Techniques and Problem-Solving Patterns

While backtracking problems may appear different in form, most of them follow a small set of powerful logical techniques. These techniques help structure recursive decisions, control branching, eliminate duplicates, and track the current state of the solution. Mastering these patterns allows learners to solve a wide variety of backtracking problems with confidence and consistency.

Inclusion–Exclusion Strategy

The **inclusion–exclusion strategy** is one of the most fundamental backtracking techniques. For every element or choice, the algorithm decides between two possibilities:

- **Include** the element in the current solution.
- **Exclude** the element from the current solution.

This naturally forms a binary recursion tree and is commonly used in problems such as:

- Subset Generation (Power Set)
- Subset Sum
- Decision-Based Combination Problems

At each level of recursion:

- One branch explores the path where the current element is included.
- The other branch explores the path where it is excluded.

This strategy guarantees that **all possible combinations are explored exactly once**. It also provides a clean and intuitive way to express problems that require selecting or skipping elements.

Fixing One Element and Recurring

In this pattern, the algorithm **fixes one position or one element at a time** and then recursively solves the rest of the problem for the remaining elements. Instead of choosing include/exclude, it focuses on **placing elements in a specific order**.

This pattern is widely used in:

- Permutation Generation
- N-Queens Problem
- Arranging Objects under Constraints

For example, in permutations, the first position is fixed by choosing each available element one by one, and the rest of the positions are solved recursively. In N-Queens, one queen is fixed in each row, and the next row is solved using recursion.

This technique simplifies complex arrangements by reducing them to a sequence of smaller placement decisions.

Handling Duplicates with Sorting or Visited Arrays

Duplicate elements in the input can cause **repeated solutions** in backtracking if they are not handled carefully. To ensure that only **unique solutions** are generated, certain control techniques are applied.

The most common approaches are:

- **Sorting the Input First:** Sorting places identical values next to each other, which makes it easier to detect duplicates during branching.
- **Skipping Duplicate Elements at the Same Recursion Level:** If the current choice is the same as the previous one and the previous one was not chosen at this level, the current choice is skipped.
- **Using Visited Arrays:** A Boolean visited array marks which elements have already been used in the current recursive path, which prevents the repeated selection of the same element in the same position.

These techniques are essential for problems such as:

- Subsets II
- Permutations II
- Combination Sum II

Without careful duplicate handling, backtracking would produce redundant results and waste computation time.

Using Auxiliary Space to Track State

Most backtracking problems require **temporary storage** to keep track of the current partial solution and decisions made so far. This auxiliary space helps maintain state across recursive calls.

Common forms of auxiliary space include:

- **Lists or Arrays:** Used to store the current combination, permutation, or partition
- **Boolean Arrays:** Used to indicate whether an element is currently in use (for example, permutations)
- **Frequency Maps or Hash Maps:** Used to track how many times a number or character has been used

This space is continuously updated as the algorithm moves forward and backward:

- When a choice is made, the state is updated.
- When backtracking occurs, the state is restored to its previous form.

This careful state tracking ensures correctness, while allowing for multiple solution paths to be explored independently.

Visualization and Debugging in Backtracking

Backtracking algorithms rely heavily on recursion and systematic exploration of choices. While the logic is powerful, it can be difficult to understand and debug if the flow of execution is not visualized properly. Visualization techniques such as recursion trees and trace tables, along with careful step-by-step dry runs, make backtracking easier to understand, analyze, and correct. Debugging recursive algorithms also requires a different mindset compared to iterative programs.

Drawing Recursion Trees for Tracing

A **recursion tree** is a graphical representation of how a backtracking function explores different choices. Each node in the tree represents a recursive call, and each branch represents a decision made at that call.

When drawing a recursion tree:

- The **root node** represents the initial call with an empty or starting state.
- Each **level** of the tree corresponds to one recursive depth.
- Each **branch** represents a different choice.
- Each **leaf node** represents either a complete, valid solution or a dead-end that was pruned.

Recursion trees help students:

- Clearly see how many paths are being explored.
- Understand where pruning occurs.

- Visualize exponential growth in backtracking problems.
- Trace how the algorithm reaches a solution.

By sketching recursion trees for small inputs, learners can gain a deep intuitive understanding of how backtracking navigates the solution space.

Understanding Recursive Branch Expansion

Recursive branch expansion refers to how new recursive calls are created from existing ones as decisions are made. At each level of recursion:

- A new choice expands the search into a new branch
- The algorithm continues moving deeper until a stopping condition is reached
- Once no further progress is possible, the function returns and the branch collapses

This expansion-and-collapse behavior explains:

- Why does backtracking explore one full path before moving to another?
- How does Depth-First Search (DFS) naturally arise from recursion?
- Why does stack memory grow and shrink during execution?

Understanding branch expansion also helps estimate the **time complexity**, since each additional decision level multiplies the number of possible paths.

Dry-Running Backtracking Problems Step by Step

Dry running means manually simulating the algorithm step by step using small inputs, while writing down:

- The current recursive call
- The partial solution
- The available choices
- The constraint checks
- The points where backtracking happens

For example, while dry-running a subset or permutation problem, students should track:

- Which elements are chosen at each level
- When a solution is added to the result
- When the algorithm returns and removes the last element

Dry running helps in:

- Verifying the correctness of logic
- Detecting missing backtracking steps
- Understanding how and when recursion terminates

It is one of the most effective learning techniques for mastering backtracking.

In real-world **software engineering and system design**, dry-running backtracking algorithms are commonly used during the development of **constraint-based systems**. For example, in **employee shift scheduling systems**, a backtracking algorithm is used to assign shifts while respecting constraints such as availability, labor rules, and skill requirements. By dry-running the algorithm on a small set of employees and shifts, engineers can manually trace how assignments are made, how constraints are checked, and where the algorithm backtracks when a conflict occurs. Similarly, in

configuration engines used in manufacturing or cloud infrastructure, backtracking helps determine valid combinations of components or resources. Dry-running these problems allows developers to verify constraint enforcement, ensure correct backtracking steps, and validate solution completeness before deploying the system at scale. This practice directly mirrors academic backtracking exercises and strengthens confidence in both correctness and efficiency.

Common Debugging Techniques for Recursion

Debugging recursive and backtracking programs requires careful observation of how calls evolve and return. Some effective techniques include:

- **Print the Recursive State:** Display the current partial solution, recursion depth, and input parameters to understand the exact execution path.
- **Indentation-Based Tracing:** Use indentation in debug output to reflect recursion depth, making the execution flow visually clear.
- **Verify Base Cases First:** Incorrect or missing base conditions are the most common cause of infinite recursion or wrong results.
- **Check Backtracking Steps:** Ensure that every change made before a recursive call is properly undone after the return.
- **Test with Small Inputs:** Small datasets reveal logical mistakes quickly without overwhelming output.

By combining visualization with systematic debugging, students can turn complex recursive logic into a transparent and manageable process.

Common Implementation Challenges

While backtracking and recursion are powerful tools for solving complex problems, they can be tricky to implement correctly. Many errors occur not because the overall idea is wrong, but because small details in base cases, state updates, or pruning logic are overlooked. Understanding these common challenges helps learners avoid logical bugs and build reliable backtracking solutions.

Missing or Incorrect Base Cases

The base case is the stopping condition of recursion. If it is missing or wrongly defined, the recursive function may:

- Run indefinitely
- Cause a stack overflow
- Return incorrect results

In backtracking, base cases usually represent:

- A complete, valid solution
- A state where no further choices are possible

For example:

In permutations, the base case occurs when the current list has the same length as the input.

In N-Queens, the base case occurs when all rows have a queen placed. A correct base case must always be **reachable** and must correctly define when recursion should stop.

Failure to Undo State Changes

One of the most common mistakes in backtracking is forgetting to undo changes made to the solution state before returning from a recursive call. Since the same state object (such as a list or array) is reused across multiple recursion paths, failing to reverse a change causes incorrect results.

For example:

In permutation problems, if an element is marked as visited but not unmarked after recursion, it cannot be used again.

In subset generation, if an element is added but not removed after recursion, future subsets become incorrect.

Every "**choose**" step must always be matched with an "**unchoose**" (backtrack) step.

Excessive Recursive Calls Without Pruning

Without pruning, backtracking behaves like brute force and explores **all possible combinations**, even those that are guaranteed to fail. This can make algorithms extremely slow.

Examples of missing pruning:

- Not stopping a combination sum branch when the current sum exceeds the target
- Continuing queen placement even after a diagonal conflict is detected
- Filling Sudoku cells without checking row, column, and grid constraints early

Pruning:

- Eliminates invalid paths early
- Reduces recursion depth and width
- Makes backtracking computationally practical

Inefficient Duplicate Handling

If inputs contain duplicate values and they are not handled carefully, backtracking will generate:

- Redundant solutions
- Large unnecessary recursion trees
- Excessive computation

Common causes include:

- Not sorting the input before starting backtracking
- Not skipping identical values at the same recursion level
- Not using visited or frequency tracking structures

Problems such as Subsets II, Permutations II, and Combination Sum II rely heavily on proper duplicate control. Inefficient duplicate handling can turn manageable problems into time-limit failures.

Practice Exercises

To strengthen their understanding of recursion and backtracking, learners should solve problems that gradually increase in complexity. The following exercises are grouped into basic recursion, generation-based problems, and constraint satisfaction problems for balanced practice and skill development.

Basic Recursion Exercises

These problems focus on understanding recursion flow, base cases, and stack behavior.

- Write a recursive function to print numbers from 1 to n.
- Write a recursive function to compute the sum of the first n natural numbers.
- Find the factorial of a number using recursion.
- Compute the nth Fibonacci number using recursion.
- Write a recursive function to reverse a given string.
- Check whether a given string is a palindrome using recursion.
- Find the power of a number (x^n) using recursion.
- Count the number of digits in a number using recursion.

Subset and Permutation Generation Problems

These exercises strengthen inclusion–exclusion logic, order-based generation, and duplicate handling.

- Generate all subsets (power set) of a given set of integers.
- Generate all unique subsets when the input contains duplicate elements.
- Generate all permutations of a given list of distinct numbers.
- Generate all unique permutations when duplicate values are present.
- Find all combinations of numbers that sum to a given target (Combination Sum I).
- Find all unique combinations that sum to the target using each number at most once (Combination Sum II).
- Partition a given string into all possible palindrome partitions.

Constraint Satisfaction Problems

These problems apply strong pruning, constraint checks, and deep backtracking logic.

- Solve the N-Queens problem for a given value of N.
- Implement a Sudoku solver for a partially filled 9×9 grid.
- Solve the Knight's Tour problem using backtracking.
- Solve the Rat in a Maze problem with blocked and unblocked cells.
- Find all valid paths from the top-left to bottom-right in a grid with obstacles.

These exercises help learners to:

- Build a strong intuition for recursive flow.
- Master inclusion–exclusion and fixed-position strategies.
- Apply pruning and constraint checking effectively.
- Debug and optimize recursive and backtracking programs.

Regular practice with these problems will develop confidence in tackling both interview-level and real-world constraint-based scenarios.

Conclusion

In this chapter, we developed a strong foundation in recursion and backtracking, which are two core techniques that enable systematic exploration of complex solution spaces. Beginning with the fundamentals of recursion, we understood the role of base cases, recursive steps, stack behavior, and tail recursion optimization. Building on this foundation, backtracking was introduced as a powerful extension of recursive thinking. It is capable of solving problems that involve decision branching, constraints, and combinatorial exploration. Through classic problems such as subsets, permutations, combination sum, palindrome partitioning, the N-Queens problem, and Sudoku solving, students learned how solutions are constructed incrementally, invalid paths are pruned early, and the state is carefully tracked and restored using the backtracking template. Visualization using recursion trees, dry-run tracing, and structured debugging methods further strengthened the ability to analyze and correct recursive logic. By mastering these techniques and patterns, learners will be well-equipped to approach a wide range of constraint-based and combinatorial problems with clarity, efficiency, and confidence.

In the upcoming chapter, the focus moves beyond foundational structures into powerful data organizations that re designed for high-performance querying and optimization. We will explore Tries for efficient string matching and prefix searches, Segment Trees and Fenwick Trees for fast range queries and updates, and their real-world applications in competitive programming, frequency analysis, and large-scale data processing. Through comparative analysis, implementation techniques, and debugging strategies for range-based logic, the next chapter will equip learners with advanced tools that dramatically improve both time and space efficiency in complex problem-solving scenarios.

Points to Remember

- Recursion solves problems by reducing them to smaller versions of the same problem.
- Every recursive function must have a **base case** and a **recursive step**.
- Recursive calls are managed using the **call stack**, which follows LIFO order.
- Tail recursion can be optimized in some languages to reduce stack usage.
- Backtracking is an extension of recursion that builds solutions incrementally.
- Backtracking abandons invalid paths early using **pruning**.
- All backtracking problems follow the **`choose - explore - unchoose`** pattern.
- Recursion trees visually represent the entire decision space.
- Constraint checks prevent unnecessary recursive calls.
- Subsets follow the **inclusion-exclusion** strategy.
- Permutations follow the **fix one element and recur** strategy.
- Duplicate handling requires **sorting and visited tracking**.
- The state must always be restored after recursion (backtracking step).
- N-Queens and Sudoku are classic **constraint satisfaction problems**.
- Visualization and dry runs are essential for debugging recursion.

Multiple Choice Questions

1. A recursive function must always contain:
    a. Loop
    b. Base case
    c. Global variable
    d. Sorting

2. The data structure used to manage recursive calls is:
    a. Queue
    b. Stack
    c. Heap
    d. Tree
3. Backtracking mainly follows which traversal strategy?
    a. BFS
    b. DFS
    c. Level Order
    d. Greedy
4. The process of abandoning invalid solution paths is called:
    a. Sorting
    b. Pruning
    c. Hashing
    d. Mapping
5. Tail recursion is a form of recursion where:
    a. Multiple recursive calls are made
    b. Recursive call is the last operation
    c. No base case exists
    d. Stack is unused
6. Subset generation uses which strategy?
    a. Fixing one element
    b. Inclusion–exclusion
    c. Binary search
    d. Heapification
7. Which problem is a pure constraint-satisfaction problem?
    a. Fibonacci
    b. N-Queen
    c. Binary search
    d. Sorting
8. In permutations, elements are usually tracked using:
    a. Stack
    b. Queue
    c. Visited array
    d. Hash map only
9. Failure to undo changes after recursion leads to:
    a. Faster execution
    b. Incorrect results

   c. Reduced space usage
   d. Sorting errors
10. Pruning improves backtracking by:
   a. Increasing recursion depth
   b. Reducing search space
   c. Avoiding recursion
   d. Using iteration
11. Sudoku solving mainly depends on:
   a. Greedy method
   b. Dynamic programming
   c. Backtracking
   d. Sorting
12. The recursion tree is used for:
   a. Memory allocation
   b. Visualizing recursive calls
   c. Hashing
   d. Searching
13. Duplicate handling is best achieved using:
   a. Random selection
   b. Sorting and skipping duplicates
   c. Binary search
   d. Prefix sums
14. Backtracking is mainly used for:
   a. Simple arithmetic
   b. Combinatorial and constraint problems
   c. Sorting lists
   d. File handling
15. Stack overflow occurs due to:
   a. Too many loops
   b. Infinite or deep recursion
   c. Heap overflow
   d. Sorting errors

Answers

1. b
2. b
3. b
4. b
5. b

6. b
7. b
8. c
9. b
10. b
11. c
12. b
13. b
14. b
15. b

Questions

1. Explain recursion with an example. Distinguish between recursion and iteration.
2. Define base case and recursive step. Why are both essential?
3. Explain how the call stack works in recursion.
4. Describe the concept and working of backtracking with a suitable example.
5. Explain the role of pruning in backtracking.
6. Write the logical steps used in the general backtracking template.
7. Explain how permutations are generated using backtracking.
8. Describe the N-Queens problem and explain how backtracking solves it.
9. Explain the Sudoku Solver using the concept of constraint checks.
10. Describe common implementation challenges in backtracking.

Key Terms

- **Recursion:** A technique where a function calls itself to solve smaller parts of a problem
- **Base Case:** The stopping condition of a recursive function
- **Recursive Step:** The part of a recursion that reduces the problem size
- **Call Stack:** A memory structure that stores active function calls
- **Tail Recursion:** Recursion where the recursive call is the last operation
- **Backtracking:** A problem-solving method that explores choices and abandons invalid paths
- **Pruning:** Cutting off invalid branches early in backtracking
- **Recursion Tree:** A visual representation of recursive calls
- **Constraint Checking:** Validating partial solutions against problem rules
- **Subset:** A selection of elements from a set
- **Permutation:** An ordered arrangement of elements
- **Combination Sum:** Forming combinations that add up to a target
- **Palindrome Partitioning:** Dividing a string into palindromic substrings
- **N-Queens Problem:** Placing queens on a chessboard without conflict
- **Sudoku Solver:** Filling a grid while satisfying row, column, and subgrid rules

CHAPTER 14

Advanced Data Structures: Tries, Segment Trees, and Fenwick Trees

Introduction

As real-world applications continue to grow in scale and complexity, the limitations of basic data structures such as arrays, linked lists, stacks, and queues are becoming increasingly apparent. Many modern problems demand not only fast data storage but also **highly efficient querying, updating, and searching over large datasets**. This is where **advanced data structures** play a crucial role. They are specifically designed to optimize performance for complex operations that are impractical to handle using simple structures.

In this chapter, learners will step into the world of powerful non-linear data structures that enable **logarithmic or near-constant time operations** even on massive inputs. The chapter introduces **tries** for efficient string and prefix-based processing, **segment trees** for handling range queries and updates, and **Fenwick trees (binary indexed trees)** for fast prefix sum computation and dynamic frequency management. These structures form the backbone of many high-performance systems such as search engines, auto-complete features, financial analysis platforms, real-time analytics engines, and competitive programming solutions.

Alongside understanding how these structures work internally, students will also learn **when to use each structure**, their **time and space trade-offs**, and the **practical challenges involved in implementing them correctly**. By the end of this chapter, learners will gain the ability to select, implement, and apply advanced data structures effectively to solve large-scale, performance-critical problems with confidence and precision.

Structure

In this chapter, we will cover the following topics:

- Tries
- Segment Trees
- Fenwick Trees
- Co-Relation of Indexing with Tries, Hash Tables, Segment Trees, and Fenwick Trees
- Comparative Analysis of Advanced Data Structures
- Implementation Techniques

- Common Implementation Challenges
- Practice Exercises

Tries

A **trie** (pronounced as "try"), also known as a **prefix tree**, is a special tree-based data structure used to store and retrieve strings efficiently. Unlike hash tables or binary search trees, where the entire key is treated as a single unit, a trie stores characters **one level at a time**. This makes it extremely powerful for prefix-based searching. Tries are widely used in applications that involve dictionaries, autocomplete systems, spell checkers, and text processing.

Structure and Node Representation

A trie is an **m-ary tree**, where each node represents a single character of a string. The root node represents an empty string. Each edge from a node corresponds to one character, and each complete path from the root to a terminal node represents a full word.

Each trie node typically contains the following:

- An array or hash map of child pointers (for next characters)
- A Boolean flag indicating the **end of a word**
- A frequency counter or metadata (optional)

If the alphabet is fixed (just like the lowercase letters of the English language), each node can have up to **26 children**. For larger or dynamic alphabets, hash maps are preferred for flexible storage.

This level-by-level character storage allows tries to support fast prefix queries.

Insertion Operation in Trie

To **insert a word** into a trie:

1. Start from the root node.
2. For each character of the word, make sure that:
    a. A corresponding child node exists.
    b. If it is not present, create a new node.
    c. Move to the next node.
3. After inserting the final character, mark its node as the **end of the word**.

Insertion does **not depend on the number of words in the trie**, only on the **length of the word**. This gives it a time complexity of `O(L)`, where L is the length of the word.

Insertion builds common prefixes only once and saves memory when many words share starting characters.

Search Operation in Trie

To **search for a word** in a trie, follow these steps:

1. Begin at the root.
2. For every character in the word, do the following:
    a. Move to the corresponding child node.
    b. If the required child does not exist at any step, the word is not present.

3. After the last character is processed, consider the following:
    a. If the node is marked as the **end of a word**, the word exists.
    b. Otherwise, it is only a prefix, not a complete word.

Since traversal follows one character per level, the search operation also takes **O(L)** time. This predictable time performance is a major advantage of using tries instead of hashing in prefix-heavy applications.

Deletion Operation in Trie

Deletion in a trie is more complex because nodes may be shared among multiple words. The algorithm does the following:

- Traverses the word character by character
- After reaching the end of the word, it unmarks the **end-of-word** flag.
- Removes nodes **only if they are not part of any other word**

Backtracking is used to safely delete unused nodes without affecting other words. Proper deletion ensures that memory is freed only when a character is no longer needed by any word in the trie.

Applications of Tries

Tries are designed for **fast string operations**, especially when prefix searching is required. They are widely used in both system-level and user-facing applications.

Autocomplete Systems

Autocomplete features in search engines and mobile keyboards use tries to:

- Store a large dictionary of words.
- Display all words matching a given prefix instantly.
- Rank suggestions based on frequency or priority.

As the user types each letter, the trie moves one level down and retrieves all valid continuations efficiently.

Dictionary Matching

Tries are heavily used in:

- Spell Checkers
- Word Games
- Text Analyzers
- Plagiarism Detection

They allow users to rapidly validate if a word exists in a dictionary. Tries also support efficient prefix-based word matching.

Trie Implementation Using an Array

In this implementation:

- Each node contains a **fixed-size array** of length equal to the alphabet size (for example, 26 for lowercase letters).
- Child access is done using index calculations such as `index = char - 'a'`.

Advantages:

- Rapid Access Time
- Simple Implementation
- Predictable Memory Layout

Disadvantages:

- It uses a lot of memory when many child pointers are unused.
- It is not suitable for large or dynamic alphabets.

This approach is ideal when:

- Alphabet size is small and fixed.
- Speed is a priority.

Trie Implementation Using Hash Map

In this implementation:

- Each node contains a **fixed-size array** of length equal to the alphabet size (for example, 26 for lowercase letters).
- Child access is done using index calculations such as `index = char - 'a'`.

The advantages of hash map implementation include:

- Fast Access Time
- Simple Implementation
- Predictable Memory Layout

The disadvantages are as follows:

- Hash map implementation uses a lot of memory when many child pointers are unused.
- It is not suitable for large or dynamic alphabets.

This approach is ideal when:

- Alphabet size is small and fixed.
- Speed is a priority.

Compressed Tries and Suffix Tries

A **compressed trie**, which is also called a **radix tree**, reduces memory usage by:

- Merging chains of single-child nodes into a single edge labeled with multiple characters
- Reducing tree height
- Improving cache performance

A **suffix trie** stores all suffixes of a given string and is used in:

- Fast Substring Search
- Pattern Matching
- DNA Sequence Analysis

While these structures are more advanced and memory-intensive, they can greatly improve performance in string matching problems. At this introductory level, students only need to understand their purpose and use cases, instead of the full implementation details.

Segment Trees

Segment trees are powerful tree-based data structures designed to efficiently handle **range query problems** where repeated queries and updates are performed on an array. When direct array processing becomes too slow for large inputs, a segment tree provides a highly optimized way to perform these operations in **logarithmic time**. They are widely used in competitive programming, data analytics, gaming systems, and real-time applications.

Introduction to Range Query Problems

A **range query problem** involves performing repeated queries on a continuous portion (range) of an array. These queries may ask for:

- The **sum** of elements in a range.
- The **minimum or maximum** value in a range.
- The **count** of values satisfying a condition.
- The result after **updating** the values in the array.

For example:

- Find the sum of elements from index l to r.
- Find the minimum value between positions i and j.
- Update a value at a given index and reflect it in future queries.

A naive approach scans the array every time, while taking **O(n)** per query. If there are many queries, this becomes inefficient. Segment trees solve this problem by preprocessing the data into a structure that allows for **fast querying and rapid updates**.

Segment Tree: Structure and Representation

A **segment tree** is a **binary tree** where:

- Each node represents a **range of indices.**
- The root represents the entire array.
- Each internal node represents a sub-range.
- Leaf nodes represent individual array elements.

For an array of size n:

- The total number of nodes is at most **4n.**
- The tree height is **O(log n).**

Each node stores:

- A value based on the query type (sum, minimum, maximum, and so on).
- Pointers to its left and right child (or stored in an array using indexing).

The structure enables the array to be split into segments recursively. This allows for range queries to be resolved by combining only a few relevant nodes instead of scanning the entire range.

Segment Tree Construction (Build Process)

The segment tree is constructed by recursively dividing the array into smaller segments until each segment contains exactly one element. The process begins with the root node representing the full array range and continues by splitting each range into two halves.

The construction procedure is as follows:

Begin with the complete range `[0, n-1]`.

Compute the midpoint of the current range.

Recursively construct the left child for the left half.

Recursively construct the right child for the right half.

After both children are built, compute the value of the parent node by combining the values of its children (for example, summing them in a range-sum tree).

When the start and end indices become equal, a leaf node is created that stores the corresponding array element.

Since each node is processed only once during construction, the total time required to build the segment tree is **O(n)**.

Range Query Operations

Once constructed, the segment tree can answer queries efficiently. A **range query** follows three rules at every node. These rules are:

- **Complete Overlap:** If the node's range lies completely inside the query range, return the node's stored value.
- **No Overlap:** If the node's range lies completely outside the query range, return a neutral value (0 for sum, ∞ for minimum, -∞ for maximum).
- **Partial Overlap**

  Query both children recursively and combine their results.

Since each query only explores at most `O(log n)` branches, the total query time will be `O(log n)`.

Update Operations in Segment Trees

Two types of updates are commonly performed and are mentioned as follows:

- **Point Update:** Updating a single element
- **Range Update:** Updating all elements in a range

For a **point update**:

- The algorithm traverses from the root to the leaf corresponding to the index.
- The value is updated.
- All ancestor nodes are recomputed on the way back up.

Point updates take `O(log n)` time.

However, range updates become inefficient without optimization, which can result in the concept of lazy propagation.

Lazy Propagation Technique

Lazy propagation is a powerful optimization used when **range updates** are frequent.

Instead of immediately updating all values in a range:

- The update is **delayed** and stored in a separate **lazy array.**
- The actual update is applied **only when that segment is needed.**

- Pending updates are passed down to child nodes when required.

This avoids unnecessary repeated updates and ensures that:

- **Range updates run in `O(log n)`** time.
- **Queries still run in `O(log n)`** time.

Lazy propagation is essential for problems involving:

- Repeated Increment/Decrement of Ranges
- Bulk Modifications of Values
- Real-Time Data Adjustments

Applications of Segment Trees

Segment trees are used wherever **fast range queries and frequent updates must be handled together on large datasets**. Many real-world systems require repeated querying over intervals while data continues to change dynamically. A simple array becomes inefficient in such cases; however, a segment tree ensures that both **queries and updates are processed in logarithmic time**, even for very large inputs. This makes Segment Trees extremely valuable in performance-critical applications.

Range Sum Queries

Range sum queries involve calculating the **sum of elements between two given indices** multiple times. Without a segment tree, each query would require scanning the array, which would eventually result in poor performance.

By using a segment tree:

- Partial sums of different ranges are precomputed and stored.
- Only the relevant segments are combined to produce the answer.
- The query is resolved in `O(log n)` time instead of `O(n)`.

Real-world use cases include:

- Financial systems for calculating total transactions within a time range.
- Sensor networks for computing cumulative measurements.
- Game scoring systems for real-time score tracking.
- Analytics dashboards for processing large datasets quickly.

Thus, segment trees make repeated sum calculations both **accurate and fast**.

Range Minimum and Maximum Queries

In many applications, it is necessary to determine the **smallest or largest value within a given range**. Segment trees efficiently support these queries by storing the minimum or maximum value at each node of the tree.

With segment trees:

- The minimum or maximum value in any subrange can be found in `O(log n)` time.
- The structure remains efficient even after updates.

Common applications include:

- Weather analysis systems to detect the lowest and highest temperatures.
- Stock market analysis to track price fluctuations in time windows.

- Gaming systems for ranking players dynamically.
- Competitive programming tasks requiring fast Range Minimum Query (RMQ).

This makes segment trees ideal for **real-time monitoring and decision-making systems.**

Range Update Problems

Range update problems involve modifying **all elements within a given range**. Examples include adding a value to every element in a segment or replacing values within a range. Performing such updates directly on an array is often slow for large inputs.

Using segment trees with **lazy propagation includes the following**:

- The update is applied only when needed.
- Large range modifications are performed in `O(log n)` time.
- Repeated unnecessary updates are avoided.

Practical use cases include:

- Salary increments for employees within a pay grade range
- Applying discounts to product price ranges
- Bulk updates in database indexing systems
- Terrain height updates in simulation and gaming engines

Lazy propagation allows these massive updates to remain **computationally efficient and memory-safe**.

Fenwick Trees

A **Fenwick tree**, also known as a **Binary Indexed Tree (BIT)**, is a specialized data structure used to efficiently handle **prefix sum queries and point updates on an array**. It offers a balance between simplicity and performance, as it provides faster operations than a normal array while using significantly less memory than a segment tree. Fenwick trees are especially popular in competitive programming and real-time data processing tasks where cumulative values are frequently queried and updated.

Structure and Core Intuition

A Fenwick tree is implemented using a **single array**, but it internally represents a clever tree-like structure using **binary indexing**. Each index of the BIT stores the sum of a specific range of elements from the original array.

The key ideas behind Fenwick trees are:

- Each index is responsible for a **fixed-size block of values.**
- The size of this block is determined by the **Rightmost Set Bit (LSB)** of the index.
- Parent-child relationships are derived using bit manipulation.

This binary partitioning allows the data structure to:

- Aggregate partial sums efficiently.
- Jump across relevant segments quickly during queries and updates.

Unlike segment trees, Fenwick trees do **not explicitly build a tree structure**; the entire logic is embedded into index manipulation within a single array.

Point Updates in Fenwick Trees

A **point update** means changing the value at a single index and ensuring that all relevant prefix sums are updated accordingly.

When a value at index i is updated:

- The difference between the new and old values is calculated.
- This difference is added to `BIT[i]`.
- The update is propagated to all higher indices that cover this index.

The movement follows this pattern:

```
i = i + (i & -i)
```

This update process ensures that every prefix segment that depends on index i is correctly adjusted. The time complexity of a point update in a Fenwick tree is `O(log n)`, which makes it highly efficient even for large datasets.

Prefix Sum Queries Using BIT

The primary strength of a Fenwick tree lies in handling **prefix sum queries** efficiently. A prefix sum query computes the total of elements from index 1 to i.

To compute a prefix sum:

- Initialize a result variable.
- Add the value stored at `BIT[i]` to the result.
- Move to the parent index using:

  ```
  i = i - (i & -i)
  ```
- Repeat until i becomes zero.

This process jumps through only the necessary indices that contribute to the sum, while avoiding unnecessary traversal.

The time complexity of prefix sum queries is `O(log n)`, which is a dramatic improvement over the `O(n)` time required by simple arrays.

Difference Between Segment Tree and Fenwick Tree

Although both segment trees and Fenwick trees are used for range queries and updates, they differ in structure, flexibility, and performance trade-offs.

Aspect	Fenwick Tree (BIT)	Segment Tree
Structure	Single array	Explicit tree
Memory Usage	Low (O(n))	Higher (O(4n))
Query Type	Prefix sums only	Any associative range query
Updates	Point updates fast	Point + range updates
Lazy Propagation	Not supported	Supported
Implementation	Simple	More complex
Range Queries	Indirect via prefix sums	Direct

Table 14.1: *Differences between Segment Trees and Fenwick Trees*

Fenwick trees are preferred when:

- Only prefix sums or simple cumulative queries are needed.
- Memory usage must be minimal.
- Implementation simplicity is important.

Segment trees are preferred when:

- Multiple query types are required (min, max, gcd, and so on).
- Range updates are common.
- More complex querying logic is needed.

Applications of Fenwick Trees

Fenwick Trees are ideal for applications where **cumulative information must be updated and queried repeatedly in real time**. Their low memory footprint and fast performance make them suitable for large-scale systems.

Cumulative Frequency Arrays

Fenwick Trees are widely used to maintain **frequency counts** where values change dynamically. They allow for:

- Fast updates when an item count changes
- Fast computation of cumulative frequencies up to a given index

Common use cases include:

- Inventory Management Systems
- Online Polling Systems
- Event Counting in Real-Time Applications
- Histogram Processing in Data Analytics

With Fenwick Trees, frequency updates and cumulative queries remain efficient even for very large datasets.

Inversion Count in Arrays

An **inversion** is a pair of indices `(i, j)` such that `i < j` and `arr[i] > arr[j]`. Counting inversions is a classic problem in algorithm design.

However, when we use Fenwick trees:

- The array elements are processed in order.
- For each element, the number of smaller elements already processed is queried.

Thus, the Fenwick tree stores frequency information dynamically.

Each update and query runs in `O(log n)` time.

This reduces the overall inversion counting complexity from $O(n^2)$ to `O(n log n)`, which makes it practical for large arrays.

Co-Relation of Indexing with Tries, Hash Tables, Segment Trees, and Fenwick Trees

Indexing is a fundamental concept that enables fast data retrieval by organizing data in a structured and searchable form. Different data structures implement indexing in ways that suit specific access patterns and query types. **Tries** provide character-level indexing, while allowing for efficient prefix-based searches commonly used in dictionaries and autocomplete systems. **Hash tables** use key-based indexing through hash functions to offer near constant-time access for exact lookups, which make them ideal for caches and symbol tables. **Segment trees** and **Fenwick trees (Binary Indexed Trees)** implement index-based hierarchical structures that support efficient range queries and updates, such as range sums, minimums, or frequency counts. While tries and hash tables focus on fast point lookups and prefix queries, segment and Fenwick trees extend indexing to handle dynamic range-based operations efficiently. Together, these structures demonstrate how indexing strategies are adapted to different problem requirements, while balancing speed, memory usage, and query flexibility in real-world systems.

Comparative Analysis of Advanced Data Structures

Advanced data structures such as **tries, hash maps, segment trees, and Fenwick trees** are designed to solve specific categories of problems efficiently. While each of these structures improves performance over basic arrays and lists, their strengths, limitations, memory usage, and application scenarios are very different. A careful comparison helps students choose the **apt structure for the right problem**, which is a crucial skill to master in both interviews and real-world system design.

Tries versus Hash Maps

Both **tries** and **hash maps** are used for fast data retrieval, especially in dictionary-like applications, but they differ significantly in how they store and search data.

A **trie** stores data **character by character** in a tree-like structure. Each path from the root to a node represents a prefix, and complete words end at terminal nodes. A **hash map**, on the other hand, stores each key as a whole and uses a **hash function** to directly map the key to a memory location.

The key differences in their respective behaviors are as follows:

- **Search Mechanism:** Tries perform searches by traversing characters level by level, whereas hash maps use a hash function for direct access.
- **Prefix Searching:** Tries naturally support prefix-based operations such as autocomplete and word prediction. Hash maps do not support prefix searching efficiently without extra processing.
- **Time Complexity:** Trie operations run in `O(L)` time, where L is the word length. Hash maps provide `average O(1)` time but can degrade under collisions.
- **Memory Usage:** Tries tend to use more memory due to multiple node references, whereas hash maps are generally more compact.
- **Ordering:** Tries maintain lexicographical order naturally, while hash maps do not preserve any order.

When to Use Each:

- Use a **trie** when prefix searching, word suggestions, and dictionary operations are required.
- Use a **hash map** when fast direct lookups are needed without prefix relationships.

Segment Tree versus Fenwick Tree

Both **segment trees** and **Fenwick trees (BITs)** are used for range query problems, but they differ in flexibility, memory usage, and complexity.

A **segment tree** is a full binary tree where each node stores information about a specific range of the array. A **Fenwick tree** is implemented using a single array with binary indexing to store cumulative information.

Key Differences in Behavior:

- **Query Types:** Segment trees support a wide variety of range queries, such as **sum, minimum, maximum, GCD**, and more. Fenwick Trees are mainly designed for **prefix sum queries**.
- **Updates:** Segment trees handle both **point updates and range updates** efficiently through lazy propagation. Fenwick trees mainly support **point updates**.
- **Memory Usage:** Segment trees require more memory (up to **4n**), while Fenwick trees use only **n** memory.
- **Implementation:** Segment trees are more complex to implement. Fenwick trees are simpler and easier to code.
- **Performance:** Both structures perform operations in `O(log n)` time, but Fenwick trees have smaller constant factors.

When to Use Each:

- Use a **segment tree** when multiple query types and range updates are required.
- Use a **Fenwick tree** when only prefix sums and point updates are needed with minimal memory.

Space and Time Complexity Comparison

This comparison in *Table* 14.2 clearly shows that:

- Tries trade memory for prefix efficiency.
- Hash maps trade prefix support for speed and compactness.
- Segment trees trade memory for flexibility.
- Fenwick trees trade flexibility for simplicity and space efficiency.

Data Structure	Primary Operations	Time Complexity	Space Complexity
Trie	Insert, Search, Delete	`O(L)`	High
Hash Map	Insert, Search, Delete	`O(1) avg`	Moderate
Segment Tree	Range Query, Range Update	`O(log n)`	`O(4n)`
Fenwick Tree	Prefix Sum, Point Update	`O(log n)`	`O(n)`

Table 14.2: *Space and Time Complexity*

Real-World Problem Categories and Use Cases

Each advanced data structure is designed to excel in specific problem domains. Therefore, we have elaborated their respective use cases in this section.

Tries are used in:

- Autocomplete Systems in Search Engines

- Spell Checkers in Text Editors
- Dictionary Word Lookup Systems
- DNA Sequence Matching
- IP Routing and Network Prefix Matching

Hash maps are used in:

- Caching Systems
- Frequency Counting
- Database Indexing
- Session Management
- Duplicate Detection Problems

Segment trees are used in:

- Financial Analytics for Range-Based Calculations
- Gaming Engines for Score Tracking
- Signal Processing Systems
- Time-Series Data Analysis
- Competitive Programming Problems Involving Range Queries

Fenwick trees are used in:

- Online Polling Systems
- Cumulative Frequency Analysis
- Inversion Counting in Arrays
- Rating Systems
- Real-Time Statistical Updates

Implementation Techniques

Implementing advanced data structures such as **tries, segment trees, and Fenwick trees** requires more than just understanding their theory. Proper construction methods, correct index handling, efficient memory layout, and reliable debugging practices are essential to ensure that these structures work accurately and efficiently in real-world programs. This section focuses on the most important practical techniques that are used while implementing these advanced structures.

Recursive and Bottom-Up Construction Methods

Advanced tree-based data structures are commonly built using either a **recursive approach** or a **bottom-up approach**. The choice of method depends on the nature of the structure and the problem.

Recursive Construction

Recursive construction is widely used in **segment trees and tries**. The problem is divided into smaller subproblems, and the tree is built by repeatedly calling a function on smaller segments or prefixes.

In **segment trees**, recursion is used to divide the array into two halves until leaf nodes are formed.

In **tries**, recursion is often used to insert characters one by one into deeper levels of the tree.

Advantages of recursive construction include:

- Closely follows the logical structure of trees
- Easy to understand and implement
- Matches naturally with divide-and-conquer thinking

Disadvantages of recursive construction include:

- Uses additional stack memory
- May cause a stack overflow for very deep recursion, if not handled carefully

Bottom-Up Construction

Bottom-up construction is commonly used in **Fenwick trees and some iterative segment tree implementations**. Instead of recursion, values are inserted directly into an array structure and combined iteratively.

In a Fenwick tree, values are placed and propagated using bit manipulation. In bottom-up segment trees, leaf nodes are filled first, and parent nodes are built iteratively.

Advantages of bottom-up construction include:

- Memory Efficiency
- Rapid Speed due to the Avoidance of Recursion
- No Risk of Stack Overflow

Disadvantages of bottom-up construction include:

- Less Intuitive Logic
- Harder to Visualize than Recursive Construction

Both methods are correct and efficient when used appropriately.

Index Manipulation Techniques

Index manipulation is a **core skill** in implementing advanced data structures efficiently, especially for **segment trees and Fenwick trees**. Many operations depend on precise index movement rather than explicit pointers.

In segment trees:

Parent and child nodes are typically stored using index relationships such as:

```
Left child → 2 * i
Right child → 2 * i + 1
```

Proper mid-point calculation ensures the correct division of ranges.

Careful handling of low, high, and mid indices prevents incorrect tree construction.

In Fenwick trees:

Index movement is controlled using the **Least Significant Bit (LSB), as shown here**:

Update: `i = i + (i & -i)`

Query: `i = i - (i & -i)`

These bitwise operations allow fast traversal to parent and child blocks without explicitly storing a tree.

Correct index manipulation looks like:

- Ensuring accurate query results
- Preventing infinite loops
- Avoiding memory access errors
- Improving execution speed

Even a small mistake in index calculation can lead to incorrect outputs or runtime errors, which make this a critical implementation skill.

Tree Flattening Concepts

Tree flattening is a technique that converts a hierarchical tree structure into a **linear array representation** while preserving parent–child relationships. This concept is particularly useful in:

- Segment Trees
- Binary Trees
- Heavy–Light Decomposition (Advanced Applications)

In segment trees:

- Flattening allows the tree to be stored efficiently in a single array.
- It improves cache performance.
- It simplifies memory management.

Therefore, flattened trees:

- Enable faster access using array indexing.
- Reduce pointer overhead.
- Make iterative implementations possible.

Flattening is also useful while:

- Applying range queries on trees
- Performing subtree operations
- Combining multiple data structures with array-based representations

Although tree flattening is mostly hidden in standard implementations, understanding this idea helps learners write programs that are more memory-efficient and scalable.

Debugging Range Query Logic

Debugging range query structures such as segment trees and Fenwick trees requires a **careful and systematic approach**. This is because errors are often silent and produce incorrect results rather than crashes.

Common debugging techniques include:

- **Print the Internal Tree/Array:** Printing the internal structure after construction helps verify if values are placed correctly.
- **Test with Small Input Sizes:** Small datasets allow for step-by-step verification of queries and updates.
- **Verify Base Conditions Carefully:** Incorrect base ranges often lead to wrong aggregation results.

- **Check Overlap Conditions in Queries:** Ensure that the logic for full overlap, partial overlap, and no overlap is implemented correctly.
- **Validate after Each Update:** After a point or range update, re-run simple queries to confirm correctness.
- **Compare with Brute-Force Results:** For small inputs, always confirm segment tree or BIT results with direct array computation.

Debugging these structures improves logical accuracy and will help you build confidence in handling real test cases and competitive programming environments.

Common Implementation Challenges

Advanced data structures such as **tries, segment trees, and Fenwick trees** provide powerful performance benefits, but their implementations are often error-prone. Most issues arise not from misunderstanding the overall concept, but from small mistakes in indexing, boundary handling, update propagation, or memory management. Recognizing these challenges early on helps learners write correct, efficient, and reliable implementations.

Incorrect Index Mapping

One of the most frequent sources of errors in advanced data structures is **incorrect index mapping**. Since many structures rely heavily on array-based representations, even a small indexing mistake can lead to wrong query results or runtime failures.

Common causes include:

- Confusion between **0-based and 1-based indexing**
- Using incorrect parent-child index formulas in tree structures
- Mistakes in midpoint calculation during segment tree construction
- Incorrect bit manipulation in Fenwick trees

For example:

In segment trees, not using **`2*i`** and **`2*i+1`** correctly can break the entire tree structure. In Fenwick trees, a wrong update or query step (**`i & -i`**) can result in infinite loops or incorrect prefix sums.

Therefore, careful index planning, consistent indexing style, and repeated verification with small test cases are essential to prevent such errors.

Boundary Errors in Range Queries

Boundary errors occur when the limits of a query range are handled incorrectly. These mistakes are subtle, but they can significantly affect the correctness of outputs.

Typical boundary-related issues include:

- Using incorrect lower and upper limits in queries
- Off-by-one errors in inclusive and exclusive ranges
- Failing to handle edge cases such as single-element ranges
- Incorrect handling of full overlap, partial overlap, and no-overlap conditions in segment trees

For instance, a query intended to process elements from index `l` to `r` may return incorrect results, if either `l` or `r` is shifted by one position. Such errors are especially common during competitive programming, where fast coding increases the risk of oversight.

Thorough dry runs and test cases involving boundary values are necessary to detect and fix these mistakes.

Lazy Propagation Mistakes

Lazy propagation is an advanced optimization technique used in segment trees for efficient range updates. However, it is also one of the most complex parts to implement correctly.

Common lazy propagation errors include:

- Forgetting to propagate the pending update to child nodes
- Applying the lazy value multiple times
- Failing to clear the lazy flag after propagation
- Mixing up update and query operations

These mistakes can cause:

- Incorrect Query Results
- Accumulation of Outdated Updates
- Inconsistent Tree Values

Since lazy propagation defers updates intentionally, its correctness depends entirely on precise logic. Debugging such errors is often difficult without systematic testing and clear tracking of update states.

Memory Overhead Issues

Advanced data structures often trade **memory for speed**, which can become problematic when memory usage is not carefully controlled.

Typical memory-related challenges include:

- Over-allocating arrays for segment trees (for example, using excessively large fixed-size arrays)
- Inefficient node storage in tries, when many child pointers are unused
- Storing redundant information at each node
- Using heavy recursion that increases stack memory usage

In memory-constrained environments such as embedded systems or competitive programming platforms, poor memory management can cause:

- Program Crashes
- Time-Limit or Memory-Limit Exceeded Errors
- Reduced Overall Efficiency

To manage memory effectively:

- Dynamic memory allocation and hash map-based tries should be preferred wherever appropriate.
- Tree sizes should be calculated carefully.
- Recursive depth should be monitored.

Practice Exercises

Practice is essential for mastering advanced data structures such as **tries, segment trees, and Fenwick trees**. The following exercises are carefully organized from concept-building to interview-level complexity. Solving these problems will help learners strengthen implementation skills, debugging ability, and algorithmic confidence.

Trie-Based Practice Problems

These problems focus on string processing, prefix searching, and dictionary-based applications.

- Implement a trie that supports insertion and search for lowercase words.
- Design an autocomplete system using a trie that suggests words based on a given prefix.
- Implement a trie to check whether a word exists in a dictionary.
- Count how many words in the trie share a given prefix.
- Implement the deletion of a word from a trie.
- Store a set of contact names and print all the contacts that match a search prefix.
- Implement a spell checker using a trie.
- Find the longest common prefix among a set of strings using a trie.
- Implement a trie that supports both uppercase and lowercase English letters.
- Insert a list of words and count how many distinct words are stored in the trie.

Segment Tree Practice Problems

These exercises aim to strengthen your understanding of range queries, point updates, and lazy propagation.

- Build a segment tree to answer range sum queries on an integer array.
- Implement a segment tree to find the minimum value in a given range.
- Implement a segment tree to find the maximum value in a range.
- Perform point updates and verify updated range sums.
- Implement lazy propagation for range increment updates.
- Perform range update and range sum query using a lazy segment tree.
- Solve the Range Minimum Query (RMQ) problem using a segment tree.
- Given a time-series dataset, support queries for sum and updates for corrections.
- Implement a segment tree for counting even and odd numbers in a range.
- Solve range XOR queries using a segment tree.

Fenwick Tree Practice Problems

These problems will help you develop a strong command over prefix sums and fast updates using BIT.

- Implement a Fenwick tree for prefix sum queries.
- Support point updates and prefix sum queries using BIT.
- Find the cumulative frequency of elements in a dynamic dataset using BIT.
- Count the number of inversions in an array using a Fenwick tree.

- Solve range sum queries using BIT.
- Process online update and query operations on an array using BIT.
- Maintain a frequency table for a voting system using BIT.
- Implement BIT to support prefix maximum queries (conceptual).
- Solve the dynamic range sum query problem using BIT.
- Track score updates in a live competition using BIT.

Mixed Advanced Data Structure Problems

These problems require selecting and combining the right advanced data structure.

- Implement an autocomplete system using a trie and rank suggestions by frequency.
- Use a segment tree to solve a stock price range analysis problem.
- Use BIT to maintain and query leaderboard scores efficiently.
- Design a system to insert words and query prefix matches dynamically.
- Combine BIT and hashing to solve a dynamic frequency update problem.
- Process millions of range updates and query operations efficiently.
- Implement a real-time analytics engine using segment trees.
- Use a trie for IP address routing simulation.
- Solve a dynamic inversion counting problem with updates.
- Design a dictionary and prefix search system with fast lookup and updates.

Conclusion

In this chapter, we explored the world of **advanced data structures**, as we moved from the limitations of basic linear and hierarchical structures to powerful tools designed for high-performance computing. Through **tries**, students learned how modern applications efficiently handle prefix-based searching, autocomplete systems, and dictionary matching. With **segment trees**, they gained the ability to process complex range queries and updates efficiently on very large datasets, while using techniques such as lazy propagation. **Fenwick trees (Binary Indexed Trees, or BITs)** introduced a lighter yet highly effective structure for handling prefix sums and dynamic frequency operations. Alongside these structures, learners also understood their comparative strengths, implementation techniques, common pitfalls, and real-world applicability. By the end of this chapter, students will be equipped with a deep understanding of how advanced data structures enable fast, scalable, and reliable solutions in performance-critical systems.

With this strong foundation in place, the book now moves to its final and most practical phase in *Chapter 15: Applied* DSA *Patterns and* STL. This upcoming chapter brings together everything learned so far and focuses on **how to apply these concepts effectively in real problem-solving scenarios**. Learners will master widely used **algorithmic patterns** such as Two Pointers, Sliding Window, Prefix Sums, Binary Search on Answer, Greedy methods, and Bit Manipulation. The chapter also provides a comprehensive guide to the **C++ Standard Template Library (STL)** and essential **Python built-in utilities**, enabling students to write clean, efficient, and industry-ready code. With hands-on case studies, mock interview problems, and time-space trade-off analysis, the next chapter serves as the perfect bridge between theoretical DSA knowledge and real-world programming excellence.

Points to Remember

Tries store strings character by character and are ideal for prefix-based searching.

- Trie operations (insert, search, delete) run in `O(L)` time, where L is word length.
- Segment trees efficiently solve **range queries and update problems** in logarithmic time.
- Segment trees use a **divide-and-combine** tree structure over array segments.
- Lazy propagation optimizes **range updates** in segment trees.
- Fenwick trees (BITs) efficiently handle **prefix sum queries and point updates**.
- BITs use **binary index manipulation** for fast traversal.
- Segment trees are more flexible than BITs, but they use more memory.
- Fenwick trees are simpler and more memory-efficient than segment trees.
- Tries consume higher memory due to multi-child node representation.
- Advanced data structures trade **memory for speed**.
- Correct index mapping is critical in tree-based implementations.
- Boundary handling errors are a common source of incorrect outputs.
- Advanced data structures are widely used in **real-time analytics and competitive programming**.
- Choosing the right structure depends on **query type, update type, and data size**.

Multiple Choice Questions

1. A Trie stores data based on:
   a. Hash Values
   b. Prefix Structure
   c. Binary Indexing
   d. Tree Height
2. Time complexity of search in a Trie is:
   a. `O(1)`
   b. `O(log n)`
   c. `O(L)`
   d. `O(n)`
3. Segment Trees are mainly used for:
   a. Sorting
   b. Range Queries and Updates
   c. Graph Traversal
   d. Pattern Matching
4. Lazy propagation is used to optimize:
   a. Point Updates
   b. Range Updates
   c. Trie Insertion
   d. BIT Construction

5. Fenwick Trees efficiently support:
   a. Full Range Minimum Queries
   b. Prefix Sum Queries
   c. String Matching
   d. Graph Connectivity
6. BIT operations are based on:
   a. Recursion
   b. Hashing
   c. Binary Index Manipulation
   d. Queue Traversal
7. Which of the following structures supports prefix searching naturally?
   a. Hash Map
   b. Segment Tree
   c. Trie
   d. Fenwick Tree
8. Memory usage of a Segment Tree is approximately:
   a. n
   b. 2n
   c. 4n
   d. n^2
9. Which of the following structures is lighter when it comes to memory usage?
   a. Segment Tree
   b. Fenwick Tree
   c. Trie
   d. Graph
10. Inversion counting can be efficiently solved using:
    a. Trie
    b. Stack
    c. Fenwick Tree
    d. Queue
11. Range Minimum Query is best solved using:
    a. Stack
    b. Queue
    c. Segment Tree
    d. Array
12. Trie deletion is complex due to:
    a. Multiple Root Nodes
    b. Shared Node Prefixes

   c. Binary Conflicts
   d. Hash Collisions
13. Which of the following updates are efficiently supported by BIT?
   a. Range Updates
   b. Point Updates
   c. String Updates
   d. Graph Updates
14. Prefix sum computation in BIT runs in:
   a. `O(n)`
   b. `O(n log n)`
   c. `O(log n)`
   d. `O(1)`
15. Which of the following structures is the best choice for autocomplete systems?
   a. Hash Map
   b. Segment Tree
   c. Trie
   d. Fenwick Tree

Answers

1. b
2. c
3. b
4. b
5. b
6. c
7. c
8. c
9. b
10. c
11. c
12. b
13. b
14. c
15. c

Questions

1. Explain the structure and working of a trie with a suitable example.
2. Describe insertion, search, and deletion operations in a trie.
3. Explain the concept of range query problems and the need for segment trees.

4. Describe the construction of a segment tree, as well as its time complexity.
5. Explain how range queries are processed using a segment tree.
6. What is lazy propagation? Explain its importance.
7. Describe the structure and working of a Fenwick tree.
8. Explain prefix sum computation using a Fenwick tree.
9. Compare segment trees and Fenwick trees.
10. Discuss the common implementation challenges that surface while dealing with advanced data structures.

Key Terms

- **Trie:** A prefix-based tree structure used for efficient string storage and searching
- **Prefix Tree:** Another name for Trie that highlights prefix-based traversal
- **Segment Tree:** A tree structure used to answer range queries efficiently
- **Range Query:** A query performed on a continuous segment of an array
- **Lazy Propagation:** A technique to delay range updates for efficiency
- **Fenwick Tree:** A tree-based array structure for prefix sums and point updates
- **Binary Indexed Tree (BIT):** An alternate name for Fenwick tree
- **Prefix Sum:** Sum of elements from index 1 to a given index
- **Point Update:** Updating a single index value in a data structure
- **Range Update:** Updating multiple values within a specified range
- **Inversion:** A pair of elements where the left value is greater than the right value
- **Autocomplete:** A feature that suggests words based on prefix input
- **Hash Map:** A key-value data structure using hashing for fast lookup
- **Index Manipulation:** A technique of using index calculations for tree traversal
- **Tree Flattening:** Conversion of a tree structure into an array representation

Chapter 15
Applied DSA Patterns and Standard Template Library

Introduction

After building strong foundations in Data Structures and Algorithms (DSA) in the previous chapters, learners will now move into the most practical and application-oriented phase of their journey. In real programming, competitive coding, and technical interviews, problems rarely appear as isolated algorithmic concepts. Instead, they demand intelligent use of **established problem-solving patterns** and **efficient libraries** that can translate logic into fast, reliable code. This chapter focuses on widely used applied DSA patterns such as two pointers, sliding window, prefix sums, greedy with sorting, and binary search on answer. Learning about these patterns is crucial, as they repeatedly appear in real-world problem solving scenarios. Alongside these patterns, the chapter introduces the power of the **C++ Standard Template Library (STL)** and essential **Python built-ins**, which allow programmers to write clean, optimized, and expressive code with minimal effort. Through hands-on reinforcement, mock interview problems, and a guided mini project, this chapter bridges the gap between theoretical DSA learning and professional-level coding practice.

Structure

In this chapter, we will cover the following topics:

- Problem-Solving Patterns
- The Two-Pointer Technique
- The Sliding Window Technique
- Prefix Sum and Difference Arrays
- Monotonic Stack and Monotonic Queue
- Binary Search on Answer
- The Merge Intervals Technique
- Greedy Choices with Sorting
- Bit Manipulation Patterns
- STL Essentials: C++
- STL Containers

- Linear Data Structures in STL
- Pairs and Tuples
- STL Algorithms from `<algorithm>`
- Custom Comparators and Lambda Functions
- Iterators and Ranges
- Time-Saving STL Tricks for Contests and Interviews
- Python Built-ins and Standard Modules
- Core Python Data Structures
- Collections Module
- Python Algorithmic Modules
- List Comprehensions and Lambda Functions
- Hands-On Reinforcement

Problem-Solving Patterns

In real-world programming and technical interviews, problems rarely require the direct application of a single algorithm in isolation. Instead, most problems follow **recognizable logical structures or patterns** that, once identified, guide the programmer toward an efficient solution. These structures are known as **problem-solving patterns**. Rather than starting from scratch every time, experienced programmers first identify the underlying pattern, and then apply the appropriate technique with confidence and speed.

Problem-solving patterns act as a **bridge between theory and practice**. Even with strong knowledge of DSA, many learners struggle to solve new problems because they are unable to recognize which technique applies. Patterns simplify this process by reducing complex problems into familiar templates. Once the correct pattern is identified, the choice of data structure, traversal method, and optimization approach becomes much clearer.

These patterns are not limited to competitive programming or interviews. They are heavily used in **real-world software development** for tasks such as data filtering, scheduling, optimization, searching, system monitoring, and analytics. From detecting anomalies in streaming data to allocating limited resources efficiently, most real-life problems follow one or more of these standard patterns.

Another major advantage of mastering problem-solving patterns is the **dramatic improvement in efficiency**. Many beginners rely on brute-force solutions that work correctly, but fail due to poor performance. Recognizing patterns, such as sliding window, two pointers, prefix sums, greedy with sorting, or binary search on the answer, allows the same problem to be solved in linear or logarithmic time, instead of quadratic time.

Therefore, in this chapter, each important pattern is studied with its **core idea, logical framework, optimization strategy, and practical use cases**. The goal is not just to memorize techniques, but to develop the ability to **look at a problem and immediately recognize how to approach it**. By mastering these patterns, learners will gain the confidence to tackle a wide range of problems efficiently in coding interviews, competitive programming, and professional software projects.

The Two-Pointer Technique

The two-pointer technique is one of the most powerful and widely used problem-solving patterns in algorithm design. It is especially effective when working with **arrays, strings, or any sequential data structure** where relationships between pairs of elements must be examined efficiently. Instead of using nested loops that lead to higher time complexity, this technique uses **two indices (pointers)** to traverse the data in a controlled and optimized manner. The result is a significant reduction in time complexity and cleaner, more intuitive logic.

Fundamental Idea and Pointer Movement Strategies

The fundamental idea of the two-pointer technique is to use **two independent pointers that move based on the condition of the problem**, rather than exploring every possible pair through brute force. These pointers can move in different ways depending on the problem structure.

In the most common strategy, a pointer starts at the **beginning of the array** and the other starts at the **end**. Based on a comparison condition, one of the pointers moves inward. This strategy is frequently used in problems such as pair sum in a sorted array, palindrome checking, and reversing arrays.

In another strategy, both pointers start at the **same position** and move in the same direction, but at different speeds. This approach is widely used in duplicate removal, slow–fast pointer problems, and cycle detection in linked lists.

By carefully controlling how the pointers move, the algorithm avoids unnecessary comparisons and achieves optimal efficiency.

Applications in Arrays and Strings

The two-pointer technique is extensively applied in array and string problems due to its simplicity and efficiency. In arrays, it is commonly used for tasks such as finding pairs with a given sum, partitioning elements based on conditions, merging sorted arrays, and removing duplicates from sorted data.

In string-based problems, two pointers are used to check for palindromes, compare characters from opposite ends, and solve substring matching conditions. For example, when verifying whether a string is a palindrome, one pointer begins at the start of the string and the other at the end, and both move inward while comparing characters.

This technique allows such problems to be solved in **linear time**, which makes it far superior to traditional nested loop solutions.

Common Problem Categories

Several types of problems consistently rely on the two-pointer technique. These include:

- Pair-Sum and Difference-Based Problems
- Palindrome and Symmetry Checks
- Partitioning and Rearrangement Problems
- Duplicate Elimination in Sorted Sequences
- Subsequence Verification and ,Merging Operations

These categories frequently appear in coding interviews, competitive programming contests, and real-world data processing tasks.

The Sliding Window Technique

The sliding window technique is a highly effective problem-solving pattern used to process **continuous subarrays or substrings** efficiently. Instead of repeatedly recalculating values for every possible window using nested loops, this technique **maintains a window of elements and updates results incrementally as the window moves**. This approach dramatically improves performance and is widely used in array and string problems involving ranges, frequencies, and cumulative conditions.

The key idea behind the sliding window method is to treat a subset of consecutive elements as a "window" and slide this window forward, while updating the result at each step without recomputing everything from scratch.

Fixed and Variable Window Concepts

In the **fixed window approach**, the window size remains constant throughout the computation. The algorithm processes the first window of size *k*, computes the desired result, and then slides the window one step forward by removing the leftmost element, and including the next rightmost element. This continues until the end of the array is reached. This concept is commonly used in problems such as finding the **maximum sum of a subarray of size k**.

In the **variable window approach**, the size of the window is not fixed. Instead, the window **expands and shrinks dynamically** based on a condition such as sum, frequency, or distinct element constraints. A pointer extends the window to include more elements, while the other pointer shrinks it when a condition is violated. This adaptive behavior makes it suitable for problems like finding the **longest substring without repeating characters**, or the **smallest subarray with a given sum**.

Performance Improvement over Brute Force

Without the sliding window technique, many subarray and substring problems are typically solved using **nested loops**, resulting in a time complexity of `O(n²)`. Such brute-force solutions become inefficient and often fail for large input sizes.

The sliding window method reduces this complexity to `O(n)` by ensuring that each element is added to and removed from the window at most once. Instead of recalculating the entire window repeatedly, the algorithm **updates only what changes** when the window slides. This optimization makes the technique extremely powerful for large datasets and time-critical applications.

Typical Use Cases

The sliding window technique is commonly applied in problems involving:

- Maximum or Minimum Sum in a Subarray
- Longest or Shortest Valid Substring under Constraints
- Frequency-Based Substring Problems
- Subarray Product or Sum Thresholds
- Window-Based Statistical Computations

It is also widely used in **real-time data streaming, signal processing, network traffic analysis, and performance monitoring systems**, where continuous window-based computation is required.

Prefix Sum and Difference Arrays

Prefix sum and difference arrays are powerful preprocessing techniques used to solve **range query and range update problems efficiently**. Many problems involving repeated subarray sum calculations, or multiple range updates become inefficient when handled using traditional loops. These techniques transform such expensive computations into fast, constant-time operations after a one-time preprocessing step. They are widely used in competitive programming, data analysis, and real-time systems where excellent performance is critical.

Prefix Sum Construction and Usage

A prefix sum array stores the **cumulative sum of elements up to each index**. Each position in the prefix array represents the total of all elements from the beginning of the original array up to that index. Once constructed, it allows the sum of any subarray to be computed instantly.

The main advantage of prefix sums is that they eliminate the need to repeatedly add elements for each query. Instead of summing values inside a loop for every range, the sum is obtained using a simple subtraction between two prefix values. This reduces the time complexity of each range sum query from linear time to **constant time** after linear preprocessing.

Prefix sums are widely used in problems involving:

- Subarray Sum Queries
- Frequency Counting
- Cumulative Score Calculations
- Rainwater Trapping and Elevation Accumulation
- Performance Analytics and Financial Computations

Therefore, prefix sums provide an elegant and highly optimized way to handle repeated range-based calculations.

Difference Array Technique for Range Updates

The difference array technique is used when a problem involves **multiple range update operations** on an array. Instead of updating every element within each range, which would be inefficient, the difference array records only the **change at the boundaries** of each update.

In a difference array, updates are applied only at the start and end of a range. After all updates are recorded, a single prefix sum pass over the difference array reconstructs the final updated array. This approach dramatically reduces the time complexity of multiple update operations from quadratic to **linear time**.

Difference arrays are commonly used in:

- Mass Range Increment or Decrement Operations
- Scheduling and Booking Systems
- Data Synchronization Problems
- Large-Scale Batch Updates in Databases

Therefore, difference arrays offer a clean and efficient way to handle large numbers of updates without repeated element-wise modification.

Optimization of Range Queries

Together, prefix sums and difference arrays play a central role in the **optimization of range-based problems**. Prefix sums convert costly repeated range queries into instant lookups. Difference arrays convert costly repeated range updates into a single efficient transformation.

These techniques are often combined in complex problems involving both frequent updates and frequent queries. Thus, by shifting computation from repeated runtime work to a one-time preprocessing step, they achieve exceptional performance improvements, while keeping the logic simple and structured.

In real-world systems such as analytics platforms, streaming data processors, and monitoring tools, these optimizations ensure that large datasets can be handled with **high speed and low computational overhead**.

Monotonic Stack and Monotonic Queue

Monotonic stacks and monotonic queues are specialized data structure techniques designed to maintain elements in a **specific sorted order while processing them sequentially**. These structures are extremely useful in problems where we need to efficiently track the **next greater, next smaller, maximum, or minimum elements** over a range. By ensuring that elements are added and removed in a controlled monotonic order, these techniques eliminate unnecessary comparisons and achieve optimal linear-time performance in many complex problems.

Increasing and Decreasing Monotonic Structures

A **monotonic structure** is the one in which the elements are stored in either strictly increasing or strictly decreasing order.

In a **monotonic increasing stack or queue**, elements are arranged from smallest to largest. Whenever a new element arrives that violates this order, the elements are removed from the structure until the order is restored. This structure is typically used when we need to find the **next smaller elements**.

In a **monotonic decreasing stack or queue**, elements are arranged from largest to smallest. The smaller elements are removed when a larger element arrives. This structure is used when we need to find the **next greater elements**.

The key advantage of these structures is that **each element is inserted and removed at most once**, which guarantees an overall time complexity of O(n). This makes them ideal for large datasets where repeated comparisons would otherwise be expensive.

Window Maximum and Minimum Problems

One of the most important applications of the monotonic queue is in **sliding window maximum and minimum problems**. In such problems, we are required to find the maximum or minimum value within every window of fixed size as it moves across an array.

A simple brute-force solution would recompute the maximum or minimum for each window, resulting in `O(nk)` time complexity. However, a monotonic queue maintains only the relevant candidates for the maximum or minimum by removing elements that can no longer influence the result. This allows each window's answer to be computed in **constant time after linear preprocessing**.

This technique is widely used in:

- Stream Data Processing
- Image Filtering and Signal Processing
- Performance Monitoring Systems
- Real-Time Analytics Dashboards

Therefore, a monotonic queue ensures that both accuracy and speed are maintained even when you are handling massive data streams.

Histogram and Span Problem Applications

Monotonic stacks play a critical role in solving **histogram and span-based problems**, which involve finding boundaries based on relative heights or values.

In the **largest rectangle in a histogram problem**, a monotonic stack is used to efficiently determine the width over which each bar can extend without encountering a smaller height. This leads to an optimal `O(n)` solution, instead of a quadratic brute-force approach.

In the **stock span problem**, a monotonic decreasing stack is used to compute how many consecutive days a stock price has been less than or equal to the current day's price. Therefore, this problem demonstrates how monotonic stacks can efficiently track historical comparison data without repeated scanning.

Ultimately, these applications highlight the power of monotonic structures in problems that involve **range dominance, boundaries, and historical comparisons.**

Binary Search on Answer

Binary search on answer is an advanced and highly powerful problem-solving pattern used in **optimization problems where the exact answer is not directly known, but lies within a range of values**. Instead of applying binary search on a sorted array, this technique applies binary search on the **space of possible answers.** It is especially useful in scenarios where we need to **minimize or maximize a result under certain constraints** such as minimizing time, distance, cost, or maximum load.

This pattern transforms a difficult optimization problem into a simpler **decision problem**—one where we only need to check whether a proposed solution is feasible or not. By repeatedly narrowing down the answer range, the optimal solution is found efficiently with logarithmic complexity.

Search Space Formulation

The first and most critical step in the binary search on answer pattern is to **correctly define the search space**. Instead of searching through array indices, we search through a numeric range that contains all possible valid answers.

For example, in problems involving:

- The minimum time required to complete tasks
- The maximum capacity or load
- The minimum feasible distance or speed

The search space is usually defined between a **lower bound** (minimum possible value) and an **upper bound** (maximum possible value based on constraints). Thus, choosing the correct bounds is essential because an incorrect search space may cause the algorithm to miss the optimal answer or fail altogether.

Once the bounds are established, binary search is applied over this range, just like in traditional binary search.

Feasibility Checking Techniques

The heart of this pattern lies in the **feasibility check function**. For any candidate value chosen during binary search, a feasibility function determines whether it satisfies the problem's constraints.

This function usually:

- Simulates the process using the candidate value
- Verifies whether the condition can be satisfied
- Returns a Boolean result (feasible or not feasible)

If the condition is feasible, the algorithm attempts to find a **better (more optimal) answer** by moving the search range in one direction. If it is not feasible, the algorithm adjusts the search range in the opposite direction. This repeated decision-making process gradually converges into the optimal answer.

Feasibility checks often use greedy strategies, prefix sums, or counting techniques to evaluate conditions efficiently.

Optimization Problem Patterns

The binary search on answer pattern is widely used in a large class of optimization problems where brute-force solutions are too slow. Some common problem patterns include:

- Allocation problems, such as distributing workloads or resources
- Scheduling problems involving time constraints
- Capacity determination problems, such as shipping packages or loading weights
- Distance-based optimization, such as placing objects with minimum separation
- Speed-based problems, such as the minimum speed to complete tasks

These problems may appear complex at first glance, but once the **search space and feasibility conditions are identified**, they become structured and efficient enough to solve using this pattern.

The Merge Intervals Technique

The merge intervals technique is a widely used problem-solving pattern for handling problems that involve **ranges, segments, or time intervals**. Such problems are common in scheduling systems, calendar management, resource booking, and range-based data processing. The main goal of this technique is to **combine overlapping intervals into a minimal set of non-overlapping intervals**, which ensures that all covered ranges are preserved, while eliminating redundancy. This is why the merge intervals technique can transform a seemingly complex comparison problem into a well-structured and efficient algorithm.

Interval Sorting Strategy

The first and most essential step in the merge intervals approach is **sorting the intervals based on their starting points**. Sorting ensures that intervals are processed in a logical left-to-right order. This makes it easy to detect overlaps using a single pass.

Once the intervals are sorted, any overlapping ranges will always appear adjacent to each other. This removes the need for comparing every interval with every other interval. This reduces the algorithm's time complexity significantly, and lays the foundation for a clean linear merge process.

Overlapping Interval Merging Logic

After sorting, the algorithm processes each interval sequentially and compares it with the last merged interval.

If the current interval **overlaps** with the previously merged interval, the two intervals are combined by extending the end boundary to the maximum of both ends. If there is **no overlap**, the current interval is added as a new distinct range.

This simple comparison-and-merge logic ensures that each interval is examined only once after sorting. As a result, the overall time complexity becomes `O(n log n)` due to sorting, followed by a linear scan for merging. This makes the technique highly efficient even for large datasets.

Scheduling and Range Merging Applications

The merge intervals technique is extensively used in real-world scheduling and range management systems. In **meeting room scheduling**, it helps us determine overlapping meetings and calculate the minimum number of rooms required. In **calendar applications**, it merges overlapping appointments to create clean and conflict-free schedules.

It is also widely applied in **CPU task scheduling, memory allocation systems, booking platforms, network bandwidth management, and time-range analytics**. Apart from time-based problems, it is used in spatial data processing and range-based access control systems.

Greedy Choices with Sorting

Greedy algorithms are based on the principle of making the **best possible choice at each step with the aim of arriving at an overall optimal solution**. While greedy strategies are powerful on their own, many real-world problems require an additional step—**sorting the input data before applying greedy decisions**. Sorting arranges the problem elements into a meaningful order that allows the greedy logic to work correctly and efficiently. Together, sorting and greedy decision-making form one of the most widely used optimization patterns in practical problem solving.

This pattern is especially effective in problems involving **selection, allocation, scheduling, and maximizing or minimizing results under constraints.**

Greedy Decision Framework

The greedy decision framework works on a simple but strong idea: at every step of the algorithm, choose the option that **appears to offer the immediate best benefit** without reconsidering previous choices. Once a decision is made, it can never be changed.

This framework relies on two important properties, which are:

- The problem must exhibit optimal substructure. This means that optimal solutions to subproblems contribute to the optimal solution of the main problem. The problem must satisfy the greedy choice property, which implies that a locally optimal choice leads to a globally optimal solution.
- The framework typically follows these steps: evaluate all available options, select the best immediate option based on a priority rule, update the remaining problem, and repeat the process until a solution is reached.

Sorting-Based Greedy Optimization

In many problems, greedy decisions cannot be applied directly to the raw input because the elements are not in a meaningful order. **Sorting arranges the data, so that greedy choices can be made correctly and efficiently**.

For example, in scheduling problems, activities are often sorted by finishing time; in resource allocation, items may be sorted by weight, profit, or ratio; whereas, in interval selection, ranges are sorted by start or end time. Once sorted, the greedy algorithm can process the input in a single pass, while making optimal locally best decisions.

Sorting reduces ambiguity, avoids unnecessary comparisons, and ensures that every greedy choice is made in the **most informed and optimal sequence**. This combination greatly improves both correctness and performance.

Resource Allocation and Scheduling Problems

Greedy choices with sorting are heavily used in **resource allocation and scheduling systems**, where limited resources must be assigned efficiently to maximize productivity or minimize cost.

In task scheduling systems, jobs may be sorted based on deadlines, execution time, or profit before choosing which tasks to execute. In bandwidth allocation or CPU scheduling, tasks are prioritized using sorted queues. In logistics and supply-chain problems, goods are allocated based on sorted demand or transport cost.

Therefore, these applications show how sorting prepares the data, and greedy logic ensures that **resources are used in the most effective way possible** under given constraints.

Bit Manipulation Patterns

Bit manipulation refers to solving problems using the **binary representation of numbers and direct operations on bits**. Since computers internally store all data in binary form, bit-level operations allow programs to run extremely fast and use minimal memory. Many problems that appear complex at first can be solved very efficiently using simple bit operations. Bit manipulation patterns are especially powerful in optimization problems, low-level system programming, cryptography, and competitive programming. These patterns help programmers perform operations such as toggling, checking, setting, or clearing bits with precise control and high performance.

Basic Bit Operations and Masking

At the heart of bit manipulation are the following fundamental operations that work directly on binary digits:

- **`AND (&)`** is used to check whether a particular bit is set.
- **`OR (|)`** is used to set a specific bit.
- **`XOR (^)`** is used to toggle bits.
- **`NOT (~)`** inverts all bits.
- **`Left shift (<<)`** and **`right shift (>>)`** move bits to multiply or divide numbers by powers of two.

Bit masking is a technique where a specially crafted binary number (called a mask) is used with these operations to isolate, modify, or test specific bits. For instance, masking is used to:

- Check if a certain permission bit is enabled.
- Extract specific bits from a number.
- Turn off unwanted bits.

Bit masking is widely used in **file permissions, encryption systems, graphics processing, and memory-efficient state tracking**.

Power of Two Checks

One of the most common and elegant applications of bit manipulation is checking whether a number is a **power of two**. A power of two has only **one bit set in its binary representation**, such as 1 (0001), 2 (0010), 4 (0100), 8 (1000), and so on.

Using bit manipulation, this check can be performed in constant time by verifying that a number has exactly one set bit. This technique is much faster than repeatedly dividing the number by two in a loop.

Power-of-two checks are frequently used in:

- Memory Allocation Systems
- Hash Table Sizing
- Binary Tree Indexing
- Optimizing Algorithmic Operations

This simple bit-based check plays a crucial role in efficient system-level programming.

Subset Generation Using Bit Representation

Bit manipulation provides a very elegant way to generate **all possible subsets of a given set**, especially when the set size is small. Each subset can be represented using a binary number, where:

A bit value of 1 indicates the inclusion of the element.

A bit value of 0 indicates the exclusion of the element.

For a set of size n, there are 2^n possible subsets. By iterating through all binary numbers from 0 to (2^n – 1), each number directly represents one unique subset. This method avoids recursive approaches and generates subsets efficiently using simple loops and bit checks. This pattern is widely used in:

- Combinatorial Problems
- Optimization Tasks
- Feature Selection in Machine Learning
- Game State Enumeration
- Brute-Force Solutions for Small Constraint Problems

STL Essentials: C++

The **Standard Template Library (STL)** is one of the most powerful features of the C++ programming language. It provides a rich collection of **predefined data structures, algorithms, and utility functions** that help programmers write efficient, clean, and highly optimized code with minimal effort. Instead of implementing common data structures such as arrays, stacks, queues, maps, and sets from scratch, STL allows programmers to directly use tested and optimized versions. Thus, it saves both time and development cost.

In competitive programming, technical interviews, and real-world software development, STL is considered an **essential skill**. It not only speeds up coding, but also improves reliability. This is because STL components are well-tested and follow standard performance guarantees. Therefore, by mastering STL, programmers can focus more on problem-solving logic, rather than on low-level implementation details.

STL is built around three main pillars:

- **Containers**, which store data
- **Algorithms**, which process data
- **Iterators**, which connect containers with algorithms

This strong design allows programmers to combine different components flexibly and efficiently. For example, the same sorting algorithm can work on vectors, deques, or arrays simply by using iterators.

Another important benefit of STL is its **time and space efficiency**. Most STL operations are optimized to provide logarithmic or constant time complexity, depending on the data structure used. This makes STL highly suitable for large-scale data processing and performance-critical applications.

In technical interviews, candidates are often expected to:

- Choose the correct STL container for the problem.
- Apply STL algorithms effectively.
- Write concise, readable, and optimized code using STL features.

Therefore, in this section, learners will explore the most important STL components used in problem solving, including containers, linear structures, pairs and tuples, built-in algorithms, custom comparators, iterators, and contest-level STL tricks. Mastering these tools transforms raw coding ability into **professional-grade, industry-ready programming skill**.

STL Containers

STL containers are **predefined data structures provided by C++ to store and manage collections of data efficiently**. Each container is designed for a specific type of data access pattern, such as sequential access, fast searching, ordered storage, or constant-time lookup. Choosing the right container plays a crucial role in achieving optimal time and space performance in real-world applications and competitive programming.

Vectors

Vectors are **dynamic arrays** that allow elements to be stored in contiguous memory with the ability to grow or shrink in size at runtime. Unlike traditional arrays, vectors automatically manage memory and resizing, which makes them highly flexible and convenient.

Vectors provide fast random access using index-based lookup, which works in constant time. They support efficient insertion and deletion at the end of the container, while insertions in the middle may require shifting elements.

Vectors are widely used when:

- The number of elements is not fixed in advance.
- Fast indexing is required.
- Data must be stored sequentially.
- Sorting and searching operations are needed.

To elaborate further, vectors are the **most commonly used STL container** in industry and competitive programming because of their simplicity, speed, and broad compatibility with STL algorithms.

Maps

Maps store data in the form of **key–value pairs**, where each key is unique and is associated with exactly one value. Internally, maps are usually implemented using **balanced binary search trees**, which allow elements to be stored in sorted order based on keys.

Maps provide logarithmic-time complexity for insertion, deletion, and searching. As the keys are always kept in sorted order, maps are useful when **ordered traversal or range-based queries** are required.

Maps are commonly used in:

- Frequency Counting and Dictionary Applications
- Indexing Systems
- Symbol Tables in Compilers
- Ordered Data Storage and Retrieval

As is apparent from this section, we can say that maps offer structured data organization with guaranteed performance.

Sets

Sets are containers used to store **unique elements only**, with automatic sorting of elements in ascending order. Like maps, sets are also implemented using balanced search trees, which provide logarithmic-time complexity for core operations. Sets are useful when:

- Duplicate elements must be avoided.
- Fast membership checks are needed.
- Data needs to remain sorted automatically.

Given these features and advantages, sets are commonly applied in problems involving uniqueness constraints, dynamic ordering, and mathematical set operations such as union and intersection.

Unordered Containers

Unordered containers include **`unordered_map` and `unordered_set`**, which store elements using **hashing instead of tree-based ordering**. As a result, they offer **average constant-time complexity** for insertion, deletion, and search operations. However, unlike maps and sets, unordered containers do **not maintain any sorted order**. Their primary goal is speed rather than ordered traversal. Unordered containers are widely used when:

- Fast lookups are more important than sorted order.
- Large datasets need rapid access.
- Real-time applications require constant-time performance.

Additionally, unordered containers are heavily used in **caching systems, lookup tables, frequency counting, and real-time analytics platforms**.

Linear Data Structures in STL

The C++ Standard Template Library (STL) provides ready-to-use implementations of several **linear data structures** that are essential for sequential data processing. These structures follow well-defined access rules such as Last-In-First-Out (LIFO) and First-In-First-Out (FIFO), which makes them ideal for handling tasks like expression evaluation, scheduling, and priority-based processing. Using STL for these structures allows programmers to write **clean, efficient, and highly reliable code** without worrying about low-level memory management.

Stack

A stack is a **Last-In-First-Out (LIFO)** data structure. This means that the last element inserted is the first one to be removed. The STL stack is an adapter container built on top of underlying containers such as deque or vector. The stack supports three fundamental operations which are:

- Pushing an element onto the stack
- Removing the top element
- Accessing the top element without removing it

Additionally, stacks are widely used in:

- Expression Evaluation and Syntax Parsing
- Function Call Management (Using the Call stack)

- Undo and Redo Operations in Applications
- Parenthesis and Symbol Matching
- Depth-First Search (DFS) in Graphs

Therefore, the STL stack ensures that these operations are performed efficiently and safely with minimal code complexity.

Queue

A queue follows the **First-In-First-Out (FIFO)** principle, where the first element inserted is the first one to be removed. It is ideally suited for **sequential processing and scheduling tasks**. In STL, the queue is also implemented as an adapter over containers such as deque or list. The basic queue operations include:

- Inserting elements at the back
- Removing elements from the front
- Accessing the front element

Queues are heavily used in:

- Task Scheduling Systems
- Breadth-First Search (BFS) in Graphs
- CPU and Process Scheduling
- Network Data Packet Handling
- Producer–Consumer Systems

The STL queue provides a structured and optimized way to manage such linear workflows.

Priority Queue

A priority queue is a special type of queue where each element is associated with a **priority**, and elements are processed based on their priority, rather than their insertion order. In STL, the priority queue is implemented using a **heap structure**, which makes the retrieval of the highest (or lowest) priority element very efficient.

By default, the C++ STL priority queue behaves as a **max-heap**, where the largest element is always at the top. It can also be configured as a min-heap using custom comparators.

Priority queues are essential in:

- Task Scheduling (Based on Importance)
- Dijkstra's Shortest Path Algorithm
- Heap Sort
- Event-Driven Simulations
- Top-K Element Problems

They allow fast access to the most important element, and are also able to maintain efficient insertion and deletion operations.

Pairs and Tuples

In many programming problems, it is necessary to **group multiple related values together and treat them as a single unit**. The C++ STL provides two such powerful utility structures: **pairs** and **tuples**.

These structures simplify data handling, improve code readability, and reduce the need to define custom structures for simple grouped data. They are especially useful in competitive programming, graph algorithms, coordinate storage, and while returning multiple values from functions.

Pair Creation and Value Access

A **pair** is a simple container that stores exactly **two values**, possibly of different data types, as a single entity. It is defined using the pair template and is commonly used to combine related values such as coordinates, key-value data, or value-index relationships.

Pairs can be created directly using a constructor or with helper functions. Once created, the two elements of a pair are accessed using the members **first** and **second**. This makes the code intuitive and self-explanatory, as the programmer can clearly distinguish between the two stored values.

Pairs are widely used in:

- Graph Representations (To Store Node-Weight Relationships)
- Coordinate Systems to Store (x, y) Values
- Sorting Problems (Where Elements are Paired with Indices or Priorities)
- Map Insertions and Retrieval Operations
- Returning Two Values from a Function

Because of their simplicity and efficiency, pairs appear frequently in both interview problems and real-world software systems.

Tuple Usage and Unpacking Techniques

While pairs are limited to two elements, a **tuple** can store **multiple values of different data types** within a single object. Tuples are designed for situations where more than two related values must be grouped together without creating a custom structure or class.

Tuples facilitate:

- Storage of multiple heterogeneous values
- Structured grouping of function return results
- Compact representation of complex relationships

One of the most useful features of tuples is **unpacking**, where individual values are extracted from the tuple into separate variables in a single statement. This improves code readability and avoids repetitive access syntax. Tuples also support direct access to elements using their index positions.

Tuples are commonly used in:

- Multi-Property Sorting and Ranking
- Returning Multiple Results from Algorithms
- Storing Records with Several Attributes
- Complex Graph Representations
- Simulation and Modeling Systems

To summarize it all, tuples provide a clean and flexible way to handle grouped data without introducing structural complexity.

STL Algorithms from <algorithm>

The **`<algorithm>`** header in C++ is one of the most powerful components of the STL. It provides a rich collection of **ready-made algorithms for searching, sorting, counting, and manipulating data stored inside STL containers**. These algorithms are highly optimized and well-tested, besides being designed to work seamlessly with iterators. By using these built-in algorithms, programmers can write concise, efficient, and reliable code without manually implementing common logic.

One of the greatest strengths of STL algorithms is that they are **generic**; the same algorithm can work with vectors, arrays, deques, and other containers simply by supplying the appropriate iterators. This makes code more flexible, reusable, and easier to maintain.

Sorting and Searching Utilities

STL provides powerful built-in functions for sorting and searching data efficiently. The sort function is the most commonly used sorting utility and arranges elements in ascending order by default. It uses highly optimized internal algorithms that ensure fast performance even for large datasets.

For searching operations, functions such as **`binary_search`**, **`lower_bound`**, and **`upper_bound`** are widely used. These functions operate on sorted data and allow programmers to quickly determine whether an element exists in a container or where it should be inserted while maintaining sorted order.

These utilities are essential in:

- Ranking and Ordering Problems
- Efficient Lookup in Sorted Data
- Interval and Range-Based Problems
- Duplicate Handling and Frequency Control

Thus, using STL's sorting and searching utilities ensures both correctness and optimal performance with minimal code effort.

Min, Max, and Bounds Functions

STL also provides simple yet powerful functions to determine **minimum and maximum values** and to operate within value boundaries. Functions such as min and max are used to compare two values, and return the smaller or larger one, respectively. For collections, **`min_element`** and **`max_element`** scan a range of elements, and return the iterators to the minimum or maximum element.

The bounds-related functions, **`lower_bound`** and **`upper_bound`**, are used to locate the range of values corresponding to a specific key in a sorted container. These functions are extremely useful in problems involving **frequency counting, range searching, and ordered data processing**.

Together, these functions simplify many comparison-based tasks, and eliminate the need for manual loops and conditional logic.

Accumulate, Count, and Find Operations

The **`<algorithm>`** and **`<numeric>`** headers work together to offer powerful aggregation and search utilities. The accumulate function is used to compute the **total sum of a range of values** with a single function call. It can also be extended to perform custom accumulation using user-defined operations.

The count function returns the number of times a specific value appears in a given range, while **`count_if`** counts elements that satisfy a particular condition.

The find function searches for the first occurrence of a value in a container, and returns an iterator to it if found. These functions play a major role in:

- Frequency Analysis
- Data Verification
- Filtering Tasks
- Statistical Computations

They enable programmers to perform common data-processing tasks in a clear, concise, and highly efficient manner.

Custom Comparators and Lambda Functions

While STL provides powerful default sorting and searching utilities, real-world problems often require **custom ordering and personalized comparison rules**. This is where **custom comparators and lambda functions** become essential. They allow programmers to precisely control how elements are compared, sorted, filtered, or processed, which makes STL far more flexible and adaptable to varied problem requirements.

Using custom comparators and lambda expressions, programmers can implement complex logic directly within STL operations without writing long helper functions. This leads to **cleaner, shorter, and more expressive code**, which is especially valuable in competitive programming and professional software development.

Comparator Design for Sorting

A **comparator** is a function or rule that defines how two elements should be compared with each other. By default, STL sorting functions arrange elements in ascending order. However, many applications require custom sorting, such as descending order, sorting by secondary attributes, or sorting based on computed values.

In comparator-based sorting, the programmer defines a condition that returns true when the first element should appear before the second. This allows sorting based on:

- Custom Priorities
- Multiple Fields (For example, sorting objects by one attribute and tie-breaking using another)
- Absolute Values
- Ratios or Weighted Values

Custom Comparators are widely used in:

- Sorting Pairs (Based on the Second Value)
- Scheduling Problems with Deadlines and Priorities
- Sorting Objects (Based on Multiple Criteria)
- Greedy Algorithms Combined with Sorting

Therefore, a well-designed comparator ensures that sorting aligns exactly with the logic required by the algorithm, while preserving both correctness and efficiency.

Lambda Expressions for Inline Logic

Lambda functions are short, anonymous functions that can be written directly inside expressions. They allow programmers to define temporary logic without creating a separate named function.

In STL, lambda expressions are especially useful for providing **inline comparison rules, filtering conditions, and transformation logic**.

Lambda expressions help make code:

- More compact and readable
- Easier to modify
- Closer to the logic of the algorithm
- Free from unnecessary helper functions

They are commonly used with functions such as sort, `find_if`, `count_if`, and `transform`. For example, instead of writing a full comparator function, a simple lambda can define the comparison logic directly within the sort call.

In modern C++, lambda functions also support **capturing external variables**, and allow the comparator or condition to depend on values defined outside the function. These features greatly enhance flexibility and expressiveness.

Iterators and Ranges

Iterators connect **STL containers with STL algorithms**. They behave like generalized pointers that allow programmers to traverse through container elements in a **uniform and container-independent manner**. Instead of accessing elements using direct indexing, iterators provide a flexible way to move through different data structures, such as vectors, lists, sets, and maps, using a consistent interface.

Ranges define the portion of a container over which an operation is performed. Almost all STL algorithms work on ranges defined using iterators, which makes understanding iterators and ranges essential for writing efficient and reusable C++ code.

Iterator Traversal Methods

Iterators support movement across container elements using increment and decrement operations. By advancing an iterator step by step, the programmer can traverse through the entire container in sequence. Different containers provide different types of iterators based on their structure, such as:

- Forward iterators for single-direction traversal
- Bidirectional iterators for two-way movement
- Random access iterators for direct movement using arithmetic

Through these traversal methods, iterators enable:

- Sequential scanning of container elements
- Integration with STL algorithms such as sort, find, and count
- Uniform data access without knowing the internal structure of the container

In this way, the highlighted abstraction makes C++ programs **more generic, flexible, and reusable**.

Begin and End Operations

Every STL container provides two important functions: **`begin()`** and **`end()`**. The **`begin()`** function returns an iterator pointing to the **first element** of the container, while **`end()`** returns an iterator pointing just **after the last element**.

These two iterators define the **range of elements** over which an STL algorithm operates. For instance, when a sorting or searching algorithm is applied, it processes all elements between **`begin()`** and `end()`. This design allows algorithms to work on any container type without modification, as long as the container supports the required iterator type.

Therefore, using `begin()` and `end()` ensures **safe access**, prevents out-of-bound errors, and maintains consistency across different container types.

Range-Based Loops

Range-based loops provide a **modern, clean, and readable way to traverse containers** without explicitly using iterators. Instead of manually controlling iterator variables, the loop automatically visits each element in the container.

These loops:

- Reduce boilerplate code.
- Improve readability.
- Lower the chances of logical errors.
- Make the intention clear to the reader.

Range-based loops are widely used in modern C++ for printing, modifying, and processing container elements. They combine the power of iterators with the simplicity of traditional loops, which makes them ideal for both beginners and professional developers.

Time-Saving STL Tricks for Contests and Interviews

In competitive programming and technical interviews, **time management is just as important as accuracy**. Even a perfectly correct algorithm can fail due to time limits if the implementation is slow. The C++ STL offers several built-in techniques and optimizations that help programmers **write faster code, reduce boilerplate, and improve execution speed**. Mastering these time-saving STL tricks will allow candidates to focus more on logic, and less on implementation details.

Fast Input-Output Techniques

Input and output operations often become the **main performance bottleneck** when programs process large volumes of data. Hence, standard input/output methods may be too slow by default, and are not too apt for competitive environments.

Therefore, to improve speed, programmers synchronize input streams efficiently and reduce unnecessary flushing of output buffers. Using fast input methods allows programs to read millions of integers quickly, while fast output techniques ensure that results are printed without delays. These practices are crucial in:

- Large Dataset Problems
- Real-Time Input Processing
- Competitive Programming Contests
- Online Coding Assessments

It is important to remember that fast input-output techniques do not change the algorithm itself, but can **significantly reduce execution time**. This often determines whether a solution passes or fails within time limit.

Common STL Shortcuts

STL provides many **built-in shortcuts that reduce code length and improve clarity**. Using these shortcuts eliminates repetitive loops and manual operations.

Examples include:

- Direct Container Initialization and Resizing
- Built-in Swapping and Reversing Operations
- Using Auto for Type Inference
- Using Predefined Algorithms (Instead of Writing Custom Loops)

To state further, these shortcuts allow programmers to **express complex logic in fewer lines of code**, which make solutions easier to debug, understand, and modify. In interviews, clean and concise code also leaves a strong positive impression on interviewers.

Performance Optimization Using STL

STL is internally optimized for **high-performance operations**, but choosing the correct container and algorithm is essential to fully benefit from these optimizations. These benefits can show up as follows:

- Using vectors instead of arrays enables dynamic resizing with cache-friendly access.
- Using unordered containers provides constant-time average lookup.
- Using priority queues enables fast retrieval of extreme values.
- Using efficient algorithms such as **`sort`**, **`lower_bound`**, and accumulate minimizes computational overhead.

Another important aspect of STL-based optimization is avoiding unnecessary copying of data by passing containers using references and using move semantics where applicable. Therefore, these small technical decisions can often make a **major difference in execution speed and memory usage**.

Python Built-ins and Standard Modules

Python is one of the most preferred languages for algorithmic problem solving due to its **simple syntax, rich built-in data structures, and powerful standard library support**. Unlike low-level languages that require detailed memory management, Python allows programmers to focus directly on **logic, problem formulation, and optimization**. Its inbuilt features drastically reduce code length while maintaining efficiency, and thus make it ideal for interviews, competitive programming, scripting, and rapid application development.

The strength of Python lies in its **ready-to-use core data structures such as lists, dictionaries, and sets**, which provide efficient storage, fast lookups, and flexible data manipulation. Along with these, Python's **standard modules** extend functionality for priority queues, combinatorics, binary searching, caching, and functional programming. These modules are internally optimized and widely used in production-level systems.

Therefore, by mastering Python built-ins and its standard modules, learners gain the ability to **write concise, expressive, and high-performance solutions** without implementing low-level logic manually. The following sections will equip students with the essential Python tools that will allow them to solve real-world algorithmic problems efficiently and confidently.

Core Python Data Structures

Python provides several powerful built-in data structures that form the **foundation of most algorithmic and real-world programming tasks**. Among these, **lists, dictionaries, and sets** are the most widely used due to their flexibility, efficiency, and simplicity. These structures allow programmers to store, retrieve, and manipulate data efficiently without worrying about low-level memory management. Therefore, a strong understanding of these core structures is essential for effective problem-solving in Python.

Lists

Lists are **ordered, dynamic collections of elements** in Python. They can store items of any data type and allow duplicate values. Lists are implemented as dynamic arrays internally, enabling fast index-based access and flexible resizing.

One of the biggest advantages of lists is their versatility. They also support features like:

- Direct Indexing and Slicing
- Easy Insertion and Deletion of Elements
- Iteration Using Loops
- Use as Stacks and Queues (With **append** and **pop** Operations)

Lists are commonly used to represent arrays in algorithmic problems, store sequences of input data, maintain intermediate results, and support sliding window and two-pointer techniques. Due to their dynamic nature and ease of use, lists are the **most frequently used data structure in Python-based DSA solutions**.

Dictionaries

Dictionaries store data in the form of **key–value pairs** and provide **average constant-time access** using hashing. Each key is unique, and it maps directly to a corresponding value. This structure enables extremely fast searching, insertion, and deletion operations.

Dictionaries are widely used in:

- Frequency Counting Problems
- Caching and Memoization in Dynamic Programming
- Indexing Large Datasets
- Mapping Relationships between Objects
- Graph Representations Using Adjacency Lists

Due to their speed and flexibility, dictionaries play a central role in optimization problems where fast lookups are required. They are especially powerful in scenarios involving **real-time data processing and large-scale data analysis**.

Sets

Sets are **unordered collections of unique elements**. They automatically eliminate duplicates and provide fast membership testing using hashing. Sets do not store elements in any specific order, but they enable extremely efficient operations for checking existence.

Sets are commonly used for:

- Removing Duplicate Values from Collections

- Fast Membership Testing
- Finding Intersections and Unions between Datasets
- Cycle Detection in Graph Algorithms
- Tracking Visited Nodes in Search Algorithms

As sets support mathematical set operations efficiently, they are often used in problems involving **distinct elements, filtering, comparisons, and validation tasks**.

Collections Module

The collections module in Python is a powerful extension of the core data structures and is designed to provide **specialized container data types that improve both performance and code clarity**. While lists, dictionaries, and sets handle most general-purpose tasks, the collections module introduces optimized alternatives for specific use cases such as frequency counting, double-ended queues, and automatic default value handling. These structures are highly efficient and are therefore widely used in competitive programming, data processing, and real-world applications.

Counter

The Counter class is a dictionary-based container designed specifically for **counting the frequency of elements in a collection**. It automatically maps each unique element to the number of times it appears.

Instead of manually writing loops to track frequencies, Counter performs this task efficiently in a single line. It is commonly used in:

- Character and Word Frequency Analysis
- Array Element Counting
- Anagram and Permutation Problems
- Statistical and Data Analysis Tasks

It also supports operations such as retrieving the most common elements and performing arithmetic operations on frequency counts, which make it extremely useful in optimization and pattern-matching problems.

deque

The deque (abbreviated from Double-Ended Queue) is a highly optimized data structure that allows **fast insertion and deletion from both ends**. Unlike Python lists, where inserting at the beginning is slow, a **deque** performs such operations in constant time.

Deque is widely used in:

- Queue and Stack Implementations
- Sliding Window Algorithms
- Breadth-First Search (BFS) in Graph Traversal
- Task Scheduling Systems
- Producer–Consumer Models

Due to its balanced performance at both ends, deque is preferred over lists whenever frequent front insertions or deletions are required.

`defaultdict`

The `defaultdict` is a specialized dictionary that **automatically assigns a default value to a key that does not yet exist**. This eliminates the need to explicitly check whether a key is present before using it.

`defaultdict` is especially helpful in:

- Frequency Counting
- Grouping Elements
- Graph Adjacency List Construction
- Accumulating Results in Dynamic Programming

Thus, by eliminating repetitive key-existence checks, `defaultdict` makes code **cleaner, safer, and more readable**, while also reducing logical errors.

Python Algorithmic Modules

Python offers several specialized standard modules that are designed to handle **common algorithmic operations efficiently and elegantly**. These modules reduce the need for manual implementation of complex logic and provide optimized, ready-to-use solutions for priority handling, combinatorial generation, binary search operations, and functional programming. The most widely used algorithmic modules include **`heapq`, `itertools`, `bisect`, and `functools`**. Together, they form a powerful toolkit for solving advanced problems with high performance and minimal code.

`heapq`

The `heapq` module implements a **priority queue using a min-heap structure**. In a min-heap, the smallest element is always maintained at the top, which allows for fast access to the minimum value.

This module is extensively used in:

- Scheduling and Task Prioritization
- Shortest Path Algorithms (like Dijkstra's Algorithm)
- Top-K Element Problems
- Event-Driven Simulations

Additionally, `heapq` supports efficient insertion and removal in logarithmic time, which makes it ideal when frequent priority-based retrieval is required. Therefore, it plays a critical role in real-time systems and optimization problems.

`itertools`

The itertools module provides **fast, memory-efficient tools for generating combinations, permutations, and infinite iterators**. Instead of creating large intermediate lists, itertools generates values on the fly, which saves memory and improves performance.

It is commonly used in:

- Generating Permutations and Combinations
- Cartesian Product of Multiple Sets
- Sequence Manipulation and Pattern Generation
- Backtracking and Combinatorial Optimization Problems

itertools enables programmers to explore large solution spaces efficiently without unnecessary memory overhead.

`bisect`

The bisect module offers tools for **binary search and sorted insertion in lists**. It allows programmers to maintain a list in sorted order while still performing fast insertions and searches.

Bisect is widely used in:

- Maintaining Dynamically Sorted Sequences
- Efficient Searching in Sorted Data
- Insertion without Breaking Order
- Range Query and Ranking Problems

Therefore, by replacing manual binary search logic, bisect makes sorted list handling both **efficient and conceptually simple**.

functools

The functools module provides utilities for **functional programming and performance optimization**. It includes tools for function wrapping, partial function application, and automatic caching of computation results.

`functools` is highly useful in:

- Dynamic programming through memoization
- Reducing repeated computation in recursive functions
- Cleaner implementation of higher-order functions
- Code optimization in complex recursive algorithms

Its caching capability significantly improves performance in problems involving **overlapping subproblems and repeated function calls.**

List Comprehensions and Lambda Functions

List comprehensions and lambda functions are two powerful features of Python that support a **concise and expressive functional programming style**. They allow programmers to perform data transformations, filtering, and small computations with minimal code while maintaining clarity and efficiency. These features are widely used in algorithmic problem solving because they **reduce verbosity, improve readability, and often enhance performance** when compared to traditional looping constructs.

Together, list comprehensions and lambda expressions encourage a clean, declarative coding style where the focus shifts from *how* a task is performed to *what* result is required.

Syntax and Practical Usage

A **list comprehension** provides a compact way to create a new list by applying an expression to each element of an existing iterable, optionally with a condition. It replaces multiple lines of loop-based code with a single expressive statement. List comprehensions are commonly used for:

- Filtering elements from a list
- Transforming values into a new form

- Flattening nested lists
- Generating sequences based on conditions

A **lambda function** is a small anonymous function defined in a single line. It is typically used when a short piece of logic is needed temporarily, such as inside sorting, filtering, or mapping operations. Lambda functions are commonly used with higher-order functions that process lists, sets, and dictionaries.

In practical programming, list comprehensions and lambda functions often work together—for example, applying a lambda condition inside a comprehension to filter or transform data in a clean and compact way.

Functional Programming Style

List comprehensions and lambda expressions promote a **functional programming approach**, where computation is expressed using transformations instead of step-by-step procedures. This style emphasizes:

- Immutability of data
- Expression-based computation
- Clear data flow through transformations
- Reduced side effects

In algorithmic problem solving, this approach helps in writing **more predictable and easier-to-debug code**. Functional constructs are widely applied in data processing, filtering pipelines, feature selection, and algorithmic optimizations.

This style also integrates seamlessly with Python's standard modules, such as map, filter, sorted, and many tools from the `itertools` and `functools` modules.

In functional programming, the transformation factor refers to expressing complex logic as a series of **data transformations** rather than explicit control flow. Instead of modifying data step by step, inputs are transformed into outputs through chained operations such as mapping, filtering, reducing, and aggregation. In high-intensive data structure computation environments — such as big data analytics, machine learning pipelines.

Performance Advantages

In many cases, list comprehensions are **faster than equivalent for-loops**, because they are optimized at the interpreter level. They reduce overhead by:

- Avoiding repeated function calls
- Minimizing variable lookups
- Using optimized internal iteration

Lambda functions also introduce minimal overhead compared to full function definitions, making them suitable for short, one-time computations. Together, these features help achieve **both concise code and efficient execution**, which is especially important in competitive programming, large data processing, and interview environments where both clarity and speed matter.

Hands-On Reinforcement

Learning Data Structures and Algorithms becomes truly effective only when concepts are **applied to real problems and tested through structured practice**. This section is designed to strengthen conceptual understanding by connecting theory with real-world use cases, interview-level challenges, and optimization-driven decision making. Through carefully designed case studies, mock problems, and performance analysis, learners develop the confidence to apply DSA patterns and STL/Python tools in practical scenarios.

Real-World Case Problems

Real-world case problems simulate how DSA concepts are used in **actual software systems and production environments**. These problems integrate multiple techniques such as two pointers, sliding windows, greedy strategies, heaps, hash maps, and interval processing into a single cohesive solution. Learners work with scenarios such as:

- Log file analysis and event stream processing
- User activity tracking and frequency analytics
- Scheduling and resource allocation systems
- Search and recommendation engines
- Financial transaction aggregation

Each case problem emphasizes **end-to-end solution design**, beginning with problem understanding, followed by optimal data structure and pattern selection, implementation using STL or Python modules, and finally performance evaluation. This process builds **industry-ready analytical and implementation skills**.

Mock Interview Problems

Mock interview problems reflect the **actual structure, difficulty level, and time pressure of real technical interviews**. These questions are curated from frequently asked problems across product-based and service-based companies.

This subsection helps learners:

- Practice under strict time constraints
- Improve clarity of logical explanation
- Strengthen pattern recognition and decision-making
- Build confidence for live coding scenarios

Each mock problem is supported with a detailed solution approach and complexity discussion, enabling students to understand not just *what* the solution is, but *how to think through it systematically*. This prepares learners for **real interview environments rather than only academic evaluations**.

Time-Space Trade-Off Analysis

Every efficient program is the result of a **careful balance between time complexity and space complexity**. This subsection focuses on developing analytical thinking for comparing alternative solutions.

Students learn to:

- Evaluate multiple valid solutions for the same problem
- Decide when extra memory can be traded for faster execution
- Recognize constraints that demand memory-efficient design
- Justify optimization choices clearly during interviews and technical discussions

This ability to reason about trade-offs is critical in real-world software systems as well as in high-level technical interviews.

Mini Project

The mini project serves as the **capstone activity** of this chapter, enabling learners to integrate multiple DSA patterns and STL/Python tools into a complete working solution. The project workflow includes:

- Understanding a real-world inspired problem statement
- Selecting appropriate data structures and algorithmic patterns
- Designing the overall solution architecture
- Implementing the solution using STL or Python standard modules
- Performing detailed time and space complexity analysis

Students are also encouraged to **test their solutions using diverse datasets and evaluate scalability under different constraints**, helping them develop a professional engineering mindset.

Practice Exercises

Practice exercises are structured to progressively move from **concept reinforcement to interview-level optimization challenges**. The problems are grouped to cover:

- Pattern-specific exercises
- Multi-pattern integration problems
- Optimization-focused challenges
- Competitive programming and interview-level problems

Regular practice of these exercises builds **speed, accuracy, and confidence**, which are essential for real interview environments and coding assessments.

Common Implementation Mistakes

This subsection highlights frequently observed mistakes made by learners, such as choosing inappropriate STL containers, incorrect iterator usage, ignoring boundary conditions, and unnecessarily applying brute-force logic when optimized patterns are available. These mistakes often result in **runtime errors, time limit exceeded (TLE) issues, or incorrect outputs** in competitive and interview environments. By studying these pitfalls, students develop the ability to **debug faster, avoid repeated errors, and write more robust and reliable solutions**.

Conclusion

This chapter brought together the complete journey of Data Structures and Algorithms by focusing on their **practical application through industry-relevant problem-solving patterns and modern programming tools**. Learners explored powerful techniques such as Two Pointers, Sliding Window, Prefix Sums, Binary Search on Answer, Greedy with Sorting, Monotonic Structures, and Bit Manipulation—each of which forms the backbone of efficient algorithmic thinking. The chapter also provided in-depth exposure to **C++ STL and Python built-in utilities**, enabling students to convert theoretical solutions into clean, optimized, and professional-grade code. Through real-world case studies, mock interview problems, time-space trade-off analysis, and a structured mini project, learners developed not only technical accuracy but also design thinking and optimization awareness. This chapter transforms students from concept learners into **confident problem solvers ready for real-world and interview-level challenges**. As the next step in this learning journey, *Chapter 16, Smart*

Coding Practices, Interview Preparation and Emerging Tech Trends, shifts the focus from algorithms alone to **career-oriented mastery and professional readiness**. It equips learners with clean coding principles, structured thinking for interviews, resume-building strategies, mock interview preparation methods, and insights into how DSA powers modern technologies such as Artificial Intelligence, Cloud Computing, Cybersecurity, Blockchain, and IoT. Together, this and the next chapters ensure that learners are not only strong in problem-solving but also **fully prepared for industry expectations and long-term career growth**.

Points to Remember

- Applied DSA patterns help convert theoretical algorithms into efficient real-world solutions.
- The two-pointer and sliding window techniques optimize subarray and substring problems to linear time.
- Prefix sums and difference arrays enable fast range query and range update operations.
- The binary search on answer technique is used when the search space is monotonic.
- Greedy strategies combined with sorting solve many scheduling and allocation problems efficiently.
- Bit manipulation allows constant-time optimization using binary representation.
- C++ STL offers highly optimized containers, algorithms, iterators, and utility functions.
- Python built-ins and standard modules reduce coding overhead, while maintaining performance.
- Choosing the right data structure is as important as choosing the right algorithm.
- Time-space trade-off analysis is critical for interview and industry-level optimization.
- Mock interviews simulate real coding environments and improve confidence.
- Mini projects integrate multiple patterns into a single practical solution.
- Avoiding common implementation mistakes prevents logical and performance errors.
- Clean, readable code improves debugging and maintainability.

Multiple Choice Questions

1. The two-pointer technique is primarily used to:
    a. Solve graph problems.
    b. Optimize array and string traversal.
    c. Handle recursion.
    d. Perform hashing.
2. The sliding window technique is best suited for:
    a. Tree Traversal
    b. Fixed and Variable Range Problems
    c. Graph Traversal
    d. Matrix Multiplication
3. Prefix Sum is mainly used to:
    a. Sort arrays.
    b. Optimize range query computations.

   c. Apply greedy strategies.
   d. Perform recursion.
4. Difference arrays are mainly used for:
   a. Searching
   b. Range Updates
   c. Sorting
   d. Pattern Matching
5. Binary Search on Answer is applied when:
   a. Input is random.
   b. Search space is monotonic.
   c. Data is unsorted.
   d. Graph traversal is needed.
6. Greedy with sorting is commonly used in:
   a. Graph Coloring
   b. Job Scheduling
   c. Tree Balancing
   d. String Matching
7. A monotonic stack is mainly used to:
   a. Store unique values.
   b. Solve next greater/smaller element problems.
   c. Handle recursion.
   d. Perform hashing.
8. Bit manipulation is especially useful for:
   a. Matrix Problems
   b. Constant-Time Optimizations
   c. String Pattern Matching
   d. Binary Trees
9. Which STL container provides dynamic resizing with fast indexing?
   a. List
   b. Vector
   c. Map
   d. Set
10. Which STL container is implemented using a heap?
   a. Queue
   b. Stack
   c. Priority Queue
   d. Deque

11. Which Python structure provides key-value mapping?
    a. List
    b. Tuple
    c. Dictionary
    d. Set
12. The Python module used for priority queues is:
    a. bisect
    b. heapq
    c. itertools
    d. functools
13. Lambda functions in Python are used for:
    a. Long multi-line functions
    b. Inline short functional logic
    c. File handling
    d. Threading
14. Time-space trade-off refers to:
    a. Ignoring memory
    b. Ignoring execution time
    c. Balancing memory usage and speed
    d. Only optimizing code length
15. STL shortcuts are mainly used to:
    a. Increase memory usage.
    b. Reduce code clarity.
    c. Improve performance and reduce code length.
    d. Replace algorithms.

Answers

1. b
2. b
3. b
4. b
5. b
6. b
7. b
8. b
9. b
10. c
11. c
12. b

13. b
14. c
15. c

Questions

1. Explain the importance of applied DSA patterns in real-world software systems.
2. Describe the two-pointer technique with suitable applications.
3. Explain the sliding window technique and its performance benefits.
4. Discuss the role of prefix sums and difference arrays in optimization.
5. Explain the concept of binary search in an answer with examples.
6. Describe the use of greedy strategies with sorting in scheduling problems.
7. Explain monotonic stacks and their applications.
8. Discuss how Python built-in modules simplify algorithmic problem-solving.

Key Terms

- **Two-Pointer Technique**: A method that uses two indices to optimize array and string traversal
- **Sliding Window**: A technique to efficiently process subarrays or substrings of fixed or variable size
- **Prefix Sum**: A precomputed array used for fast range sum queries
- **Difference Array**: An array used for efficient range update operations
- **Binary Search on Answer**: A method that applies binary search on the solution space instead of direct data
- **Greedy Algorithm**: An approach that makes locally optimal choices at each step
- **Monotonic Stack**: A stack that maintains elements in increasing or decreasing order
- **Bit Manipulation**: Using binary operations for fast computation
- **STL**: Stands for 'Standard Template Library' in C++, which provides optimized data structures and algorithms
- **Vector**: A dynamic array in C++ STL
- **Priority Queue**: A queue that always removes the highest-priority element
- **Dictionary**: A Python data structure that stores key-value pairs
- **Lambda Function**: A small anonymous function in Python

CHAPTER 16
Best Tips and Trends for Interviews

Introduction

Mastering Data Structures and Algorithms (DSA) is only the first step toward becoming a successful software professional. In real-world scenarios, what truly sets a strong programmer apart is their ability to **write clean and efficient code, think logically under pressure, communicate solutions clearly, and adapt to evolving technologies**. Hence, this chapter is designed to bridge the gap between academic knowledge and real-world industry expectations by focusing on **smart coding habits, structured interview preparation, and the growing importance of DSA in modern technologies**. In today's competitive job market, employers look for more than just correct answers; they value **code quality, problem-solving approach, optimization mindset, and the ability to justify design decisions**. Therefore, this chapter will guide learners through proven strategies for tackling coding interviews with confidence, from understanding a problem statement and choosing the right data structure, to optimizing solutions and managing time effectively during interviews. It will also provide practical guidance on **resume building, mock interviews, and self-assessment** to help students present their technical skills professionally. Beyond interviews and placements, this chapter will also highlight how **DSA powers emerging technologies** such as Artificial Intelligence (AI), Machine Learning (ML), Big Data, cloud computing, cybersecurity, blockchain, and the Internet of Things (IoT). Thus, by understanding these connections, learners can gain clarity on how the fundamental concepts they studied throughout this book are applied in real-world systems at scale. By the end of this chapter, students will develop a **holistic perspective on programming**—not just as a subject of study, but as a professional skillset that includes clean coding, disciplined practice, ethical responsibility, and continuous learning. Hence, this final chapter will ultimately prepare learners to transition confidently from classrooms and labs into **interviews, industry roles, and lifelong growth in technology**.

Structure

In this chapter, we will cover the following topics:

- Smart Coding Practices
- Algorithmic Thinking for Interviews
- Coding Interview Preparation Strategy
- High-Frequency Interview Topics in DSA

- Resume Building for DSA and Software Roles
- Mock Interviews and Practice Protocol
- Emerging Technology Trends Using DSA
- Industry-Relevant Problem-Solving Case Studies
- Ethical Coding and Responsible Computing
- Career Roadmap for DSA Learners
- Practice and Assessment

Smart Coding Practices

Smart coding practices form the foundation of professional software development. Writing code is not just about making a program work; it is about making it **easy to understand, easy to maintain, safe from errors, and efficient in performance**. These practices help programmers build reliable systems, collaborate smoothly with teams, and perform confidently in interviews and real-world projects. Hence, this section will explain the essential habits every programmer must develop to become a smart and responsible coder.

Writing Clean, Readable, and Maintainable Code

Clean code **explains itself through its well-outlined structure and clarity**. A reader should be able to understand what the program does without struggling to decode complicated logic or confusing syntax. Readable code uses meaningful variable names, proper indentation, consistent formatting, and simple logic.

Maintainable code is just as important as clean code. Software often needs updates, bug fixes, and feature enhancements. If the original code is well structured and easy to read, future changes become smoother and safer. Thus, clean and maintainable code:

- Reduces debugging time
- Improves teamwork and collaboration
- Increases software reliability
- Reflects professional coding standards

A good habit is to write code as if someone else will maintain it in the future—even if that person will be you.

Importance of Modular Programming

Modular programming means **to break down a large program into smaller, independent, and reusable modules or functions**. Instead of writing everything in one long block, the program is divided into logical units, where each performs a specific task.

- The benefits of modular programming are:
- Simpler understanding of program flow
- Faster debugging and testing
- Better reuse of code across projects
- Improved team collaboration
- Scalable and flexible software design

For instance, instead of writing all logic inside main(), separate functions can handle input, processing, and output. Therefore, this separation of concerns makes programs more organized and professional.

Naming Conventions and Structured Documentation

Meaningful naming and proper documentation can greatly improve the clarity of a program. Variable names, function names, and class names should clearly describe **what they represent or what they do**. Ambiguous names like x, temp, or data1 should be avoided, unless they are used in a very small, local scope.

Here are some good naming practices you should keep in mind:

- Use descriptive names (`totalMarks`, `searchIndex`, `calculateAverage`).
- Follow consistent naming styles (`camelCase`, `PascalCase`, `snake_case`).
- Avoid unnecessary abbreviations.

Structured documentation includes comments, function headers, and brief descriptions of logic where needed. Comments should **explain why something is done**, and not what is already obvious from the code. In other words, well-documented code becomes much easier to review, debug, and enhance.

Error Handling and Defensive Coding

Errors and unexpected situations are unavoidable in real-world software. Smart programmers anticipate these situations and design code that can **handle failures safely and gracefully**. This practice is known as defensive coding.

Error handling includes:

- Checking for invalid input
- Using exception handling where required
- Preventing illegal memory access
- Handling file and resource errors properly
- Ensuring proper cleanup of system resources

Defensive coding reduces system crashes, improves application stability, and enhances user experience. Instead of allowing a program to fail silently or abruptly, it should ideally respond with clear messages and controlled behavior.

Input Validation and Edge-Case Handling

No program can assume that the input will always be valid. Users may enter incorrect values, empty inputs, large numbers, or unexpected formats. **Input validation ensures that only valid and safe data is processed**. Common validation checks include:

- Data Type Verification
- Range Checking
- Empty or Null Value Checks
- Format Validation

Edge cases refer to **extreme or special input conditions** such as zero elements, maximum limits, duplicate values, or boundary indexes. Ignoring edge cases can cause logic failures even in well-written algorithms. Therefore, smart programmers should always test their code against both normal inputs and edge cases.

Code Optimization Strategies

Code optimization focuses on improving the **time efficiency, space efficiency, and overall performance** of a program. While correctness is the first priority, performance becomes critical when dealing with large inputs and real-time systems.

Common optimization strategies include:

- Choosing efficient data structures
- Reducing unnecessary loops
- Avoiding repeated computations
- Using appropriate algorithms for the problem size
- Minimizing memory usage

However, premature optimization should be avoided. The correct approach will be to first ensure that the program works correctly, and then optimize the parts that consume the most time or memory.

Balancing Readability and Performance

A common challenge in programming is maintaining the right balance between **code readability and performance**. Highly optimized code can sometimes become difficult to understand, and very clean code may not always be the fastest.

Smart programmers aim for the following features:

- Clear Logic
- Measurable Optimization (Only Where Required)
- Avoiding Over-Complex Solutions
- Writing Efficient and Understandable Code

To add further, readable and maintainable code is often preferred over extreme micro-optimizations in professional environments, unless the application is performance-critical.

Algorithmic Thinking for Interviews

Cracking technical interviews is not only about knowing the basics of DSA; it is about how you think, how you approach a problem, and how you design a solution under time pressure. Interviewers closely observe a candidate's reasoning process, and not just the final answer. This is where algorithmic thinking comes in—it trains you to analyze a problem logically, break it into manageable pieces, select suitable tools, and arrive at an efficient solution. Thus, this section will explain the key components of algorithmic thinking that every interview candidate must master.

Understanding Problem Statements Effectively

The first and most critical step in solving any interview problem is to **properly understand the problem itself**. Many candidates lose marks not because they lack knowledge, but because they misinterpret what is being asked.

Therefore, effective problem understanding involves:

- Carefully reading the full question before jumping to a solution
- Identifying the exact input format and expected output
- Understanding constraints such as input size, range of values, and time limits

- Clarifying ambiguous statements by asking questions, if allowed

Additionally, a good practice is to **rephrase the problem in your own words** before starting. This ensures conceptual clarity and prevents logical mistakes that might emerge later in the solution.

Breaking Complex Problems into Sub-Tasks

Most interview problems appear difficult because they are presented as a single large challenge. Smart problem solvers **decompose the problem into smaller, simpler sub-problems**.

This includes:

- Identifying independent components of the problem
- Separating input processing, core logic, and output generation
- Solving simpler versions of the problem first
- Gradually building toward the complete solution

To sum up, decomposition reduces mental burden and makes it easier to debug and optimize later.

Identifying Appropriate Data Structures

Once the problem is understood and broken into parts, the next step is to choose the **right data structure**. This decision often determines the efficiency and simplicity of the final solution.

You can make any of the following choices, depending on the nature of the problem:

- Arrays and Strings (For Direct Indexing and Sequence Processing)
- Hash Maps (For Fast Lookups and Frequency Counting)
- Stacks and Queues (For Sequential Processing)
- Trees for Hierarchical Data
- Graphs (For Network-Like Relationships)

Interviewers often test whether candidates can **map a problem to the correct data structure,** based on access patterns and constraints.

Choosing Correct Algorithms

After selecting the data structure, the next step is choosing a suitable algorithmic strategy. This includes recognizing which algorithmic paradigm fits the problem best, such as:

- Sorting-Based Logic
- Greedy Approach
- Divide-and-Conquer Approach
- Dynamic Programming
- Backtracking
- Binary Search

A correct algorithm should satisfy both functional correctness and performance efficiency. A brute-force solution may work for small inputs but fail for large constraints. Therefore, algorithm selection must always be guided by the problem's time and space limits.

Recognizing Hidden Constraints

Many interview problems appear simple but contain **hidden constraints** that influence the choice of solution. These include:

- Extremely Large Input Sizes
- Repeated Queries
- Hardware Memory Limitations
- Real-Time Processing Requirements

For instance, a problem that allows only one pass through the data demands a linear-time solution. Hence, recognizing such constraints early prevents you from spending unnecessary effort on inefficient approaches.

Transition from Brute Force to Optimized Solutions

Interviewers often expect candidates to **first describe a brute-force solution, and then optimize its reasoning step by step**. This demonstrates logical maturity and deep understanding.

The typical optimization journey involves:

- Starting with a simple, straightforward solution
- Identifying bottlenecks, such as nested loops or repeated computations
- Reducing time complexity through better data structures
- Applying advanced techniques such as prefix sums, binary search, or dynamic programming

Therefore, the ability to refine a solution is a strong indicator of problem-solving skill and technical depth.

Coding Interview Preparation Strategy

Preparing for coding interviews is a structured journey that combines technical knowledge, consistent practice, mental preparation, and strategic planning. Success in interviews does not come solely from memorizing algorithms; it comes from understanding how to apply concepts under the pressure of limited time, while communicating solutions clearly, and maintaining confidence. Hence, this section will explain the key components of an effective coding interview preparation strategy that helps learners perform at their best across different interview formats.

Types of Technical Interview Rounds

Technical interviews usually consist of multiple rounds, each designed to evaluate different skill sets of a candidate. Common types include:

- **Screening Round:** A basic filtering stage that checks fundamental programming and logical skills
- **Technical Coding Round:** Focuses on solving algorithmic problems using DSA concepts
- **System Design Round:** Tests the ability to design scalable and efficient systems
- **Behavioral and HR Round:** Assesses communication skills, attitude, and cultural fit

To put it simply, understanding the purpose of each round helps candidates prepare in a focused and structured manner, rather than studying randomly.

Online Coding Assessments

Online coding assessments are often the **first formal stage of recruitment**, especially in campus placements and large tech companies. These tests are conducted on digital platforms and usually include:

- Multiple Choice Questions (MCQs) on Programming and CS Fundamentals
- (One or More) Coding Problems with Time Limits
- Automated Evaluation (Based on Correctness and Efficiency)

Therefore, to perform well in online assessments, candidates must:

- Practice writing code quickly and accurately.
- Be comfortable with input-output handling.
- Optimize solutions to pass hidden test cases.
- Manage time efficiently across multiple problems.

Additionally, regularly practicing on competitive programming and coding platforms will be helpful in building confidence for this stage.

Whiteboard and Live Coding Rounds

In whiteboard and live coding rounds, candidates are asked to **solve problems in front of interviewers**, either on a physical board or using a shared online editor. The focus here is not only on the final answer but also on the **thinking process, clarity of explanation, and step-by-step approach**.

The key expectations in these rounds include:

- Understanding and restating the problem clearly
- Explaining algorithm choice and complexity
- Writing clean and structured code
- Handling edge cases during the discussion
- Debugging logically when errors occur

Therefore, it is advised that candidates practice explaining their solutions aloud, as communication plays a crucial role in these rounds.

System Design Interview Overview

System design interviews test a candidate's ability to **design large-scale, real-world software systems** rather than just writing small algorithms. These interviews evaluate:

- Understanding of Scalability and Performance
- Appropriate Use of Databases, Caching, and Load Balancing
- Selection of Suitable Data Structures and Algorithms
- Trade-Offs between Speed, Memory, and Reliability
- High-Level Architecture and Component Interaction

Even at the beginner level, candidates are expected to demonstrate structured thinking, logical decomposition, and the ability to justify design choices.

Time Management during Coding Interviews

Time is a critical factor in every interview round. Effective time management involves:

- Avoiding excessive time on understanding the problem
- Not getting stuck on a single approach for too long
- Switching to simpler alternatives when needed
- Testing code with minimal, but meaningful test cases
- Prioritizing correctness before micro-optimization

Therefore, a smart candidate should allocate their time wisely between thinking, coding, and verifying the solution. Practicing timed mock tests also helps in building this skill.

Handling Pressure and Building Confidence

Interview environments naturally create pressure. Nervousness, fear of failure, and stress are common challenges faced by candidates. However, confidence can be built with the right mindset and preparation.

Effective techniques include:

- Attempting regular mock interviews
- Practicing under time constraints
- Positive self-talk and focus on calm reasoning
- Accepting mistakes as learning opportunities
- Entering interviews with a problem-solving attitude rather than fear

Confidence grows when preparation is systematic and consistent. A calm and clear-headed approach often results in better logical decisions during interviews.

High-Frequency Interview Topics in DSA

DSA forms the core of most technical interviews. While the syllabus may be vast, a specific set of topics appears repeatedly across coding interviews in product-based companies, service companies, and competitive programming platforms. Mastering these high-frequency areas not only strengthens fundamental understanding, but also significantly increases the chances of success in technical interviews. This section highlights the most important DSA topics, along with their relevance and typical problem patterns.

Arrays and Strings

Arrays and strings are among the most commonly tested topics in interviews because they represent basic data storage and manipulation. Problems typically focus on traversal, searching, sorting, subarrays, substrings, and pattern-based techniques.

Common interview problem areas include:

- Two-Pointer Techniques
- Sliding Window Problems
- Prefix Sums
- Subarray Sum Problems
- String Reversal, Palindromes, and Pattern Matching

These problems test a candidate's ability to handle indexing, optimize brute-force solutions, and manage memory efficiently.

Linked Lists

Linked lists are used to evaluate understanding of dynamic memory allocation and pointer manipulation. Interviewers often test both conceptual knowledge and implementation accuracy.

Typical problem types include:

- Reversal of a Linked List
- Detecting and Removing Cycles
- Finding the Middle Element
- Merging Sorted Linked Lists
- Removing the nth Node from the End

These problems assess problem-solving using pointer logic, rather than array indexing.

Stacks and Queues

Stacks and queues test a candidate's understanding of order-based data processing. Their applications in real-world systems make them a key interview topic.

Common interview applications include:

- Parenthesis Matching
- Expression Evaluation
- Next Greater Element
- Queue Implementation Using Stacks
- Sliding Window Maximum

The mentioned problems focus on managing sequential constraints efficiently.

Trees and Binary Search Trees

Tree-based structures are central to many advanced interview questions. They test recursive thinking, hierarchical processing, and structural properties.

Frequently asked problems include:

- Tree Traversals
- Height and Diameter of a Tree
- Lowest Common Ancestor
- Validating a Binary Search Tree
- Insertion and Deletion in BST

These problems are important as they evaluate both theoretical understanding and practical recursion skills.

Heaps and Priority Queues

Heaps are used to solve problems that require fast access to the minimum or maximum element. They appear frequently in scheduling and optimization problems.

Typical interview problems include:

- Finding the kth Largest or Smallest Element
- Merging k Sorted Lists
- Running Median of a Stream
- Priority-Based Task Scheduling

Therefore, these problems assess understanding of heap properties and priority queue operations.

Graphs and Graph Algorithms

Graph-based problems test a candidate's ability to model networks, relationships, and paths. These questions assess both theoretical concepts and implementation skills.

High-frequency graph problems include:

- Breadth-First Search (BFS) and Depth-First Search (DFS)
- Detecting Cycles
- Shortest Path Problems
- Connected Components
- Topological Sorting

Graph algorithms demonstrate a candidate's strength in traversal and optimization strategies.

Sorting and Searching

Sorting and searching form the backbone of many algorithmic problems. Interviewers often expect candidates to know both the working principles and the complexity trade-offs of these techniques.

Common questions include:

- Binary Search Implementation and Its Variants
- Sorting Algorithms and Their Stability
- Search in Rotated Sorted Arrays
- Finding the First and Last Occurrence

These problems test algorithm selection and performance analysis skills.

Greedy Algorithms

Greedy algorithms are used to solve optimization problems where local decisions lead to global solutions. These problems test logical reasoning and decision-making ability.

Frequently asked greedy problems include:

- Activity Selection
- Fractional Knapsack
- Job Scheduling
- Minimum Number of Platforms
- Huffman Coding

Interviewers evaluate whether candidates can justify their greedy choices through these questions.

Dynamic Programming

Dynamic programming is one of the most important and challenging interview topics. It tests a candidate's ability to break problems into overlapping sub-problems and store intermediate results.

High-frequency DP problems include:

- Fibonacci Series
- Climbing Stairs
- House Robber
- Knapsack Variants
- Longest Common Subsequence
- Edit Distance

These problems check state formulation, transitions, and optimization techniques.

Recursion and Backtracking

Recursion and backtracking assess logical depth, problem decomposition, and exhaustive search capability.

Common interview problems include:

- Permutations and Combinations
- Subsets Generation
- N-Queens Problem
- Sudoku Solver
- Palindrome Partitioning

These problems test whether a candidate can manage recursive states and backtracking correctly.

Resume Building for DSA and Software Roles

A resume is often the **first impression** a candidate creates in the mind of a recruiter. Even with strong technical skills in DSA, a poorly structured resume can reduce the chances of getting shortlisted. A well-crafted technical resume should clearly communicate **skills, projects, problem-solving ability, and professional potential** within a short span of time. This section explains how to design an effective resume specifically for DSA-focused and software development roles.

Structure of a Strong Technical Resume

A strong technical resume follows a **clean, logical, and professional structure,** so that recruiters can quickly locate essential information. The typical structure includes:

- **Header Section:** Name, contact details, professional email ID, and portfolio or GitHub link
- **Career Objective or Summary:** A brief statement highlighting technical interests and career goals
- **Technical Skills:** Programming languages, data structures, algorithms, tools, and platforms
- **Projects:** Academic, personal, or professional projects with technical details
- **Internships and Experience:** If applicable, with responsibilities and technologies used
- **Education:** Degree, institution, year of passing, and academic performance

- **Certifications and Achievements:** Relevant technical certifications, hackathons, or coding competitions

A well-structured resume allows recruiters to scan important information within a few seconds.

Highlighting Projects and Technical Skills

For DSA and software roles, **projects and technical skills form the core of the resume**. Recruiters look for proof of practical application of concepts.

Here are some important points to consider while updating this section of your resume:

- List programming languages clearly (such as C++, Python, Java).
- Mention core DSA topics you are confident in.
- Include tools and technologies used (databases, frameworks, version control systems).
- Prioritize recent and relevant projects.
- Include links to GitHub repositories or live demos if available.

Projects demonstrate not just knowledge, but also **problem-solving ability, design thinking, and hands-on experience**. Drafting your resume as per the mentioned points will help you draw a compelling picture of your skills and expertise.

Writing Effective Project Descriptions

Project descriptions should focus on **what problem was solved, how it was solved, and what technologies were used.** Instead of general statements, precise technical details should be highlighted.

An effective project description should include the following:

- Problem Statement or Objective
- Key Features Implemented
- Algorithms and Data Structures Used
- Tools, Libraries, or Platforms Involved
- Performance Improvements or Outcomes Achieved

For example, instead of writing "*Built a sorting application*", it will be more effective to write "*Designed and implemented a C++ application using Merge Sort and Binary Search to efficiently process and query large datasets.*"

This approach will allow recruiters to understand your technical depth quickly.

Quantifying Achievements

Quantifying achievements adds **credibility and impact** to a resume. Numbers make your accomplishments measurable and compelling.

Examples of quantification include:

- Reduced processing time by a certain percentage
- Processed a specific volume of data
- Ranked within a certain percentile in a coding contest
- Solved a given number of coding problems on platforms

For instance, "Optimized search algorithm reducing execution time by 40%" is stronger than a vague statement like "Improved algorithm efficiency".

ATS-Friendly Resume Guidelines

Many companies use **Applicant Tracking Systems (ATS)** to filter resumes before human review. An ATS-friendly resume ensures your profile is not rejected automatically.

Here are some important ATS guidelines to remember:

- Use standard fonts and simple formatting.
- Avoid excessive graphics, tables, and images.
- Use standard section titles like **Skills; Education; Projects**.
- Include relevant keywords from the job description.
- Save the resume in commonly accepted formats such as PDF or DOCX.

An ATS-friendly resume increases the probability of your resume reaching the recruiter's desk.

Common Resume Mistakes to Avoid

Even skilled candidates often lose on opportunities due to common resume errors. Some of the most frequent mistakes include:

- Spelling and Grammatical Errors
- Overly Long Resumes with Unnecessary Details
- Irrelevant Personal Information
- Poor Formatting and Cluttered Layout
- Exaggeration of Skills
- Lack of Project Clarity
- Missing GitHub or Portfolio Links

Therefore, avoiding these mistakes is indicative of **professionalism, attention to detail, and seriousness about career growth.**

Mock Interviews and Practice Protocol

Preparing for technical interviews requires more than just studying concepts; it demands **consistent practice in a simulated interview environment**. Mock interviews and structured practice play a vital role in transforming theoretical knowledge into confident real-time performance. Therefore, this section will explain how students can use self-assessment, peer interaction, online platforms, and feedback analysis to build a strong, continuous improvement cycle for interview success.

Self-Assessment Techniques

Self-assessment is the foundation of effective preparation. It allows candidates to **identify their strengths, weaknesses, and knowledge gaps** before facing real interviewers.

Here are some commonly used self-assessment methods:

- Solving coding problems without external help
- Timing yourself while attempting interview-level questions
- Maintaining a personal error log to track recurring mistakes
- Regular revision of weak topics
- Rating confidence levels across different DSA areas

Self-assessment encourages honesty and self-discipline. It helps learners focus their efforts on areas that need the most improvement instead of revising only familiar topics.

Peer-to-Peer Mock Interviews

Peer interviews recreate the **pressure and interaction of real technical interviews** in a low-risk environment. When students interview each other, they experience both sides of the process—that of the candidate and the interviewer – which eventually strengthens problem understanding and communication skills.

Benefits of peer mock interviews include:

- Practicing clear explanation of solutions
- Learning alternative approaches from peers
- Developing confidence in speaking about code
- Improving logical thinking under time constraints
- Receiving immediate constructive feedback

In this way, regular peer mock sessions build both technical skill and interview temperament.

Platform-Based Practice Strategies

Online coding platforms provide structured and scalable environments for interview preparation. These platforms simulate **real online assessments and competitive coding environments**, and offer timed tests, difficulty levels, and performance statistics.

Effective platform-based strategies include:

- Daily practice of mixed-difficulty problems
- Weekly topic-wise revision sets
- Participating in monthly coding contests
- Tracking accuracy and speed metrics
- Revisiting previously incorrect problems

Therefore, using online platforms consistently builds speed, improves accuracy, and increases familiarity with automated testing systems used by companies.

Analyzing Mock Interview Feedback

Feedback is meaningful only when it is **carefully analyzed and acted upon**. After each mock interview, candidates should review both technical and non-technical feedback in detail.

Some key aspects for analysis are:

- Clarity of Explanation of a Given Problem
- Speed and Correctness of Solution
- Use of Appropriate DSA Components
- Handling of Edge Cases
- Code Readability and Structure
- Communication and Confidence Level

Therefore, instead of viewing feedback as criticism, candidates should treat it as **a roadmap for targeted improvement**.

Continuous Improvement Cycles

Interview preparation is not a one-time process; it is a **continuous cycle of improvement and considering areas that can do with more work.** Each round of practice, feedback, and revision should lead to measurable progress.

A typical improvement cycle involves:

- Practicing new problems
- Taking mock interviews
- Analyzing feedback
- Revising weak areas
- Reattempting improved solutions

Therefore, this cycle ensures steady growth in both technical competence and interview performance.

Emerging Technology Trends Using DSA

DSA forms the **backbone of every modern technology system**. No matter how advanced a technology appears on the surface, its efficiency, scalability, and reliability are deeply rooted in how well data is organized and processed behind the scenes. From intelligent machines to global cloud platforms and secure financial networks, DSA plays a decisive role in shaping the performance of emerging technologies. Therefore, this section explains how core DSA concepts directly power today's most influential technology domains.

Role of DSA in AI

AI systems rely on **fast data processing, intelligent decision-making, and real-time responses**. Behind these capabilities lie fundamental data structures and algorithms.

DSA applications in AI include:

- Trees and Graphs (For Decision Trees and Knowledge Representation)
- Priority Queues (For Best-First and A* Search Algorithms)
- Hash Tables (For Fast State Lookups)
- Dynamic Programming (For Optimization Problems)
- Graph Traversals (For Path Planning and Robotics)

Therefore, efficient algorithms ensure that AI systems can analyze large datasets, choose optimal actions, and respond in real time.

Role of DSA in ML Systems

ML involves training models on massive datasets and performing repeated computations efficiently. Without strong DSA foundations, ML models would become too slow and memory-intensive.

DSA supports ML by:

- Using arrays and matrices for feature storage
- Applying trees in decision tree models and random forests
- Using heaps for top-K prediction selection
- Employing hashing for fast feature indexing
- Using dynamic programming in optimization routines

Efficient data handling directly impacts training speed, prediction accuracy, and scalability of ML systems.

Role of DSA in Big Data Analytics

Big Data systems deal with **huge volumes of structured and unstructured data** that must be processed efficiently in limited time.

DSA contributes to Big Data by:

- Using hash maps and trees for indexing large datasets
- Applying sorting and searching algorithms for data filtering
- Using queues and streams for real-time data processing
- Applying graph algorithms for relationship analysis
- Using distributed data structures for parallel computation

DSA ensures that Big Data platforms can analyze terabytes of information quickly and reliably.

Role of DSA in Cloud Computing

Cloud computing platforms manage millions of requests, virtual machines, and data operations simultaneously. Efficient resource management depends heavily on DSA.

DSA applications in cloud systems include:

- Queues (For Request Scheduling)
- Heaps (For Load Balancing)
- Hashing (For Distributed Data Storage)
- Graphs (For Nctwork Routing)
- Trees (For Metadata Indexing)

Without optimized algorithms, cloud platforms would suffer from delays, overloads, and unreliable performance. Therefore, mastering DSA components is important to devise effective solutions for these problems.

Role of DSA in Cybersecurity

Cybersecurity systems must detect threats, analyze network traffic, and protect sensitive data in real time. These tasks require **high-speed data access and processing**, which is made possible through DSA.

Here are some important uses of DSA for cybersecurity:

- Hashing (For Password Storage and Data Integrity)
- Graph algorithms (For Intrusion Detection)
- Pattern matching (For Malware Detection)
- Trees (For Access Control Systems)
- Queues (For Network Traffic Monitoring)

Therefore, strong DSA implementation improves threat detection speed and system reliability in security-critical environments. Therefore, integrating these components with cybersecurity practices can make your system environment impervious to upcoming threats.

Role of DSA in Blockchain Technology

Blockchain technology relies on **secure, distributed, and verifiable data storage**, which is fundamentally algorithm-driven.

DSA plays a central role in blockchain through the following components:

- Hashing (For Block Creation and Validation)
- Merkle Trees (For Transaction Verification)
- Linked Lists (For Block Chain Structure)
- Graph Structures (For Peer-to-Peer Networks)
- Cryptographic Algorithms (For Secure Transactions)

Hence, the efficiency and security of blockchain systems directly depend on robust algorithm design.

Role of DSA in Internet of Things (IoT)

IoT systems involve **millions of interconnected devices** generating continuous streams of real-time data. Efficient management of this data is impossible without optimized data structures and algorithms.

DSA supports IoT by:

- Using queues for sensor data buffering
- Using graphs for device network modeling
- Using trees for hierarchical device control
- Using hash tables for fast device identification
- Streaming algorithms for continuous data analysis

Through these components and actions, DSA ensures that IoT platforms remain scalable, responsive, and energy-efficient.

Moreover, rapidly emerging **Low-Code/No-Code (LCNC)** and **Vibe Coding** platforms aim to simplify application development by abstracting implementation details. However, behind their visual workflows and auto-generated code, these platforms still rely heavily on core **DSA components**. Workflow execution engines use graphs and trees, data binding relies on hash maps and indexing, scheduling engines depend on queues and priority queues, and optimization logic often applies greedy or dynamic programming techniques. Hence, understanding DSA enables developers to customize, optimize, debug, and scale LCNC-generated solutions effectively, while ensuring peak performance, reliability, and correctness even in highly automated development environments.

Industry-Relevant Problem-Solving Case Studies

Real-world software systems operate on massive volumes of data, serve millions of users, and demand high performance, reliability, and scalability. At the core of every such system lie carefully selected **DSA components** that make efficient processing possible. Therefore, developing a thorough understanding of how DSA is applied in real industry scenarios can help learners connect theoretical knowledge with practical system design. Hence, this section explores key real-world case studies where DSA plays a central role in building high-performance technology solutions.

Real-Time Data Processing Systems

Real-time data processing systems are designed to handle continuous streams of data with minimal delay. Examples include stock market platforms, live sports analytics, sensor networks, and online monitoring systems. These systems require immediate processing as data arrives, which makes speed and memory efficiency critical goals to achieve.

Queues and deques are used for buffering incoming data streams, while hash tables provide fast access to records. Heaps are used for prioritizing time-sensitive tasks, and sliding window algorithms help process recent data efficiently. Graphs may also be used to model event dependencies. Therefore, using DSA aptly results in low latency, high throughput, and accurate real-time decision-making in such platforms.

Search Engine Indexing and Ranking Basics

Search engines must store and retrieve billions of web pages within fractions of a second. The foundation of this capability lies in advanced indexing and ranking algorithms.

Tries and inverted index structures are used to store keywords and document references for fast lookups. Hash maps enable quick access to metadata, while graphs represent the web as interconnected pages. Ranking algorithms rely on graph traversal techniques and priority queues to determine the relevance of each page. Hence, without optimized searching, sorting, and graph algorithms, modern search engines would not be able to deliver accurate results at a high speed.

Recommendation System Foundations

Recommendation systems power applications such as e-commerce websites, video streaming platforms, and social media feeds by suggesting relevant products or content to users. These systems analyze large volumes of user behavior data to generate accurate personalized recommendations.

Arrays and matrices store user-item interaction data, while hash maps store user preferences. Additionally, priority queues help identify top recommendations, and graph-based techniques model relationships between users and items. Sorting and searching algorithms are heavily used to rank recommended content. Efficient DSA ensures that recommendations are generated quickly, and are updated dynamically as user behavior changes.

Financial Analytics Platforms

Financial analytics platforms process large-scale transactional data for banking systems, investment portfolios, fraud detection, and risk management. These systems must guarantee accuracy, speed, and security.

Segment Trees and Fenwick Trees are widely used for real-time financial range queries such as cumulative transactions and rolling analytics. Hashing supports quick account lookups, while heaps handle priority-based transaction processing. Graph algorithms are used to detect suspicious transaction patterns. Thus, efficient algorithms enable these platforms to handle millions of transactions per second without degrading performance.

Network Routing and Traffic Management Systems

Modern communication networks rely on intelligent routing and traffic control systems to ensure fast and reliable data transmission. These systems continuously calculate optimal paths for packets across dynamic networks.

Graphs are used to represent network nodes and connections. Shortest path algorithms help determine optimal routing paths, while queues manage packet flow and scheduling. Heaps optimize route selection, and hashing ensures fast lookup of routing tables. Thus, efficient DSA allows networks to dynamically adapt to congestion, failures, and varying traffic loads while maintaining high data transmission efficiency.

Ethical Coding and Responsible Computing

As software systems increasingly influence every aspect of human life—from healthcare and finance, to education, communication, and governance—the responsibility of a programmer extends far beyond writing correct and efficient code. Hence, ethical coding and responsible computing focus on **how technology should be built and used in a way that protects individuals, promotes fairness, and ensures social trust.** To elaborate further, DSA gives systems their power, but ethics decides how this power should be applied. Thus, this section will build upon the key principles that guide responsible software development in the modern digital world.

Data Privacy and Security Principles

Data privacy refers to the right of individuals to control how their personal information is collected, stored, and used. Modern applications continuously process sensitive data such as personal identities, medical records, financial transactions, and location details. Ethical responsibility demands that programmers treat this data with **strict confidentiality and respect**.

From a technical perspective, secure data structures and algorithms are essential to protect sensitive information from unauthorized access. Hashing is used to store passwords securely, encryption algorithms protect data during transmission, and access control structures regulate who can read or modify data. Beyond technical protection, ethical developers must also follow legal and regulatory frameworks related to data protection. Therefore, respecting user privacy builds trust and safeguards users from identity theft, fraud, and misuse of personal information.

Algorithmic Fairness and Bias

Algorithms increasingly influence decisions related to hiring, lending, medical diagnosis, content recommendation, and law enforcement. Therefore, if they are trained on biased data or designed with hidden assumptions, they can produce **unfair or discriminatory outcomes**.

Algorithmic fairness requires developers to ensure that automated decisions do not unfairly disadvantage individuals or groups based on gender, race, religion, disability, or socioeconomic status. From a DSA perspective, bias can emerge not only from data but also from **how algorithms prioritize, filter, and rank information**. Ethical computing demands continuous testing, transparency in decision logic, and careful validation of outputs across diverse user groups. Thus, a responsible programmer must always ask whether an algorithm is treating all users equitably, and if its decisions can be logically justified.

Secure Coding Practices

Secure coding is a vital part of responsible computing. Many real-world cyberattacks arise not from weaknesses in hardware but from **poorly written or carelessly designed code**. Vulnerabilities such as buffer overflows, injection attacks, and improper memory handling can expose systems to serious security breaches.

Responsible developers follow strict secure coding practices that include validating all inputs, avoiding unsafe memory operations, using secure libraries, and handling errors safely without exposing sensitive system details. Data structures must be used carefully to prevent unauthorized access to memory regions, and algorithms must be designed to avoid predictable behavior that attackers could exploit. Therefore, secure coding is not an optional enhancement; it is a fundamental obligation of every software professional.

Responsible Use of Data and Algorithms

Beyond security and fairness, ethical computing also involves the **responsible use of data and algorithms in decision-making systems**. Just because an algorithm can process massive amounts of data does not mean that it should be used without accountability or human oversight.

Responsible use requires transparency in how algorithms work, explainability in automated decisions, and caution in deploying systems that may have significant social impact. For instance, recommendation systems should not manipulate users unfairly, surveillance systems should not violate civil liberties, and prediction algorithms should not replace human judgment blindly in critical domains such as healthcare and justice.

Therefore, programmers must remain aware that their technical decisions shape not only system performance, but also **human lives, social structures, and ethical boundaries**.

Career Roadmap for DSA Learners

Learning DSA is a long-term journey that gradually transforms a beginner into an industry-ready software professional. A clear roadmap helps students stay focused, measure progress, and build confidence at every stage of learning. Hence, this section presents a structured career pathway that guides learners from foundational programming skills, to advanced problem-solving, competitive programming excellence, and successful interview readiness. It will also touch upon the importance of continuous learning in a rapidly evolving technology landscape.

From Beginner to Industry-Ready Developer

The journey typically begins with mastering the fundamentals of programming using languages such as C++, Python, or Java. At this stage, learners focus on understanding basic syntax, control structures, functions, and simple data types. Once the programming foundation is strong, they move on to core structures such as arrays, linked lists, stacks, queues, and hash tables. This phase will build your confidence in handling data efficiently, and solving basic algorithmic problems.

The next stage involves advanced topics including trees, graphs, heaps, sorting and searching algorithms, greedy strategies, dynamic programming, and backtracking. As learners progress, they start recognizing patterns across problems and develop the ability to design optimized solutions independently. Alongside DSA, students should also work on real-world mini projects that integrate these concepts into practical applications. By this stage, they will be no longer just learners but problem solvers who can design, implement, test, and optimize software solutions, which is an essential requirement for becoming industry-ready.

Competitive Programming Roadmap

Competitive programming provides an excellent platform for sharpening algorithmic thinking, speed, and accuracy. The roadmap typically begins with solving easy-level problems focused on arrays, strings, and simple mathematics. Gradually, learners move toward medium-level problems involving stacks, queues, recursion, and basic dynamic programming.

As your confidence strengthens, advanced topics such as segment trees, graph algorithms, and optimization techniques can be introduced through complex problems. Participating regularly in contests will help you improve time management, logical thinking under pressure, and exposure to diverse problem patterns. Over time, consistent practice in competitive programming strengthens intuition, improves debugging skills, and builds resilience. These qualities are highly valued in coding interviews and technical roles.

Interview Preparation Timeline

Interview preparation should ideally begin alongside advanced DSA learning rather than waiting until the final phase of college. In the early phase, students focus on revising fundamental concepts and solving topic-wise problems. As interviews approach, preparation should ideally become more targeted, with significant emphasis on frequently asked interview questions, coding patterns, and time-bound practice.

The timeline then shifts to mock interviews, resume refinement, and system design exposure. Candidates can start practicing explanation skills, whiteboard coding, and real-time debugging. In the final phase, revision of weak areas, stress management, and confidence building should be your primary focal points for preparation. Hence, a balanced interview timeline ensures that you are not overwhelmed at the last moment and enter interviews fully prepared both technically and mentally.

Continuous Learning and Upskilling Strategies

Technology evolves constantly, which makes continuous learning a lifelong requirement for every software professional. Even after securing a job, DSA learners must keep upgrading their skills to stay relevant in the industry. This includes learning new programming frameworks, exploring advanced algorithms, understanding system design concepts, and staying updated with emerging technology trends such as AI, blockchain, and cloud computing.

Upskilling also involves participating in coding competitions, contributing to open-source projects, attending technical workshops, and following research and industry updates. Therefore, you must undertake regular self-assessment, learn new tools, and revisit foundational concepts to ensure that your skills remain sharp and adaptable. It is important to remember that learning transforms a good programmer into a long-term successful technologist.

Practice and Assessment

Practice and assessment form the final and most crucial phase of preparation for a successful software engineering career. Therefore, learning concepts alone is not enough; real mastery comes from **applying those concepts repeatedly under realistic constraints**. Practice strengthens problem-solving ability, while assessment helps measure progress, identify gaps, and build confidence. This section focuses on three essential categories of evaluation, which are interview-level coding problems, design-thinking problems, and case-based technical questions. Hence, you must remember that regular practice will help prepare you for real-world technical challenges and professional interviews.

Interview-Level Coding Problems

Interview-level coding problems evaluate a candidate's ability to **apply DSA components efficiently under pressure**. These problems are designed to test logical reasoning, algorithm selection, edge-case handling, and coding accuracy in a limited time frame. Unlike academic exercises, interview problems often involve carefully hidden constraints and require both correctness and optimization.

Through consistent practice of such problems, students can learn how to analyze a problem statement quickly, choose the most suitable data structure, design an efficient algorithm, and implement it cleanly. These problems also build debugging skills, speed of execution, and familiarity with automated testing environments used in real recruitment processes. Therefore, repeated exposure to interview-level coding challenges will help you develop confidence and also reduces anxiety during actual interviews.

Design-Thinking Problems

Design-thinking problems focus on a candidate's ability to **plan, structure, and justify solutions rather than only writing code**. These problems require students to think at a higher level, considering constraints such as scalability, performance, reliability, and maintainability. Instead of producing a single correct output, learners must explain how they would design a system or algorithm for a given real-world scenario.

Such problems help students understand how DSA is used beyond small programs, in large and complex systems. They enhance architectural thinking, logical decomposition of requirements, and the ability to evaluate trade-offs. Hence, design-thinking exercises play a vital role in preparing candidates for advanced technical interviews and system-level discussions.

Case-Based Technical Questions

Case-based technical questions present learners with **realistic problem scenarios drawn from industry applications**, such as data processing systems, recommendation engines, traffic management platforms, or financial analytics tools. Students will be expected to analyze the scenario, identify the underlying computational challenges, and propose suitable data structures and algorithms to solve them.

These questions test not just theoretical knowledge, but also skills like **practical reasoning, decision-making ability, and domain awareness**. By solving case-based questions, learners can gain significant experience in translating abstract requirements into concrete algorithmic solutions. This prepares them to handle unpredictable real-world problems where there is no single textbook answer for a given problem.

Practice and assessment ensure that learners move from passive understanding to **active problem-solving excellence**. Interview-level coding problems build speed and precision, design-thinking problems strengthen architectural reasoning, and case-based questions develop real-world analytical ability. Together, these assessment methods prepare students to perform confidently in coding interviews, system design discussions, and professional software development environments.

Conclusion

This chapter has provided a comprehensive roadmap that connects **technical knowledge with professional readiness**. While mastering DSA builds a strong foundation, true success in the software industry depends equally on how effectively you apply this knowledge, besides communicating it and continuously refining your skills. Through the smart coding practices underlined in this chapter, learners will be able to grasp the importance of writing clean, secure, and maintainable code. Moreover, by exploring algorithmic thinking and structured interview preparation strategies, they can develop the mindset required to approach complex problems with confidence and clarity. The chapter also highlighted the growing importance of DSA in modern technological domains such as AI, ML, Big Data, cloud computing, cybersecurity, blockchain, and IoT. Furthermore, real-world case studies demonstrated how fundamental algorithmic concepts power large-scale industry systems, while discussions on ethical coding emphasized the responsibility that comes with building technology that impacts society. The career roadmap and practice strategies further prepared learners to move from academic learning to professional excellence with discipline and purpose. Therefore, this final chapter brings together **conceptual understanding, practical application, professional ethics, and continuous learning** and combines them into a single integrated perspective. Students who follow these principles will not only perform well in interviews, but will also grow into responsible and adaptable software engineers. With strong foundations in DSA, smart coding habits, and a commitment to lifelong learning, learners are now well-equipped to face the challenges of the ever-evolving technology industry with confidence and competence.

Points to Remember

- Smart coding focuses on writing clean, readable, maintainable, and secure programs.
- Algorithmic thinking is essential for breaking down complex problems into solvable steps.
- Interview success depends on both problem-solving ability and clear communication.
- Online coding tests evaluate speed, accuracy, and optimization skills.
- Whiteboard and live coding rounds test real-time thinking and explanation ability.
- System design interviews focus on scalability, performance, and architectural decisions.
- Mock interviews help simulate real interview pressure and improve confidence.
- Resume structure plays a major role in shortlisting for technical roles.
- DSA forms the foundation of emerging technologies such as AI, ML, Big Data, and cloud computing.
- Ethical coding ensures fairness, privacy, and responsible use of algorithms.
- Continuous learning is necessary to remain relevant in the technology industry.
- Case-based problems test real-world application of DSA concepts.
- Time management is a critical skill during coding interviews.
- Security and input validation are essential parts of professional coding.
- DSA learning does not end with placement and must continue throughout one's career.

Multiple Choice Questions

1. Clean code mainly improves
   a. Compiler Speed
   b. Code Readability and Maintainability
   c. Hardware Performance
   d. Internet Speed
2. Which of the following interview rounds primarily tests large-scale system planning?
   a. HR Round
   b. Coding Round
   c. System Design Round
   d. Aptitude Round
3. Mock interviews are mainly useful for:
   a. Memorizing Syntax
   b. Reducing Exam Syllabus
   c. Simulating Real Interview Conditions
   d. Increasing Typing Speed Only
4. Which of the following is an ATS-friendly resume feature?
   a. Heavy Graphics
   b. Standard Section Headings
   c. Multiple Fonts
   d. Images and Charts

5. Which technology heavily relies on graphs and search algorithms?
   a. Blockchain
   b. IoT
   c. Search Engines
   d. Cloud Storage
6. Algorithmic bias primarily affects
   a. Program Compilation
   b. Execution Time
   c. Fairness of Automated Decisions
   d. Memory Allocation
7. Which skill is essential for whiteboard interviews?
   a. Internet Browsing
   b. Clear Explanation of Logic
   c. Database Indexing
   d. File Handling
8. Competitive programming mainly improves:
   a. GUI Design
   b. Coding Speed and Logical thinking
   c. Resume Formatting
   d. Presentation Skills
9. Which domain uses queues extensively for buffering data?
   a. Cybersecurity
   b. IoT Systems
   c. Blockchain Mining
   d. Image Processing
10. Secure coding helps prevent:
    a. Syntax Errors
    b. Algorithm Complexity
    c. Cyber Attacks
    d. Logical Errors
11. Continuous upskilling is required because:
    a. Technology remains constant.
    b. DSA changes every month.
    c. Technology evolves rapidly.
    d. Programming languages expire yearly.
12. Case-based questions mainly test:
    a. Theoretical Memorization
    b. Real-World Problem Analysis

c. Syntax Accuracy

d. Typing Speed

Answers

1. b
2. c
3. c
4. b
5. c
6. c
7. b
8. b
9. b
10. c
11. c
12. b

Questions

1. Explain the importance of smart coding practices in professional software development.
2. Discuss the role of algorithmic thinking in technical interviews.
3. Describe the different types of technical interview rounds.
4. Explain how mock interviews help improve interview performance.
5. Discuss the importance of resume building for DSA roles.
6. Explain the role of DSA in AI and ML.
7. Describe ethical challenges in modern software development.
8. Explain the career roadmap for a DSA learner from beginner to industry level.

Key Terms

- **Smart Coding:** Writing software that is clean, secure, efficient, and maintainable
- **Algorithmic Thinking:** The process of solving problems using structured logical steps
- **Mock Interview:** A simulated interview conducted for practice
- **ATS (Applicant Tracking System):** Software used to filter resumes automatically
- **System Design:** The process of designing scalable and efficient software systems
- **Algorithmic Bias:** Unfair outcomes produced by biased algorithms
- **Cybersecurity:** Protection of systems and data from digital attacks
- **Continuous Learning:** Ongoing process of updating technical skills
- **Case-Based Question:** A real-world technical problem scenario
- **Ethical Coding:** Practicing fairness, privacy, and responsibility in software development

Index

Symbols

A

C

M

N

O

P

T

U

V

W